1991

W9-AED-575

ALLY ACKER

REEL WOMEN

PIONEERS OF THE CINEMA
1896 TO THE PRESENT

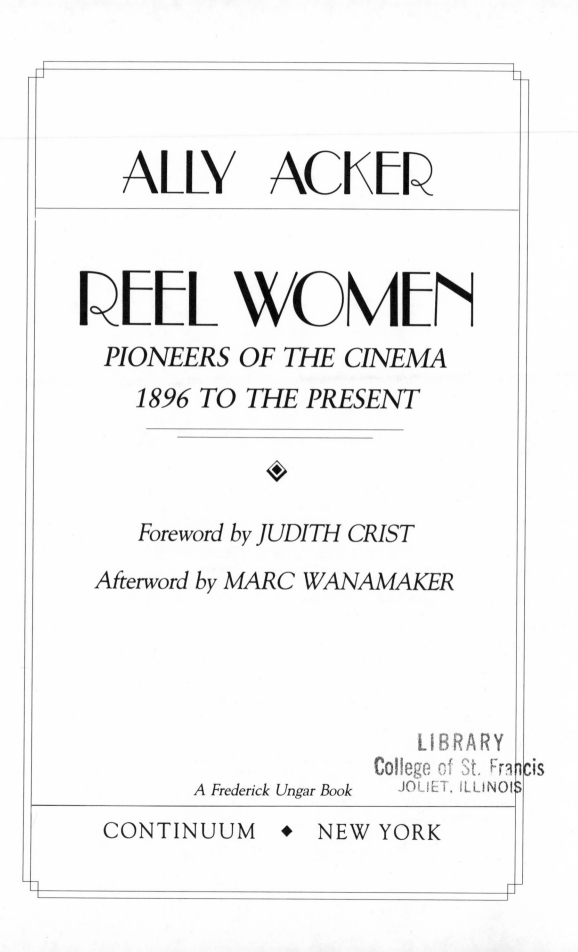

Foreword by JUDITH CRIST

Afterword by MARC WANAMAKER

A Frederick Ungar Book

CONTINUUM ◆ NEW YORK

1991

The Continuum Publishing Company
370 Lexington Avenue, New York, NY 10017

Library of Congress Cataloging-in-Publication Data

Acker, Ally.
    Reel women : pioneers of the cinema, 1896 to the present /
Ally Acker ; foreword by Judith Crist ; afterword by Marc Wanamaker.
        p.   cm.
    Includes bibliographical references and index.
    ISBN 0-8264-0499-5
    1. Women motion picture producers and directors—United States—
Biography.   2. Motion picture industry—United States—History.
I. Title.
PN1998.2.A24   1991
791.43'0233'0922—dc20
    [B]   90-43743
                                                        CIP

for my father,
mortimer acker (1920–1990),

without whom no portion
of the reel women book or films
could have been realized

for muggie, my wild swan,
in peace and freedom wherever you fly

for alana, some models for you
to follow

and for the women named
and unnamed in these pages
whose middle name is courage

here is my endless love letter to you

CONTENTS

◆ ◆ ◆

* Birth and/or death dates not available. Note: Due to complaints of "ageism" by many contemporary women in the industry, birth dates not included for those still alive and working. Birth dates only included for those women still alive but no longer working.

A.A.

ACKNOWLEDGMENTS

◆　◆　◆

First and foremost, loving thanks to my father, Mortimer, a long-standing visionary pioneer in his own right. When I mentioned this project his first words were, "It's an idea whose time has come." My mother, Nora, typed, made photocopies, and did whatever needed to be done, lovingly, generously and, as is par for the course with great women, without ever expecting credit.

My friend and colleague, Marc Wanamaker, initially enlightened me to this subject many moons ago, generously wrote the Afterword, checked for inaccuracies, and supplied the priceless, beautiful photographs you see before you.

Tom Stempel took on the huge task of reading the first draft, and he did so with a gentle toughness and a generosity of spirit. His comments had me laughing through notes of corrections where another commentator would have left an author sobbing. Bruce Cassiday was likewise a diligent, relentless, and most careful copy editor.

Kevin Brownlow always had an ear for my questions and an encouraging word.

Thanks to Judith Crist for her invaluable comments on the first draft manuscript. Her feedback was crucial to the structural as well as to the contextual design of the book. Steve Friedman at NBC provided the initial opportunity for me to interview many of the important women included here, by ask-ing me to produce a special segment on women behind the scenes for "The Today Show." Thanks also to NBC's Jim Brown for expertly conducting some of those interviews. Colby Atlas, in the Burbank bureau, helped faciliate all this.

Mark Hollis went beyond the call of duty many times for *Reel Women,* not the least of which was a donation of a hard disk for my computer! Miriam Hipsh provided her friendship as well as moral and financial support which allowed many of the important interviews to be conducted. Terrance Murray artfully photographed a number of the interviews for the documentary films of the same title (see About the Author), which of course translated into invaluable research for this book. I am deeply grateful to the many women in film who gave of their time to be interviewed. They know who they are. You provide great courage by your examples.

This book would not have been possible without the resources and people at the following museums and libraries: Charles Silver at the Film Studies Center at the Museum of Modern Art in New York, Madeleine Matz and Paul Spheer at the Library of Congress, Kristine Krueger, Sandra Archer, Alison Pinsler, and Sam Gill of the Margaret Herrick Library of the Academy of Motion Picture Arts and Sciences.

Thanks to all the indispensable librarians

and research people who invariably get overlooked. Ronnie Turcik of the Alice and Hamilton Fish Library in Garrison, New York who performed miracles with interlibrary loans. Lori Styler did imperative last minute research with a microscopic eye.

Mabel Haddock of the National Black Programming Consortium in Columbus Ohio, and Jacquie Jones of *Black Film Review* in Washington, D.C. generously provided current information on black and third world women in film.

My kind and generous editors and friends, Michael Leach, Kyle Miller, and all the people at Continuum, who made my first book the most pleasant experience any author could hope for. Gene, Debbie, Evander, Barbara, thank you.

Thanks to The Blue Mountain Center, where much of the early research for this project was completed. A special thanks to Kaye Burnett ("The Buddha"), for her magical way of knowing and of giving without being asked. Thank you for your kindnesses and for the time I needed there.

An endless list of friends helped me to keep the big picture in perspective: my life-long friend, Donnis Newman, Margorie Bair, Judy Chaikin, Irene McKinney, and my agent, Phyllis Wender, all provided me with encouragement one step ahead by their very fine examples. I also want to thank Janis Whitney, Jolie Barbiere, John Ramo, Janis Strout (who started me touring with *Reel Women*), Magda Schoenfeld, and the Women's Spirit Group in Garrison, New York.

To all of the women I met as I traveled on lecture tour all over the United States whose words, "Thank you for doing this!" encouraged me more than they knew. This book is largely *for* and *because of* you.

The indefatigable Vanilla never had a bad word to say in all the dark nights. Van, the winter would have been a lot colder without you.

And last in this listing, but first in my life, Joan Campbell, whose tireless encouragement, support, love, not to mention expert editorial input as a writer I both respect and admire, helped me stay grounded and hopeful during the long haul. Her vision of joy and beauty assist me in more ways than she will ever know.

"You ask me 'Is it difficult to be a *woman* director?' I'd say it is difficult to be a director period! It is difficult to be free; it is difficult not to be drowned in the system. We have a lot of women in the film industry—It is in terms of consciousness that we have not got it right."

—Agnes Varda

FOREWORD

◆ ◆ ◆

They were always there behind the screen—but who knew it?

Certainly for my generation—the post-radio, pre-television children of Loew's Paradise—it was the women *on* the screen who shaped our lives in those once-a-week (limited by the Great Depression even at 10-cents-before-5 P.M. box-office prices), one-on-one encounters in the dark. Movies set dress regulations (shoulder pads and ankle straps from **Joan Crawford,** sweater-and-skirt from **Betty Grable**), class distinctions (white telephones meant wealth), and even domestic sexual patterns. (If hands met and clasped while turning out the light on the night-table between the twin beds it was going to be a hot time ahead, but one that would, by morning, leave our heroine's hair unmussed, the pretty bedtime bow therein untouched.) Sex without marriage, need I note, meant agony and death by fadeout time.

More important, however, were the role models presented. It was **Katharine Hepburn**'s Jo in LITTLE WOMEN and **Hepburn** thereafter who set standards for action and independence, albeit only until the final clinch. It was **Marlene Dietrich,** in everything, who sent the message that true glamour covered both trampishness and a heart of gold. It was, at least for me, **Bette Davis** who stood for character—good or bad—self-determination, control of one's life, and

cigarette-smoking as an adjunct thereto. And **Vivien Leigh**'s Scarlett, a creature of the 1930s despite the Civil War setting, taught us that breaking the rules—going your own way and making it in a man's world, let alone coveting your best friend's husband—left you bereft of child and Clark Gable, with only a hope for a better tomorrow.

Certainly as young moviegoers we were mindful only of what was on the screen and there were relatively few film critics to raise our consciousness, to bring us an awareness of who—male or female—created and operated the dream machines. Beyond the "buffs" among us (film enthusiasts as opposed to star-worshiping "fans"), few even read the brief credits that in those days only preceded the movies. Probing my own memory I realize that the first female name I became aware of in credits was that of **Natalie Kalmus,** first wife of the inventor of Technicolor, who insisted on being listed as "color consultant" on all films that used that process from 1933 until their patent expired in 1949.

But from the very beginning, as Ally Acker reveals in this groundbreaking and invaluable work, there were women in all walks of filmmaking. Oscar, for example, was only two years old when **Frances Marion** became the first behind-the-screen woman to win a statuette for writing for

THE BIG HOUSE (1930), and won again for THE CHAMP (1931). (**Marion** has been quoted as writing that she saw the Oscar as "a perfect symbol of the picture business: a powerful athletic body clutching a gleaming sword with half of his head, the part which held his brains, completely sliced off.") But ask Oscar's parent Academy of Motion Picture Arts and Sciences how many other women have won Oscars and you draw a blank there and from other sources. An unofficial name count from my own record books yielded some eighty-five among the hundreds of Oscars dispensed over more than sixty years: seven other women won writing awards; ten won for film editing, five for art direction, one for set decoration, two for special effects, one for choreography, seven for music, eighteen for documentaries and short films, and there were thirty-two Oscars awarded to women for costume design, of which seven went to **Edith Head,** five to **Irene Sharaff,** and two apiece to **Helen Rose** and **Dorothy Jeakins.**

It's also difficult to get a head count from the guilds. The Directors Guild of America, which has taken the lead in trying to increase the number of women and minorities in the industry, reports a continuing growth thereof but the figure is still only at 18 percent, some 1,620 of its 9,000 members. Women constitute 13 percent of the production managers; 23 percent of the first assistant directors; 33 percent of the second assistant directors; 38 percent of the associate directors in tape, and 23 percent of the stage managers. The Producers Guild of America reports that 50 of its 416 active and inactive members are women and that there's been steady growth in their numbers in recent years. The Writers Guild of America reports that 38 percent, some 3,914 of its 10,300 members are women, but this includes those who write for both television and film or television exclusively, as well as newswriters. There's no breakdown of screenwriters.

All this underlines the importance of Ally's work, indeed an archeological survey as well as a sociological, cultural, and feminist study. Its virtue is that it is not the definitive encyclopedia of women in film: it is a personal and passionate work that will, I know, inspire others. Welcome.

—Judith Crist

INTRODUCTION—
THE FEMINIZATION
OF FILMMAKING

◆ ◆ ◆

In 1985, I took a proposal called "Reel Women: Pioneers of the Cinema" to the Corporation for Public Broadcasting requesting funds to produce a documentary on the subject. I was told, quite off the record but nonetheless glibly, "the closest this administration is getting to funding women's issues is quilts in women's lives." Are quilts, I wondered, a woman's *issue?* The 80s may be over, yet the *real* issues that lingered even before the guise of a "post-feminist" era continue to haunt our lives.

The first director in history of a narrative film was a woman. The highest paid director in the silent days was a woman. Even **Helen Keller** got into the act and formed a production company to produce and star in her own film drama in 1918.

We know about Méliès, Eisenstein, Griffith, and Truffaut. But what about **Blaché, Weber, Dulac,** and **von Trotta?** These women are as integral and transformative to the cinema as the men above, and yet their stories have consistently remained untold.

This is a book about the manipulation of history. About history as a fabrication and a lie. About the myth of history as a col-

lection of unchangeable data recorded by "objective" and unimpassioned record keepers.

The film industry is over ninety years old. All through these ninety years women have held important positions as directors, producers, editors, studio owners, writers, and technicians.

As Anthony Slide wrote in *Early Women Directors* (1977), "During the silent era, women might be said to have virtually controlled the film industry."[1] Not only were most of the important stars women, but many of those actresses, of both major and minor import, had their own production companies. Film buffs have been aware for some time that women were equal in numbers and importance with men in the screenwriting trade from the turn of the century through the midtwenties.

In 1984, while working as a television producer in Los Angeles, I was assigned to do a two-part program entitled, *Remarkable Women in History*. Determined not to cover personalities already familiar to the general public, I set myself on what was to become a six-year archaeological journey.

I began to contact archivists of old photographs, and in the process befriended Marc Wanamaker, head of the Bison Archives, a unique collection of rare motion picture stills. It was Marc who first showed me snapshots of women that completely altered my concept and my understanding of history. Here were women pictured on the set, in obviously influential positions behind the scenes. I asked Marc if he could identify them. A short article he had written for a local film journal identified some, and then went on to unadornedly state that *"more women worked in decision-making positions in film before 1920 than at any other time in history"* (italics mine). If the history books forgot to convey this no-so-small detail, does it make the fact of it any less true? Does it make the work that these women produced any less significant? What was the difference, I wondered, between an omission from history and a lie?

I contacted historians like Kevin Brownlow, who generously pulled other esoteric female names I hadn't heard of out of the closet. He put me onto other people, other sources of oral history. Lost periodicals like *Moving Picture World* and *Photoplay* told stories of yet more women who not only had impressive records of achievement in film, but also went against the grain of a Victorian world that told women flat out not to make waves and definitely not to be innovators.

Hundreds of days were spent looking through these pages, long buried in time, stashed away in perhaps three libraries in the country, where rare artifacts were hidden: names and pictures not mentioned or seen in the film books written by the men who began to tell the story of the film industry beginning in the 1940s.

It soon became clear to me that I had more than a documentary on my hands. Perhaps this was a *series* of films, and most certainly this was a book—a book containing information that should have been known to anyone who had ever read anything about the film industry. Instead, these primary movers and changers were fading away in the aging memories of a few, scattered in lost, obscure periodicals, and sometimes luckily found as addenda to a story regarding some influential male mogul.

With my first thought of a long film, I left my job at KABC TV, and began to do interviews with "great women" in the movies who had been around the business a long time. What I found was that each of these oral histories was inspiring, moving, life-changing.

Why wasn't I finding these women's stories, or the tales of their early predecessors, in "respected" historic texts on film such as William K. Everson's *American Silent Film* (1978), or in Lewis Jacob's *The Rise of the American Film* (1939, 1969)?

Although in relation to men the actual number of women I was unearthing was small, it didn't seem to justify their being left out of the records altogether. Why had this surprisingly vast, uncharted history of how women created, transformed, and even controlled the movies gone unrecorded?

Part of the answer doesn't need much explanation. In a less-enlightened era, Andrew Sarris once dismissed the contributions of two generations of women filmmakers as "little more than a ladies' auxiliary"—a statement he was later to revise and retract. It's no news that women's work, whether inside or outside the home, has traditionally been devalued. But it's tough to pinpoint exactly *how* this condescension rears its ugly head.

There's the myth we've always been told: "There have been no great women artists."

Sometimes we are told this audaciously and directly, as in the case of the art historian, H. W. Janson. As the author of one of the most widely read art history books in the world, *The History of Art* (1962), Janson said in an interview in 1977, on the anniversary of the book's second printing:

There is not a single woman artist, so far as I know, in my book. . . . There are hundreds of women artists from the fifteenth century on . . . But none of them has had enough of an impact or development on the history of art . . . Women artists have often done very interesting variations on themes that ultimately go back to somebody else who turns out to be a man. One has to be extremely selective.[2]

Such autonomous selectivity brings us to perhaps the moral of our tale: He who has access to major publishers gets to make history.

The question is not what is great art? Rather the question is, who *decides* what the great classics are? and by whose standards do we define them? Is ALL QUIET ON THE WESTERN FRONT (1930) a greater picture than THE WILD PARTY (1929) because the former deals with "big issues" like war, while the latter focuses on the friendships and love between women in a sorority? Is war *more important* than personal human relations?

History has been just that: *his story*. At the movies, it is important to remember that what we see is what the camera sees. The camera is not an objective eye, but a subjective view of one particular storyteller. From the films readily accessible to us, and deemed important enough to archive and pass on (not to be confused with the hundreds of films made by women and lost by archival neglect), this interpretive eye has most often been the eye of a man. When women watch themselves on the mythic silver screen, they generally watch themselves from a male point of view.

Even in the heyday of "the woman's film," the 'glorious forties' decade of great female stars, the shapes of those large women were born out of male fantasy. Yet one has only to peruse the results of the history put before you now—a history born of scattered, nearly-lost oral history sources—to know its truths.

As late as 1986, while in graduate school in film at Columbia University, I attended courses that examined in detail the contributions of "the Great Directors": D. W. Griffith, Sergi Eisenstein, François Truffaut. Not until much later did it dawn on me that not even my women professors thought to offer courses on the films of **Alice Guy Blaché, Lois Weber, Dorothy Arzner, Ida Lupino, Maya Deren,** or **Margarethe von Trotta.** Most likely, they didn't know enough about the women or their films to do so.

The significance of these filmmakers has never been acknowledged. Discussions about their work in books of serious scholarship are either nonexistent or else narrowcast to discussions about specific genres. For instance, in reading about "the German New Wave" you might see mention of the name **Margarethe von Trotta.** If you are reading an article in a film journal about "Early Women Directors" you might also bump into the names of **Alice Guy Blaché** and **Lois Weber.** It's as if to study them as serious filmmakers needs some sort of qualifying. Their very omission from major historic film texts is a testament to how women's work has been minimalized.

Women have not been highly visible in the British film industry. However, in television, particularly with the arrival of Channel Four television in 1982, women are now prominent as directors, producers, writers, and editors. In reading about British documentary filmmaking, you will come across the names of such pioneering women as **Jill Craigie,** and **Mary Field** (1896–1968). While there have been very few British women feature directors some women of note are **Muriel Box, Wendy Toye, Sally Potter, Beeban Kidron,** and **Lezli-An Barrett.**

What follows is by no means meant to be a comprehensive listing of every woman who has ever made a motion picture. First, because of sheer limitations of time and space, I decided to limit my look to women who made features. The exception to this applies to many of the women who worked in the very early days, when the concept of "feature" had not yet taken form. Two and three reelers were being churned out at the rate of two and three a week, and many of these women were responsible for the cinema's early attempts. Another exception made here was to women of color who simply have not had the kind of economic or political access to making features that others have had. In the meantime, the work these women are doing in short films, in video, and in documentaries have a kind of artistic eclecticism not known in these media before.

Most importantly, I wanted to deal with "pioneers," women who blazed trails and forged paths where certainly other women, and in many cases, other filmmakers in general, had not gone before. Women who in some way pushed over boundaries that had not been crossed before.

And even if I had not been restricted in any way to do so, it would be impossible to make mention of every single woman in cinema. What is formulated here is what happens in *all* recountings arrogantly dubbed "history." What manifests itself finally is a selective and subjective accounting.

Invariably there will be those who complain that their favorite women have been omitted. I regret that I do not have the room to profile editors like **Blanche Sewell** and **Dorothy Spencer**, producers like **Harriet Parsons** and **Gale Ann Hurd,** writers like **Nancy Dowd** and **Nora Ephron,** directors like **Amy Heckerling** and **Randa Haines.** I hope only that someone will follow my lead and write a second volume. We need all of the unearthing of great pioneers our energies can provide.

My interest here was to focus on mainstream cinema. I wanted to look at the women who pursued, grappled with, tried to transform, or merely wanted to be a part of that all-powerful, mythmaking machine called HOLLYWOOD—the one industry that, for better or worse, has succeeded in completely changing our lives since its inception in 1896.

As one of the most powerful media in existence (a medium that Woodrow Wilson knew, as early as 1916, was powerful enough to help him win a presidential election), film has set our fashions, fantasies, mores, and moral trends for the last five generations.

From the moment film codified itself into an industry that deified profit over art, Hollywood films sculpted, molded, and glorified the female image according to male desire. Even in films like Howard Hawks's, HIS GIRL FRIDAY (1940), we are less interested in the competence of the strong and powerful Hildy as a journalist than we are in whether she will buckle under the inevitable pull of her "female emotions" and end up with her man.

It would not be until the seventies, with films like **Claudia Weill's** GIRLFRIENDS (1978), that women would finally (and of course, *independently*) see their real lives on the screen—women intensely absorbed, as men on the screen have always been absorbed, by their work. Finally, women were no longer prisoners of their emotions.

Images of women that kept both men and women prisoners of culturally imprinted roles were finally beginning to crack. The old Hollywood lens, even for one brief, shining moment, began to be called into question. The very powerful act of using film to explore women's personal lives as the primary content—giving women's lives a kind of public credence—advanced the possible existence of "a female gaze" one giant step.[3]

In the eighties, consciousness on the part of independent women filmmakers about the existence of something called "the controlling male gaze," began to free us all. Finally, women had a language to explain our confinement. The language proved a key with which we could, as Aldous Huxley said, "pass through a door of perception." There was no turning back. Women began speaking about their own lives with a boldness and a depth never before seen on the screen.

Canadian filmmaker **Patricia Rozema's** I'VE HEARD THE MERMAIDS SINGING (1987) comes to mind, harking back in an odd way to **Barbara Loden's** WANDA (1971) more than fifteen years before—two films that represented a multitude of women's experiences, women who were lost and homeless in their souls, strangers in their own homeland. The land their foremothers had found solace in was no longer viable, and women filmmakers were finally able to talk about it.

After a lifetime of male coming-of-age tales, **Joyce Chopra's** SMOOTH TALK (1985) finally focused on the confusions surrounding an adolescent woman's rites of passage. ENTRE NOUS (1983) spoke the unspeakable taboo of two women falling in love, not from the vantage point of male eroticism, but from the stable, emotional threading that can only be characterized as inherently female. And **Donna Deitch** daringly, erotically, beautifully portrayed two women making love in DESERT HEARTS (1985). For the first time on the screen, and for a mainstream audience, it was being done from a woman's point of view.

If there were clouds of confusion surrounding what, if anything, determined a "female gaze," then certainly the smoke was clearing. The choice of woman-centered content was what separated the girls from the boys. Then came the decisions about how to handle that content.

With DESERT HEARTS came the question of *how* and when a female sensibility crosses over into a lesbian sensibility. The issue is often a thin, dicey, and ambivalent line. Director **Francine Parker,** who must be commended for resurrecting **Dorothy Arzner** in the midseventies, said to me, "One got the feeling that if she [Arzner] was lesbian, she was closeted even to herself. My opinion is that if she had been born later she might have openly been gay." But despite any possible ambivalence about her sexuality, nearly all of the films that Arzner directed focused upon women's lives, and did so with a passionate gaze. She wrote

about "women in all phases of consciousness, wrestling for love, career, independence, integrity. George Cukor, 'woman's director,' sympathizes with his women characters. **Dorothy Arzner** . . . *empathized* with hers."[4] From 1927 to 1943, her women were bold decision makers. They were unconventional women who made unconventional choices, as Arzner did herself, which left them outside the bounds of society and its rules.

Margarethe von Trotta, who in film after film passionately gazes upon women's experiences and lives, denied to me ever feeling any sort of interest in pursuing the lesbian theme in her private life. Yet the women in many of her films get so intimate that the issue of an erotic charge becomes inevitable. In SHEER MADNESS (1985), according to Barbara Quart, "Olga is in a bare sundress so that Ruth's repeated touching of her must suggest something erotic."

Quart says that von Trotta denied such filmic evidence when she interviewed her, "speaking instead of 'a sort of attachment, or fascination for another woman . . . to be very close to her thoughts and her soul and all that but it has nothing to do with sex.' "[5]

It is interesting to explore the feminist/lesbian ambivalence and continuum in instances where real-life characters in films were lesbian, but this aspect of their lives is absent from the fictional retelling. For the most part one finds that women filmmakers have admittedly feminist leanings (if they are also lesbian, they are generally careful to be closeted to the press), and a kind of unresolved tension is evident in the final product. This shying uncomfortably away from the truth of their characters' lives generally comes from a desire not to lose a potentially wider viewership. About the real-life Karen Silkwood, portrayed in SILKWOOD (1983), screenwriter **Nora Ephron** said:

Karen was very sexual and pretty much up for grabs. She certainly had a couple of experiences with women. The question was, did we want to do that film? . . .

The real question is, if, hypothetically, Karen Silkwood had actually been a lesbian, would we have done that on film? I don't know.

If she weren't only a slightly unbalanced woman who'd given up her children but a slightly unbalanced lesbian mother who'd given up her children, who knows how the audience might have reacted?[6]

On the anniversary of the opening of ENTRE NOUS by **Diane Kurys** in 1984 (a film based on a true story), she speaks of her reluctance to have the film billed lesbian, "suspecting it would narrow or skew her audience and blind viewers to the nuances of the story."[7]

Thus, her predilection to show these women's "natural" inclinations toward heterosexuality by creating affairs with men, and men other than their husbands. In this way it was perhaps more permissible to show their deep and yearning affections towards one another. "I have their letters," said Kurys, "they were passionate. My mother said they tried to have sex but it didn't work—they just laughed . . . I wonder if it wasn't the pressure of the period and the gossips that prevented anything more . . . it lasted twenty-five years and there wasn't a day they didn't see each other, not a day."[8]

Even a film about two historically acknowledged lesbians like Gertrude Stein and Alice B. Toklas, **Jill Godmilow**'s WAITING FOR THE MOON (1987) was "a beautiful, literate and civilized film but strangely without emotional intimacy." This, according to Vito Russo, was largely because Godmilow made no secret of the fact that she wanted to avoid making a "lesbian film." But as Russo says, "If you don't want to make a lesbian film then don't make a film about two lesbians."[9]

The difference between a female and a lesbian sensibility will no doubt continue to be a cloudy one until we can advertise a lesbian film as an acceptable mainstream product. That may be a very long time in coming. In the meantime, we can at least claim less difficulty in distinguishing a woman's eye behind the camera from a man's—all of which has to do with responsibility and consciousness of attitude on the part of the filmmaker.

It should be emphasized that films of the "conscious" filmmaker are most often, if not always, produced either independently or on foreign soil—far away from a Hollywood that is slow to let go of the old ways of seeing. And yet, prior to 1970, an abundance of women had given their blood and sweat to a system that continued to represent them falsely.

I wanted to know why certain women were crazy enough to want to penetrate that system. What kind of woman was she, who bravely, intentionally—masochistically?—went against the grain of an entire culture?

I mostly omitted the actresses whose box-office appeal allowed them an overwhelming power to influence, control, and essentially produce their own product. "The women with the power, but not the credit" would be an apt description for these early screen actresses. **Norma Talmadge, Clara Kimball Young, Gloria Swanson,** and **Katharine Hepburn,** are only a few examples.

Contemporary actresses who are following the legacy of those early women's footsteps are also left out: **Sally Field, Jessica Lange,** both committed, enormously talented women who are making an important contribution for women on and off of the screen. Their conscious choices to empower women (**Field's** NORMA RAY [1979]) as well as to heal the earth (**Lange's** COUNTRY [1984]) have served to change the image of *people* on the screen forever.

Jane Fonda has more than once committedly stuck her neck out for what she has believed in and then been brave enough publicly to stand tall. She has become a kind of cultural symbol for women who hope to transform their own lives. Beginning as a

Jane Fonda

brainless sex object in BARBARELLA (1967), Fonda slowly woke to consciousness with her generation and wore the faces of those changes in her films. Always under public scrutiny, she came to represent different sorts of women—women in control of their own bodies and their own destinies: a woman of mind and public conscience—CHINA SYNDROME (1979); a woman of heart—COMING HOME (1978). "I just wanted to be an actress—that's what I was trained for," said Fonda in 1985. "No one told me I would end up having to negotiate and produce . . . but it's come to that. Now that I'm over forty-five, I find it's hard to get interesting roles, so I'm creating my own. With the decline of the studio system, which has its up side and its down side, it's up to actresses to develop their own projects. COMING HOME, CHINA SYNDROME, NINE TO FIVE, ON GOLDEN POND, and ROLLOVER are all films that we've created and developed—and it's been very rewarding."[10] Fonda has proved herself to be one of those screen personae whose essence is often more powerful than the two dimensional requirements of the script. Certainly she follows in a proud line: Davis, Hepburn, Garbo.

Where I detour to speak about independent, avant-garde artists like **Maya Deren,** it is because I believe they have taken the medium of film and stretched its capacity in some large and visionary way beyond socially acceptable or expected realms. For instance, without the cultural support of the women's movement of the seventies, Deren took a knife to male and female role playing as early as the 1940s.

Women in the forefront of the seventies, generally over fifty, and reared in a world prior to the women's movement are also included. **Elaine May**'s films are predominantly male-centered because of the cultural climate in which she was raised.

And yet, women like May helped to blaze the trail when the support of other women directors was simply not available. With these filmmakers one is intrigued to look closely at "the equation of woman with body, woman as sexual sign, the central way woman has been viewed in patriarchal films."[11] One wants to see if and how women filmmakers are similar to or different from men in their approach to the treatment of women on the screen. What, if anything, in their lives has brought them to their filmic conclusions?

I was interested in exploring the diversity of all of these individual biographies—women's lives so much more layered than their male contemporaries whose struggles are not complicated by career versus family concerns, or by the guilt that obtrudes as a result.

The most empowering discovery throughout the course of my research was how consistent and steadfast women have been as innovators in film. It is important, therefore, to place the pioneer woman of cinema into the historic context of which she is so indelibly a part.

Between 1913 and 1923, at least twenty-six women directors have been counted in Hollywood. But one of the reasons they were allowed to direct during these formative years was the fact that directing was not yet considered a glamorous job. As Marjorie Rosen says in *Popcorn Venus* (1973), "Before it became a powerful elitist operation, the industry's hunger for material and moviemakers left little room for sexual prejudice."[12] It was literally possible for almost anyone to walk off the streets and, direct a movie. Production costs were meager. Salaries were low.

In his introduction to *The Silent Screen and My Talking Heart* (1987), an autobiography of **Nell Shipman,** Peter Morris explains that in 1912 filmmaking was a casual operation. People could, and did, move easily between acting and writing and directing, often on the same picture. The budgets were low. Biograph, for instance, a leader in production values, spent around five hundred dollars on each film with expected returns of about fifteen hundred. It was possible to set up your own production company with very little money. But by the early twenties a feature was costing two hundred thousand to make, and major epics were running close to a million.

Morris says that the new kind of film that became rampant in the twenties—with Hollywood's highly structured star system, division of labor, and control by a centralized management—was mirroring changes taking place in US industry in general. Henry Ford, for example, was applying exactly the same principles to making cars.[13]

So as film began to be a big business and only secondarily an art form, women were promptly shown the door. Labor unions made it quite clear that women were not to be solicited as members.

We need to remember that because the contributions of women filmmakers are not recorded, it doesn't mean they didn't exist. Since the person one grows up to be is directly connected to the role models one sees projected, those real and imagined, then both sexes are bereft if those models are rendered invisible. It might have *appeared*in history books that women screenwriters

and editors evaporated from the thirties until recently, but as far as the truth of the working industry was concerned, they consistently remained steadfastly on the job.

What I have tried to do in these pages is change the lens of an old camera. The impetus for this book stems from one little-known fact: the first director of a story film in history was a woman, and to this day, even with significant persuasive evidence, historians either insist it isn't true, or else belittle the magnitude and the effect of her contribution.

In *The Dictionary of Filmmakers,* published in 1968 by Georges Sedoul, the first director in history, **Alice Guy Blaché,** is listed in this way:

> **Guy Blaché, Alice**. . . . Originally Leon Gaumont's secretary when he was still only making film equipment. She began making short films intended for use as demonstrations for clients. She made her first film, LA FÉE AUX CHOUX [1896] *some months before Méliès,* thus becoming the first *woman* director in the world [italics mine].

The entry under "Méliès" in the same book describes him as the first director of "story films." Not the first *man* director, but the first director. Although Blaché's film was not specifically made as an entertainment vehicle, it was certainly a fictional, story film. (LA FÉE AUX CHOUX [*The Cabbage Fairy*], concerned a fairy who "made" children in a cabbage patch.) Yet Sedoul chose to invent a subcategory "woman director" for Blaché, presumably in order to reserve the title "first director" for a man.

But this cannot negate the facts. Blaché directed over two hundred films in her lifetime—every genre and manner of film: romances, adventures, comedies, even a science fiction film called, IN THE YEAR 2000 (1912), in which women rule the world.

Such unconscious manipulation of the truth answers the question as to why the major contributions of women have been so neatly scratched out. There are volumes upon volumes of information about Méliès, and virtually all his films are available to see—but there are barely a handful of articles on the work of Blaché and very few of her films still exist.[14] In fact, only her short films exist, none of her features. The few shorts that are still about are locked away in museum vaults, or held in private collections.

And what about the woman who *did* succeed in mainstream Hollywood? How did her *female* vision reflect her artistic creation? What did women filmmakers bring as *women* to movies? Is there such a thing as a "female gaze" in moviemaking? And once she succeeded in entering the industry, did the woman filmmaker change the system, or did the system change her? Did gender even enter into the picture? And, maybe most importantly, have the movies of Hollywood undergone a visible transformation because of her appearance on the scene? In short, I wanted to know what determined a "pioneer"?

In her comprehensive study, *Women Filmmakers: A Critical Reception,* Louise Heck-Rabi devised a list of what she believed to be common traits of women filmmakers. Among these:

> Most are . . . considered attractive, restless, dynamic, energetic. . . . Most have had previous training in the arts. . . . Most are married and work in collaboration with men.[15]

I have come up with my own additions to the list:

1. From very early on these women see the world in a unique way. They often see themselves as outsiders.
2. They are born in families that range from middle-class to well-to-do, and are generally highly educated. They are given the opportunity to pursue eclectic, wide-ranging interests— hence, with the barest handful of exceptions, the stark absence of women of color.
3. Most would consider themselves workaholics.
4. Most have a tremendous drive, and feel that the necessity to make films is a "mission."
5. The majority of women in the directing category did not have children. (**Alice Guy Blaché** and **Nell Shipman** are two notable exceptions.)
6. Many in the early period came to sad or tragic endings. Divorces and nervous breakdowns were particularly prevalent in many of the careers.
7. Many, especially from the early group, didn't tend to think of themselves as "women" in their professions. Their gender, as women, never entered their consciousness.

This last observation is very much in keeping with the general consciousness of a homogeneous, male industry that has no interest in any challenge to its power structure.

I asked **Margaret Booth,** the pioneering film editor who supervised every film at MGM from the thirties through the sixties, if she ever felt lonely. "Lonely?" she asked, genuinely puzzled with my question. "No. I had all these men around me."

The childlike innocence of her response was revelatory. Startlingly bright, sophisticated, tough, savvy, Booth had no awareness of what I meant. That I was specifically asking about her experience in being one of the only women in an all-male studio system seemed strange to her. When I clarified my question, she said without emphasis, "I was one of the boys."

And indeed, many of the pioneers felt as such in order to be assimilated into this alien world in which they wanted to work.

Many of the overlooked filmmakers of the early part of this era went against fashion and convention. They had no books to study on how a movie was supposed to look. They made up the rules as they went along. As a result, they became visionaries. Whether they came up with technical innovations (**Dorothy Arzner** with the "fish-pole" microphone), conceptual achievements (**Maya Deren**'s "trance" films), **Natalie Kalmus**'s brainchild of a "package deal" that would make "color" movies an attractive notion to studio producers), or advancements for filmmakers as well as for women (**Dede Allen** winning solo credit for editors on the screen), these women contributed in changing our perspective on the world forever.

My greatest hope is that the reward of such a long and circuitous unearthing will inspire those in other arts and industries to do the same; to dig into the unconventional sources—letters, journals, word of mouth—from their own pasts. It is my belief that if so many jewels were buried in the world's most visible medium, then certainly similar female powerhouses wait to be uncovered in other fields.

The consequence of suppressing important female models is that we all suffer. As Anne Ross Muir has pointed out in THE FEMALE GAZE (1989), children are presented with a lopsided view of the world, women are cut off from a vital source of self-expression, a great loss of talent befalls the entire industry, a feeling of isolation among women perpetuates and stifles communication options, and the images created by both women and men continue to be far from reality as invisibility perpetuates more invisibility.

Our his/toric texts keep perpetuating a lie.

I now spend a great deal of my time traveling to universities and film festivals speaking to students—changing for them, as was changed for me, the lens of this old camera. I show these remarkable, rare photographs so lovingly preserved by Marc Wanamaker to whom I will ever be indebted for his important work—this overt pictorial evidence that so dramatically reverses everything we have been taught about film. I tell the stories I've learned—stories of courage from these great women who have so informed, inspired, and changed my life. I tell them in hopes that the lies of history will cease once and for all.

What becomes most apparent is that women's voices, although silenced, have never been absent. An unmistakable chord has resonated consistently ever since the movies were born. With these stories between the pages of a single source, it is my hope that, in Barbara Quart's words, "an unmistakable interwoven whole reveals itself, the long silenced voice of women."[16]

As both men and women, we need to know the visions our foremothers had if we are to pass on the truth of what life can be. We need to know what visions have been made in order to discover what visions might be made. We need to re-vision female filmmaking in order to determine what possible female filmmaking can be.

Trying to right a wrongful omission, telling the tales of some remarkable female eyes who changed our vision by showing us their own, is but a beginning.

Ally Acker
New York, 1990

· 1 ·

REEL WOMEN DIRECTORS

Unsung, the noblest deeds will die.
—Pindar, *Fragment 120*

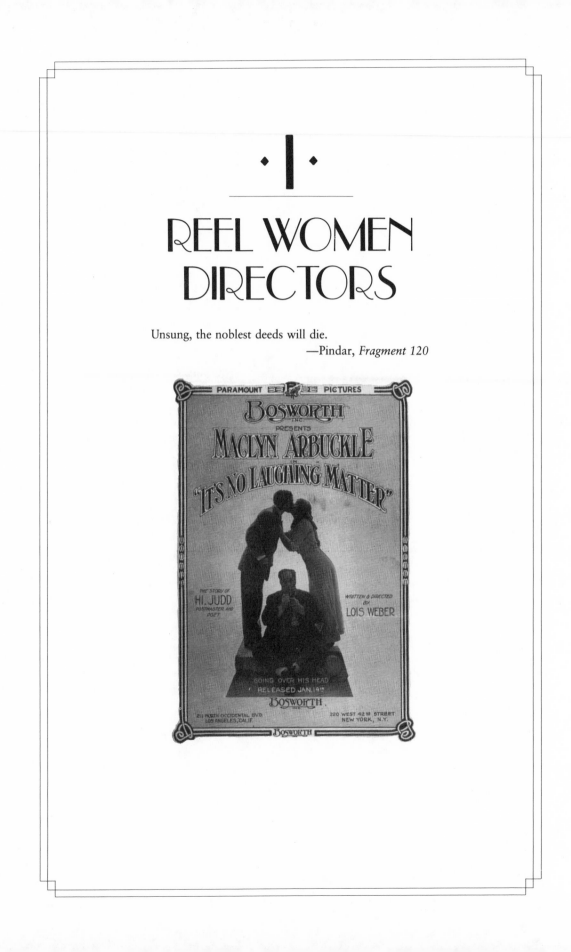

PREVIEW

How profoundly their unholy assumption of directorial power
must have challenged the gender definitions of their time.

—Barbara Koenig Quart

While it may be obvious to many as it was to **Dorothy Arzner** (1900–79) that "if one was going to be in the movie business, one ought to be a director," it was a far from natural concept to the culture at large. The notion of a woman at the helm, decisively taking charge and dispensing orders, went against the very grain of gender definitions so embedded into every aspect of our lives.

One out of every two articles I came across profiling women directors in magazines before 1920 spent the first half in praise of the fact that she "attacked" her assignment as well as any competent man. The latter half catalogued in great detail the recipés she most liked to cook in her spare time—to prove that in fact, she was a "real" woman, should the reader harbor doubts.

Substantial evidence has it that **Alice Guy Blaché** (1875–1968) was the first director in history ever to put a narrative story on celluloid. This, however, has never sat well in traditional historic accounts of the film business, all of which were then written by men. Some prefer to say that the business of "firsts" in film is mere rumor based on hearsay, and should not be trusted, others belittle the contribution of Blaché by attacking the consequence of her subject matter.

Often her topics focused on domestic issues, which is mostly what you find when you read about her work. But when she *was* involved in overtly political productions, she was careful never to talk about them in interviews. And when asked about them directly, she would disavow any overtones, suffragette or otherwise, as being a part of her filmic intentions. What she was reacting to was an unspoken rule of the industry—if you are too radical, or convicted to your approach, you're going to alienate your box office, and put your career in jeopardy.

From the onset of movies, **Blaché** was constantly on her toes with regards to her public image. Whenever a reporter was present, she was careful to be demure and soft-spoken—in short, a "lady" every inch of the way. The result from the press was praise and acceptance. This unsaid practice was to be picked up by many women directors, including **Dorothy Arzner** fifteen years later, as is evidenced by a newspaper headline of 1934: "Hollywood's Only Woman Director Never Bellows Her Orders."

Lois Weber (1882–1939) became known as a filmmaker *because* of her independent stance and her staunch political tirades. Yet she too always disavowed suffragette affiliations. As a role model, the women's movement needed her badly, and Weber knew it. But she also knew that the correct invisibility of a woman was the key to longevity in a directing career. The message from the culture was loud and clear: "If you want to play in this business, you play like a man, or you're out. And if you happen to be a woman, better not mention it to anybody."

Weber's ideology revolved around controversial issues, and so it is interesting that she is usually remembered in conventional historic accounts as a "domestic" filmmaker. Reiterating such a skewed vision serves its purpose. The unspoken derogatory assumption is that since personal topics do not hold the weight of grand-scale world affairs, Lois Weber must not have been a terribly important filmmaker.[1]

By the thirties, **Dorothy Arzner** felt more comfortable looking like a man since she was standing in one's shoes. But the costume enabled her to put her best foot forward for women in work with feminist overtones such as CHRISTOPHER STRONG (1933) and DANCE, GIRL, DANCE (1940).

Ida Lupino (1918–   ) would later take on the position of being referred to as "mother" on the set, publicly declaring how she detested working with other women behind the scenes unless they were actresses. She stated forthrightly that she'd certainly rather be a good wife and mother than have to do "this career thing" for the money.[2]

Still prior to the women's movement, filmmakers like **Elaine May** were allowed to make films in the mainstream as long as they appropriately subjugated their femaleness. As Barbara Koenig Quart has said, "**May** disparages everyone in her movies, but she "aims a particular animus at her women characters and works through male protagonists."[3]

Claudia Weill and **Joan Micklin Silver**

took bold strides (albeit independent ones) after the women's movement to stand up for what they believed in for women, as well as remain true to their own, authentic voices. **Stephanie Rothman** stood steadfast and conscious for feminism in the most unlikely of genres: slice-and-dice movies. The result of all of this was eclectic and interesting moviemaking, with heartily unique female visions emerging. Feminism had become the umbrella under which the new woman director could not only get out of the rain, but could scream her 'femaleness' while doing so.

As in all things, however, didacticism dies hard. The women directors that followed later didn't feel compelled to discuss gender overtly in their films. And as the Reagan administration got increasingly under way, they were subtly encouraged not to.

On foreign ground, far from Hollywood's golden gates, feminist allies, with a megaphone they didn't have to hide, were increasing in number and recognition. Their governments gave these pioneer filmmakers the kind of economic support that allowed them the freedom to use the medium of film to speak their minds. **Margarethe von Trotta** in a mere decade had directed six superlative pieces, placing herself in a class as a major director. Her work, as Barbara Quart notes in *Women Directors,* "is of special interest because it is a woman-centered and woman-affirming cinema of a kind still a rarity—women looked at with intensity and love by the woman behind the camera."[4] **Von Trotta** is only one of several foreign women directors whose gifted eyes are filling an immense abyss for women.

As of this writing, the statistics for women in Hollywood look bleak. A survey by the Directors Guild of America (DGA) in 1980 revealed that only 14 of the 7,332 features made in Hollywood in the previous thirty years were directed by women. By 1986, however, figures were increasing. Thirty-six features that one year were directed by women. One statistic has it that between 1949 and 1979, one-fifth of 1 percent of all films directed by major studios were directed by women.[5]

Out of the approximately 5,081 members in the DGA, only 8.8 percent, or 448, are women. But just because one has membership in the guild does not mean one is working. By no means. In the past thirty years, less than 1 percent of all prime-time television and all feature films have been directed by women.[6]

This means that that "eye of the camera," that vision, still remains almost entirely in the province of men.

And yet, the latest female voices are giving us all reasons to stand up and cheer. Although in equality of numbers we still have a long way to go, the *quality* of content, as evidenced by these new courageous filmmakers, gives us much hope when looking toward the future for "the female gaze."

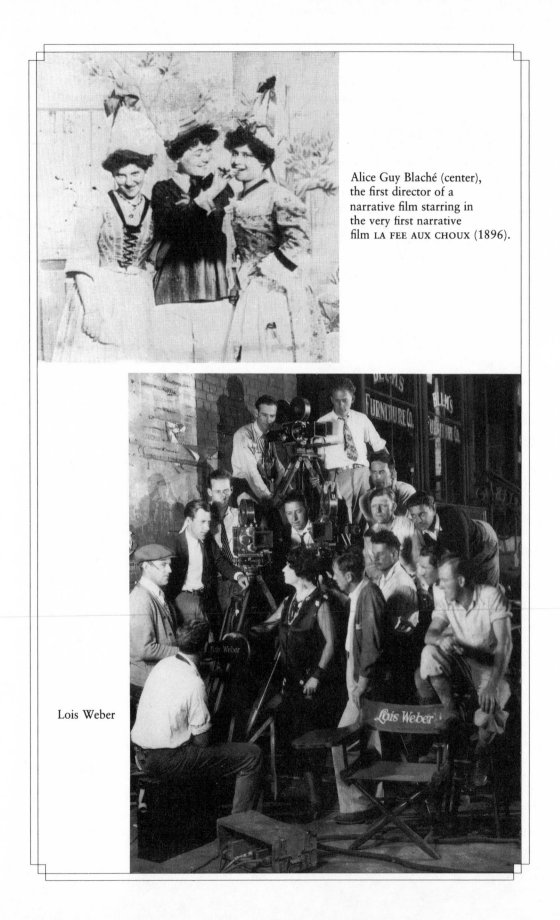

Alice Guy Blaché (center), the first director of a narrative film starring in the very first narrative film LA FEE AUX CHOUX (1896).

Lois Weber

THE SILENTS

◆ ◆ ◆

She is never ruffled. Never agitated. With a few simple
directions, uttered without apparent emotion, she handles the
interweaving movements like a military leader might the
manoeuvers of an army.
—Reporter of *Moving Picture World*
observing director **Alice Guy Blaché** on the set,
1912

Alice Guy Blaché (1875–1968)

History is lies agreed upon by the victors.
—Anonymous

Never has an axiom proved truer than in
the case of the motion-picture pioneer, **Alice
Guy Blaché.** The first woman film director
in history (and arguably the first director,
male or female, to bring a narrative film to
the screen), Blaché directed, produced and/
or supervised nearly three hundred films in
her lifetime. She then spent the rest of her
life attempting to prove to others that she
had done so.[1]

Who's Who in the Motion Picture World
of 1915 credits her with starting the production of multiple reels in the United
States, where she arrived to direct in 1910.[2]
Charles Ford in his article, "The First Female Producer," tells us that she tackled
every genre and manner of film: fairy tales
and fantasies, romances and comedies, religious parables, myths, trick films, and
paintings that came alive.[3] She even pro-

duced a science-fiction film entitled IN THE
YEAR 2000 (1912) in which women rule the
world.[4]

As early as 1906 Blaché filmed one of the
first movies ever to be shot in color (LA FÉE
PRINTEMPS [the spring fairy]). And throughout 1906–1907 she was busy directing
about a hundred sound movies, running a
minute or two in length, on an early device
called the "Chronophone," which combined sound recorded on a wax cylinder
with the filmed image.[5]

Born in Paris, the remarkable Blaché—
née Alice Guy—was the youngest daughter
of a bookseller who, "imbued her with a
love of literature and the arts."[6] An independent spirit from the word go, Blaché
took it upon herself to learn shorthand and
typing when her father died so she could
earn a living, a still-rare accomplishment for
women of pre–turn-of-the-century France.[7]
In 1885, she took a job as a secretary for
the Gaumont organization when Gaumont

was only making still-photography equipment. In 1895, Louis Lumière paid Gaumont a visit to show him a new contraption that Lumière had just invented: a camera that made still photographs appear as a series of moving images. Charles Ford tells us that Alice Guy was fascinated with what she saw.[8] Some time after, Gaumont, an inventor in his own right, made his own version of Lumière's 60mm camera.[9] Although he and his staff took pictures with the contraption, he couldn't figure out any practical use for it. On the other hand, Alice Guy realized almost immediately that in order to sell the gadget, it would have to intrigue, mystify, and entertain its potential buyer. She said:

> I thought I could do better. . . . Gathering up my courage, I timidly proposed to Gaumont that I would write one or two short plays and make them for the amusement of my friends. If the developments which evolved from this proposal could have been foreseen, then I probably never would have obtained his agreement. My youth, my lack of experience, my sex all conspired against me.[10]

Gaumont, who never took the invention seriously, was taken aback. "What! What! All right, if you *want* to," he is credited with saying. "It's a child's toy anyhow."[11]
He would let her have her fun on the condition that her secretarial duties did not suffer. LA FÉE AUX CHOUX *(The Cabbage Fairy)* was shown that same year (1896) at the International Exhibition in Paris.[12] The plot was based on an old French fable about a fairy who "produces" children in a cabbage patch.
Her experiment was so successful in selling Gaumont's equipment, that she was completely relieved of her secretarial tasks. From then on, she was put in charge of Gaumont's newly formed production entity. Richard Koszarski informs us that she established Gaumont's filmmaking arm, produced nearly all the films made by them

through 1906 (specializing in the talking Chronophone films), and trained such future luminaries of the French cinema as Louis Feuillade and Victoria Jasset.[13]
Her early sound films were ambitious undertakings—scenes from operas, including the Paris Opera, *Fra Diavolo, Carmen,* and *Mignon.* Still others utilized popular singers of the day.[14]
Nor did she lose interest in "tougher" subjects, shooting a series of "military scenes," most of which were among the world's first cowboy pictures.[15]
Many of her films of this period utilized cinematic tricks generally attributed almost exclusively to George Méliès. In PIERROT'S CHRISTMAS (1897), for instance, "she used masking and double exposure, and in A HOUSE DEMOLISHED AND REBUILT (ca. 1906) she ran film backwards.[16]
Her technical advisor, Frederic Dillaye, helped her refine the tricks. "In experience acquired day by day," she related, "by mistake, by chance, I discovered small tricks such as film turned inside out allows a house to collapse and be reconstructed again like magic. A person can tumble from a roof and go back up again instantly."[17]
As Richard Henshaw writes:

> The problems she faced were not unlike those of George Méliès, whose chronology in the years before 1900 were roughly parallel to [Alice] Guy's. . . .
> In France, the "contrived scenes" of Guy, Méliès and Ferdinand Zecca of Pathe were the premiere efforts in the establishment of a narrative cinema. Guy's importance in this regard should henceforth be understood and synthesized into the annals of film history, and Méliès' ultimate position as the more inventive of the two should not obscure Guy's prominence as an instigator of fictional film.[18]

While Alice Guy was filming bullfights in Nîmes, she met and soon after (1907) married an English cameraman in charge of Gaumont's London office, Herbert Blaché.

For nearly three years she abandoned her career for domesticity.

The Blachés moved to America. For a brief stint, they lived in Cleveland, then moved to New York, where Alice gave birth to a daughter. In 1910, while her husband was running Gaumont's branch office, Alice was quickly growing bored with domestic life and decided to go back to directing. *Who's Who in Directing* in 1912 claims that Blaché "with her own money," and quite on her own accord, organized "The Solax Company."

October 1910–June 1914, under the trademark of a blazing sun, the Solax company produced some 325 films of assorted lengths and types. At least 35 (possibly as many as 50) of them were directed by the company's lady president.[19]

Blaché's mission was to cater films specific to American tastes and acted in by American artists. Because of her good business sense, Gerald Peary said, "the history of Solax was, from its inception, an almost unbroken line of success."[20]

She was so successful in fact that soon she was able to move to Fort Lee, New Jersey, and construct what has been called probably the best-equipped moving-picture plant in the world. At a cost of an unheard of $100,000, the new Solax contained carpentry shops, prop rooms, hotel-like dressing rooms, five stage sets, laboratories, darkrooms, and projection rooms.[21]

Blaché ran Solax, "with the kind of total authority that leads to theorizing about 'the studio head as auteur.' "[22] Motion-picture trade papers of the day (1912) never failed to note, "The happy atmosphere of the Solax studio, banked together, like the happy family which they are."[23]

In *Women Who Make Movies* (1975) Blaché's daughter, Simone, said about her mother: "In many respects she was a nineteenth-century person. She believed in the family structure. And yet, she had strong feminist views. She was enthused by everything she saw and heard that was feminist in any way."[24]

If Blaché felt herself to be feminist, she certainly didn't let anyone know. Perhaps she thought it would be more diplomatic not to ruffle anyone's feathers with her political views. As Gerald Peary pointed out, her public views on the "nature of woman" leaned much closer to the Victorian male's.[25] Blaché wrote:

Not only is a woman as well fitted to stage photodrama as a man, but in many ways she has a distinct advantage over him because of her very nature and because much of the knowledge called for in the telling of the story and the creation of the stage setting is absolutely within her province as a member of the gentler sex. She is an authority on the emotions. For centuries she has given them full play while man has carefully trained himself to control them. She has developed her finer feelings for generations. In matters of the heart her superiority is acknowledged, her deep insight and sensitiveness in the affairs of Cupid. . . . It seems to me that a woman is especially well qualified to obtain the very best results, for she is dealing with subjects that are almost second nature to her.[26]

After bowing her head in this "geisha girl" gesture, by acknowledging, as a man might, woman's "proper place," she comes in for a more emphatic finish—the confidence and true conviction of her heart:

There is nothing connected with the staging of a motion picture that a woman cannot do as easily as a man, and there is no reason why she cannot completely master every technicality of the art.[27]

More important than what a person says is what she does. Gerald Peary explains her public nonpolitical stance by theorizing that as a woman she felt

she should stay away from editorializing about something so close to her situation—

rather than taking the opposite and more tenable view that she should make personal movies on women's rights precisely because the question was so relevant to her.[28]

He goes on to point out that Blaché is actually,

slightly misrepresented if she is seen as totally avoiding women's issues, for there are a few Solax movies which . . . do offer some rather strange perspectives to their story content.

He gives the following examples from two of her films from 1912:

THE CALL OF THE ROSE, said Peary, was about a young professional opera singer named Grace Moore, who marries a miner and goes West. For a brief time she is contented to watch her husband dig for gold. But she soon finds her inactive existence empty, and she leaves her husband to go back east and resume her career. The miner goes back east to find her and they are reunited. The plotline, however, neglects to say whether or not Grace keeps her career.

WINSOME BUT WISE involved a young impecunious woman, full of energy, who goes out West, and discovers she could make money by capturing a notorious bandit. The cowboys laugh at her, but our young heroine uses her ingenuity, captures the bandit, and turns him in for the reward.[29]

Despite the high level of suffrage activism of the day, publicity mongers were not beyond ignorant sexist reductions. Louis Reeves Harrison of a June 1912 *Moving Picture World* filters his vision through a Victorian lens,

Madame Blaché is, "never ruffled, never agitated, never annoyed by the obtrusive effects of minor characters to thrust themselves into prominence. With a few simple directions, uttered without apparent emotion, she handles the interweaving movements like a military leader might the maneuvres of an army.[30]

The subtleties of his language here are interesting to note.[30] The allusions to "lack of emotion" and to "militaristic maneuvers" are there as firm proof for the reader that Blaché is entitled to be a director because she can behave like a man.

After Solax, Blaché continued her career successfully, forming two subsequent companies with her husband, Herbert. However, by 1919, it was becoming nearly impossible for *any* independent to compete with the onslaught of the growing monoliths of Hollywood—the major studios. She began to hire out her talents to the larger companies, but it was clear that her career as an independent voice in the industry was all but finished.

A time of great personal strife ensued. Her company fell into decline and so did her marriage. Demoralized and defeated, she returned to France in 1922 with her two children (a son, Reginald, was born in 1911, one year after she began Solax), hoping to pick up the pieces of her career in her homeland. She was without prints of her films, and by this time, a middle-aged woman; no one would employ her. "Mother was really cherished in the United States," said her daughter, Simone. "The situation in France was quite the reverse."[31] "Cherished," in indepenent filmmaking, perhaps, but not in the new studio system where she couldn't find employment.

In 1927, reports Louise Heck-Rabi, she returned to the States to search for her films. But a visit to the Library of Congress, as well as several film depositories uncovered nothing at all.[32]

Blaché began supporting herself by producing conferences at universities on "feminine psychology and filmmaking." She wholeheartedly believed in both marriage and in a working life for women. So why did it become necessary for her to spend years of unrelenting energy to correct historian's records to prove what she had in fact done? Perhaps as early as the early twenties she knew it would be the only way, as Heck-Rabi has said, "to assure herself of the place she had earned in the history of film."[33]

Heck-Rabi goes on:

Many of her films were cited as works by others. No one realized and tried to correct published errors more assiduously than Mme. Blaché herself. She anticipated that directing and producing credits for her films would be falsely assigned to her co-workers. She knew that her name, unintentionally or purposefully, would be omitted, or ignored or demoted in the histories of French and American film.[34]

Georges Sadoul wrongly credited her for directing LES MEFAITS D'UNE TETE DE VEAU (The misdeeds of a calf's head). In an interview, she said that she was honored, but this was one of the few Gaumont pictures that she did *not* direct.[35] She *did*, however, direct an important film of that period, LA VIE DU CHRIST (1906), a picture that Sadoul credited to Victorin Jasset, her assistant on the film.[36] Says Blaché, "M. Sadoul . . . was poorly informed and in all good faith no doubt . . . attributed my first films to those who were at the Gaumont studios as figureheads, ignoring my name."[37]

Blaché approached Sadoul with documents "by which I tried to persuade him that the films in question were my work. He promised to correct this in his next edition, which in all honesty he did so, but his list [of her films] once again, contained errors."[38]

At the age of seventy-eight, Blaché was finally honored in France as the first woman filmmaker in the world, at the Cinematheque Francais, and made a knight of the French Legion of Honor.

But in Mahwah, New Jersey, the state in which she changed the course of film history and made her most entrepreneurial triumphs, she died anonymous. Not one newspaper carried her obituary. She was ninety-five years old.

ALICE GUY BLACHÉ

1896	Cabbage Fairy, The
1897	Bewitched Fiancé, The
	Black Maria
	He
	I Have a Maybug in My Trousers
	Pranks of Pierrette, The
1897–1906	Ballet of Monkeys
	Delightful Rustle
	Enchanted Bean, The
	Legend of St. Nicholas
	Midnight
	Moving Out in the Night
	Pierrot's Christmas
1899	Dangers of Alcohol, The
1901	Cavalry Officers and Shop-girls
	Dance of the Seasons, The
1903	Thugs Are Not Lucky
	Willing Sacrifice, The
1904	Assassination of the Courier of Lyons
	Baptism of a Puppet
	Crime on Church Street, The
	First Cigarette, The
	Infants' Abduction by Gypsies
	Rehabilitation
	Small Cutters of Bois-Vert, The
	Young Painters
1905	Crinoline, The
	Paris Night
1906	A House Demolished and Rebuilt
	La Vie du Christ
1912	Call of the Rose, The
	Canned Harmony
	Detective's Dog, The
	Fra Diavolo
	Girl in the Armchair, The
	Hotel Honeymoon
	In the Year 2000
	Mickey's Pal
	Winsome But Wise

1912–14	Hater of Women a.k.a. His Better Self		Hook and Hand
	Her Double		House (or Castle) of Cards
	Idol Worshipper		Lure, The
	Marvelous Cow, The		Michael Strogoff
	Officer Henderson		Monster and the Girl, The
	Our Poor Relations		Ragged Earl, The
	Sewers of New York, The		Shooting of Dan McGrew, The
1912–20	*Films made in the US*		Tigress, The
	Dreadnaught		Yellow Traffic, The
	Eyes That Could Not Close		Woman of Mystery
	Honeymoon	1915	My Madonna
	Snake Temple		Sea Wolf, The
	Way of the Sea		Vampire, The
1913	A House Divided	1916	Eternal Question, The
	Beasts of the Jungle		What Will People Say?
	Dick Whittington and His Cat		Woman's Fight
	Fortune Hunters	1917	Adventurer, The
	Kelly from the Emerald Isle		Auction of Virtue, The
	Little Hunchback Tailor, The		Behind the Mask
	Matrimony's Speed Limit		Empress, The
	Pit and the Pendulum, The		Man and a Woman, A
	Rogues of Paris, The		Soul of Magdalene, The
	Shadows of Moulin Rouge		Spring of the Year
	Star of India, The		When You and I Were Young
	Terrible Night, A		Whoso Findeth a Wife
1914	Beneath the Czar	1918	Great Adventurer, The
	Dream Woman		Social Hypocrytes
	Fight for Freedom of Exiled to Siberia, A		Soul Adrift, A
	Fighting Death	1919	Brat, The
	Heart of a Painted Woman, The		Divorcée, The
			Out of the Fog
		1920	Tarnished Reputations

Lois Weber (1882–1939)

Film trivia: Who was the first woman to direct, star, coauthor, and produce a major motion picture? **Barbra Streisand?** Yes, if you're thinking of sound films, but she had a predecessor whose reputation is now as silent and forgotten as the nearly four hundred films she alternately directed, wrote, starred in, and produced.

First and foremost, this woman was a social realist. **Lois Weber** refused to associate her name with a film unless she unswervingly supported its moral stance. At a time when people were still discovering what a "movie" was, Weber's rebellious instincts came up with plots that ranged from abortion to racism, from prostitution to capital punishment.

Her films most often focused on women, although she was loath to pledge her allegiance to the suffragists, or to any other special-interest group. More important to Lois Weber was to attempt to change people's attitudes. She was the first to see how film could drive home a moral through story telling. From God's mouth to Weber's lens to the eyes of the masses.

Lois Weber began her career as a street-corner evangelist, singing hymns in the industrial slums of Philadelphia and New York in the late 1890s. But desperate finances and a zealous commitment to spread the doctrines of the Bible led her to take up an uncle's suggestion and try a more accessible soapbox. "Filled with a great desire to convert my fellowmen," said Weber later, "I went on the stage."

In a 1905 road company melodrama propitiously titled, *Why Girls Leave Home,*[1] she met and married the company's manager, Phillips Smalley. For a time, the couple continued their separate careers, and Weber achieved critical success as an actress at the great Hippodrome in New York. Perhaps it was not so coincidental that right after this, Smalley encouraged his wife to try her hand at what women have always been so good at: permanent housekeeping.

Two years of homemaking turned out to be quite long enough for Lois Weber. In 1908, she took a job at the Gaumont Film Studio in Fort Lee, New Jersey, where filmmaking began in this country, under the tutelage of Herbert Blaché, husband of the pioneer film director, **Alice Guy Blaché.**

Weber had finally found the perfect outlet for her evangelism. "Now I can preach to my heart's content," she said. "And with the opportunity to write the play, act the leading roles, and direct the entire production, if my message fails to reach someone, I can blame only myself."[2]

Her frank depictions of modern life gained her a reputation as a director/writer who stirred audiences to passionate outrage. Weber was at last on her way, and

her way was controversy! In the pervading atmosphere of a changing Victorian morality, the public was both ripe for and wary of her subject matter. But with her high-minded, fundamentalist eye, Weber's themes of birth control, divorce, abortion, and promiscuity ended up being a synchronistic complement to the social barometer of the day. Many of her topics were viewed as "sensational," although her purpose, she insisted, was not exploitation. Her movies often faced censorship hearings and were closed down by the police. At another point in history, her career might have been in jeopardy, but because the movie industry was just finding its feet, Weber won a lot of free press instead. Her films became commercial sure bets.

By 1916, with her husband now riding her coattails in a writer/director partnership, Weber was employed by Universal Studios as the top-salaried director of the silent era. She earned an astonishing five thousand dollars a week, and was elected "The Mayor of Universal City." Her plum assignment came with the Russian ballerina Anna Pavlova and the Ballet Russe in the only dramatic film Pavlova ever made. Now a classic, THE DUMB GIRL OF PORTICI (1915) was a historic costume drama set in Spain in the late 1600s. It was not Weber's favorite material, but the movie's moderate success won her the freedom to do the pictures she really wanted to do.

HYPOCRITES (1914) was a fascinating risk for Weber as well as a terrific success. Its concern was corruption in the modern world. According to Anthony Slide, the male protagonist, Courtenay Foote, played "a dual lead of a monk who sees the hypocrisy of the world and a minister stoned to death by his congregation for unveiling a statue of 'The Naked Truth.' "[3] According to Slide, "The Naked Truth" was a nude girl whose real identity is dubious to this day. Some say Weber, unable to find a willing player, played the role herself.[4] But Kevin Brownlow disagrees with this assertion stating, "The nude in HYPOCRITES is a petite young girl—probably wearing a bodystocking—and could not possibly be Weber."[5]

The Ohio Board of Censors banned the film and the mayor of Boston demanded that clothes be hand-painted on "The Naked Truth," frame by frame. The critics were astonished. *Variety* in November 1914 wrote, "After seeing it, you can't forget the name of Lois Weber!" The film caused riots at New York's Strand Theatre. Always assured of a moral tale in an entertaining context, audiences quickly learned to spot Weber's trademark as well as they could Griffith's.

Her favorite and most famous foray came with the five-reel "spectacular," WHERE ARE MY CHILDREN? (1916). It advocated birth control while speaking forthrightly against abortion, or "race suicide," as it was referred to in the film. Tyrone Power (the elder) plays a district attorney who longs for children. His selfish wife and her social butterfly set, however, take due care that none of their social engagements are upset by "interventions of nature." The crisis is precipitated when the brother of the attorney's wife impregnates the housekeeper's daughter. The wife suggests to her brother that he consult her doctor who she knows performs illegal abortions. When the girl dies by the doctor's hand, he is brought to trial, and prosecuted by the district attorney. Power discovers his wife's involvement in the affair and berates her harshly. She admits to him that she's also physically "unable to wear the diadem of motherhood." "And all their lives together," say the concluding subtitles, "she must face that mute question, 'Where are my children?' "

The film was sufficiently controversial to stir up a sleepy 1916 Victorian audience. It was banned by the Philadelphia Board of Censors. *Motion Picture News* in October 1916 wrote, "Dr. Ellis P. Oberholtzer, a member of the board [of censors] expressed himself freely, 'The picture is unspeakably

vile . . . I would have permitted it to pass the board in the state only over my dead body. . . . It is not fit for decent people to see.' . . . The Reverend John C. Wheeler [another board member] and spiritual director of the Federation of Catholic Societies said, '. . . One may not be able to say that the film is openly immoral, but most likely it is even worse in its suggestive situations.' "

The religiously dominated Philadelphia Board of Censors was soon in the minority of opinion. Censorship trials sprang up all over the country, creating just the kind of publicity the film needed to turn hundreds of curious viewers away from many screenings. WHERE ARE MY CHILDREN? grossed the happy, fledgling Universal Studios three million dollars. Universal President Carl Laemmle said in tribute to Weber, "I would trust Miss Weber with any sum of money that she needed to make any picture that she wanted to make. I would be sure that she would bring it back. She knows the motion picture business as few people do and can drive herself as hard as anyone I have ever known."[6]

As Weber grew as a filmmaker, her style became more subtle. After the excessive reaction to her five reeler, she felt she no longer needed to hit audiences over the head quite so hard to get her messages across. Instead, she followed with a string of successful, theatrical soap operas with sugary moral plots.

SHOES (1916) speaks to the issue of child labor. THE PEOPLE VS. JOHN DOE (1916) attacked the evils of capital punishment. The very contemporary message of THE LEPER'S COAT (1914) was that "science has proven that fear of disease will produce its symptoms more surely than contagion, and that thought governs the body."

By late 1916, she was at the height of her career. *Moving Picture Stories* hailed her as, "the greatest woman director."[7] In 1917 she attained the highest goal of any director of that period: Universal sponsored, built, and provided Weber her own studio far from the bustling lot. On the occasion of this major coup she wrote in *Motion Picture Magazine,* "The public as a whole is sentimental and . . . unless you give them what they want you're not going to make any money. And let those who set themselves up as idealists chatter as much as they please about their art, the commercial side cannot be neglected. We're all in business to make money. You can pander to the whim of the moment; or you can build with an eye to the future. Personally, I prefer the latter."[8]

By 1920, her success was unprecedented. Paramount lured her away from Universal with a $50,000-per-picture contract, and half of all profits.[9] The very next year she turned out five features. Her most successful, and one still in existence today, THE BLOT (1921) (independently made and released by F. B. Warren Corporation), concerns itself with the pride of a poor family who would rather starve than accept charity. One critic called it "a brilliant, lively fugue of urban vs. rural values."[10]

"I'll never be convinced that the general public does not want serious entertainment rather than frivolous,"[11] she said in a 1921 interview. Yet it was specifically this stubborn resistance to reading the pulse of a changing time that was the beginning of her demise. For the twenties was the era of the jazz age. People were no longer interested in being preached to. They wanted to go to the movies to have fun.

Weber's films started to fail at the box office. By the mid-1920s she lost her company, divorced her husband Smalley, and suffered a nervous breakdown.

She returned to directing briefly in the late 1920s with SENSATION SEEKERS (1927), a film that did not mask her underlying disapproval for the era's easing of moral standards. A fashionable girl of the Long Island Jazz set runs around with two men at the same time: a wealthy bachelor and the reverend of the church. When the offended

church community takes the matter up with the bishop, she runs off with the bachelor to his yacht. The bachelor drowns in a yacht accident, but the girl is saved by the reverend and the bishop, who finally decides that the best thing of all is for the reverend and the girl to marry. "It is disconcerting to watch the young girl of today grow into manhood!" says the film's protagonist.

Cecil B. De Mille gave her a chance in 1927 to direct her last silent film about "loose women" entitled, THE ANGEL OF BROADWAY with **Leatrice Joy** and written by **Lenore Coffee**. According to film historian Richard Koszarski, "A cabaret dancer burlesques the innocence of a salvation army girl—an oblique but bitter allusion to Weber's own early days."[12]

Its initial run closed to bad reviews and the film was refused further distribution because of its subject matter. The career of Lois Weber was all but over.

For the next decade, she struggled to make a comeback. But it was increasingly clear, except to Weber herself, that her skills lay mainly in depicting her own inner vision, not in entertaining audiences in the way they now were demanding to be entertained. One of only three talkies she ever made, WHITE HEAT (1934), concerned miscegenation and racism on a sugar plantation. Shot on location in Hawaii, a white sugar planter marries a native on the island.

Critics attacked the film as "humorless," and distributors in 1934 saw the topic as lethal. The film never saw the light of the silver screen after its initial run in Los Angeles.

The final proof of Weber as a thinker far ahead of her time came with her pioneering notion in 1937 to use film as an audiovisual aid in schools.[13] Although newsreels and nature movies had been shown around the country since World War I, the concept of producing films specifically for the educational market was not yet popular. Professional use of 16mm film was introduced in the 1920s, and 28mm and 9.5mm film distributors listed educational films in their catalogues. Still, Weber's idea was viewed as a costly "scheme," and would not be realized until the 1940s, when 16mm projectors became as common in schools as VCRs are today.

Like many of the silent screen's pioneers, Weber found the transition to talkies difficult. The form was wrong for her now anachronistic and preachy style. Unable to obtain work again as a director during the last five years of her life, she humbled herself to free-lancing as a script doctor and to testing "starlets" for Universal Studios. Lonely and bereft in the Hollywood of 1939, this most successful woman director died penniless and ignored by an industry she helped create.[14]

No filmmaker before or since achieved what Lois Weber achieved. "Not only was she . . . the most important female director the American film industry has known," remembers one encyclopedia of filmmakers,

but, unlike many of her colleagues up to the present, her work was regarded in its day as equal to, if not a little better than that of most male directors. She was a committed filmmaker in an era when commitment was virtually unknown.[15]

LOIS WEBER

1913	Eyes of God, The
	Jews Christmas, The
1914	False Colors
	Hypocrites
	It's No Laughing Matter
	Leper's Coat, The
	Like Most Wives
	Merchant of Venice, The
	Traitor
1915	Cigarette, That's All Gold Seal, A
	Dumb Girl of Portici, The
	Scandal
	Sunshine Molly
1916	Alone in the World
	Discontent
	French Downstairs, The
	Hop, the Devil Brew
	John Needham's Double
	People vs. John Doe, The
	Rock of Riches, The
	Saving the Family Name
	Shoes
	Where Are My Children?
1917	Even As You and I
	Hand that Rocks the Cradle, The
	For Husbands Only
	Man Who Dared God, The
	Mysterious Mrs. M., The
	Price of a Good Time, The
	There's No Place Like Home
1918	Borrowed Clothes
	Doctor and the Woman, The
1919	Forbidden
	Home
	Mary Regan
	Midnight Romance
	Scandal Managers
	When a Girl Loves
1921	Blot, The
	To Please One Woman
	Too Wise Wives
	What Do Men Want?
	What's Worth While?
1923	Chapter in Her Life, A
1926	Marriage Clause, The
1927	Angel of Broadway, The
	Sensation Seekers
1934	White Heat

SHORT TAKES

◆ ◆ ◆

Ida May Park (?–1954)

Virtually forgotten because her pictures have been lost, **Ida May Park** was one of several prominent women directors[1] at Universal Studios in the late 1910s, and certainly one of the most prolific. Like **Lois Weber,** Park was primarily and prominently a director, while many of the other women in film of the period were actresses with one or two directorial attempts.

In 1920 *Motion Picture News* announced the formation of Park's own firm. "The Andrew J. Callaghan Productions is pleased to announce the creation of a new unit to be known as the Ida May Park Productions. Officials of the company have long been aware of the distinctive quality of Miss Park's directorial work . . . [We have] the highest faith in Miss Park. We are able to take this step as a means of recognition for her own producing unit."[2]

Park, like many early women in film, entered the medium as a teenage actress on the stage. She later branched out into writing, and then into directing as a team with her husband, the actor Joseph De Grasse. At Universal, as Anthony Slide notes in *Early Women Directors,* the couple made as many as twelve features in eleven months.[3] By 1917 Park was directing solo with many of Universal's biggest stars. One

of them was Lon Chaney, the famous "Phantom" of Rupert Julian's film. Park, with no directing credits listed post-1920, seems to have continued as a writer for her husband's directorial efforts.

Richard Koszarski differentiates Park from Lois Weber: "Weber was totally committed to the cinema as a tool for moral betterment . . . one of the cinema's few true idealists. Park on the other hand . . . was the very model of a modern studio functionary. . . . She subordinated all else to getting the product out on time and under budget."[4] From such evidence, one could deduce that Weber used her privileged stance to revolutionize cinema, while Park was just happy to be working in the industry, reluctant to upset the apple cart. And yet, one can never be certain about such deductions.

In a lengthy 1918 interview with Park in *Photoplay Magazine,* she spoke about directing:

> It has been said that a woman worries over loves, and works for her convictions exactly as though they were her children. Consequently, her greatest danger is in taking them and herself too seriously.
>
> Directing is a recreation to me, and I

want my people to do good work because of their regard for me and not because I browbeat them into it. I believe in choosing distinct types and then seeing that the actor puts his own personality into his parts, instead of making every part in a picture reflect my personality.[5]

In answering a request to write a chapter on women and directing for the 1920 anthology, *Careers for Women,* Ida May Park agreed with **Alice Guy Blaché** when she wrote, "As for the natural equipment of women for the role of director, the superiority of their emotional and imaginative faculties gives them a great advantage. Then too, the fact that there are only two women directors of note in the field today [i.e., she and Weber] leaves an absolutely open field."[6]

This attitude was apparently not always one Park possessed, as is evident from an interview done with her in *Photoplay* from 1918:

"It was because directing seemed so utterly unsuited to a woman that I refused the first company offered me. I don't know why I looked at it that way either. A woman can bring to this work splendid enthusiasm and imagination; a natural love of detail and an intuitive knowledge of character. All these are supposed to be feminine traits, and yet

they are all necessary to the successful director."[7]

But as Koszarski points out, "If [women] had an advantage, Hollywood took no use of it. When *Careers for Women* was reissued . . . in 1934, the entire entry on motion picture directing was dropped. There was only one woman director [**Dorothy Arzner** then] working in Hollywood."[8]

IDA MAY PARK

1917	Bondage (Director, Scenario)
	Fires of Rebellion (Director and Author)
	Flashlight, The (Director, Scenario)
1918	Bread
	Broadway Love
	Model's Confession, The
	Risky Road (Director, Adaptation)
	Vanity Pool
ca. 1918	Boss of Powderville
1919	Amazing Wife (Director, Scenario)
1920	Butterfly Man, The (Director, Scenario)
1921	Bonnie May
	Midlanders, The

Ruth Ann Baldwin

A newspaper woman and publicist, **Ruth Ann Baldwin** turned to motion pictures early on as a writer of serials in 1915 for Universal. One of her first assignments, according to Anthony Slide, was the Herbert Rawlingson-Anna Little serial, THE BLACK BOX (1915). It was an enormous success. A year later, she was assigned her own company of players and "became a full-fledged director"[1] with her own production unit to direct RETRIBUTION. The picture was re-

leased in August of 1916 and starred **Cleo Madison,** another Universal actress turned director. *Photoplay Magazine* of 1916 said of her, "She has long been regarded as one of the most capable of Universal's staff."[2]

RUTH ANN BALDWIN

1915	Arrangement with Fate, An
	Black Box, The
	Double Deal in the Park, The

1916	Recoiling Vengeance, The		Twixt Love and Desire
	Retribution		When Liz Lets Loose
1917	Black Mantilla, The		Wife on Trial, A
	Butterfly, The		Woman Who Could Not Pay, The
	Is Money All?	1918	Mother's Call, The
	It Makes a Difference	1919	Broken Commandments
	Rented Man, The	1920	Devil's Ripple, The
	Soldier of the Legion, A	1921	Marriage of William Ashe, The
	Storm Women, The		Puppets of Fate
	Three Women of France		

Elizabeth Pickett

If **Elizabeth Pickett** is forgotten today, she was remembered by John Ford as a model and an inspiration for his own work. Her short, THE KING OF THE TURF (1923), shot in her native Kentucky, was a model for Ford's later feature KENTUCKY PRIDE (1925).[1] Pickett edited and titled the Ford feature.

After graduating from Wellesley and taking charge of her family's tobacco farm, Pickett began a new career of making prop-aganda shorts for the Red Cross. Anthony Slide points out that she wrote eleven hundred of the fifteen-hundred-pages of *The History of the Red Cross*.[2]

In 1923, Pickett made the first "short series" films for Fox Film Corporation, writing and directing about forty, and soon became their West Coast supervisor.

Gerald Peary once noted that Pickett never directed a feature film, but later evidence has proved him wrong. In 1928 she

Elizabeth Pickett

Marguerite Bertsch

announced in *Moving Picture World,* that "I want to write and direct my own pictures."[3] Presumably, this meant features. Paramount picked up on this, and gave her the opportunity with REDSKIN in 1929.[4]

ELIZABETH PICKETT

1923   "Short Film Series" (for Fox)
1929   Redskin

Marguerite Bertsch (?–1967)

Marguerite Bertsch was head of Vitagraph's scenario division for many years before turning her talents to directing in 1916 with THE LAW DECIDES. Anthony Slide called her Vitagraph's most important woman director of the silent days.[1]

When asked by *Moving Picture Stories* what she first felt as a director she said, "To be perfectly frank with you I didn't feel at all. You know, I never wrote a picture that I did not mentally direct. Every situation was as clear in my mind as though the film was already photographed."[2]

Bertsch was also the author of a best-selling book of the period, *How to Write for Moving Pictures* (1917).[3]

MARGUERITE BERTSCH

1916   Law Decides, The

THE SOUND ERA

◆ ◆ ◆

Dorothy Arzner (1900–1979)

My philosophy is that to be a director you cannot be subject to anyone, even the head of the studio. I threatened to quit each time I didn't get my way, but no one ever let me walk out.

—Dorothy Arzner in an interview with Francine Parker

"You see, I was not dependent on the movies for my living, so I was always ready to give the picture over to some other director if I couldn't make it the way I saw it. Right or wrong, I believe this was why I sustained so long—twenty years."[1]

This extraordinary woman held her own in an all-male Hollywood of the thirties and forties. She directed seventeen features between 1927 and 1943.[2]

Her most interesting films confronted the struggle for sexual equality in relationships. She bravely chose actresses whose screen presences expanded beyond the two-dimensional boundaries of the script. Her women were never meek nor boring, her protagonists bravely fought no-win battles of commitment to marriage and career versus commitment to the self.[3] She was, and remains after her death, the only woman able to build up a coherent body of work *within* the Hollywood system.

Dorothy Arzner was the only director in mainstream Hollywood to work with *all of* the major female stars of her day,[4] including: **Clara Bow, Rosalind Russell, Lucille Ball, Merle Oberon, Claudette Colbert, Sylvia Sidney, Joan Crawford, Katharine Hepburn,** and to give many their important debuts.[5]

Her 1933 classic, CHRISTOPHER STRONG brought Kate Hepburn boldly into public view. MERRILY WE GO TO HELL (1932) was Sylvia Sidney's first starring role (and was one of the highest-grossing films for a period of forty years). With ANYBODY'S WOMAN (1930), **Ruth Chatterton** became known as "The First Lady of the Screen." THE WILD PARTY (1929) launched Fredric March successfully into his motion picture career (and was Paramount's first "talkie"). THEODORA GOES WILD (1936) had Arzner in the role of producer and story developer. The film was also instrumental in turning **Irene Dunne** into a star of comedy. And Arzner's CRAIG'S WIFE (1936) transformed Roz Russell into a major screen personality.

"She was a remarkable woman," said Katharine Hepburn. "She just did what she wanted, working along quietly, and no-

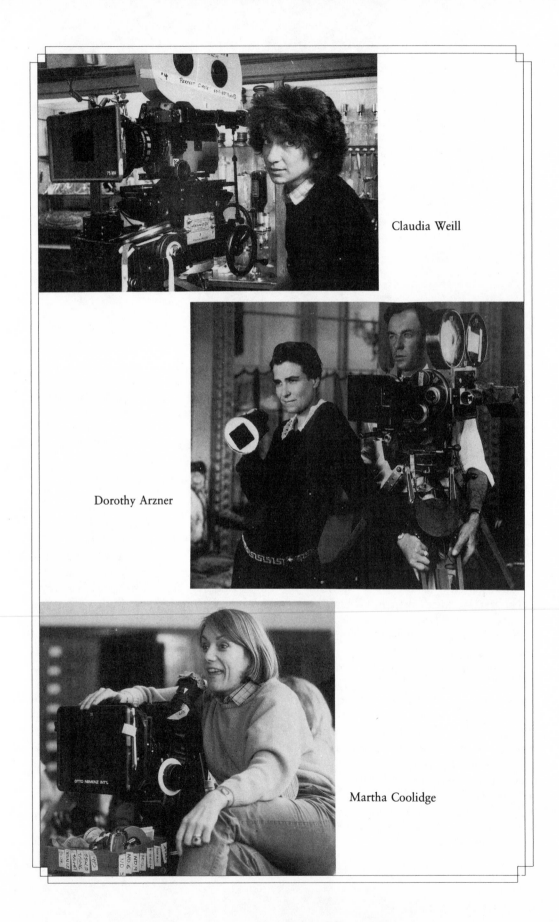

Claudia Weill

Dorothy Arzner

Martha Coolidge

Susan Seidelman

Donna Deitch

Joan Tewkesbury

Joan Micklin Silver

Karen Arthur

body thought a damn about it. Of course, looking back, it seems queer as the dickens, but not so then. Ladies just did a lot of things without talking about them. . . . But remarkable that she could occupy that job fifty odd years ago and have no one say, 'Miss Hepburn, would you mind working with a woman?' 'Not at all!' Now I would consider it slightly peculiar!"[6]

Arzner started out with aspirations of becoming a doctor. "I wanted to be like Jesus, 'Heal the sick and raise the dead,' instantly, without surgery or pills."[7] After a few short months observing a surgeon and becoming disillusioned that medicine didn't pay homage to such lofty fantasies, she astutely moved over to the industry that did—the movies.

Soon after, she impressed William De Mille, Cecil's brother, by telling him that the only job she would consider was that of typing his scripts. Seeing his surprised reaction, Arzner asked him if there was any other way to learn an industry *except* from the ground up?

Within six months, such tenacity took her to the cutting room where she said she learned more about the business of making movies than she could have anywhere else. Assigned to Paramount's subsidiary, Realart Studio, Arzner was the only editor among cameramen and a full studio department—and certainly the only woman —and was quickly crowned as chief editor. She ended up cutting fifty-two pictures during her two-year tenure as chief.

In 1923, Arzner was recalled to the parent company to edit the silent classic, BLOOD AND SAND. It was to be the turning point of her career. The problem in this Rudolph Valentino epic (Valentino was earlier plucked out of anonymity and made a star in THE FOUR HORSEMEN OF THE APOCALYPSE because of the pioneering foresight of **June Mathis**) was how to double Valentino into the "corrida" in Madrid. Arzner thought of cutting three bullfights into the scene from Madrid bullfight stock, saving

Paramount costly double exposures. She then shot close-ups of Valentino to match the longer shots.[8] Her ingenuity worked. And Paramount chiefs were duly impressed.

She wrote and edited other big pictures with director James Cruze. THE COVERED WAGON (1923) was perhaps the first great giant American Western. "We used five tribes of Indians," says Arzner, "and oxen were broken to the yoke."[9] After OLD IRONSIDES (1926) she decided to leave Paramount for a chance at directing for the then-smaller firm of Columbia. Dorothy Arzner recalls the day of this monumental decision:

> It was late afternoon. I decided I should say goodbye to someone after seven years and much work: B. P. Schulberg. But Mr. Schulberg's secretary told me he was in conference. So I went out to my car in the parking lot, had my hand on the door latch, when I decided after so many years I was going to say 'goodbye' to *someone* important and not just leave unnoticed and forgotten. . . .
>
> I returned and asked the secretary if she minded if I waited for the conference to be over. She *did* mind. Mr. Schulberg would not see anyone. It was late then . . . but Walter Wanger passed in the studio . . . I called out, "Oh, you'll do!" "What's that?" And I told him I was leaving Paramount after seven years, and I wanted to say goodbye to someone *important*. . . .

When Arzner told Wanger she was leaving, he all but panicked and instantly got Schulberg out of his meeting. Schulberg couldn't believe his ears. Their dialogue was as good as any one of Arzner's best pictures:

> SCHULBERG
> What do you mean you're leaving?
> ARZNER
> I've finished IRONSIDES. I've closed out my salary, and I'm leaving.
> SCHULBERG
> We don't want you to leave. There's al-

ways a place for you in the scenario department.

ARZNER
I don't want to go into the scenario department. I'm going to direct for a small company.

SCHULBERG
What company?

ARZNER
I won't tell you because you'd probably spoil it for me.

SCHULBERG
Now Dorothy, you go into our scenario department and later we'll think about directing.

ARZNER
No, I know I'd never get out of there.

Schulberg saw that there was no persuading her and that he was up against the wall. He knew that he only had one alternative:

SCHULBERG
What would you say if I told you that you could direct here?

ARZNER
Please don't fool me, just let me go. I'm going to direct at Columbia.

SCHULBERG
You're going to direct here at Paramount.

Next, we know, Arzner is going for broke. Just how far, she wondered, could he be pushed?

ARZNER
Not unless I can be on a set in two weeks with an "A" picture. I'd rather do an "A" picture for a small company and have my own way than a "B" picture for Paramount.

And with that, Schulberg walked away from her saying, "Wait here." He returned minutes later with a play in his hand and said to her,

141,784

SCHULBERG
Here. It's a French farce called, *The Best Dressed Woman in Paris*. Start writing the script and get yourself on the set in two weeks. New York is sending Esther Ralston out to star. . . .[10]

And that is the story of how Dorothy Arzner became a director. The announcement in the papers the following day read, "Lasky Names Woman Director."[11]

Arzner brought her first picture in on time and under budget. The year was 1927. Her next vehicle starred Clara Bow and Buddy Rogers. By this time, Arzner had truly won over not only B. P. Schulberg, but also his progressive wife. Some say in fact, that it was Mrs. Schulberg who initially leaned on her husband to give Arzner the chance to direct.[12]

Buddy Rogers recalled that at the time it was the start of his career and he didn't much care *who* it was directing him, just as long as *someone* was directing him.[13] Clara Bow was a bit fussier. As Tui Lorraine recalls,

> She bitched to me about having a woman director. After all, girlfriends like me she could lose, but a gorgeous man was 'divine,' and Dorothy Arzner was going to make one less man around.[14]

Men were about the last thing on Arzner's mind. In fact, Arzner did her best to set Clara Bow straight on that account. "Now, I don't want a lot of men around here, and I don't want any nonsense going on."[15] From that moment forward, star and director understood one another. They were inherently different enough to get on quite well. Bow had a childlike elegance that charmed and impressed Arzner, and maybe even awed her a little. Opposites attracting, perhaps Arzner felt she could learn from Clara's instinctual way of dealing directly and candidly from her heart. A 1932 article entitled, "Feminine Director Depends on

Reason, Discards Intuition," quotes Arzner as saying:

> Men think analytically. Women rely on what they call intuition and emotion . . . but those qualities do not help any one in directing. A director must be able to reason things out in logical sequence.[16]

Arzner was stiff and restrained in her manners on the set, Clara was just the opposite.

> Arzner insisted on a cathedral hush, with everyone talking in low-pitched voices—no hammers, no saws, no laughter. . . . Nobody ever dared call Miss Arzner "Dorothy"—let alone Dotty.[17]

The last scene of GET YOUR MAN was memorable. It was 4:00 A.M., the final scene of the movie. Arzner was exhausted and called to Bow and Rogers through her megaphone: "Now you come together, meet in the middle, and we fade out." Everyone burst into hysterics with a stunned, sheet-faced Arzner wondering what she had said.

> Clara rushed over to Arzner and threw her arms around her. "She didn't know what she said!" yelled the star in defense of her mortified director. Then, Clara comforted Arzner . . . "the boys'll try ta twist everythin' into a double meanin' on ya, see. Anythin' for a laugh." Her dignity restored, Arzner got the shot and brought in [the film] for $200,000.[18]

This was not only on time, but 15 percent below the budgets of two previous Clara Bow "formula" films.[19]

THE WILD PARTY, Arzner's next film with Clara Bow,[20] was an extraordinary achievement on many fronts. It was the first "talkie" that Paramount ever produced. Next, it is probably the first film in America to deal with the subject of female bonding in a positive, affirming way. There is a heterosexual love affair, but it falls a quiet sec-

ond to the female friendships. The women stand up for each other, take the rap for each other, and ultimately, the Clara Bow character allows herself to be expelled from school in order to save a girlfriend's reputation. Perhaps it is the first (certainly it is a rare) case in the cinema where relationships among women are shown to be anything other than catty.

Another salute for this picture is Arzner's technological achievement. It was becoming a problem that the actors had to do their acting pantomimes, then come to the front of the room to the stationary microphones in order to deliver their lines. On the second day of shooting, Arzner suggested to the soundman that he attach a fishpole to the microphone and instead, follow the actors around. Thus, the industry's "boom microphone" was born.[21] She used her ingenuity to turn her megaphone into double usage, and make it also into a viewfinder.

Despite Clara Bow's "constant fear" throughout making THE WILD PARTY,[22] the finished product played to packed houses nationwide.

By the time Dorothy Arzner entered movies, the industry was really beginning to coalesce into a "business," replete with profits and losses, careers and reputations at stake. By the early thirties, the nepotistic unions simply did *not* let women join.[23]

Yet with all of the resistance she faced, it is generally agreed that Dorothy Arzner directed from a woman's point of view. What does that mean? According to Sharon Smith,

> She sought to undo the stereotypes of women characters as scheming witches, and light-hearted husband chasers, and depicted them instead as persons of intelligence, humor and humanity.[24]

A case in point was CHRISTOPHER STRONG. It was one of those rare films for the early thirties that featured, as its protagonist, a strong woman who had a career.

The film would be Katharine Hepburn's second appearance on celluloid after her debut in BILL OF DIVORCEMENT (1932), and it would set her on the road to stardom. This 1933 phenomenon has Hepburn playing a woman aviator forced to choose between her career and her love for a married man. It was a no-win situation for the woman of the 1930s, and Arzner had Hepburn do the only sensible thing a woman in her situation could have done in that time: commit suicide kamikaze style.

Sarafina Batherick, a women's history scholar and professor at Hunter College in New York, put it this way, "She [Hepburn's character] was supposed to be challenging the altitude record for flying. But metaphorically, by society's standards, she had in some sense 'flown too high.' Suicide was really her only option."[25]

Marjorie Rosen queried Dorothy Arzner while she was alive as to what she thought the differences were between masculine and feminine viewpoints. Arzner depicts a moment in CRAIG'S WIFE, when Roz Russell is alone in her house. "The audience hated her up to that point," explained Arzner,

> and I only had one close-up left with which to turn their emotion to sympathy. Russell did it so perfectly that in movie theatres handkerchiefs began coming out. . . .

And yet in speaking with George Kelly, the author of the original play, it was clear that he and Arzner had very different ideas about Mrs. Craig's character. Said Arzner,

> I told him I was following [the play] as faithfully as possible . . . but that I believed Mr. Craig should be down on his knees to Mrs. Craig because she'd made a man of him. I believe he'd been dominated by his mother who, before she died, had told his aunt to stand by him because she didn't approve of Mrs. Craig. So the aunt is in his house throughout the play.

At this, Arzner reports that George Kelly rose to his six-foot height and said,

> "That's not my play! Harriet Craig is an SOB and Craig is a sweet guy."
> So there you are—a woman's point of view vs. a man's.

Arzner continues to defend her position:

> Kelly even had Harriet Craig tell how her mother had slaved for her father and how he had gone off with another woman and left her penniless. So we know what made Harriet Craig what she was. But it made a man of Craig, and she received enlightenment: "A woman who loves her home more than her husband is generally left alone."[26]

Arzner was aware as early as 1932 that men and women might see distinctly differently as filmmakers when she said in an interview:

> There should be more of us directing. Try as any man may, he will never be able to get the woman's viewpoint in directing certain stories. . . . A great per cent of our audience is women. That too is something to think about.[27]

Arzner directed seventeen films, most of them box-office successes, for Paramount, RKO, Columbia, and MGM. She nearly directed a picture called STEPDAUGHTERS OF WAR (never made) with **Marlene Dietrich,** when the war broke out with Nazi Germany. She wanted to show in her own words "how war makes women hard and masculine." Curiously, this is precisely what the motion-picture industry did to Arzner.

Her contributions to the war effort were a series of short films for the WAC's, as well as training for women to cut and edit these movies. Apparently they were successful since the US military activated Dorothy Arzner and bestowed upon her the rank of Major! An "honor" that she turned down because, as she said, "I never wanted to be in the army."[28]

Arzner returned to Columbia after seven years absence to direct a remarkable film about the anti-Nazi resistance, FIRST COMES COURAGE (1943), with **Merle Oberon.** As usual, Arzner has her female protagonist in an unconventional role: a screen persona more typical for that of a man. Oberon plays a calculating, brilliant member of the Norwegian underground—a dangerous, death-confronting role that she assumes to appropriate heroic proportions. Arzner employed her favorite editor for the project, **Viola Lawrence,** who was also one of Hollywood's first women editors.

Arzner contracted pneumonia with a week to go on shooting, and the picture was completed by another director. But still, she found the picture too violent for her liking.[29] She made the brave decision in 1943 to leave Hollywood and never return.

"I was led by the grace of God to the movies," said Arzner much later in her life. "I would like the industry to be more aware of what they're doing to influence people for good and for bad. There's no doubt that we're affected by our environment."[30]

In the years that followed, Arzner began the first film courses at the Pasadena Playhouse on a nonexistent budget. She made over fifty Pepsi commercials for her old friend, **Joan Crawford.** She taught filmmaking at UCLA for four years in the 60s. She retired to the desert and died at the age of 82. She did, however, live to see the Director's Guild of America throw a large benefit in her honor (with **Ida Lupino** presenting the film clips), in 1975.

Why was she the only woman director? In a 1976 interview for the *New York Times* she said:

I don't honestly know. Maybe producers felt safer with men; they could go to a bar and exchange ideas more freely. But I made one box-office movie after another, so they knew they could gamble a banker's money

on me. If I had a failure in the middle, I would have been finished. Today, of course even the stars are all men. When men do put women in pictures, they make them so darned sappy, weeping all over the place, that it's disgusting.[31]

"Re-visioning" history, as poet Adrienne Rich once suggested, is not only an act of cultural history, it's an act of survival. Dorothy Arzner was well aware of using the medium of film as a tool for transformation—the powerful transformation of positive, strong image-making of woman on the screen. Marjorie Rosen said:

During the late twenties, Arzner played down the fact that she was a woman, even refusing to allow her directorial credit to appear alone on the screen . . . Still, the press treated her as an oddity.[32]

Arzner never married. One of the most frequent questions I am asked on the lecture circuit is whether or not Arzner was lesbian. The answer is, if she was she was careful that the fact was never known. In order to achieve her Sisyphian feat, she knew that the rules included never discussing one's personal life in the same breath as work. Emotions do not have a place in the all-male world of business, especially if one is a lesbian.

Dorothy Arzner was, and still is, the only American woman director to develop a substantial body of work in the mainstream Hollywood system.[33] What's more remarkable is that Arzner never sold herself, or the integrity of her screen characters, short in order to accomplish her remarkable task.

DOROTHY ARZNER

1927 Get Your Man (Director)
 Fashions for Women (Director)
 Ten Modern Commandments
 (Director)

1928	Manhattan Cocktail (Director)	1933	Christopher Strong (Director)
1929	Wild Party, The (Director)	1934	Nana (Director)
1930	Anybody's Woman (Director)	1936	Craig's Wife (Director)
	Behind the Makeup (Co-director)		Theodora Goes Wild (Producer,
	Charming Sinners (Co-director)		Story developer)
	Paramount on Parade (Director)	1937	Bride Wore Red, The (Director)
	Sarah and Son (Director)		Last of Mrs. Cheyney, The (Co-
1931	Honor among Lovers (Director)		director)
	Working Girls (Director)	1940	Dance, Girl, Dance (Director)
1932	Merrily We Go to Hell (Director)	1943	First Comes Courage (Director)

Joan Tewkesbury

An early 1970s *MS Magazine* article described her as "a suburban housewife turned spartan screenwriter." At the age of thirty-seven, before the women's movement had coalesced enough to give any kind of real support, **Joan Tewkesbury** left a marriage of thirteen years, left her two children to be raised by her husband, sold her big Santa Monica house, and sublet a furnished apartment. "I live like a man now," she told the *MS* reporter, "For the first time in my life, I am able to support myself emotionally and financially."[1]

Tewkesbury took courage by leaping into the unknown and wrote what became one of the unique visionary films of the decade. NASHVILLE (1975) wove six complex plots into a contemporary epic, and became a hit for director Robert Altman.

But the real story of courage is the personal one. Giving up children for a career is still the same scandalous treachery in our culture it was for Nora in Ibsen's *A Doll's House*.[2] Speaking of the guilt she faced she said: "It has to do with the cultural attitudes of what a mother should do. . . . It was always as though I was missing the jump rope." Ten years later she said, "You still suffer with it."[3]

Tewkesbury moved from a full-blown suburban life, replete with nannies for the children and caretakers for the garden and the swimming pool, to "an all-white monastic high-rise one room apartment . . . white walls devoid of pictures . . . a work table that serves as her desk and the couch that folds into a bed."[4] Unlike many women pioneers unfairly forced to choose between work and family, Ms. Tewkesbury's decision was deliberate. Her room in Santa Monica was described as "the room of a woman whose work has become tantamount to a religious vocation."[5]

> The whole process of being alone is very important in terms of what you want to do in the industry. Yes, it's an industry of people . . . and collaboration. But if you can't be alone at night when you go home . . . you're in big trouble. . . . I get really isolated when I'm shooting a film. I move into a hotel room really in earnest. I just don't come out except to work, and I love it.[6]

Having the feeling as many women pioneers in the industry do of always feeling like an outsider ("I was an only child who desperately wanted to be normal," but "I was always on the outside looking in"[7]), Tewkesbury began her career as a Los Angeles stage director, choreographer, and dancer, with dance being the prime focus. In fact, her youthful claim to "outsider" fame at age eighteen was as **Mary Martin's** "flying understudy" in the stage version of *Peter Pan*. Dancing would eventually leave its mark on Tewkesbury, the writer/director:

> I worked with too many choreographers, Jerome Robbins being a classic example. . . . In *Peter Pan* . . . I had to move my eyeballs . . . to so many counts every night. I thought, This is a way to make your living? . . . I learned about being contained and refined and precise and professional. But I said, "I'm not going to spend the rest of my life counting."[8]

Although she didn't know it at the time, this was the beginning of Tewkesbury, the pioneer, learning to count to the beat of her own rhythm.

But she made one more try for her almost-extremist desire for normalcy. She gave up dancing altogether, married a financier, had two children, spent all her time shopping for expensive dresses she never wore, and fought with her husband.

For a while, the nine-to-five–ness appeased something in her. But at age thirty, after nearly a decade of admittedly feeling lost, Tewkesbury felt something inside her blowing up. It had nothing to do with political or intellectual motivations about "feminism"; it had to do with the denial of an artistic spirit quietly going mad:

> People think I'm a feminist. I'm not a feminist. I'm for folks. Which is not to say a lot of things don't piss me off. I'm very angry, or I wouldn't sit down at that desk to write. But mine is not the kind of rage that's expressed in one avenue. Mine gets spread out over lots of issues.[9]

In 1970 she learned that Robert Altman had liked one of the scripts she had written for the stage, and asked if she might observe him on MCCABE AND MRS. MILLER (1971). He made her script supervisor[10] on the project, and it gave them the opportunity to get to know each other artistically. A script collaboration, THIEVES LIKE US (1974) followed, and Tewkesbury was on her way.

"On her way" has never meant box-office stardom with a sensibility like Tewkesbury's. She works with a kind of depth and realism about her characters, never interested in black-and-white portrayals of good guys and bad guys. Often, she says, she covers the gray areas of emotions in people's relationships. The highly structured, most unusual in terms of form, but thoroughly tight NASHVILLE is a perfect example.

The blond, small-boned Joan Tewkesbury broke into directing with a feature, OLD BOYFRIENDS (1979), starring John Belushi and **Talia Shire**. "I actually waited around a few moments for Altman to say, Action! before I realized that that was my job now."[11] At about the same time she broke into television when Carol Burnett asked her to write and direct THE TENTH MONTH (1979). This was followed by another television drama, THE ACORN PEOPLE (1981), about handicapped children for NBC. The script won her a Writer's Guild of America Award in 1981.

Like many women directors in the industry, Tewkesbury would have one or at the most two feature debuts[12] before turning the bulk of her attentions toward the more available medium of television. But TV is not a medium Tewkesbury turns her nose up at.

> To me, television is not the weekly shows that numb everybody's brain. Television is doing something controversial enough to make an impact on the audience, about doing something so special that it pierces your heart and brain.[13]

In a different interview, she qualifies that,

> I'm not a social filmmaker. If I say something to you, I don't go out of my way to say it to you. The quickest way to turn me, as an audience, off, is to say, "Look at that.

Now do something about it because you've been shown the light. . . . As a filmmaker, I want to show you all I can, but let you draw your own conclusions.[14]

Does Tewkesbury believe in a "female sensibility?"

I hate the idea of a woman's viewpoint; . . . a viewpoint is a viewpoint is a viewpoint. It's colored by more things than just what sex you are. It's colored by where you grew up, who you spend time with, who you loved, and whether that was good or rotten.[15]

JOAN TEWKESBURY

1974	Thieves Like Us (Writer)
1975	Nashville (Writer)
1979	Old Boyfriends (Director)
	Tenth Month, The (TV) (Writer, Director)
1980	Acorn People, The (TV) (Writer, Director)
1982	A Night in Heaven (Writer)
1987	Accused, The (Writer, No screen credit)
1988	Almost Grown (TV series) (Director)
1989	Cold Sassy Tree (Cable TV) (Writer, Director)
1990	Sudie & Simpson (Cable TV) (Director)

Claudia Weill

With GIRLFRIENDS in 1978, **Claudia Weill** broke open a long, unacceptable taboo in films. She made it possible for women to make the subject of their personal lives important enough to put on the screen. For among the first moments in American films since perhaps **Dorothy Arzner's** THE WILD PARTY (1929), these women were bonding in a way that was neither catty, nor coy, nor clawing—the three terrible C's for women on the screen. Their focus and goal were on themselves, their careers, and each other—not on winning the heart of a man.[1]

The question, "Is there a female gaze"? is one that will ever remain fraught with complexities and ambiguities. But perhaps an admission that a friendship between two women deserves our undivided attention puts a part of that question to rest.

The choice of such subject matter as important enough to make the focal point of a feature was previously viewed as suspect in Hollywood. Weill did the film the only way such a film could have been completed—independently.

GIRLFRIENDS proved a big critical, though not a huge commercial, success. Although the film brought in only a million dollars in rentals, it is remembered as a hit. Even with the New York newspapers on strike in tandem with the movie's release, the movie's word of mouth recommendation brought the audiences into theaters.

Weill assisted at what she didn't know then—the beginning of a transformational change for women in cinema. Women were learning the power of their own voices on and off the screen.

GIRLFRIENDS's debut coincided with a gradually coalescing independent film community. Before that, unless you had someone wealthy on your bankroll, the fate of your feature (including creative decisions regarding content) was in the political hands of studio heads. The chance of a film like GIRLFRIENDS escaping from the studio gates unscathed was negligible.

Raised in the affluent suburb of Scarsdale, New York, Weill was a Radcliffe graduate in still photography. While spending her summers as a gofer on various documentaries, she found that she was far more interested in the pictures when they started to move.

After college she teamed up with friend and filmmaker, **Joyce Chopra,** to codirect JOYCE AT 34 (1972), for PBS, as well as twenty short films for *Sesame Street.* **Shirley MacLaine** recruited her skills, and they set sail with the first women's delegation to China, where Weill directed, edited, and shot THE OTHER HALF OF THE SKY: A CHINA MEMOIR (1974). The film was nominated for an Academy Award. The attention enabled her to get access to key grants that made what eventually became GIRLFRIENDS possible.

After GIRLFRIENDS, the studio offers arrived. The result was her second feature, IT'S MY TURN (1980), starring **Jill Clayburgh.** Like JOYCE AT 34, the film was about women

> committed to having a profession, but having a life as well . . . having a home, a family, and other such "old-fashioned" pleasures. Weill is intensely sympathetic toward this desire to have it all: "It's hard to do everything," [says Weill] "but I think it's important to try."[2]

Mysteriously, male filmmakers with a couple of features under their belt seem to continue to have long careers in features, even when their films do not do well at the box office. The trend for talented women, however, seems to steer them into oblivion, or else into television, where Claudia Weill currently does much of her work.

Perhaps this has something to do with Weill's press in the midseventies. She was labeled "one of the few active women, not to mention feminist, filmmakers in the United States." But *feminist,* as journalist **Linda Ellerbee** has said, is a four-letter word, especially in the political arena of Hollywood, where being unpopularly pegged can ruin your career. Weill was well dubbed after the release of GIRLFRIENDS. She characterized herself as a filmmaker who was also a feminist, although she qualified that admission by saying she didn't believe in making didactic or rhetorical films. "You can only change people by making them laugh or cry."[3]

A few years later, she would undub herself entirely. She denied being a feminist despite the dramatic content of her first feature.

After the success of VALLEY GIRL (1983), director **Martha Coolidge** remembers being asked if she was a feminist. "Of course I'm a feminist," she said, "but I knew that if I said yes, I'd lose the job. So I said no."[4] One can scarcely blame Weill, or the scores of women who followed her example. Unless one chooses to move to Europe where the culture makes it possible for women like **Margarethe von Trotta** and **Márta Mészáros** to examine their personal voices, American women are prisoners of an exhausting and defeating game.[5]

What is important to remember in the light of GIRLFRIENDS's history is that it was a breakthrough film that reflected the feelings of an entire generation of American women. Hollywood accepted and distributed the film only after it had won accolades at the European festivals. Europe had to discover this American talent first before her own native land would acknowledge her.

CLAUDIA WEILL

1968   Metropole
        Radcliffe Blues
1969   Putney School
1970   This Is the Home of Mrs. Levant
        Graham
1971   IDCA—1970

Joan Micklin Silver

One of the few women directors on any-one's list in the seventies, **Joan Silver** became a symbol of hope for women on the outside wanting to get in. At a time when that "list" included **Elaine May** (who had the star stature of her name to depend on), and for a short time, **Barbara Loden** and **Shirley Clarke,** the virtually anonymous Silver had directed three features before 1980.

She is a champion for bringing noncommercial subjects to the screen and proving Hollywood wrong on its box office assessments. Her stunning first attempt, HESTER STREET (1975), preceded **Claudia Weill**'s GIRLFRIENDS (1978). But Silver did not mean the film to be "feminist" as much as she intended it as an homage to the strong women of her Jewish heritage. As though it wasn't a bold enough move to make the protagonist of a film a woman at this early juncture, Silver made her a Jewish woman! Double trouble in Hollywood terms.[1] On this topic, Silver said about her later film, CROSSING DELANCY (1988),

Well, there seems to be good ethnic and bad ethnic. And good ethnic seems to be Italians, especially if they're Mob Italians. I don't think that makes Italians very happy at all. Susan [Sandler—the playwright] had a person from a studio say to her that if she would change [her play] and make it about Italians, she could get her movie deal. So there is this sense, for some reason, felt by a lot of the Jewish people who run the studios, that Jewish material is not going to be commercial. Woody Allen seems to have persisted despite it, but I think that all of you who want to write about something besides mainstream white America should be aware of it.[2]

HESTER STREET was hailed more than many other of Silver's subsequent films, because the heroine begins as a dishrag and by the end of the film comes to recognize her own strengths.

"I'm a feminist, by all means," said Silver in 1980,

but I don't consider it my mission in life to illustrate that over and over. I want to tell all sorts of stories. I don't think I would ever make a film against my political beliefs—a sexist film. On the other hand, I don't think it's my duty to show powerful women, or women triumphing against all odds, unless that happens to be the particular story I want to tell.[3]

Barbara Koenig Quart points out that instead of turning envyingly toward the gentile world, as does **Elaine May** in her film, THE HEARTBREAK KID (1972), Silver's HESTER STREET turns back toward the traditional world of European Jewry in a way unusual among American Jews. "It celebrates *shtetl* values above the new American values."[4] No one in HESTER STREET is idealized, painted, or romanticized, either with star or stereotyped casting. All of the characters are real to their bones.

The other side of women's skill in handling the world is that the less macho man, gentle and always formally dressed, usually sitting and reading, is by far the more attractive man in HESTER STREET. (Streisand's casting her male lead in YENTL [1983] as appealingly sexy as a hip Hollywood actor, involved no such risk.)[5]

Joan Micklin Silver's first break came in 1967 after she raised three daughters in Cleveland, Ohio and the family moved to New York. Producer **Linda Gottlieb** (DIRTY DANCING [1987]) hired Silver as a freelance writer for an educational film. Together, they sold a screenplay, LIMBO (1972) to Universal.

Beginners luck in writing was recoiled by continual rejection at Silver's attempts to direct. "Flagrant sexism,"[6] encouraged her to form Midwest Film Productions in partnership with her husband.

Silver readily admits that she might never have become a film director if it weren't for her husband. "I was a good little girl in the 1950s," she said, "I went from college to marriage and had my first child at twenty-two."[7]

Raphael Silver was a real-estate entrepreneur who became frustrated at seeing his wife continually buffeted by the system. In honest belief of her talents, he raised enough money for her to complete her first feature effort, as well as her second, BETWEEN THE LINES (1977). "Ray only got into the film business to help me," said Joan Silver. "He was so aggravated to see me shut out. Then, once he got into it, he liked it."[8]

Silver, who was once described by an interviewer as "bearing an overwhelming resemblance to a suburban housewife from some affluent community on Long Island," was born in Omaha, and is a graduate of Sarah Lawrence College. She got through school writing scripts for educational film companies and persuading them to allow her to direct them.

Silver's BETWEEN THE LINES, would sur-

prisingly anticipate the sentiments, as Barbara Koenig Quart points out, of John Sayles's THE RETURN OF THE SECAUCUS SEVEN (1980), as well as the glossier, less-impressive Hollywood version, THE BIG CHILL (1983). In BETWEEN THE LINES, which delicately captures the nostalgia and idealism of the sixties without sentimentality, Silver cast the then-unknown John Heard and Lindsay Crouse.

As one of the first directors to work consistently after the consciousness of the women's movement, it is interesting to note how Joan Micklin Silver "handles her women." In her second film, we see the character Laura follow her man to another city. Yet verbally, she voices a fear that this may be the wrong thing to do—a consciousness unavailable to such a character only a few years before. "Silver opts for couples though cognizant of the difficulties they pose, especially for women—which is really a major subject of each film. She also opts for gentle, intellectual men."[9]

In her third feature, CHILLY SCENES OF WINTER (1979) (re-titled HEAD OVER HEELS and rereleased in 1981) based on the book by Ann Beattie, Joan Silver wrote the screenplay herself. And while many women in powerful positions will pay lip service to hiring female colleagues who might not otherwise get opportunites, Silver has always put her money where her mouth is. She made a point of hiring many women in her crew ranks.

CROSSING DELANCY (1988) reclaimed the charm and singular vision of HESTER STREET through dealing with the conflict of the old Jewish traditions as they butt against the new American values.

LOVERBOY (1988), is the only film that Silver has thus far directed where she wasn't also involved in development. Maybe this was at the root of the film's problem. The material is an oddity in Silver's oeuvre, and although she termed it "a well-constructed farce,"[10] the piece (about a pizza delivery boy suspected by husbands of delivering more than just pizza to their wives), leans more toward the kind of vapid, exploitation material Hollywood is so famous for. Why Silver took on the task, one can only surmise. One would imagine that after nearly two decades of struggle to develop films independently, it must have been a relief to be solicited by a studio. But regardless of the financial and crew support, when you answer to someone else for the bill your work pays a price.

Silver may still, however, be the one American woman filmmaker who has been able to find that fine balance between pleasing the studio and not compromising her own unique voice. The reason for this may be because she began her career in tandem with a man who had a strong financial base, and she never *needed* to make her movies.

She may be like **Dorothy Arzner** who said that if her films were strong it was because she was willing to give them up at every turn. She would never have gone another step if she were at all prevented from realizing her vision in just the way she saw fit. Joan Micklin Silver can, in a similar way, pursue her vision luxuriously. She will not go hungry if she never makes another movie. We, as cinema viewers, on the other hand would be sadly depleted at the loss of her intelligent visions.

JOAN MICKLIN SILVER

1975   Bernice Bobs Her Hair (TV)
         Hester Street
1977   Between the Lines
1979   Chilly Scenes of Winter
1981   Head over Heels (Rerelease of
         Chilly Scenes of Winter)
1984   Finnegan, Begin Again (HBO)
1988   Crossing Delancy
1989   Loverboy

Karen Arthur

Karen Arthur's story answers the question of why a bright, successful woman director, with two well-received independent features under her belt, would give up the idea of pursuing theatrical features as a career and turn her attentions instead toward television. The reviews of her first piece LEGACY (1975) were everything that a first-time director would want to hear. Comments like, "A rare and beautiful first film"[1] So why do we see so many women directors with rare, unique voices routinely disappearing into television instead of becoming auteurs like men? What does she prefer about working in television?

the fact that I don't have to wait eight long years to do it! . . . I'm a director, and a director *directs*. Instead of spending years trying to get a film made, in television I'm saying "Action" often. And, ultimately,

what excites me most is the *process* of doing it. . . . That's the sacred part.[2]

Process is something that Arthur has been familiar with since she was a child. Born in Omaha, she moved at an early age to Florida where, like many women directors, she trained as a dancer.[3] At the age of fifteen she was a featured soloist, and from fifteen to eighteen, she choreographed four full-length ballets. She ended that period dancing in a ballet at London's Strand Theatre.

She moved on to New York City, then to Hollywood, where dancing led to acting, and acting to directing. She took a crash course in filmmaking at UCLA, and six weeks later, came out with her first short film, HERS (1974). The piece enabled her to compete for and win hard-to-win grants, and the timing was right for her to be invited into the prestigious first cycle of the

American Film Institute's (AFI) Directing Workshop for Women. The year was 1974—the same year she won the Independent Filmmaker Program Grant from the AFI that enabled her to make LEGACY, her first feature.

LEGACY was a success artistically, but not commercially. Her next independent piece, THE MAFU CAGE (1978), starred **Carol Kane** and **Lee Grant**. Once again Arthur spent years calling on all the money people she knew. She succeeded in raising $1 million (against LEGACY's $70,000) and hoped the film would bring wider recognition.

But Arthur's life could serve as a sample guide to the independent filmmaker on the dangers and pitfalls of the independent world. Although the film premiered the Directors' Fortnight at Cannes, a prestigious honor, she couldn't get the film distributed in America. When she tried to distribute the film herself (as time-consuming an occupation as directing a feature) the exhibitors refused her the box-office returns. "You can't show the kind of muscle that the big studios do," she said at the end of a long struggle. The film continues to be a cult classic with film lovers.

What happened to Karen Arthur happens to too many film artists who shouldn't be tangling in a system really set up for bankers and gamblers.

> I was exhausted with trying to raise money. . . . As an independent filmmaker, you get used to making all the creative decisions and never budging. But there are times to fight and times not to fight.[4]

She learned some hard lessons after THE MAFU CAGE won her the legendary meetings and a three-picture studio deal. They asked her, What do you want to do now? She wanted to do a film about "psychological rape." The studios didn't understand. They asked for violence. They asked for blood. She wanted to talk about sexual and verbal violence, not physical violence. They wanted to make the man a psychopathic killer.

> you go into meetings with studio executive . . . and fight for what you want. . . . I made the mistake time and time again of winning the battles but losing the war. . . . There are times you should just sit there, like when they say: "We're going to have an orangutan play the lead. We've seen this orangutan, and she's very talented. Got a hit single out and we just know this orangutan is going to the top. And you explode. . . . Wrong. You should say, "Orangutan. Very interesting. Always liked the little hairy people. Right. Yes. Can see the possibilities." . . . Save the muscle for the time when the orangutan is actually being hired. *Then* do something about it.[5]

So she fought too hard at the wrong time. She wouldn't give up her point. Finally, eight long years and many studios later LADY BEWARE (1987) was made by a smaller studio, which chopped it up and released a film that wasn't the film she directed. Important, tough lessons in Hollywood. A town where people don't talk movies over lunch. They talk bankroll and percentages.

So Karen Arthur took her talents and turned them toward television. She won an Emmy for "Heat," a *Cagney & Lacey* episode. She became the first woman to direct an American miniseries, CROSSINGS (1986), for Aaron Spelling, and then a six-hour miniseries for Australian television. She did made-for-TV movies like THE RAPE OF RICHARD BECK, which won Richard Crenna a Best Actor Emmy. But no more movies that have that unique trademark stamped, "Made by Karen Arthur."

"I don't want to make little films [meaning independent films] anymore," said Arthur after her tough, but, for Hollywood, relatively routine experiences. "There's just no art market for American independent filmmakers. It's a great tragedy, because I'd still like to make those films."

A tragedy for us all, because those art

films are where the unique voices of American filmmakers lie.

What is it like for Karen Arthur to be a "woman" director?

> Like being a director, thank you very much. I just wear pantyhose and you don't . . . but once you've got a body of work, that's what speaks for you. Actors and crews can tell in fifteen minutes if you're a good leader, and if you are, they'll be beside you whether you're a man or a woman or a buffalo.[6]

KAREN ARTHUR

1975	Legacy
1978	Mafu Cage, The
1980	Charleston
1982	Return to Eden
1984	A Bunny's Tale
	Victims for Victims
1985	Rape of Richard Beck, The
1986	Crossings
1987	Cracked Up
	Lady Beware
1988	Bridge to Silence
	Evil in Clear River
1991	Bump in the Night (TV)

Martha Coolidge

"I spent twenty years getting to where I am, which is at the beginning of my career."[1]

Within the company of a new generation of filmmakers to arrive in Hollywood fresh out of film school—and a small number of the women in this group who found their break into directing through teen movies—**Amy Heckerling, Lisa Gottlieb—Martha Coolidge** stands out.

Perhaps it is because she was a serious independent director for many years before she got her hard-won break in Hollywood, and she is ever aware of the cost. More to my thinking, it is because she is a filmmaker with a consciousness that thankfully won't quit. With enough bad breaks, and the numerous obstacles of sexism that would have made a less-tenacious woman give up, Coolidge has more than just managed to keep her head above water; she has managed to keep her integrity.

Her political integrity has a fixed eye on "moral rights" legislation for artists. When her film, VALLEY GIRL (1983) had to be cut down for television, Coolidge wasn't so much as informed.

In countries like France and Italy, just because you own a work of art doesn't mean you can do anything you like to it. They recognize ownership, but they also recognize inalienable authorship rights. You can buy a Picasso, but you can't cut it into little pieces and sell mini-Picassos. But the law in this country is based on English law, which only recognizes property rights—even the Bill of Rights is an anomaly. . . . The whole idea [is] that once a work of art is completed, it shouldn't be altered without the approval of the artist.[2]

"I believe sincerely, that as a man I would have been working in this town ten years before I was as a woman," she told me. Considering her political awareness, and her often publicly demonstrative feminist leanings, it's somewhat ironic that her first big break in mainstream cinema came with VALLEY GIRL.

One of the most successful independent feats in Hollywood's history, VALLEY GIRL cost $350,000 and grossed $17 million in box-office returns, suddenly putting Coolidge in a whole new class. Although the breadth of her experience to that point was

in feminist documentaries—OLD FASH-
IONED WOMAN 1974 was about her grandmother, and NOT A PRETTY PICTURE, was a
1975 autobiographic account of her own
rape—Coolidge was "offered every single
teen sex comedy in Los Angeles. Stacks of
them. Some of them I had to read all the
way through because I couldn't believe that
people in their right mind could offer this
picture to me, a woman, even if they didn't
know me."[3]

Her next movie, THE JOY OF SEX
(1984)—a script she describes as the least
offensive of all the teen sex movies sent to
her—was a self-admitted disaster. The studio's strategy was to make it as cheaply as
possible and recoup all the development
money that by then had soared into the triple digits. Coolidge was taken off the picture in postproduction when it was recut.
She hoped the experience wouldn't end her
career, although she might not particularly
have minded it getting her out of the youth
market.

But teen films have had their advantages
for Coolidge. Aside from giving her an un-
anticipated entry into the studio system, she
has learned how to access her own unique
female vision in places not imagined possible. For instance, she was nearly not hired
on VALLEY GIRL because the studio was
afraid they'd be "women's-libbed to
death." There were four nudity scenes in
the script, and seeing them as the picture's
commercial viability, the studio wanted
them in. Coolidge agreed to keep them, but
she said she'd do them in her own way. Her
own way went something like this: Jilted
boyfriend tries to get back at the girl who
turned down his ring by trying to make it
with her best girlfriend . . . and rumor had
it, an "easy" girl. However in the middle of
the full-breasted screen seduction, the confused young woman asks, "Does this mean
we're going steady?" Coolidge's view of the
scene was that the seducer stomps out with
a "What? *No!*," leaving the audience
watching the hurt victim who suddenly be-

comes aware she has been used. "From a
male director, the scene's ending might have
followed our Romeo back into the locker
room to concentrate on his frustra-
tion. . . . As it was, I felt the emotion was
quite well expressed."[4]

Her next studio film, REAL GENIUS
(1985), was also a teen picture, with an all-
male cast that "broke through a well-established sexual barrier that had roped off
boys, science and multi-million dollar special effects budgets as male turf."[5] Coolidge
was pleased with the picture. She says, "I
was attracted by the chance to do men dealing with men, because women bring a fresh
perspective to male characters. I'll opt to
show them as more vulnerable than a male
director would."[6]

Barbara Quart has noted, "The most important element of REAL GENIUS that sets
it apart from the other youth films is that
it is built around respect for the mind,"[7]
a clear reflection of Martha Coolidge's
hand.

Since she was raised to be a visual artist,
it is not surprising that Coolidge has been
able to maintain her integrity regarding her
art, even when the vehicle's association to
the "art form" is questionable. Both her
mother and father were architects, and
Coolidge grew up in an intellectual enclave
in New Haven, where her father taught at
Yale.

After a brief stint as a folk singer—"If I
had gotten into a rock band, I think I probably would have been a singer, and God
knows I probably would be dead by
now"[8]—she enrolled to study printmaking
at the Rhode Island School of Design. While
there she made her first film, an animated
short. "The minute I did that film, I felt I
had to be a director." After completing
three more short films at RISD, she packed
her bags for New York and tried to enroll
in film school at New York University.

When I applied, the guy told me I couldn't
be a director. He said to me, "You can't

name five women directors in the world," and he was right, I could name one [**Elaine May**] but that didn't seem to me to be a reason not to pursue it.[9]

Discouraged but undaunted, she followed her boyfriend to Canada instead, where she was given the opportunity to direct a dramatic children's piece for television. Issues of seniority found her back at NYU's gates the next year, enrolled in directing. Award-winning documentaries made in graduate school were Martha Coolidge's entry into mainstream cinema.

Francis Ford Coppola was impressed with NOT A PRETTY PICTURE, and put Coolidge on the payroll for two-and-a-half years, before financial setbacks forced Zoetrope Studios to close.

Another return to Canada, and the CBC (Canadian Broadcasting Corporation) would be the place where Coolidge would find her big break in dramatic features. The well-produced CITY GIRL (1983) would never be released, but it would bring her the opportunity for VALLEY GIRL, and another, perhaps final move to Hollywood.

Since 1985, Coolidge has mostly directed television while continuing to develop feature scripts she would be proud to have her name on. Of all the scripts that pass through her hands, few have both commerical *and* artistic possibilities. REAL GENIUS opened up opportunities to direct such "unlikely female" territory as THE TWILIGHT ZONE. One feature, PLAIN CLOTHES, gave her the opportunity to direct adults again after feeling pigeonholed into teen subjects, but the film only saw a limited eleven-city release.

Finally, in 1990, after five years of trying to find a backer, Martha Coolidge found herself directing the kind of material for which she has waited twenty years. RAMBLING ROSE (1991) starring Laura Dern is one of those rare and wonderful coming-of-age stories about a young woman. Based on a Calder Willingham novel, Rose's tale

is one of "flowing sexuality, and the crisis it caused in the family and the town she came to in the Great Depression,"[10] at a time in the South when women were punished with clitorodectomies and ovarectomies for "hysterical" and sexually promiscuous behavior. Before Coolidge discovered the script in 1985 in a "dead script" pile, it spent twelve years being passed to various producers, unable to generate support. This is not the kind of material that RAMBO's hollywood bets its box-office on.

But thankfully, Coolidge was persistent and found a sympathetic reader in Renny Harlis who agreed to produce the film independently. "They [the studios] don't develop material for women," said Coolidge. "And writers are not necessarily putting strong emphasis on writing female characters. There hasn't been a call for it commercially."[11]

The image most people have is that the director is completely in control of the film. But that's not exactly the case. The director is the sandwich person. . . . You're the inspiration and guide to everyone on the set, but you're under all these other people you're working for . . . the employee . . . The biggest lesson was discovering how to find the most effective avenue of creative expression in the areas where you have no control or power. And oh. The most important thing for a director is to have a good pair of shoes. It's murder on your feet.[12]

MARTHA COOLIDGE

1971   Passing Quietly Through (Producer, Editor)
1972   David: On and Off (Producer, Writer, Director, Editor)
1973   More Than a School (Director, Writer, Editor)
1974   Old Fashioned Woman 1974 (Producer, Director, Writer, Editor)

1975	Not a Pretty Picture (Producer, Director, Writer, Co-editor)
1978	Bimbo (Producer, Director, Editor)
1979	Trouble Shooters, The
1980	Strawberries and Gold (TV)
1983	City Girl (Producer, Director) Valley Girl

1984	Joy of Sex, The
1985	Real Genius
1988	Plain Clothes Roughhouse
1989	Trenchcoat in Paradise
1991	Rambling Rose

Susan Seidelman

Susan Seidelman is one of a handful of contemporary American women directors who are developing a body of work since **Ida Lupino**. A body of work becomes essential when trying to determine "a female gaze." Trends, stylistic traits of voice, patterns unique to one specific eye, become impossible to identify without a substantial oeuvre.

The bad news is that what we're seeing as Seidelman continues on her lone journey is not all that exciting. Since the fresh vision of SMITHEREENS (1982), which made Seidelman the new darling of the Cannes film festival, and presented to the world the promise of a major, eclectic new voice, Seidelman's choice to access a more mainstream sensibility has perhaps robbed her of that first flair for danger, ironically so marketable at the time because it was so unique. But attempting to encapsulate a formula for something that will strike gold is the beginning of the end; the essence is already lost. Essentially this has been true of her subsequent movies. Her second film, DESPERATELY SEEKING SUSAN (1985) was Seidelman's first attempt at a movie with a big studio budget. It was a great success at the box office, with the auspicious timing of Madonna's debut video playing a major role. DESPERATELY SEEKING SUSAN cloned a similar situation to SMITHEREENS, but with a more conventional Hollywood rhythm governing the script, making the film entertaining to a broader market. Seidelman

garnered the praise she needed from the mainstream to allow her to go on and continue working, a coup in itself. From our conversation in 1988 she was eminently aware how quickly women directors disappear with just a single box-office flop. Vincent Canby praised her: "With DESPERATELY SEEKING SUSAN ... Miss Seidelman successfully takes the long, potentially dangerous leap from the ranks of the promising independents to mainstream American movie-making, her integrity, her talent and her comic idiosyncrasies intact."[1]

Idiosyncrasy is the key word. Idiosyncrasy is what determines a director's very specific vision, her unmatchable "gaze." Seidelman's idiosyncrasies are first, a kind of indescribable and spontaneous "let's-try-it-and-see-what-happens" sensibility. Another is her brilliant choice of music that echoes the very blood and pulse of the protagonist. And probably her most bankable trait is her knack for offbeat casting—witness the choice of Meryl Streep in SHE-DEVIL (1989) as comedy star, and the unusual debut of rock-star turned film-star Madonna. As one Hollywood insider puts it, the ingredients of a Seidelman film are "quirky casting, a lot of camera energy, a lot of motion, and a certain amount of pink."[2] But neither pink nor offbeat casting does a bad movie save, and the subsequent trials such as MAKING MR. RIGHT (1987)[3], and COOKIE (1989) have been all but forgettable.

Although Seidelman is ironically now engendering the kinds of shopping-mall movies she was hell-bent to avoid as an adolescent—"I knew nothing about movies. My favorite film was THE PARENT TRAP [1961] with Hayley Mills"[4]—her original intents heralded something more promising. She grew up in the suburbs of Philadelphia set upon being a fashion designer, and took herself off to the Drexel Institute of Technology. It wasn't long before she realized that this life would mean long hours before a sewing machine, leading Susan to thinking alternatively about her future. "As a kid . . . my film knowledge was limited to the movies playing at the shopping mall. In college, when I got bored, I started to go to movies as a way just to cut classes." For almost lack of anything else to try, she applied to NYU film school and was accepted.

"It was right after a lot of changes, after our battles had been fought for women. So in reaping some of the benefits of the women's movement at that time, I just assumed I could be a director. I never questioned that I couldn't, and as a result I was kind of ignorant. But I also think that ignorance is bliss. I wasn't aware how bad the statistics really were for women."

What she *was* aware of was that the handful of other women directors on the scene were primarily producing product that was about the experience of being a woman. It was almost an unwritten mandate at the time. But just because one called oneself a feminist and was grateful for the advantages it provided one (which Seidelman admittedly did and was), one did not have to narrowcast one's movies that way. Men certainly didn't. Politically bent movies simply were not Seidelman's calling. She describes her interests instead as sociological ones.

With money she scraped up from family and friends, Seidelman teamed up with a graduate writing student at Columbia University's Screenwriting program and did the script for SMITHEREENS. "I wrote the story, but none of the dialogue," she said. "I'm not a writer. It's important to know one's limitations." Her reasoning for giving herself this large task was this: "I knew if I was to go out to Hollywood and start to knock on doors, the chances of me saying, 'Hey, I want to direct a movie,' and getting one, were pretty nil. So I figured, 'No one is going to make that happen, so I'd better make it happen for myself.' "

It was obvious by the time she had completed film school that she had a much more accurate picture of the movie business than when she began. Her instincts were savvy and right on the money. SMITHEREENS was chosen as the first independent American feature to be shown in competition at Cannes. And although the movie didn't garner any awards (it should have) it was clear from the media barrage that she was the new darling of the movie world.

Many of Seidelman's films, such as MAKING MR. RIGHT, were made concurrently with Seidelman's questions about her own life. How can I integrate my professional and personal life? "I'm really consumed by my work, but I'd be really sad if I thought I couldn't also have a personal life with someone in it."[5] Her own "Mr. Right" would be found only a couple of years later in the form of Jonathan Brett, a onetime assistant to the president of Arista Records and now the producer of Susan's movies. In 1989, the two of them were maried and in 1990 had a child.

Seidelman continues to uphold her public image as the fiercely independent director, "creator of insouciant heroines." Feisty and insouciant or not, it is disappointing to see films like SHE-DEVIL that reinforce the negative mythology of women on the screen— that is, that they claw at one another (in this case literally) for the love of a man. Women whose only reason for living, in fact, is to have someone like Ed Begley, Jr., validate their existence. In recent interviews she says she wants to keep making "personal films" about "how I see the world,"[6]

"For women directors," she says, "because there are so few of us—" She stops. In the past Seidelman has said that they have an obligation to put female experience on the screen, but she seems less didactic—or more polite now. "I'm disppointed when women make generic films. There are enough men around to do that."[7]

It's not easy to be a first, with the eyes of the world gawking to see whether or not you will strike gold. External pressures are great on Susan Seidelman. Orion pictures, which professed to give her so much leeway as a first director, took away her final cut on DESPERATELY SEEKING SUSAN. Seidelman must be praised for carrying off her first studio deal so well with the multitude of compromises she was forced to make.

Yet one can't help thinking that the system is to blame and that Seidelman is only one of many pawns. How can a system whose bottom line is box-office returns hope to engender art as a by-product? Perhaps it's time to look toward European cinema for an education and transformation in filmic thinking. In the meantime, Susan Seidelman must be praised for covering the kind of tough ground that few women directors under a studio contract have been able to achieve since **Dorothy Arzner**. Her tenacity, and her determination are models for encouragement.

SUSAN SEIDELMAN

1982   Smithereenes
1985   Desperately Seeking Susan
1987   Making Mr. Right
1989   Cookie
　　　 She-Devil

Donna Deitch

DONNA DEITCH is the first female filmmaker to take a taboo sexual topic and turn it into a box-office smash. DESERT HEARTS (1985), adapted from the Jane Rule novel, *Desert of the Heart* (1964), was the first lesbian love story to obtain mainstream distribution. "At least," Deitch told me, "the first one that has a hopeful ending for lesbians. All the others ended in suicides, murders, or convoluted bisexual triangles."[1]

Indeed, the other two well-known American mainstream films dealing with a similar theme end unhappily. John Sayles's LIANNA (1983), and Robert Towne's PERSONAL BEST (1982) both show the unfortunate pitfalls that await a woman who chooses an alternative life-style, and point up the benefits for opting to be heterosexual.

Deitch (along with **Susan Seidelman**, **Amy Heckerling**, and **Martha Coolidge**), is part of the new generation of young filmmakers graduating into feature production from film school. "You sort of knew that women had been directors before you," she says, "even if you had to read it between the lines. Names like **Lupino** and **Arzner** kind of slipped in, though you were never informed about their work directly.

"Role models," she insists, "are crucial. If you're a woman filmmaker or black or Hispanic or whatever—you see other people of your own ethnicity or gender. There's an inclination to think, 'Yes, I can,' if someone preceded you."

Deitch did her undergraduate work as a painter before moving to film. She got hooked on photography after a few classes. "Until," she said, "the pictures started to move." She pursued documentary work, such as WOMAN TO WOMAN (1975). She described the film as being about "hookers, housewives, and other mothers." Her rebellious, pioneering roots came through early, while she was attending graduate school in film at UCLA.

"I did a one-minute film for design class entitled, FOR GEORGE, LOVE DONNA [1975]. It was a kind of tight shot of an erection. I thought it was an opportune time to strike back at all the sexist films the male students were turning out. That kind of adolescent, puerile mentality that becomes—I don't know what . . . Hollywood." Deitch says that the normally animated auditorium fell into dead silence at the end of the screening. She was pleased, if one will pardon the expression, that the film had made its point.

Deitch attributes her mother to being her role model. "She was the breadwinner of the family. A real American fantasy story, more than a dream. She was a Hungarian refugee who worked in a sweatshop, and worked her way up to being a dress designer. She had this attitude of 'You can do anything you want to do.' My dad gave up his career as a dentist to be her manager."

Deitch spent two years raising money for her first feature, DESERT HEARTS.

"Most of my investors were women who felt like me—They wanted to see just a regular old love story, except with two women, on the screen. And a happy ending!

There hadn't been a love relationship between two women handled in a frank and real way. . . . I wanted to make the film so badly. But I knew the only way to do it was to do it myself. I just figured I'm going to go out and use all this energy, and I could put it into trying to make the film through a studio and wind up not getting anything.

I didn't want them to buy the film off me, then wind up being made an associate producer or something. I wanted to direct. Now I'm probably going to give the studio

setup a try. You can't go on raising money like that. You can't continue that kind of energy."

After the terrific popularity and success of DESERT HEARTS, Deitch accepted the opportunity of directing **Oprah Winfrey** in the TV miniseries, THE WOMEN OF BREWSTER PLACE (1989). How did she find television different from the independent life?

"When you're on your own, you don't have Standards and Practices people coming at you on the set saying, 'Listen Donna, we just want to remind you that there is to be no open-mouth kissing in this miniseries. And *no saliva*, please.' I mean, we had never discussed the possibility of saliva—but they just wanted to make sure I understood this, coming from the world of saliva and independent filmmaking.

When I made DESERT HEARTS I didn't have anyone standing over me telling me how they think I should make my movie. The only restrictions I had were my own dollars and cents. It's important to stick true to your own vision, and that's hard to do when a thousand other hands are on your work."

Does Deitch think there is such a thing as "a female gaze?" "With DESERT HEARTS, people would tell me that the love scene feels more 'female.' I think men more easily objectify a love scene. Women are more subjective with their sexuality. They *need* more subjectivity and emotion connected to love-making. I'm speaking generally, of course. But it's rare with sex scenes directed by men where orgasm is a mutually shared, joyous experience.

But I think there's definitely a female gaze. . . . It's hard to define it now, because we can't look back on it. If there were a group of women filmmakers in the fifties or sixties, we could look back on that communal body of work.

But not enough women have established a body of work. When women are making films in similar numbers to men, when it's as normal and commonplace for a woman to make a film as a man, we'll be able to answer that question. Not before."

DONNA DEITCH

1968 Berkeley 12 to 1
1969 Memorabilia P P 1
1970 She Was a Visitor

1972 Portrait
1975 "For George, Love Donna" (Short)
      Woman to Woman (Documentary)
1978 The Great Wall of Los Angeles
      (Documentary)
1985 Desert Hearts
1989 Women of Brewster Place, The
      (TV)

SHORT TAKES

♦ ♦ ♦

Joyce Chopra

Can a Brandeis intellectual who can't type find her way through the circuitous maze of Hollywood and come out singing? For **Joyce Chopra**, who had made career jumps from running a sixties' coffeehouse for folk-ies,[1] to eclectic documentary filmmaking,[2] to directing a dramatic feature, the answer seems to be yes.

SMOOTH TALK (1985), based on the famous Joyce Carol Oates short story, "Where Are You Going, Where Have You Been?" was praised as one of the most assured new narratives of the eighties. More important, it gave a language to a hardly touched screen topic: a young girl's coming of age. Coming-of-age tales for boys seem to flourish in the movies, but for young girls the screen models are few.

SMOOTH TALK was one of the few teen films to address realistically and seriously the endless psychic confusions of female adolescence: shopping malls, boredom, restlessness, mortification with parents, budding sexuality. Chopra has said that she never recovered from her own adolescence, that all the feelings of being an outsider are still with her.

Chopra makes her home close to the land in Kent, Connecticut, with SMOOTH TALK's screenwriter, and Chopra's husband, Tom Cole.

Joyce Chopra

Subsequently to filming her first feature, Chopra spent two months filming a documentary in Nigeria. She says that after the journey of SMOOTH TALK, with all the potential development deals, then no deals, then deals again, she found the culture of LA "equally fascinating, if not more so than Africa."

JOYCE CHOPRA

1972   Joyce at 34
1985   Smooth Talk

Stephanie Rothman

Roger Corman did more for the screen than slice and dice. Seeing inexpensive talent directly under his nose, he gave many women filmmakers their beginnings, including his wife, **Julie Corman. Stephanie Rothman** was another Corman graduate. She became known in the early seventies as "the only woman director who makes exploitation movies with a message." As Dannis Peary wrote:

> Rothman's pictures are all centrally about interesting contemporary women, exploring new occupations, relationships, and living situations, and confronting the ever changing values of the 1970s. . . . Instead of showing her women in conflict with a male-dominated world, she likes to place them in cinematic situations in which they are already men's equals. . . . Her heroines are independent young women, aggressive, healthy, and open in their sexual attitudes. They get along fine with their women associates; and their relationships with men are mutually supportive. . . . It is unfortunate that few feminist cinema researchers are familiar with [her] series of features (1966–74).[1]

IT'S A BIKINI WORLD was her first feature for Corman as early as 1967. It's a film that Rothman didn't really feel was indicative of her work. But it gave her a start. This was followed by such unforgettable terror titles as THE STUDENT NURSES (1970), THE VELVET VAMPIRE (1971), and TERMINAL ISLAND (1973).

She directed six features in eleven years, giving her the distinction (through the mid-seventies) of being Hollywood's most prolific woman filmmaker since **Ida Lupino**.

A Rothman film might typically deal with issues like abortion, social reorganization, and political activism. Her pictures also try to forge a humane and rational way of coming to grips with the vicissitudes of existence. They're not always about succeeding, they're about fighting the good fight."[2]

Within the limitations of much sex, violence, and material strong enough to receive an R rating, Rothman was pretty much free to mold and script the material the way she wanted. Within those limitations, the self-proclaimed feminist Rothman (who was frequently described as a woman who could pass for a Modigliani model) tried "to create female characters who fight for the right of self-determination."[3] One reviewer called THE STUDENT NURSES the "first exploitation picture about the Chicano revolution."

It was Ingmar Bergman's THE SEVENTH SEAL (1958) that changed Rothman's life. She dropped out of graduate work in sociology, and applied to the University of Southern California's School of Cinema at a time when women simply weren't accepted.

She became the first woman to win a fellowship for directing work from the Director's Guild of America. As the vice president in charge of Dimension Pictures in 1972, Rothman made a concerted and publicized effort to locate and hire women.

Rothman said in 1970 that she was encouraged by her parents to be ambitious. They never told her that she couldn't do something because she was a girl, she said, "or that my role was to be a wife and mother—nothing else. I wouldn't change my sex if I could."

This was in defense of a situation that Rothman had no idea she was pioneering, a situation that she would help alter dramatically over the next fifteen years. An interview in 1979 showed her foresight:

A great deal of the problem women have today is that they don't demand change. If you don't complain, no one knows you have a complaint. What roles women will play in the future depends on what women expect and want to happen to them. It isn't up to men. . . . And men have to realize it's all right to be what they want, even if the role is traditionally female. I wish the women's liberation movement could be followed by a men's liberation movement.

Rothman went on to acknowledge the crucial part that role models played in her development as both a woman and as an artist.

I want my films to be judged on their own merits. But at the same time, I feel that calling attention to the fact that I am a woman might suggest to other women that

they too could become directors. It might make the possibility of accomplishing this seem a little less bleak. When I left film school [in 1965] I found the fact that at least one woman, **Shirley Clarke**, was actively working in a field otherwise monopolized by men, was a source of reassurance to me that I might be able to do it too.[4]

"Stephanie Rothman is important," writes Dannis Peary,

because she is that rare commercial filmmaker who has consistently shown a concern for women in her work, who clearly *likes* women. . . . Rothman not only repects her women, but she sets her standards high for the men she will allow them to wind up with: a macho man is either converted or deserted.[5]

STEPHANIE ROTHMAN

1966   Blood Bath
1967   It's a Bikini World
1970   Student Nurses, The
1971   Velvet Vampire, The
1972   Group Marriage
1973   Terminal Island
        Working Girls, The

·II·

REEL WOMEN
ACTRESSES
TURNED DIRECTOR/
PRODUCER

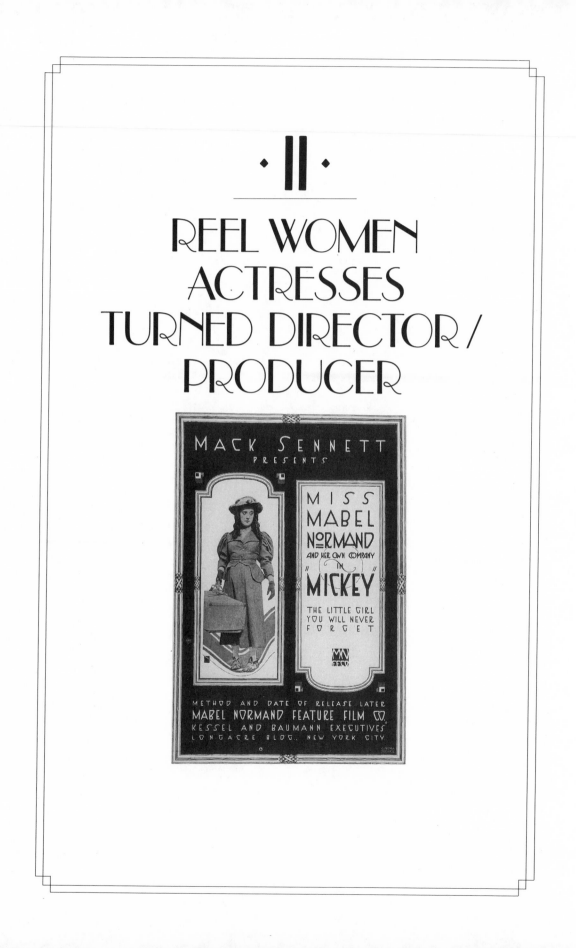

PREVIEW

◆ ◆ ◆

No one would argue that the path to major screen directing is no less than a Sisyphian feat. But since cinema's earliest days, certain actresses have understood their power well enough to form their own production firms and reap the profits from their talent. And several of these actresses had the right combination of clout and personality to also be lucky enough to catapult themselves into directing. **Constance Talmadge** (1900-1973), sister of Norma, was one, as well as the great Russian star, **Alla Nazimova** (1879-1945), who in 1922 directed the grandiose SALOME but gave away the directing credit to her husband, Charles Bryant.

The idea of "taking credit" for directing didn't have the cachet in the early days of cinema that it does today. Producing had far more prestige, and so artists such as **Nell Shipman, Gloria Swanson**, and **Mary Pickford** concentrated their efforts as such. Besides, it would have broken all illusion, as well as many hearts, for audiences to think their "Girl with the Golden Curls" was as commanding off the screen as an Erich von Stroheim.

But as cinema evolved, our cultural notions of what were acceptable male and female traits followed suit. Directing gained respectability, and women gained the self-respect to demand a kind of acknowledgment they were long overdue. Refusing a directing credit as an actress because you

Alla Nazimova in SALOME (1922).

thought it would alienate your box-office was now the notion of a day long past.

Included here are some of those actresses whose off-the-screen careers illuminated people's lives as powerfully as when they were "on."

Nell Shipman
(in BACK TO GOD'S COUNTRY,
1919, a film she also directed).

Mabel Normand

Mary Pickford

Lillian Gish (directed her sister,
Dorothy, in the 1920 feature,
REMODELING HER HUSBAND).

THE SILENTS

♦ ♦ ♦

Mary Pickford (1893–1979)

It would be no exaggeration to state that Mary Pickford . . . exerted more influence on American productions than anyone else in the industry, apart from D. W. Griffith. And by 1920, even Griffith's importance was on the decline.

—Kevin Brownlow

Interestingly enough, 1920 was precisely the time that **Mary Pickford** had reached her peak. By then, the little "girl with the golden curls" was at the creative helm of all of her pictures.

Even without the consistent practice of screen credit in those days, it is doubtful whether Pickford would have taken it. First and foremost a savvy businesswoman, Pickford was aware that the slightest moves might throw her box office out of kilter. Playing little girls well into her thirties is what her public wanted. They wouldn't have wanted to know that she was as shrewd as the best studio moguls around. As she recounted to Kevin Brownlow in *The Parade's Gone By . . .* (1969),

I didn't want what happened to Chaplin to happen to me. When he discarded the little tramp, the little tramp turned around and killed him. The little girl made me. I'd already been pigeonholed . . . I could have done more dramatic performances . . . but I was already typed.[1]

It is important to dispel the myth of Pickford's on-screen image being in any way connected with the Pickford off-screen. On-screen, audiences loved her as the tragic, naive little orphan, at the mercy of the hard, cruel world and what its fate might offer. In real life, nothing could have been further from the truth. She controlled every aspect of her business and career with an iron hand. Brownlow describes her as "one of the few great stars who was also a great producer."

It is not my prerogative as an actress, to teach (the public) anything. They will teach *me. They* will discipline *me* . . . I am a servant of the public. I have never forgotten that.[2]

But that same faithful public would abandon her each and every time she attempted to grow up on screen. STELLA MARIS (1918), one of the many brilliant pictures written for Pickford by **Francis Marion**, had Pickford playing two roles, a Cockney slave, and Stella Maris, a protected, rich girl paralyzed since childhood. When Stella Maris finally confronts reality, she berates her foster parents, "by trying to shield me you have destroyed my happiness and my faith in humanity." As Brownlow astutely points out, "The message was loud and clear, but the public preferred Mary in the one part they knew so well."[3]

From capitalizing on that one part, Mary Pickford became the first performer in history ever to become a millionaire from the craft of acting. When she and her second husband, Douglas Fairbanks, arrived at the Moscow train station on a holiday trip around the world in 1926, they were greeted by three hundred thousand fans. "The Soviets even made their own Mary Pickford picture," said Brownlow,

> by incorporating shots of Mary Pickford taken during the tour with a story of a cinema usher who imagines he's Douglas Fairbanks. One scene brings them together— and Pickford obligingly throws her arms around the comedian and kisses him. The rest of the film shows the comic pursued by film-crazy Russians, determined to tear strips from his clothes as souvenirs. Satire it may have been, but "A Kiss from Mary Pickford" represented the most graphic possible comment on the success of the American star system.[4]

England went equally wild about the couple. It was the first time in history that people could see flesh-and-blood versions of bona fide screen idols.

Indeed, it was Mary Pickford virtually in and of herself, who *created* the star system. Before her appearance, producers refused the notion of giving "credit" on the screen for fear it would inflate egos, and thus the *salaries* of the creative players. As history would prove, their fears were warranted.

Mary Pickford had confidence in her worth early. When she first met D. W. Griffith she told him, "You must realize I'm an actress and an artist. I've had important parts on the real stage. I must have twenty-five a week guaranteed, and extra when I work extra." She got what she demanded. At the time, she was sixteen.

Such business acumen apparently came from her mother. "Adolph Zukor was one of the cleverest men in the business," said Kevin Brownlow, "but he was outclassed by Mrs. Pickford at every turn. And soon, at a time when a skilled worker was earning twenty-five dollars a week, Mrs. Pickford had Mary earning ten thousand dollars."[5] They gauged this wage on what her contemporary, Charlie Chaplin, was making. At every turn of the scale, Mary Pickford demanded equal footing with men. At every turn, she got it.

Brownlow goes on to say in *Hollywood: The Pioneers* (1979):

> Mary Pickford [displayed] an unnerving knowledge of her own value as a star. Adolph Zukor excited her with his plans for Famous Players, and with her mother, Charlotte, acting as her agent, Mary Pickford squeezed from him a salary of five hundred dollars a week.... Zukor knew that to control stars meant controlling the industry, and he fought hard to keep Pickford, offering her a vast sum to stop work— anything to prevent her falling into the hands of his competitors.[6]

As the historian Benjamin Hampton said, "She was the only member of her sex to become the focal point for an entire industry."[7]

Pickford left Zukor at his top dollar when he would not grant her the right to approve her scripts. She went to First National, which offered her $675,000 a year and 50 percent of the gross. Next she did something smarter. She offered *herself* a job, by forming her own studio with Fairbanks and Chaplin in 1919, where she received 100 percent of the gross.

Now, as star, studio owner, director, and executive producer of United Artists, Pickford knew she had *better* keep her credit of "director/producer" off the screen if she wanted to stay in business—although her cameraman, Charles Rosher said, "She did a lot of her own directing. The director would often just direct the crowd. She knew everything there was to know about motion pictures."[8]

Pickford herself confirmed:

Nobody ever directed me, not even Mr. Griffith. I respected him, yes . . . but when he told me to do things I didn't believe in, I wouldn't do them. I would not run around like a goose with its head off, crying, "Oooo . . . look! A little bunny!" That's what he taught his ingenues, and they all did the same thing. "I'm a grown girl," I said, "I'm sixteen. . . . I won't do it!"[9]

Pickford was so intricately tied in to her public image (i.e., her business) that it ran her private concerns as well. When she fell in love with Fairbanks, their double divorce could have proved a double career disaster via scandal, and Pickford knew it.

According to the famed newspaper columnist and screenwriter, Adela Rogers St. Johns,

Mary came to me one day and said, "You're a judge of public opinion, so I want to ask you a question." I can see her now. She was so tiny, that her feet didn't touch the floor. And all of a sudden she just leaned forward and with tears in her eyes, she said, "Adela, if I divorce Owen and marry Douglas Fairbanks, will my people ever forgive me?" And she meant just that—"will my people ever forgive me?"—like a queen. And it was a hard question to answer, because in those days we did not regard divorce as just another game that you played before breakfast. I said, "I believe—and I can only tell you what I believe—that they will forgive you anything."[10]

The public did more than forgive Pickford and Fairbanks, it wildly applauded them. Little were they able to see at the time,

but they were two archetypes doing a huge, cultural mythological service: the adventurous hero who slays dragons wins the heart and hand of the beautiful, innocent princess. To have their two favorite screen idols wed in holy matrimony is just what the public's fantasies demanded. What the public couldn't do in their own ordinary lives, *someone* should be able to do up on Mount Olympus!

By the midtwenties, the jazz age was advancing, and the public's tastes were changing. The flapper's autonomous outrageousness demanded that women liberate themselves from the Victorian mothers once and for all. There was suddenly little room in the consciousness of America for a naive little girl who never heard of the word . . . S-E-X.

Suddenly, her box office was deserting her. "America's Sweetheart," Mary Pickford, the girl/woman who practically created motion pictures with her comedic foibles and the hilarity of her follies, became an obsolete artifact in the prime of her life.

The world remains indebted to her. A believer in abundance—she always said her talent wasn't *hers*, but a divine gift—Pickford never believed in backbiting, or in competition. In fact, it was Pickford who introduced her greatest rivals, the Gish sisters, to D. W. Griffith.

And yet, with all of her savvy, Mary Pickford's films were the ultimate escapist visions of a woman's life: a grown woman masquerading about as a little girl.

If Mary Pickford successfully used her business acumen to design a multibillion-dollar image of what a woman's life *wasn't*, one has to wonder what American movies might have looked like if she had made stories about what women's lives really *were*. In the case of Mary Pickford, one has to ask, What might a nonescapist vision of a woman's life look like on film?

MARY PICKFORD

1909 Little Teacher, The (Coscript)
1910 In the Season of Buds, May and
      December (Script)
1912 Lena and the Geese (Coscript)
1914 Hearts Adrift (Coscript)
1915 Girl of Yesterday (Coscript)

Starring Roles
1921 Little Lord Fauntleroy (Producer)
      Love Light (Producer)
      Through The Back Door
      (Producer)

1922 Tess of the Storm Country
      (Producer)
1923 Rosita (Producer)
1924 Dorothy Verdon of Haddon Hall
      (Producer)
1925 Little Annie Rooney (Producer)
1926 Sparrows (Producer)
1927 My Best Girl (Producer)
1929 Coquette (Producer)
      Taming of the Shrew, The
      (Producer)
1931 Kiki (Producer)

Mabel Normand (1894–1930)

She is most often remembered as an actress; the genius comedienne of the silent screen. Less well-known is the fact that she directed all productions in which she starred at Keystone. *The Moving Picture World*, said in December 1913, "**Mabel Normand**, leading woman of the Keystone Co. since its inception, is in the future to direct every picture she acts in. This will undoubtedly make Keystone more popular than ever, and give Miss Normand the opportunity of injecting some of her comedy."

Backhandedly, and without conscious malice, Mabel Normand has been "praised" as a female Charlie Chaplin. But the *real* story is more than likely the other way around, as Sam Peeples says in *Classic Film Collector*:

Perhaps (Chaplin's) greatest debt is owed Mabel Normand. A study of her films, made before Chaplin came to this country, show entire routines, gestures, reactions, expressions that were later a part of Chaplin's characterizations.[1]

Normand's talents were infectious, and Chaplin borrowed from her liberally. In MICKEY (1918), the film known by most as

her masterpiece, Normand gave it everything she had. She picked every player, chose the director, starred, and helped in the editing.

"If it was for a laugh, nothing was too much trouble," wrote Joe Franklin in *Classics of the Silent Screen* (1959). "She was the proverbial workhorse."[2] She was man-handled, tied to railroad tracks, dragged through muddy lakes, and plastered with various sorts of goo. Like **Lillian Gish**, Normand was well aware of the dissecting eye of the camera, and so, insisted on doing her own stunt work. "She enjoyed doing roles that required a little more strenuous effort than usual," said Franklin.[3]

Even before Normand was directing, she was doing her own stunts. In SQUAW'S LOVE (date not available), D. W. Griffith cast her as an Indian girl, forced to struggle with her pursuer on top of high rocks. She then dives deeply into the river below and gallantly swims to wreck the canoe of her evil-doers.

And yet, for such remarkable fearlessness of spirit, one *contemporary* historian, Ivan Butler, said by means of compliment (I think), "Mable Normand's MICKEY . . . was a rollicking comedy-drama with action thrills almost worthy of a female Douglas Fairbanks.''[4]

In reality, Normand should neither be insulted as a female Fairbanks nor as a reverse gender Charlie Chaplin. She was her own indomitable, talented self. And certainly that was pioneering enough. From the start, Normand knew she was breaking new turf:

Since all previous laughs had been achieved through the spoken word, and in our early days, through slapstick hokey, I had to cleave a path of laughter through the wilderness of the industry's ignorance and inexperience. I created my own standard of fun. [I simply let] spontaneity and my inborn sense of what is mirth-provoking guide me, for no director ever taught me a thing. . . . I had no precedent, nothing to imitate.[5]

Normand's comic trademark was the art of looking directly into the camera when exasperated, confused, or about to be wicked or sly. It was the old "aside" from the legitimate stage, with the actor betraying the framework and conventions of the scene to make a casual remark to the audience as confidant. Normand knew from the start that the close-up lens of the camera could turn this age-old theatrical trick into magic. She was right.

Without taking credit, Normand directed, as well as starred in, many Keystone Comedies for Mack Sennett, several of which costarred Charlie Chaplin. According to Sam Peeples, Chaplin wrongly states in his biography that Normand was just starting to direct when she first directed Chaplin at Keystone.

The record shows that Mabel Normand directed at least two Keystone Comedies before Chaplin came to the lot: WON IN A CLOSET (released Jan. 22, 1914), and MABEL'S BARE ESCAPE (released Jan. 31, 1914). Just as the record shows that Mabel Normand directed several of Chaplin's films, MABEL AT THE WHEEL (with Chaplin),

CAUGHT IN A CABARET (starring Chaplin); and that Mabel Normand and Chaplin directed at least two more.[6]

Normand and Chaplin appeared side by side in the very first American feature comedy, TILLIE'S PUNCTURED ROMANCE in 1914. Mabel later told her biographer that she was proud of the fact that Chaplin always acknowledged his indebtedness to her, and loved her for all she had taught him.

In her youth, Normand rivaled her famed boss, Mack Sennett, in ambition. Both had an equally driving compulsion to succeed. But when Sennett made his move to Keystone, it was with the understanding that Normand's talents was one of the key elements that could make him rich. Teaming Mabel with Fatty Arbuckle eventually paid Sennett the kind of phenomenal dividends that allowed him to take other entrepreneurial chances.[7]

In 1924, Mabel Normand disappeared from sight. She was hoping to recover from ill-fated press over her association with the infamous murder of William Desmond Taylor. Upon her attempt to return to her career, Mack Sennett, forever jealous over the years of Normand's many admirers, refused to find her a picture.

It wasn't until 1926 that time would wash away all bad omens for Normand, and she was able to return once again to the movies, where she belonged. Hal Roach had wired her with an offer. But as Sam Peeples tells it, she was older, sadder, beaten down in spirit. An almost-frozen silence greeted her return to Hollywood. One gray morning she opened to this letter, reprinted in every Los Angeles paper,

Welcome back to the screen, Mabel Normand! . . .

You have that rare thing, that possession above price, Mabel Normand, the charm of spontaneity. Ever since I first saw you on the screen I have tremendously and sincerely admired your gifts and abilities as an artist. These with your kind heart and mind make you the screen's very own and we are all proud of your splendid work.[8]

The letter was signed, "Mary Pickford."

A kind gesture, but the years had taken their toll. Although her three-reeler comedies for Roach were successful and her career seemed to be on the upswing at last, Normand's health and spirit never quite revived.

> Just as Mabel seemed to be recovering from the effects [of the William Desmond Taylor scandal], her chauffeur was found standing over the body of . . . a Hollywood millionaire. The pistol in his hand was said to have belonged to Mabel. The double scandal shattered her completely.[9]

In January 1927 the doctors discovered a serious advance of tuberculosis. "Life wrote FADE OUT to Mabel Normand on February 23, 1930," writes Sam Peeples. It was a long and difficult dying. Normand was thirty-five. Perhaps, suggests Peeples, she wrote her own epitaph in the closing words to her biographer:

> I'm afraid that never again will the world find such things to laugh at as it used to find when Charlie Chaplin and Roscoe Arbuckle and Ford Sterling and Charlie Murray and I made our comedies together.[10]

It is for these pages to celebrate the woman whom Mack Sennett once called "the most gifted player who ever stepped before a camera." It is for these pages to crown her acting and directing achievements, and put her in her rightful place among the greatest pioneers of classic cinematic comedies.

MABEL NORMAND

1913 Champion, The
      Zuzu, The Band Leader

1914 Alarm, The
      Caught in a Cabaret
      Fatal Mallet, The
      Fatty's Jonah Day
      Fatty's Wine Party
      Friend the Bandit
      Gentleman of Nerve
      Getting Acquainted
      Glimpse of Los Angeles, A
      Hello, Mabel
      His Trysting Place
      How Heros Are Made
      Love and Gasoline
      Lover's Post Office
      Mabel at the Wheel
      Mabel's Bare Escape
      Mabel's Blunder
      Mabel's Busy Day
      Mabel's Latest Prank
      Mabel's Married Life
      Mabel's Nerve
      Mabel's New Job
      Mabel's Stormy Love Affair
      Mabel's Strange Predicament
      Mack at it Again
      Misplaced Foot, A
      Sea Nymphs, The
      Those Country Kids
      Tillie's Punctured Romance
        (First Feature)
      Won in a Closet

1915 Fatty and Mabel at the San Francisco Exposition
      Fatty and Mabel's Married Life
      Little Band of God, The
      Little Teacher, The
      Mabel and Fatty Viewing the World's Fair at San Francisco
      Mabel Lost and Won
      Mabel and Fatty's Simple Life
      Mabel and Fatty's Wash Day
      Mabel, Fatty, and The Law
      Mabel's Willful Ways
      My Valet
      Stolen Magic
      Their Social Splash
      Wished on Mabel

1916	Bright Lights, The
	Fatty and Mabel Adrift
	He Did and He Didn't
1918	Back to the Woods
	Dodging a Million
	Floor Below, The
	Joan of Plattsburgh
	Mickey
	Peck's Bad Girl
	Perfect 36, A
	Venus Model, The
1919	Pest, The
	Pinto
	Sis Hopkins

	Upstairs
	When Doctors Disagree
1920	Slim Princess, The
	What Happened to Rosa
1922	Head Over Heels
	Molly O
1923	Extra Girl, The
	Suzanna
1926	Anything Once
	Nickel Hopper, The
	Our Hour Married
	Raggedy Rose
1927	Should Men Walk Home?

Nell Shipman (1892–1970)

Nell Shipman, like many early women film-makers, was born in a highly respected, cultured family. She was brought up in the sophisticated environs of Victoria, British Columbia, and also like many early women filmmakers, she ran off romantically to make her name as an actress in vaudeville. At the turn of the century, the stock-company life was commonplace for young women. As writer Peter Morris points out;

> Developing societies have a greater tendency than established ones to encourage women to play an active part. . . . Literature in Canada in the nineteenth century was dominated by women writers while the writers in the United States were predominantly male.[1]

The career of Nell Shipman, Morris declared, was also to some degree a microcosm of what happened to women filmmakers—a shift from a position of centrality in an industry to marginality.[2]

In 1914, when she was only eighteen years old, Shipman established a reputation as a talented writer for the early mainstream studios. Her book, *Under the Crescent* (1914), was translated into one of the "First" series for Universal by Carl Laemmle. That same year her script, SHEPHERD OF THE SOUTHERN CROSS (1914), was another "first" to be produced in Australia.[3]

She continued to write and direct her first three feature films for Universal Studios, and to star in all of them. In 1916, Shipman's GOD'S COUNTRY AND THE WOMAN became a huge success, and established her as a major independent producer/director/actress.

But by the early twenties, her films failed to get major release, and she was forced to close her company. As Peter Morris points out, this unfortunate turn of events wasn't due to a sudden loss of talent on Shipman's part, or even to a sudden shift of audience taste. It was due to the "changes that had taken place in the film industry since she had written her first film in 1912."[4]

> Her collaborative approach to production and strong sense of independence soon made her an anachronism in the emerging hierarchical film industry. Her films failed

because they were clear witness to a vision and technique absolutely opposed to that offered by the new industrial capitalism. . . . [a vision] that did not include portraits of self-sufficient women, nor any sensitivity toward nature except as something to be exploited.[5]

Nor did it include shooting on real locations as she liked to do in a collaborative process with her crew.

It was in such a world that eighteen-year-old Nell Shipman moved with her young husband Ernest to Southern California in 1912. Within only two years, she established her reputation as a talented writer for companies like Vitagraph, Selig, and Universal.[6]

GOD'S COUNTRY AND THE WOMAN, released in 1916, was the very first feature-length wildlife adventure film in history,[7] and it made Nell Shipman a star. The film was probably the first feature-length movie shot almost entirely on location. It was also the first picture ever to use an enclosed dark stage for its interiors.[8] It took an unheard-of three months to shoot and it was a huge success. Now, along with stars such as **Mary Pickford**, Nell Shipman could literally call her own shots.

For the next few years, she continued with a string of successes that seemed to have gotten increasingly stronger after her divorce from Ernest in 1920. These included BACK TO GOD'S COUNTRY (1919), and THE GIRL FROM GOD'S COUNTRY (1921).

Shipman raised an entourage of nearly two hundred animals that she both trained for her films and traveled with. In a film called THE GRUB STAKE (1922), a bear, deer, fawn, and wild porcupine are all part of the ensemble cast, and garner as much attention as the human actors. In fact, animals and actors in Shipman films usually got equal billing.

It's an amazing spectacle to watch as Nell lovingly interacts with the kind of wildlife

that would awe most rangers. Her deep understanding that humanity is only a single aspect of our environment was the trademark that made Shipman's pictures unlike anyone else's. Ironically, it was also the ultimate cause of her downfall.

Her technical applications were unusually innovative. In one of her films, she employed a now-antiquated technique called a triptych. This was a kind of keyhole to see what was happening in one time and place, while superimposed in two upper triangles of the picture were simultaneous occurrences happening elsewhere. It must be remembered that in the mid-1910s, when such experiments were being employed, the craft of editing was still in its elemental stages. Filmmakers were newly playing around with concepts such as "matching" close-up shots to wide shots to medium shots, etc., so to employ an idea that literally defied notions of time and space on the screen was somewhat revolutionary.

In terms of her characters, most heroines of the day were melodramatic, swooning and fainting if someone so much as breathed at them. And of course, the big problems were always solved by the men. But in Shipman's GOD'S COUNTRY AND THE WOMAN the main female protagonist is determined to be the mistress of her own destiny.

Though threatened throughout the film by the villain, she constantly uses her own skills, intelligence and, not least, her sympathetic rapport with a ferocious dog, to evade his clutches. . . . She is the one who rescues her husband in the climax of the film. . . . The film more than hints that male authority figures may not have a right to that authority.[9]

There is a constant reminder in her movies about living in sympathetic and humble accord with the natural world.

The fascination of Nell Shipman was this: her decision to remain staunchly independent in an emerging corporate, nonintuitive

Hollywood. She believed in film as a collaborative process. She believed in shooting on real locations—which was becoming an antiquated notion in the new Hollywood that found shooting on studio-built sets more efficient.

The changes occurring in the quickly transmuted industry reached their peak in 1922 and 1923. Nell found them intolerable and moved herself and her two hundred four-legged friends to Priest Lake, Idaho. And although the new films she made there, "embody the same perceptions of life and nature, the same sense of creating out of, and with nature, with the same admirable female characters,"[10] the films failed miserably at the box office. It wasn't Nell's lack of talent. It certainly wasn't bad filmmaking. It was due to a shift in emphasis in the industry. Like **Mary Pickford**'s "Sweetheart," Nell Shipman's mode and method of moviemaking became antiquated entities while she was in the prime of her life.[11]

Although she was forced to sell her company and give her animals to the San Diego Zoo,[12] Shipman was far from retired.

She remarried in 1925, moved to Spain and had twins in 1926,[13] moved back to the States that same year, and continued to write for the movies. Most notably now she wrote for "talkies." She also wrote several books, including *Get the Woman* (1930), which was serialized in *McCalls* as *M'Sieu Sweetheart,* and chosen as a comeback vehicle for **Clara Bow**. It was a project doomed to be unrealized, but Shipman didn't lose faith. She went on to become the author of THE EYES OF THE EAGLE, a film that William De Mille was supposed to direct and Shipman was supposed to produce. And yet, the "powers that be" shifted the movie out West where the producership was taken out of her hands. Her script, retitled WINGS IN THE DARK (1935), would star Cary Grant and **Myrna Loy**.

In 1969, when she was in her midsixties, Nell Shipman wrote an autobiography entitled *The Silent Screen and My Talking Heart*—an engrossing read for anyone interested in the silent days. One might wonder if such a woman would have become a saddened sentimentalist, broken by Hollywood. Not this outdoor pioneer! She is remembered by one film writer who interviewed her in her old age "as young as the dawn of a new day and as contemporary as tomorrow. . . . She can also scratch, spit and sting. . . . We old fans associate [her] with dog-sleds, snow-shoes, parkas and canoes rushing towards a raging waterfall. She is the beautiful girl who is so well able to take care of herself, and most times, the hero also."[14]

If you asked Nell Shipman in her later years if she was sorry that she turned down Sam Goldwyn's offer of a seven-year contract, she would have said perhaps it wasn't her wisest move. But the humor betrayed in the last pages of her autobiography makes it stunningly clear that she could never have survived in the rigid and lifeless structure that Hollywood was adopting. "There they go," she wrote. "Free from woe / Forgetting me / Aw, Gee!"[15]

Perhaps Peter Morris sums Nell Shipman's story up best:

That the years since her death have seen her values become more central in American thought is not only a tribute to her perspicacity and pioneering spirit but also a belated recognition of a truly fine creative mind.[16]

NELL SHIPMAN

1916 God's Country and the Woman
1919 Back to God's Country
1920 Something New
1921 A Bear, a Boy and a Dog
      Girl From God's Country, The
1922 Grub Stake, The
1923 Light on Lookout, The
      Trail of the North Wind

Lillian Gish (1896–   )

"I never had a double or a stand-in," **Lillian Gish** remarked to me proudly, "I did it all myself. The blizzard (in WAY DOWN EAST [1920])—I was facing it. The wind on the peninsula was terrible. The snow as it came against my face melted, and on my eyelashes—icicles! And Griffith yelled at the cameraman, 'Billy, Billy get that face!' And he said, 'I will if the oil in the camera hasn't frozen,' and he got that face!" And thus, is told the story behind how D. W. Griffith filmed his very first close-up.

"But why did you do it if you knew you might have died?" I asked.

Her look at me was one of kind impatience.

"Because the camera would know it!" she said as though it were self-evident. "That camera is more dissecting than anything that's ever been invented. You stay in front of it long enough, and it tells, as John Barrymore said, what you had for breakfast. You can't fool it! And had it been another person lying on that ice, you'd know it from the way they moved. It would tell on you."[1]

Such characteristics mark the pioneer. Actions born out of necessity. But aside from doing her own stunt work (something that wasn't unusual for either women or men of the early silent era), Lillian Gish was put in the director's seat by D. W. Griffith in 1920 with a picture called REMODELING HER HUSBAND (1920). The picture starred and was written by Lillian's sister **Dorothy**. Griffith believed that, since Lillian and Dorothy were all but linked at the hip, Lillian would be able to extract a kind of able, insightful, comedic performance out of her sister that might elude even Griffith. "He confidently assured Lillian," says Marjorie Rosen in *Popcorn Venus*, "that because she was a woman, she'd be in a better position to deal with financial and production hassles than he was."[2]

All lapses in such logic aside, he seemed to be right—especially when you consider Griffith's well-publicized, poor reputation for handling finances. Gish brought the picture in on time and under budget. It cost $50,000 and saw a sweet return of $460,000. It ultimately became the second biggest money-maker of all of **Dorothy Gish**'s comedies.

Given a totally free hand at their choice of material, they decided on a funny piece of business that Dorothy had spotted in a magazine. The story told of a husband who accuses his wife of being too dowdy. Says Marjorie Rosen:

> No more than an amusingly expanded one-liner, in the hands of a female director and star, this film evolved into a novel approach to handling masculine dissatisfaction and feminine pliability. . . . How many male directors would have permitted—or utilized—a story which, though light, mocked men and their eccentric notions of beauty?[3]

Although the picture was a moderate success, Lillian Gish said, "Directing is no career for a lady."[4] Apparently, the administrative hassles were more than she cared to handle. Yet don't let this Victorian modesty fool you—for that's exactly what it was. Griffith left a number of pictures in the able hands of Gish. She produced many of her own films after 1920, even if she didn't always take the credit. After her official directorial debut, Gish

> then starred in several major films of minor companies that gave her control over scripts and choice of directors. She received the same privileges when she joined

MGM in 1925 and chose King Vidor and Victor Seastrom to direct her in LA BOHEME [1926] and THE SCARLET LETTER [1926] respectively.⁵

When she was doing ORPHANS OF THE STORM (1922), she had to come down the steps from the guillotine, after she was released from a beheading, and she met her sister:

"I hadn't cared for the way Griffith had rehearsed and done it," said Gish, "He used to tease me by calling me Miss 'GEEESH.' "Apparently Miss 'GEEESHE' (she mimics Griffith) doesn't like what we're doing." "Oh, it's as good as a scene in any of your other films, Mr. Griffith. I just think more is expected of you."
He says, "If you're so smart, get up there and do it better!"
Well, I got down the steps and played it the way I felt it should be played. There were fifty to a hundred extras there. He got down on both knees and kissed my hand and said, "She's always right!"⁶

As his number one box-office attraction, Griffith would be foolish *not* to listen to what Gish had to say. He once remarked, "She is not only the best actress in her profession, but she has the best mind of any woman I have ever met."⁷ Fortunately, they respected each other mutually as artists and as people and were able to work out a collaboration that would benefit the entire world for generations to come.
Although Gish was wed countless times on the screen, she never married in real life. The reaction to such independence and loyalty to her career was the rise of nasty rumors of an incestual relationship with her sister, Dorothy. Resolved to keep her private life private, she was nonetheless hounded, quite unsuccessfully, by one George Jean Nathan.⁸ She later confessed:

What kind of wife would I have made? A good wife is a seven day a week, twenty-four-hour-a-day job. I was devoted to the studio. I loved many beautiful men but I never ruined their lives.⁹

Not unlike women in other time-consuming lines of work, women in film seem to feel that marriage to your work precludes any other type of personal allegiances.
Gish won a special Oscar for her cumulative work in 1970. After a long screen absence, she returned for a special appearance in Robert Altman's THE WEDDING (1978), and kept on going with her 104th film in THE WHALES OF AUGUST (1987) with **Bette Davis**. At the time, Gish was ninety-one.

LILLIAN GISH (Selected List)

1912	Unseen Enemy (First Film)
	Musketeers of Pig Alley, The
	New York Hat, The
1914	Battle of Elderbush Gulch, The
	Battle of the Sexes, The
	Hunchback, The
	Judith of Bethulia
1915	Birth of a Nation
	Enoch Arden
	Lily and the Rose, The
	Sold for Marriage
1918	Greatest Thing in Life, The
	Hearts of the World
1919	Broken Blossoms
	Trueheart Susie
1920	Remodeling Her Husband (Only Credited Directorial Piece)
	Way Down East
1922	Orphans of the Storm
1923	White Sister, The
1924	Romola
1926	La Boheme
	Scarlet Letter, The
1927	Annie Laurie

1928	Enemy, The	1960	Unforgiven, The
	Wind, The	1966	Follow Me, Boys!
1947	Duel in the Sun	1967	Comedians, The
1949	Portrait of Jenny		Warning Shot
1955	Night of the Hunter	1978	Wedding, The
1958	Orders to Kill (UK)	1987	Whales of August, The

SHORT TAKES

◆ ◆ ◆

Ruth Stonehouse (1893–1941)

Originally a dancer from Indiana, **Ruth Stonehouse** joined Carl Laemmle's Universal lot in 1916. She began her multifaceted role of directing/acting/writing with a two-reeler, DOROTHY DARES (1916). Because of her "little girl" stature a la **Mary Pickford**, she created a series for Universal entitled, MARY ANN KELLY STORIES, in which she also starred, directed, and cowrote.

A book published in 1916 called *The Life Stories of the Movie Stars* said about Stonehouse,

> She's a good actress, she's a wonderful housekeeper, she's an omnivorous reader—and there you are! Some combination, don't you think? Perhaps no one has been more wronged than she in pictures. She's ever the poor, persecuted, sad and solemn little person, pitting her feeble powers that be. . . . Miss Stonehouse in real life is the wife of Joe Roach, a scenario writer, and they're just as happy as a couple of proverbial turtledoves. They've both been in picture work for about four years.[1]

The portrait could have referred to **Mary Pickford**. Grown women masquerading about as little girls was a popular and even understandable notion for women in motion pictures in the silent days, being birthed directly out of the womb of Victorian mothers.

As Anthony Slide notes, "Her star years were over by 1920. She continued to play character roles well into the sound era."[2]

RUTH STONEHOUSE

1916 Dorothy Dares
      Heart of Mary Ann, The
      Mary Ann in Society
1917 Cocky Sue's Romance
      Dividend Dan
      Lies of Satin, The
      Puppy Love
      Stolen Actress, The
      Walloping Time, A

Lule Warrenton   Ruth Stonehouse   Margery Wilson

Cleo Madison

Lucille McVey (1890–1925)

She was a Southern girl born in the far south of Missouri in the late 1890s. Known as "Mrs. Sidney Drew" to her audience, **Lucille McVey** joined Vitagraph in 1913 to costar with her husband in a series of remarkably successful domestic comedies. *Photoplay Magazine* noted, "I give Mrs. Drew 75 percent of the credit for the conception of the Drew comedies. . . . She is the team member who selects the idea and builds it."[1]

With her husband's death in 1919, McVey gave up her acting career, but blossomed out in directing such successful productions as COUSIN KATE in 1921, starring **Alice Joyce**.[2]

LUCILLE MCVEY

1917	Close Resemblance, A
	Her Anniversaries
	Her Lesson
	His Curiosity
	Lest We Forget
	Patriot, The
	Pest, The
	Rubbing It In
	Shadowing Henry
	Safety First
	Too Much Henry
1918	Before and After Talking
	Gas Logic
	Help Wanted
	His First Love
	Special Today
	Why Henry Left Home
1919	Bunkered
	Gay Old Time
	Once a Man
	Squawed
	Romance and Ringo
1920	Emotional Mrs. Vaughan
	Stimulating Mrs. Barton
1921	Cousin Kate

Lule Warrenton (1863–1932)

A stage actress all her life, **Lule Warrenton** came to films in middle age, doing mother roles in 1913. By 1916 Universal set Warrenton up in her own company where she directed shorts with child stars.

Only a year later, she left the studio to form her own company, Frieder Film Corporation. In 1917 the *Moving Picture World* wrote,

"Mother" Warrenton is now the first and only woman producer with a studio and company all her own. . . . She plans to present the comedies and the tragedies and the dramas of childlife just as they appear to the child mind. She believes that by writing her own scenarios and directing her own scenes, and supervising the entire production, she can produce photoplays that will be intensely interesting."[1]

Her first production, A BIT O' HEAVEN (1917) was a huge success, gleaning praises like, "a feast awaits the picture-going public, man, woman, child in this production."[2] Two further features were announced in the trades that year, THE LITTLEST FUGITIVE, and HOP O' MY THUMB, but for unknown reasons, Warrenton returned in September 1917 to Universal as an actress. The pressures to begin her own firm at a fairly late stage in life might have been too great for her. Only five years later, she retired from the screen altogether.[3]

Outside of motion pictures, Warrenton is remembered as the founder of the Hollywood Girls' Club.

1917   Bit o' Heaven, A

Cleo Madison (1883–1964)

I have known—I have known
The dawn of fame—a glitter shown
One glowing hour—a gilded throne
And then—alone!

I have felt—I have felt
The heart's death sob—mirages melt
My dazzling world—a desert veldt
And there—I knelt![1]

This little ditty by **Cleo Madison** could have served alternately for the story of Hollywood as well as for her own sad and short-lived career. This pioneer is best remembered as possibly the earliest feminist director with HER BITTER CUP in 1916. *Photoplay Magazine* said of the film, "With the lovely but militant Cleo at their head, the suffragettes could capture the vote for their sex and smash down the opposition as easily as shooting fish in a bucket."[2] And about her directorial prowess, "She is so smart and businesslike that she makes most of the male population of Universal City look like debutantes when it comes right down to brass tacks and affairs."[3]

HER BITTER CUP is remembered as one of the earliest suffragette classics. The film was shot on a freak, opportune day—a snowstorm fell on Hollywood! Madison and her crew caught it on film.

Cleo Madison began as a vaudeville actress in Bloomington, Illinois, at the turn of the century. She turned to acting for the "flickers" with Universal in 1913. Almost instantly, she was swept up in the popularity of serials established by **Grace Cunard** and her partner, Francis Ford. Soon, Cleo Madison's face was synonomous with a box-office smash. She made several films with Lon Chaney, not yet known as "The Man of a Thousand Faces."

THE TREY O' HEARTS (1914) was a Saturday matinee serial, in which Madison played the double role of twin sisters. The vehicle turned her into a star—so much of a star that ambition took her over and she insisted on directing and producing her own product. "When Cleo made up her mind that she wanted to direct, the company balked," said William M. Henry of *Photoplay*. "Her request was refused. Nothing daunted, Cleo decided that what she couldn't get by asking, she would force them to give her."[4]

Her basic plan was that she would made every director's life under whom she worked as an actress so miserable that no one would want to work with her. Having a reputation that compared her with **Sarah Bernhardt** helped. ("The old timers at Universal scoff at Bernhardt or Petrova as compared to her.")[5] Madison was soon at the helm of her own company.

She directed at least three films before taking on the additional task of writing HER BITTER CUP, a five-reel feature. An enormously versatile woman, Madison could (as **Ida Lupino** would) handle westerns with the best of them. SEALED ORDERS (1914), as Buck Rainey points out in *Classic Images*, "is replete with roof-top chases, a la Ken Maynard and a fierce gun-fighting episode as Cleo's honor is protected."[6] Madison told *Moving Picture Weekly*:

Every play in which women appear needs the feminine touch. Lois Weber's productions are phenomenally successful, partly because her woman creations are true to the spirit of womanhood. I believe in doing most of the work before the camera is called into action. It should never be necessary, except in the case of accident, to retake a scene.[7]

When she was asked if she was scared at all on the day of her first directing task, she replied, "Why should I be? I had seen men with less brains than I have getting away with it, and so I knew that I could direct if they'd give me the opportunity."[8] The experience was not really all that new to her, having been her own stage manager with "The Cleo Madison Stock Company" years before. When her directing opportunity presented itself, she was more than prepared.

Her reputation on the Universal lot with the crews went something like this, according to one of her assistant cameramen. "Cleo has taken up the methods of the best directors in 'The City.' She's second to none. There isn't a director on the lot that's got the flow of language or can exhibit the temperament she can."[9]

One favorite story about Cleo Madison is a profile that was done on her in *Moving Picture Weekly* in 1916. After describing the tough, no-nonsense approach she had about her career, the writer softened the blow about this "unusual" woman to his readers thus:

Another of Miss Madison's accomplishments, when she is under the influence of her domestic personality, is cooking. . . . She enjoys nothing more than donning a big apron and setting to work to cook a real old fashioned chicken dinner. Can you imagine . . . the temperamental "Rethna" of HER BITTER CUP concoction a plate of biscuits that simply melt in your mouth? Do you think that La Tosca knew very much about coconut icing?[10]

But somehow, the reviewer had to tell the truth, the whole truth, and nothing but the truth about his subject, no matter how "unsavory" she might appear. After all, there was a good chance that Madison herself might read this article! So only two paragraphs later, the author admits: "The domestic Cleo confessed with frankness . . . that she is not very happy on the top of a kitchen ladder."[11]

Madison found herself much in demand during the heyday of the early studio, but by 1921, she suffered from nervous exhaustion. She was able to resurrect her career briefly in the midtwenties, then mysteriously disappeared from the screen for good. She died as many of the women film pioneers did, alone and forgotten in a Hollywood she helped to create.

"One of these days, men are going to get over the fool idea that women have no brains," said Madison, "and quit getting insulted at the thought that a skirt-wearer can do their work quite as well as they can. And I don't believe that day is very far off."[12] "Far off" may be the most relative concept known to women's history. But one thing is certain, Cleo Madison's contributions have helped to push that day a little nearer.

CLEO MADISON

Mystery of Wickham Hall, The
Sealed Orders
Sin of Olga Brandt, The
Trey O' Hearts, The
Unjustly Accused
1915 Alas and Alack
Crystal, The
Dancer, The
Duchess, The
Extravagance
Fascination of the Fleur De Lis,
    The
Fiery Introduction, A
Flight of a Night Bird, The
Haunted Hearts
Liquid Dynamite
Mother Instinct, The
Mother's Atonement, A
Mystery Woman, The
People of the Pit, The
Pine's Revenge, The
Power of Fascination, The
Ring of Destiny, The
Their Hour
Ways of a Man, The
Wild Irish Rose
Woman's Debt, A
1916 Alias Jane Jones
Black Orchids
Chalice of Sorrow, The
Crimson Yoke, The
Cross Purposes

Eleanor's Catch
Girl in Lower 9, The
Guilty One, The
Her Bitter Cup
Her Defiance
His Return
Priscilla's Prisoner
Severed Hand, The
Soul Enslaved, A
To Another Woman
Triumph of Truth
Virginia
When the Wolf Howls
1917 Daring Chance, The
Girl Who Lost, The
Sorceress, The
Web, The
1918 Romance of Tarzan, The
1919 Girl from Nowhere, The
Great Radium Mystery, The
1920 Price of Redemption, The
1921 Ladies Must Live
Lure of Youth, The
1922 Dangerous Age, The
Woman's Woman, A
1923 Gold Madness
Souls in Bondage
1924 Discontented Husbands
Lullaby, The
Roughneck, The
True as Steel
Unseen Hands

Margery Wilson (1898–1986)

Best remembered as "Brown Eyes" from D. W. Griffith's INTOLERANCE (1916), and as the author of several of the earliest self-help books on the market—*Charm* (1928), *The Woman You Want to Be* (1942), *How to Live Beyond Your Means* (1945).[1] Sara Strayer changed her name to **Margery Wilson** (her idol was President Wilson's daughter, Margaret) so as not to disgrace her family due to her profession. She was, after all, an actress. She appeared in several fea-

tures, playing opposite great players of the day, Douglas Fairbanks, Sr., **Dorothy Gish**, and William Desmond.

Sara Barker Strayer from Gracey, Kentucky was a leading lady by the age of fourteen with the John Lawrence Players of Ohio. In 1914 the self-dubbed Margery Wilson took herself to Los Angeles with the excuse of finding work for her sister in the movies. The first company she approached was Reliance-Mutual, where a young man named D. W. Griffith was director-in-chief. What happened to Miss Strayer's sister remains a mystery, but "Brown Eyes" Margery Wilson found a home in the new industry.[2]

Thomas Ince, who also gave **Dorothy Davenport Reid** her directorial beginnings, gave Wilson a shot at directing and starring in THAT SOMETHING in 1920. She followed this by directing two other features—INSINUATION (1922), and THE OFFENDERS (1924)—as well as several shorts. Wilson claims that she was the first person to make a film on location, "without a single set."[3] Though she was mistaken about this—director/writer/actress **Nell Shipman** beat her to it by two years—Wilson nevertheless seemed to do a spendid job of directing. She also wrote INSINUATION, produced it and sold it, "for fifty thousand dollars, which I thought was a million at the time."[4]

Upon the release of INSINUATION, *The Moving Picture World* said, "It is absolutely refreshing to review a picture like INSINUATION, whose real value and appeal lies, at the outset, in its naturalness and which does not have to rely upon artificiality or luxurious props to aid in the telling of the story. . . . INSINUATION will be classified among the top-notchers."[5]

In 1927, five years after INSINUATION, Wilson went into premature retirement. She married a man who, she said, "didn't want me to do anything."[6] She was rescued by her own self-help books, which she wrote until her death in 1986.

MARGERY WILSON (Selected List)

1920	That Something
	Two of a Kind
1922	Insinuation
1924	Offenders, The

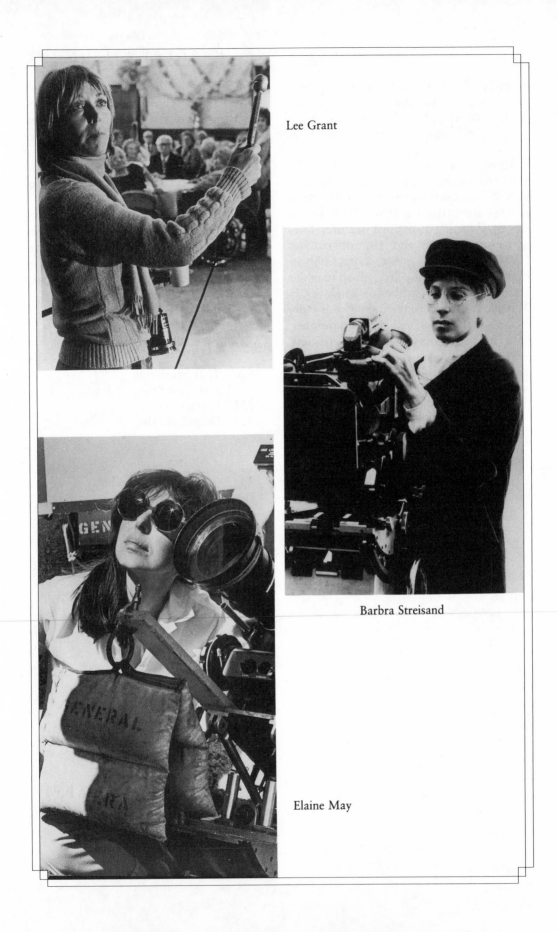

Lee Grant

Barbra Streisand

Elaine May

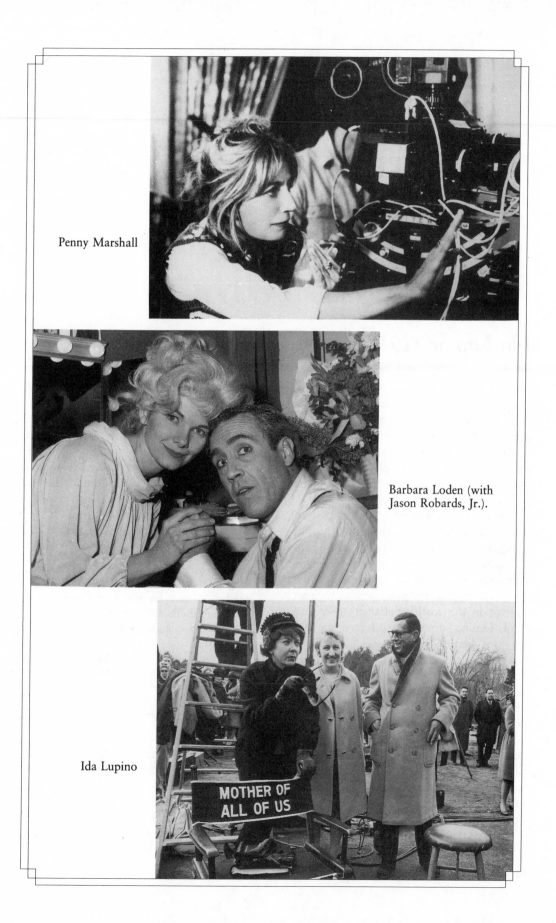

Penny Marshall

Barbara Loden (with Jason Robards, Jr.).

Ida Lupino

THE SOUND ERA

❖ ❖ ❖

Ida Lupino (1918–   )

The back of her director's chair read, "Mother of Us All . . . ," a nom de plume that **Ida Lupino** solicited, encouraged, and used fully to her own subversive advantage. It was armor against a time when women needed to be sexless to be effective in the industry. It was an attitude that for a while proved ingenious.

Taking into account both her feature film work and her later television work that brought her into maturity,[1] Ida Lupino holds the crown as the most prolific American woman director in history. And possibly, even to date, the most prolific woman director in the world. Between 1949 and 1954, Lupino wrote and directed six features for her own company, "The Film-makers," while starring in seven features directed by others. Later, for television, her filmography catalogues work for over thirty series such as *Thriller, Have Gun Will Travel,* and *The Fugitive.* She frequently directed up to nine episodes for one program. Her biographer, William Donati, says he can safely estimate at least one hundred episodes directed in her career; Lupino's claim is that she directed hundreds.[2] Although she is pigeonholed as a social realist, as Barbara Scharres of the Art Institute of Chicago has pointed out, a study of Lupino's television work expands that narrow range to "westerns, tales of the supernatural, situation comedies, murder mysteries and gangster stories."[3] Scharres also brings to light the fact that the poorly documented television work shows a Lupino ambitious with her camera and technically ahead of her time. She cites one *Thriller* episode from 1961:

> In one continuous close-up shot [the actress] reaches for the sponge, her hand hovers over it in a moment of indecision, she reaches instead for the chocolates; just when you think she's safe, her hand darts back to the sponge, grasps it, and she is electrocuted. Comedy, suspense, and a tour-de-force display of Lupino's wittiness come together in one shot. In contast to the often static camerawork of Fifties and Sixties television, Lupino made extensive use of the moving camera.[4]

As an actress, Lupino reached her full potential in the forties in film noir pictures like Raoul Walsh's HIGH SIERRA (1941). Ironically, it was her experience of powerlessness as an actress (initially she was dubbed "the English **Jean Harlow**") that drove her to want to control her own career, and hence, to directing.

Because Lupino began directing independently, she did not have to pass the potential subject matter of her films by anyone. And so, as Richard Koszarski has said:

> Her films display the obsessions and consistencies of a true auteur. . . . What is most interesting about her films are not her stories of unwed motherhood or the tribulations of career women, but the way in which she uses male actors: particularly in THE BIGAMIST [1953] and THE HITCHHIKER [1953], Lupino was able to reduce the male to the same sort of dangerous, irrational force that women represented in most male-directed examples of Hollywood *film noir*.[5]

She became so adept at directing tough "action" pictures, that she had a hard time convincing studio heads that she could do a love story.

> "You don't tell a man," Lupino once said, "You suggest to them. 'Let's try something crazy here. That is, if it's comfortable for you, love.' I'd say, 'Darlings, Mother has a problem. I'd love to do this. Can you do it? It sounds kooky, I know. But can you do this [lit'l ol' thang] for Mother?' And they do it—they just go and do it. I loved being called Mother."[6]

If it sounds perverse or manipulative in our age, it was in perfect tenor for the woman of 1950. Especially if that woman was the only woman directing in an all-male Hollywood.

If she was terrified on the set (or off for that matter) she knew enough not to show it. "Brittleness is the keystone of a Lupino performance," wrote Carrie Rickey, "but the way she played it, the toughness was a facade, protective covering for her most vulnerable of characterizations."

As if to comment on the woman herself, a character in her film THE BIGAMIST (directed by Lupino in 1953) says about the woman Lupino plays in the movie, "She fools us with that flip, hard act of hers." As Rickey says, "She's really a marshmellow underneath."[7]

Perhaps she came into the business as she came into life, with a chip on her shoulder, with something to prove. A little cast down, a little bitter, but always ready to face the fate life seemed to pose for her. By the forties she was known as "the darling of the Tough Guy school of directing"—along with some of her favorites: Raoul Walsh, Fritz Lang, William Wellman. " 'There was none of this nonsense,' said Lupino characteristically, 'I mean, you got your backside in there, baby, and you did it.' "[8]

Show business was literally in Ida Lupino's blood. She had to be an actress. She had no choice in the matter. Her family had its roots on the stage nearly ever since show biz began—the Renaissance. "Neapolitan jugglers and dancers who would eventually be banished from Italy for their politics and emigrate to England," [9] as Carrie Rickey describes them. A prophetic tale for what would become of Lupino in the political jungle of Hollywood. Her father was the music-hall comedian, Stanley Lupino, and her mother, **Connie Emerald**, an actress who would lose a movie role to her thirteen-year-old daughter, Ida.

From the start, Lupino would not be able to do what she dreamed of doing. "I had no desire to crash a man's world," she said in 1975. Ever since she was a kid, she wanted to be a writer. Instead, she did what she thought would make her father proud of her. "I knew it would break his heart if I didn't go into the business."

Lupino was enrolled in one of the most prestigious acting schools in England, the Royal Academy of Dramatic Arts. Her agent at the time told her that she would be the **Janet Gaynor** of England; she would play all the sweet roles. Instead, at the tender age of thirteen, she started on a path of playing nothing but hookers.

She was plucked out of RADA for her first movie role in Allan Dwan's HER FIRST AFFAIR (1932). Ida, in turn, plucked her eyebrows, dyed her hair blond, and was known to audiences from the debut as, "the English **Jean Harlow**." From a film called MONEY FOR SPEED (1933), done soon after, Lupino was discovered by Hollywood, who literally thought they had found that next Alice in Wonderland.

> Paramount scouts had heard of me. [In the film,] I had played a dual role. They only saw the section where I was this sweet little blond, not the part when I was the hooker. . . . When I finally got to Hollywood for the screen test, they said, "What have we got here? She ought to play the catepillar or something." But they were stuck with me for five years.[10]

Paramount had no idea what to do with such an odd mixture of beauty and toughness. About the only good thing that happened to Lupino at Paramount was that she met her best girlfriend there, **Ann Sheridan**. The two of them did several innocuous pictures, when **Hedda Hopper** saved her by giving her some good advice. She told her to take that junk off her face, let her eyebrows grow in, and remember that first and foremost she was an actress. It worked. She began to get parts that mattered. She soon became pegged, "the poor man's **Bette Davis**."

In the early fifties, when McCarthyism was reaching new heights of viciousness and inhumanity, the movies resorted more and more to escapist fare. Just before this period, Lupino explains,

> For about eighteen months in the mid-forties, I could not get a job [as an actress] in pictures. . . . I was on suspension. . . . When you turned down something you were suspended.[11]

And so she turned to directing because, "I had to do something to fill up my time."[12]

She was bored to tears with standing around the set while "someone else seemed to be doing all the interesting work." So Lupino teamed up with her second husband, Collier Young, and formed her own company. "Her work for the Filmmakers," says Carrie Rickey, "could serve as a model of modern feminist moviemaking. Not only did Lupino take control of production, direction, and screenplay, but each of her movies addresses the brutal repercussions of sexuality, independence, and dependence."[13]

Like the pioneering director, **Lois Weber**, who directed in Hollywood thirty years before her, Lupino chose controversial, socially conscious issues for the themes of her movies: rape, bigamy, polio, unwed motherhood. Like **Weber**, she handled these topics at a time when they would, to say the least, elicit controversy. But unlike **Weber**, Lupino was first and foremost an entertainer, not a preacher. Actors felt comfortable and confident taking orders from her because she was also a performer. She knew the game from their side.

And her films, like life, posed problems, though not necessarily solutions. Rarely did her films have pat resolutions. Something unexpected would interrupt the flow of her characters' day, and their whole lives were suddenly changed: a bookkeeper walking home alone gets raped (in an era when no one mentioned the word *sex*), a hitchhiker whom someone innocently picks up turns out to be a psychopath. People whose actions we can't possibly predict bring into question the whole moral fiber of our world, just as in real life. There are no easy answers. Lupino was wise enough as a filmmaker not to give any. Her films stay openended. In this way, she is most akin to contemporary European filmmakers like **Margarethe von Trotta**.

"Lupino's are unlike other American

movies of their time (1949–1954)," says Rickey. "All made for less than $160,000, without stars, without studio ('I suppose we were the "New Wave" of the time,' said Lupino), and astonishingly without liberal piety."[14]

Ronnie Scheib astutely points out, "The 'problem' [for Lupino's characters] is not how to reintegrate them back into the mainstream; the 'problem' is the shallowness of the mainstream and the void it projects around them—the essential passivity of ready-made lives."[15]

The typical Lupino character is one who rides buses. Real live people who

> when they eat out it's at a diner or lunch counter. They're not dissatisfied with their lower-middle-class lot (the way **Joan Crawford** is in MILDRED PIERCE), because they're basically optimists . . . all dreaming for Mr. Right to save them, only to discover painfully there's no Mr. Right. No other Hollywood movies of the time promoted such bitter wisdom.[16]

If you were lucky enough to be able to interview Ida Lupino in the days when she was still giving interviews, but were unlucky enough to broach the question of feminism, she would have lashed out at you with something like, "Any woman who wishes to smash into the world of men isn't very feminine. Baby, we can't go smashing. I believe women should be struck regularly—like a gong. Or is it, Bong?"[17]

She made no bones about the fact that she did not like to work with other women.

> I didn't see myself as any advance guard, or feminist," she said. "I had to do something to fill up my time between contracts. Keeping a feminine approach is vital—men hate bossy females. Instead of saying, 'Do this,' I tried to make everybody a part of it. Often I pretended to a cameraman to know less than I did. That way I got more cooperation."[18]

By 1972, however, when she was more removed from the situation and competition was not an issue, Lupino became more compassionate to others of her sex.

> I'd love to see more women working as directors and producers. Today it's almost impossible to do it unless you are an actress or writer with power. . . . I wouldn't hesitate right this minute to hire a talented woman if the subject matter were right.[19]

After the demise of her company, "The Filmmakers" in 1954, Lupino was suddenly in great demand for the budding medium of television. Norman Macdonnel, longtime producer of *Gunsmoke* said of Lupino, "You used Ida when you had a story about a woman with some dimension, and you really wanted it hard-hitting." Richard Boone, who also liked his direction hardboiled, wanted Lupino for a script by Harry Fink, "famed for his graphic descriptions of physical violence, which included rape, murder, and sandstorms."

She soon became typecast as the director who could *only* do action sequences. She wanted to do a love story badly, but no one thought she could handle it. Finally, the GE Television Theatre gave her a shot at a love story between **Anne Baxter** and Ronald Reagan.[20] Routinely in those days, she'd be called in to rescue producers from their self-imposed mayhem.

Here is a snippet of Lupino dialogue as she directs one of her TV westerns:

> Any rocks up there to give you a problem, darlin'? Now, Walter, baby, while we're here we might as well take the posse through. I want my camera here. . . . That's right. You read my mind, love. . . . Now the posse won't be coming through at such a clip. Start out at a reasonable speed. . . . That's it, sweetheart. . . . Now, are we lathering the horses in this sequence, sweetie? If not, we should be. . . . That's divine, love. OK, follow Mother, here we go, kiddies![21]

In later years, she left Collier Young for Howard Duff, with whom she had a daughter, Bridget. She said in 1973 that any good woman who has a man who loves her should stick by him. Lupino directed less and less after her marriage to Duff, deferring more and more to his career.

"A decision I think she regretted," said Lupino spokesperson, Mary Ann Anderson. "It's only my opinion, but I think that Ida felt very unacknowledged by the film world. I think she regretted pushing Duff's career instead of her own. And now she resents being forgotten."[22]

"You could say that Ida Lupino's career foreshadowed a world where sexism is no longer an issue," said Barbara Scharres,

for she directed films as if it weren't. Her women are just as likely to outsmart and outthink their men as the men are likely to be passive and indecisive. Women are as likely to be villains as heroines. They use everything they've got, including their sexuality, to maneuver in the world, just as a man would. Finally, perhaps most importantly, they are subject, without discrimination, to the rules of the world at large—the rules of convention, the laws of gravity and the morality of sixties television, but no more than any man. . . .

Scharres then turns from the unconventional choices Lupino made in her films, to the similar kinds of choices she made in her personal life.

She regarded her own directorial career as an unconventional choice for a woman, and had remarked in an interview that she'd rather be cooking her man's dinner. However, the content and technical virtuosity of her work belie this statement and point to a very wily director who knew the uses of conventionality as a tool.[23]

Necessity saw to it that on the set Ida Lupino felt herself to be "one of the boys."[24] But how lucky for women's film history that she wasn't.

IDA LUPINO

1949 Not Wanted (Director)
1950 Never Fear (Director)
      Outrage (Director)
1951 Hard, Fast, and Beautiful (Director)
1953 Bigamist, The (Director)
      Hitchhiker, The (Director)
1966 Trouble with Angels, The (Director)

Barbara Loden (1932–1980)

When **Margarethe von Trotta** was asked if there was one American film that had most influenced her work, she said without a moment's hesitation, "**Barbara Loden**'s WANDA."[1]

WANDA (1971) was the film that had most exhilarated and exasperated women in the early seventies. At the time there were stormy, controversial arguments as to whether WANDA was a profeminist or an antifeminist film.

Neither mythologized nor romanticized, WANDA concerns a poor, working-class woman who is fired from a job in a clothes factory because she works too slowly. She is tardy to her own court divorce proceedings, appearing finally in hair curlers, capri pants, and sneakers.[2]

In 1971, Rex Reed described the film as

a portrait of people for whom nothing ever happens, in which Miss Loden is simply brilliant as an ignorant [woman] from the coal mines of Appalachia who does nothing, thinks nothing, gives up her children to a judge because they'll be better off, and heads down the highway toward a depressing encounter with a bank robber and ends up with an empty life of greasy hamburgers eaten in lonely motel rooms and a future blank and gray as a mortuary slab.[3]

Wanda is a stranger in a strange land; a woman who is passive, defenseless, and stranded in a world of Marilyn Monroe projections, with finally nowhere to go. She is lost to her own soul in a world of male-driven vehicles zooming past her. She is the ultimate victim of a sexist and capitalistic culture that has no use for her.

Demoralizing and pessimistic, the story was based by Loden on a true account found in a newspaper article in the *Sunday Daily News* entitled "Did Justice Triumph?" It catalogued the story of a woman who was an accomplice to a bank robber. Loden explained to an interviewer:

Though the robbery didn't come off, and she botched it up, she still was sentenced to twenty years in prison with no appeal. When the judge sentenced her, she thanked him. She seemed glad to get the sentence. That's what struck me: why would this girl feel glad to be put away?[4]

Loden says the incidents about the woman's life only spurred what eventually would become a story about her own life— not the actual events, but the feelings she had in a world where she felt devalued. Described once as having "eyes like pools of melted cobalt, beautiful hair the color of sunflower petals and a soft, vulnerable shyness with a trace of the Southern backwoods in her voice,"[5] one doesn't know whether or not to take Loden seriously.

"All I remember about my desperate childhood is sitting behind a stove in my grandmother's kitchen." Loden says by way of explanation that she fantasized about all the good things that would happen to her someday.

I was nothing.
I had no friends, no talents, I didn't learn

a thing in school. . . . I came to New York when I was sixteen with one hundred dollars in my pocket, got a job modeling for detective stories and romance magazines, then I danced in a chorus line at the Copacabana night club from seven at night until four in the morning and learned from the other girls how to wear make-up. . . .

I hated the movies as a child. . . . People on the screen were perfect and they made me feel inferior. I knew that I could never dress, walk, or talk like that. I was very passive and resigned to numbness, very much like Wanda, except I had more emotional poverty than physical poverty in my youth.[6]

Loden realized she would not literally have to place Wanda behind bars, as in the real-life model, for anyone to be fully aware that she was already in prison.

She not only played the title role of Wanda in the film, but Loden wrote, directed, and cut the film as well. She is perhaps the first of the contemporary generation of women filmmakers who dared to show real life for a woman on the screen. Here's the way she put it to Rex Reed:

I know WANDA is crude but I wanted to make an antimovie, to present a story without manipulating the audience and telling them what their responses should be. To do that you have to take chances and you can't depend on anyone else.[7]

When the film finally appeared at the Venice Film Festival as the only American film considered important enough to be accepted in competition in 1971 and then walked away with the International Critics Prize, no one was more surprised than Loden.

I couldn't get anyone to direct it, so I had to do it myself. I didn't know anything about the camera. I only had three people in the crew. . . . There are only two professional actors in it, the rest are local people. My wardrobe cost $7 at Woolworth's, and

Michael Higgins, who played the bank robber, wore Elia [Kazan]'s old clothes. . . . I paid myself union scale [$200 in 1971]. The total budget came to $100,000, which may be cheap by Hollywood standards, but much too expensive by mine. I wasted money because I didn't know what I was doing. My next film will be made much cheaper. [8]

But an unfortunate turn of destiny for Loden would prevent her "next film," from ever occurring.

A 1972 review of WANDA in *MS* said that the film shouldn't be shown on the screen. The reviewer suggested that, at that time, there was only room for films about women achieving things and setting examples. But Loden's point was to make a film about women who never get a chance; women who are anonymous.

There are those who say, "We don't want to see anybody like that." Those are the people who wouldn't want me to exist, and they would say that I was not valid or that I shouldn't be heard. [9]

Born in Ashville, North Carolina, Barbara Loden ironically *was* one of those **Marilyn Monroe** pinup projections. In fact, under the direction of her husband Elia Kazan, she would play the character based on Marilyn in Arthur Miller's *After the Fall* (1963) to great acclaim. She won a Tony Award. The press was predicting stardom for Loden. Instead, she turned down script after script, and acted only when it suited her. "I didn't enjoy the fame and sort of became a recluse," she said. "I had two sons to raise, and acting just seemed rather unimportant compared with life." [10]

Although she spent many years acting in supporting roles for Kazan—WILD RIVER (1960), SPLENDOR IN THE GRASS (1961),—he never encouraged Loden's independent creativity. Kazan's autobiography reads like an unsavory Henry Miller novel when he speaks about his relationships with women.

Regarding his early meetings with Loden, when he was still married to **Molly Day Thatcher Kazan**, he writes:

There was something improper about her . . . so I kept her in the dark, literally so. I'd rent a hotel room, arrive there first, get into bed, turn off the lights, and leave the door ajar. She'd come in wearing work clothes. I'd leave before she did. . . . We'd hardly talk, but I became accustomed to having her near me. . . . At first our affair was nothing more than dog and bitch. [11]

And later, still married to Molly, but flourishing in his affair with Loden, he cast her in *After the Fall*. As Kazan tells his story his assumption is that Loden didn't have any talent before she was lucky enough to meet him.

He recalls that one of her teachers in the Actor's Studio Theatre, Bobby Lewis, had said of her: "She's only in the training program because she's Kazan's girl." It was the general impression, Kazan goes on to say, that she was limited and that what range of talent she did have was narrow, an assessment, in Kazan's words, "again true." Here's Kazan's follow-up:

As Barbara began to work on Miller's revised second act, she won everyone's respect. There was a naked truth in her acting that we rarely see. I knew I'd made this possible by giving her confidence in her talent, encouraging her boldness, bringing her to Miller and urging him to accept her. So I was pleased. [12]

Viewed as an addendum to his own more serious life, Kazan basically saw Loden as a Kewpie doll. But WANDA would soon change all that.

Excited and frightened by her new script, Loden asked Kazan whether he might consider directing her in the piece. He said he had no interest in such a tale. "I didn't see life as she did—sentimentally." [13] He said that Loden should do it herself—a prospect that he never thought she would carry out.

What Kazan didn't know was that the necessity of directing this film was Barbara Loden's rite of pasage. Nicholas Proferes, a friend, helped Loden mold WANDA into the screenplay it was to become, and instilled her with the confidence she needed to direct. It must be remembered that the most recent other woman directing up until this time was **Ida Lupino**—who had the support of the industry as a well-known and well-respected actress.

> When I made WANDA, I didn't know anything about consciousness raising or women's liberation. That had just started when the film was finished. The picture was not about women's liberation. It was really about the oppression of women, of people. . . . Being a woman is unexplored territory, and we're pioneers of a sort, discovering what it means to be a woman.[14]

Without thoughts about making the film likable or not likable, without a notion about how to go about making a film except what she had observed, and working very much in a European cinema verité style of filmmaking, Barbara Loden made a film of worldwide and unexpected exclaim. Elia Kazan belittles the memory of that event in this way:

> Barbara was suddenly on top of the world. . . . Now she plunged into work, writing screenplays one after another. . . . They were the same kind as WANDA, small films, devoted to the neglected side of American life. . . . She didn't want to compete in a field where she was dependent on "standard figures," like me.
> I didn't really believe she had the equipment to be an independent filmmaker.

What Kazan seemed to overlook about this period is that Loden had already made it.

She was a creative, independent thinker who had no sort of home or social group into which she could share her lonely, if pioneering, ideas. Even the women's movement came tumbling after her too late, and ignorantly, it berated this artist whom it should have celebrated instead.

In preparation for directing her second venture, a self-reflexive film about a woman's awakening consciousness—**Kate Chopin**'s THE AWAKENING—Barbara Loden would die a tragically premature death from breast cancer. She was forty-eight years old.

BARBARA LODEN

1971   Wanda

Elaine May

"There's always some idiot who'll come up to you and say, 'You're a great gal, you think exactly like a man!' For Chrissake, I always thought intelligence was neuter."[1] Zany, funny, satiric, and with a vision entirely her own—that's **Elaine May**. In 1971, she nearly single-handedly opened the doors to directing for women again with A NEW LEAF—a film she both wrote and starred in.

Her talents manifested themselves early on. She was born in Philadelphia, and as a child made numerous radio and stage appearances. As a young student in Chicago, she teamed up with Mike Nichols and began touring supper clubs with improvisational skits. An album of comedy preceded their highly acclaimed show, *An Evening with Mike Nichols and Elaine May* in New York in 1960. Her first play on Broadway, *A Matter of Position* (1962), opened and closed quite quickly. May wouldn't provide the revisions the producers requested. "Cuts and revisions were made up to the point where they would change the nature of the play,"[2] May told the press. It wouldn't be the last time May would waltz off a set, or strip her name from a screenplay that had been tampered with.

She removed her name from an adaptation of Evelyn Waugh's *The Loved One* after it had been reworked in 1965. In 1971 May wrote her first full-length screenplay, SUCH GOOD FRIENDS, based on the Lois Gould novel, but withdrew her name because she was upset by the way the film was produced. Linda Malm described the piece as being about "love and desperation, handled with a touching lack of bitterness, that have become thematic trademarks of May."[3]

The film she did take the credit for was a screenplay over which she finally had full artistic control. A NEW LEAF (1971), starring Walter Matthau and May, has been described as "a tightly constructed comedy with characters that remain well-defined throughout the wacky twists of plot."[4] Although it was an artistic and financial coup, May sought an unsuccessful injunction against Paramount because she did not approve of the release cut.

For her next auteur effort, THE HEART-BREAK KID (1972), May's work was being favorably compared with Billy Wilder. The film stars May's daughter, **Jeannie Berlin** (who, by the way, adopted her last name from May's father, the Yiddish actor, Jack Berlin, and not May's ex—Marvin May).

Elaine May made significant contributions as screenwriter to both HEAVEN CAN WAIT (nominated for best screenplay in 1978), and REDS (1981). On TOOTSIE (1982), Larry Gelbart worked on the script for two years before turning it over to May who helped mold it into its present shape.[5] Tom Stempel calls May, "one of the legendary script doctors in the business."[6]

"In all Elaine May scripts," says Linda Malm, "there's an improvisational naturalness in the dialogue. . . . She presents a world where sham is exposed and innocence prevails; a crazy equality of personalities and sexual roles exists, a kind of justice dominates."[7] May's trademark seems to burn through even in those scripts she denied she contributed to.

It is impossible to describe the eclectic sensibility of Elaine May. The only way to do her justice is to quote her directly, and even then you don't get the full impact because the quote is out of context. Even in a context, Elaine May always seems to be out of context. She is ever the virtuoso comedienne. The following excerpt of an interview by Dick Lemon, conducted after May completed A NEW LEAF, should provide the reader some idea of what I mean:

I really didn't know anything [about directing], but when I told them that, they thought that was my technique. You're supposed to be crisp . . . you're suppose to say, 'Cut, print, beautiful, next setup.' You're supposed to say it for the moral of the crew, like a captain on a ship. I couldn't say, 'Cut, print, beautiful, next setup.' I couldn't even say, 'Action'. . . .

Lemon then asked May if she could describe her approach as a director.

I try to get all the furniture in the right places without interfering with the lighting equipment. Then when Walter [Matthau] comes in—we'll call him the star, I think—ask him if he knows what scene we're doing. If he says yes, I ask him if he knows the lines. If he knows all the lines, I have a bite to eat or make a few phone calls. Then he and I might rehearse the lines in the trailer, since we can't get on the set because they're still lighting. Then when they're done lighting and are ready for you, we go and rehearse the scene on the set. Then they light what we rehearsed while Walter gets into make-up and I have something else to eat.

During this time, May says, she explains to the producers why it's taking so long. Or, "I might not if they don't ask me." Sometimes, she says, she will go in and ask why it is taking so long, just so "everybody will know I'm a man of action."[8]

The incomparably funny Elaine May could be labeled, 'a genius of the non-linear.' Genius is also the word her fellow actor Jack Lemmon used.

> Elaine is touched with genius, like **Judy Holliday**. She approaches a scene like a director and a writer, not like an actor, and she can go so deep so fast on a scene, and her mind works at such great speed, that it's difficult for her to communicate with other actors. . . . She's the finest actress I've ever worked with.[9]

Still, it made Paramount a little giddy when she shot an unheard of 1.4 million feet of film on MIKEY AND NICKY (1977). In fact, she's *such* a genius of comedy that one never really knows when she's only kidding. For example, in a more seemingly serious interview in 1975 May said that directing for her is like life, anything that she thinks will work, she tries.

> I tell you, when you direct, you do anything. You beg, you shout, you discuss, you say nothing, you kid. . . . But you really do anything. I'm not a pro as a director. I'm a pro at thinking about movies. I'm a pro at talking about them. You ask me anything about a movie and I can answer you in movie language; budget, schedule, gross, net distribution . . . and that's most of it, you know. If you can do that you can get hired anytime.[10]

She managed to get hired on what would be a historic phenomenon and a box-office disaster. ISHTAR (1987), with Dustin Hoffman and Warren Beatty, was the highest budgeted film a woman has been permitted to direct to date. Beatty and Hoffman each received five million to star, while May re-ceived two million. This means that the movie exceeded the average expenses of making a film before the cameras even started to roll. The dimensions of the budget and all of the press hoopla that surrounded the film's making nearly equaled the bottomless depths to which it fell.

It is interesting to note that May will revert to kicking and screaming before she puts up with any kind of creative interference. However, it seems that she turns out her best work when she has to answer to other people. The movies on which she has had total control, ISHTAR and MICKEY AND NICKY, were complete commercial failures. How much such a blight will damage other women's chances in Hollywood in the future remains to be seen. In an interview two years before the making of MICKEY AND NICKY, May philosophized about her own limitations as a director.

> I was much smarter twenty years ago. I was much smarter in my first movie than in my second. . . . The only thing experience teaches you is what you can't do. When you start, you think you can do anything. And then you start to get a little tired.[11]

It could just be that a quirky, creative sensibility, such as the one belonging to Elaine May, is hopelessly 'out-of-synch' with an industry ruled by commercial considerations.

The movie business does not now, nor has it ever known what to do with her genius. If it tries to rein in, she serves it with lawsuits. If it gives her complete artistic freedom, it gets into financial hot water.

Perhaps Hollywood should greet the eclecticism of Elaine May as one might greet any foreigner. Bow, respect the mystery of the ineffable, and remember the words of the Chinese philosopher Lao Tzu: "Let all things take their natural course, and do not interfere."

ELAINE MAY

1971 New Leaf, A

1972 Heartbreak Kid, The
1977 Mikey and Nicky
1987 Ishtar

Lee Grant

I've always felt that I was an outsider, and
that was the right place for me to be, and
I'm happy in that place. . . . I've always
taken enormous chances with my career in
losing everything. I did lose everything.
When I was blacklisted . . . it was a very
mixed feeling. On the one hand I was hurt
and destroyed. On the other hand, it was
an enormous feeling of freedom.

—Lee Grant
Interview with author

Lee Grant is one of a few directors who has
mastered two art forms—acting and
directing—as well as three film genres—
documentaries, made-for-TV movies, and
feature films—and she continues to work
simultaneously in all of them.

A fighter from the day she was born, she
started early observing the battles of others.
Before she knew it, she was smack in the
middle of the arena herself.

"I was raised on Riverside Drive, but you
only had to walk up to Broadway to see
people beating up on people." She describes
herself as a Riverside Drive girl obsessed
with acting, who had a very strong organic
sense of injustice. "There's a part of her,"
said writer Ken Gross, "that will always
listen for the hoofbeats of the next
pogrom."[1]

There was a time in her life, faded now
into the deep recesses of memory, when she
didn't have to struggle. She grew up under
the wing of two eccentric women—her
mother, Witia Haskell and her Aunt Fremo.
They were haunted by shadowy recollec-
tions of Cossacks pillaging their village of
Odessa. That, they would make sure, would

not happen to Lee. An only child, she would
be sheltered, they decided, from any form
of persecution. But fate would write Lee
Grant a different scenario.

"My mother had been a model," she said
when I spoke with her in 1989, "and a kind
of eccentric stage mother. She had me at the
Metropolitan Opera when I was four. She
had dreams of my being a great ballerina.
I took violin lessons and French lessons.
There was a kind of pushing and squeezing
of culture into me like in a toothpaste tube.
It was a cross between Gigi and Isadora
Duncan. It left me crazed!"[2]

Grant's father, an educator in an experimental academy for boys, was a strident
believer in discipline and justice. But both
he and her mother adored Lee. "I lived,"
she said, "in a make-believe world on Riverside Drive, where there were no problems
with money, no problems with politics, no
problems at all."[3]

After high school, Grant found what she
describes as her real home. She enrolled at
Sanford Meisner's famous Neighborhood
Playhouse in New York. After all her scattered exposure to the culture of her youth,
she found a place of rest in herself with
acting. Meisner saw the spoiled child she
was and pushed her hard. It was an education that would prove invaluable, and
would endure far beyond mere training for
the theater.

In 1949 Grant got her big break on
Broadway. She was cast as the shoplifter in
Detective Story. The drama led to the movie
in 1952, which played to acclaim and
awards at Cannes. But she would turn almost overnight from a celebrity into a

cause-célèbre, and her fame would transmute into a loathsome infamy. Joe McCarthy was hot on the trail of what he labeled 'Commies' during what **Lillian Hellman** would call America's "Scoundrel Time." Grant's husband of that period, writer Arnold Manoff, was on McCarthy's list. Ironically, Grant's career was about to take off. She was nineteen. The last thing that occurred to her in her youthful naïveté was that she might hurt herself very badly by speaking out about what she believed in. She spoke out publicly against the blacklist. Before she turned around, she was added to that list. The committee wanted only one name, that of her husband. And although she could have named any one of Manoff's dozen pseudonyms, although the marriage was on the rocks—she divorced Manoff in the midsixties and he died a year later—she adamantly refused. The result was that she wouldn't be allowed to act again in films for twelve years. "By the time I won the Cannes Award, by the time I was nominated for an Academy Award, I found myself unemployable."

During those years, Grant was grateful to Sandy Meisner for providing her work as an acting teacher. The blacklist would be her college education, and the persecution so staunchly averted from her in her overprotected childhood would meet up with her face to face. Lee Grant's "organic sense of injustice" suddenly had an outlet for real excercise.

Years later, in 1989, when the nightmare was long over, Grant was able to be philosophic about her painful past.

"I like starting all over again. I really kind of set up places for me to fall from so that I never get there, wherever *there* is supposed to be. There's a wonderful poem by Cavafy which talks about the voyage to Ithaca. . . . Don't ever get to Ithaca, it says. Stop at all the ports along the way. . . . And as soon as I read it, it touched a place in me that I really recognized. Why with all

the despair did I feel so free when I was blacklisted?"

It wouldn't be until 1964 that Grant's lawyer, an influential man in the Democratic party, was finally able to end her blacklist as quickly as it had begun by making a deal for a political favor. She found herself working literally the next day. Emmy Award winning roles would follow with the TV series, *Peyton Place*.

When her acting career finally became the fait accompli that it should have been a decade before, when she at last won the highest accolades to be won by an actress—the Academy Award (SHAMPOO [1975]), two Emmys (*Peyton Place* [1966], *The Neon Ceiling* [1971]), and the Obie (*The Maids* [1964], awarded to Grant when she was still blacklisted in films), she needed a new challenge. Lee Grant's transition from acting to directing came from that same organic need to shake up her life to make sure she was alive. The opportunity came when the American Film Institute began a Women Director's Program and asked Grant to partake in their first round. The result was August Strindberg's *The Stronger*, a short dramatic piece still frequently repeated on television.

Her first feature followed soon after with TELL ME A RIDDLE (1980), based on the story by *Tillie Olson*. In it, Grant bravely pioneered a topic that was, and still is, a taboo subject for the screen—the experience of growing old. She describes the movie as an art film. She says because it didn't make the box-office capital, she wasn't offered the vied-after three-picture deal that often comes to a successful director. But ask Lee Grant if she would have accepted a movie about a teenage warthog who becomes emperor of the shopping malls and she relents, no. Probably not. Her interest has never been success, not in conventional terms, but in the process of what the journey has to offer.

Lee Grant concedes that her mission is to

talk about truth; sometimes not always a pleasant thing to look at in films. But after a decade of sharing the injustice of Mc-Carthyism, a cancer that swept through the artistic veins of the Hollywood community, Grant's rose-colored glasses from youth are long gone. "I always consider my time very limited. If I'm going to spend two years of my life on a project, I'd better love it."

The films she loves are all projects she develops herself along with her producer/partner/husband, Joseph Feury. On the anniversary of the debut of her documentary, *Why Women Kill* (1983) on HBO, Grant said, "There is a need for more than fun and popcorn today. There is a need for reality." Looking back on it, she went on: "There comes a time when you want to see a part of your life reflected back and realize other people"—the ones on TV—"are like you." She said: "I was attracted to the project because it is not the Joan of Arc's who are today's heroines, but ordinary people faced with tough situations who take a leap of faith and risk everything."

Her life had reached a comfortable niche with acting by this time, but now she craved a path more durable, less ephemeral than acting. Although her first feature, TELL ME A RIDDLE (1980), was an artistic success, no studio was coming at her with projects as if she were Sidney Lumet ("I want to be like Sidney Lumet and pick up a script and say I will make this, and then make it. Any damn thing I want."[4]) She quickly saw that if she wanted to be a director of any weight, if in fact she wanted to be a director at all, she would have to take a less-conventional route ... not a surprising alternative for Lee Grant. The path she found opened to her was making documentaries for HBO, which had seen THE WILMAR 8 and liked her style of moviemaking.

Since then, Lee Grant's plan of doing things her way has worked well. She has been able to build upon her five documentaries and from there direct several acclaimed made-for-TV films on like topics.

DOWN AND OUT IN AMERICA (1987), for instance, her Academy Award-winning portrait of the homeless for HBO, led to the dramatic, NO PLACE LIKE HOME (1990), about a typical middle-class family who through a series of everyday occurrences find themselves living in the streets. The made-for-TV route won her a shot at her second feature after a nearly nine-year wait, STAYING TOGETHER (1989).

"It's very hard for men or women to work in Hollywood and do anything near their potential of what they want to do in this world. You have to fulfill the studio's needs in order to fulfill your own. All through my career as an actress I did one for me, one for them, one for me, one for them. And sometimes, on many pictures, I was lucky when they came together."

For example, she said, "All of us, **Martha Coolidge, Joan Silver, Gillian Armstrong,** me, have to make money for them or else we just don't get hired. And that may be something that's a little tougher on us than it is on the men, but not much. You get a couple of times up at bat and either you deliver or you're out. Now we're all hanging on by our fingernails. They're bleeding here."

No matter what she may say, this is an artist who could never do a project based solely on commercial considerations. "All the films I've done I've needed to do, badly. I've needed to get them out of here [her heart] to another place where I hold up a mirror, as a Proustian, to the world that I live in and say, 'This is the world that I see.' It is not the world reflected around me, but I need to show my world with my mirror."

That mirror, full of integrity and strength is not without its fill of continuous tightrope walks. And despite a lifetime of successes, it is still not without its terrors.

"I feel there is a wind, a reactionary, anti-humanistic wind blowing through this land, with the same kind of passion and force that used to be credited to a yearning to do something good for the world. There's an enormous puff and huff of fundamentalist, antihumanist energy. And it's very frightening to me." But regarding the struggles, Lee Grant wouldn't want to live without them. "It was after I got the Academy Award that I lost my drive. I need a lot of drive. And if obstacles nurture that drive, then I need obstacles. It's much more important for me to have that drive than to have success. Boredom is the enemy. If you're passionate, then you're alive. If you get to that point where you don't care anymore, that's the dangerous place. And I've been there."

LEE GRANT

Documentaries	Battered
(Directing Only)	Down and Out in
	America
	Matter of Sex, A
	What Sex Am I?
	Why Women Kill
	Wilmar 8, The

Features
1980   Tell Me a Riddle
1987   Nobody's Child (TV)
1989   Staying Together
1990   No Place Like Home (TV)

Barbra Streisand

With YENTL (1983), **Barbra Streisand** became the first woman in history to direct, produce, coauthor, star, and sing in a major motion picture. In tandem with this, she succeeded in bursting open the conventional form of the American musical genre. The thanks she got from the film community was not a single nomination at the Oscars. The film was unfairly recognized as, "Barbra's folly"—"the hubris of a forty-year-old actress/singer/producer/writer playing an eighteen-year-old girl playing an eighteen-year-old-boy."[1] Perhaps Streisand's only folly was in trying to present a self-empowered view of a woman's life to a culture steeped in patriarchal notions, and expect that she would be greeted amorously.

Based on a story by I.B. Singer, Streisand altered the tone of her film sufficiently enough to have evoked strong objections from the author. The story is ambitious in that it tackles "the whole issue of women's position in the traditional Jewish European *shtetl* world, with its reverence for learning, from which women were excluded."[2] Singer

harshly dismissed Streisand's pop treatment of the subject, though,

> This was no commercial enterprise for Streisand but a fifteen year obsession, completed despite all obstacles, indicating something of what it meant to her.[3]

The genre of the American film musical was "a vehicle for Hollywood to sell itself to a society that had a stong Protestant work ethic and religious prohibitions against secular art form."[4] Film genres only become popular once their issues speak meaningfully to the culture. To "hook" America on Hollywood, the American musical genre took as its bait the sanctimonious state of holy matrimony, and the romance of courtship that precludes it. From OKLAHOMA! (1955), to MY FAIR LADY (1964), to THE SOUND OF MUSIC (1965), the American musical has reinforced the cultural mythology that happiness will be obtained when boy meets girl, and then girl manages in her devious way to "hook" boy.

Other casual characteristics [in the musical genre] that are significant include: man as a source of economic power, woman as a source of sexual power; man as artist, poet and teacher, woman as art object, muse and student; man as free roving source of energy, woman as stable and the one who ties him down.[5]

Witness MY FAIR LADY, a takeoff on the Pygmalion myth where "man is not only the creator of the product which is woman, he is the consumer as well."[6]

In view of this, it is easy to see why YENTL, a film whose premise rejects the idea of marriage and courtship, was so misunderstood by the film community. By embracing a set of rules so out-of-synch with the convention of the genre, Streisand was baiting a Hollywood calamity. She was not only challenging a basic premise that a fulfilled life is one in which marriage is sanctified, but she ambitiously brought into question the role and "natural inclinations" of women. Enter also the ambiguous line between friendship and eroticism among women. Here is a story about a girl who dared to want more, a girl not happy to accept a world that donned "storybooks for women; sacred texts for men."

Her interest in books rather than carp; her hopelessness at fulfilling womanly duties like cooking; her father's pride in her; her own joy of achieving, talking, arguing about ideas—all that is powerful feminism, and it does not get corrupted or diluted or betrayed by the popular form in which it is presented.[7]

Yentl's love is in learning, not in capturing a man. That love also explains the much-criticized point of why Streisand chose to sing all of the film's musical numbers, when her costar, Mandy Patinkin, could have sung many of the songs. "Streisand must sing all of the songs because in YENTL, the greatest dichotomies are not taking place between the two lovers, Hadass

and Avidor, and not between Yentl and Avidor. They take place within Yentl herself."[8] Understanding this, it becomes clear that Streisand's decision stems from an astute understanding of the musical genre form— she had ten years experience as the star of many musicals, including the much-acclaimed FUNNY GIRL (1968)—and is, in fact, a decision not to deviate from the dictates of that form.

The open-ended sort of future that Yentl opts for, instead of the comfortable, secure (read: dead) life she would be assured of with Avidor who would want her to give up learning, is not news in light of today's cultural mores, but it is news in the world of movies where we still go in America, expecting romantic love to be the cure-all for our woes. The "bursting open" of the traditional form arrives at the very gut of this film. Although "this musical will have its pair of courting lovers in Hadass and Avidor [subplots], dichotomies will be developed [instead] in Yentl herself."[9]

A near literal illustration of this is in a scene when Yentl's father dies. According to Jewish law, all mirrors are covered by black cloth in the event of death. Yentl pulls back the cloth to reveal a diagonal crack in one mirror.

At first, Yentl is positioned in the corner. She fills the small part of the mirror which is divided by the crack. When she turns to pick up the scissors, her face moves so that the crack splits her reflection in half. The film is a reflection of reality and Yentl is a split image of a woman dealing with male and female sex role orientations and identity.[10]

These orientations are directly criticized and brought into question by Streisand in the following dialogue between Avidor and Anshel/Yentl. When Anshel questions Avidor about Hadass's strange behavior over dinner he/she says, "Is she always that nervous?"

AVIDOR
She's a woman in love. What do you expect?
ANSHEL/YENTL
She doesn't say very much, does she?
AVIDOR
What does she have to say?
ANSHEL/YENTL
Don't you ever wonder what she's thinking?
AVIDOR
No. What could she be thinking? Anyway, I don't need her to think, I can do that with you.

But when Yentl reveals her true gender identity to Avidor, they can no longer share the bonds of an intellectual life. Avidor tries to persuade her to give up her ridiculous notion of "wanting more" as a woman, since even the sacred Talmud text, the book of learning that Yentl claims to love, preaches that a woman's duty is to have children. "A wise woman knows everything without opening a book and that's the greater miracle." But Yentl knows at once that she must go beyond even the sacred book of learning. Not enticed by Avidor's offer, she

> goes off alone to America, to a life of possibility, the boat journey a metaphor for a new social place. . . . [It] is not rhetoric when Yentl sings, "Papa I've a voice now,/ Papa, I've a choice now." It is feminism, it is the American Dream;[11]

Not only does Streisand push open the boundaries of the conventional, patriarchal male/female roles, but in moving, compassionate scenes with Hadass a powerful female bonding occurs. When Hadass wants to please her betrothed, Anshel, she says, "I'll study while you're away. I want you to be proud of me." Tenderly, Anshel replies, "I am proud of you. You should be proud of yourself." Not only is this important in terms of female bonding, but of "women's relationship to their process of actualization."[12] Many of the tenuous moments between Hadass and Anshel not only play upon the ambiguous nature of the two women's sexual relationship for comic effect—a classic technique—but raise significant questions about "at what point all this intense emotion can be called erotic attraction."[13] One can't be sure, as Barbara Koenig Quart points out, how consciously Streisand did this.

It's no wonder people called it "Barbra's folly." "The world is filled with Avidors that would say, 'I don't need her to think.' "[14] After all it's the same world that measures the success of a film in terms of profit.

BARBRA STREISAND

1983   Yentl

Penny Marshall

Women directors without a penchant for or a history of political leanings, tend to be the more successful clan in Hollywood. More than any other woman director, **Penny Marshall** follows most directly in the footsteps of **Elaine May**. Next to May, who also began her career as a comedian/actress be-

fore launching off into directing, Penny Marshall secured the largest budget of any Hollywood film allotted to a woman director. Yet *unlike* May, Marshall's second feature, BIG (1988), had tremendous earnings at the box office and put her on the roster for subsequent *big* projects, her most recent being AWAKENINGS (1991). Sweet revenge to be sure for this director thrown out of her first feature directing assignment, PEGGY SUE GOT MARRIED (1986), on the excuse that she was too inexperienced.

The quirky, charming Penny Marshall made herself famous as Laverne of the now-defunct *Laverne & Shirley* TV sitcom that topped the ratings for three years in a row. In interviews as well as in her TV portrayals, Marshall is the neurotic worrier. Soon you begin to see the routine for what it is, the winning part of her public persona, "a way to charm and disarm."[1] When she was asked if filming her debut feature, JUMPIN' JACK FLASH (1986) was a positive experience, Marshall said:

> That's not quite the word I'd choose. "Harrowing" would be better. . . . It was sort of fun, but while it was going on it was like hell. I always worry . . . about everything. You're under a lot of pressure, especially during premenstrual days. We'd try to hold up flags that said, "Cranky Today" or, "Cramp Day."[2]

Marshall, famous in Hollywood for her good nature (her buddy Steven Spielberg once said that if she could ring out all the tears cried on her shoulder she would flood Encino[3]) gets her sense of humor from the same place she gets her accent, the Bronx. Her family's name was originally Marscharelli. Her mother ran a dancing school in their apartment building basement, where Penny hitched up with sixteen other tappers and took the show on the road. The troupe ended up playing for the US Army, the USO and *The Jackie Gleason Show.* Penny was the youngest of three siblings. ("I was the moody, sick one," said Garry, her older brother, who is also a director. "My sister, Ronnie, was the nice, cheerful one. It didn't leave much for Penny to be but crazy."[4] Garry, director of BEACHES (1988) and PRETTY WOMAN (1989), would end up being one of her mentors.

Penny's mom wanted her to lose her New York accent so she would sound well-bred, and sent her to school in New Mexico. "[She] thought New Mexico was next to New Jersey and New Hampshire," kids Marshall.[5] She majored in math and psychology, flunked on the accent, married a football player, had a baby, divorced her football player, all in rather quick succession. The next thing she knew she was on her big-brother Garry's doorstep wondering what to do with her life.

Sometimes it helps to have a big brother in show biz, especially one who by this time was a well-established Hollywood comedy writer. Garry cast her as Jack Klugman's secretary in *The Odd Couple,* and then in an episode of *Happy Days.* The chemistry established between her and **Cindy Williams** gave Garry an idea. It was a spin-off entitled *Laverne & Shirley.*

Perhaps Marshall decided to turn to directing—she began with directing episodes of *Laverne & Shirley*—because she's so quick that she gets bored easily. Garry would say, "She caught on to things fast. When she was a dancer and the girls would line up, she always got the routine after the first two times. So she'd spend the rest of her time reaching behind their backs and unzipping their leotards."[6]

It's a bit early to determine where Marshall will go as a director. Her technical competency, especially with BIG, is undeniable, although she insists that "she doesn't know much about the technical side of filmmaking. She doesn't even make shot lists. . . . When shooting, she seems to thrive on doing the wild thing—and hope that art happens in the process."[7] She seems drawn to plots with intricacies outside realms of everyday. JUMPIN' JACK FLASH concerned a computer programmer who receives a desperate message on her terminal from a British spy. BIG was about a little boy who makes a wish at a penny arcade to be a grown-up and is granted his wish only to discover his mind didn't mature as quickly as his body. With BIG, as entertaining as it was, one can't help wishing a woman director in such a coveted position as Marshall's had chosen a female coming-of-age film instead of adding another to an already long line of films about young men.

Another film about male bonding, AWAKENINGS (1991), is Marshall's most ambitious piece to date. After the popular BIG, it would have been comfortable and easy enough for Marshall to pursue her old stomping ground of comedy. And indeed she was pursuing what she's described as a "high-concept, now-the-Martians-go-to-Earth"[8] script when AWAKENINGS was forwarded to her. Why did the producers choose Penny Marshall for a story about a doctor who awakens a patient out of a decade-long catatonia through the use of a miracle drug? Because, producer Walter Parkes says, coming off BIG, Penny Marshall was "powerful enough to get the project made right."[9] Marshall herself knew that if she ever longed to do a serious film, [she] "better go for it while she was hot."[10]

Each one of her choices in the film is daring, down to the casting of the ebullient, manic Robin Williams as the introverted doctor—a man "fearful of human contact but willful, ingenious, and kind enough to take a chance on a lost cause."[11]

Her love of the actor is apparent in every breath of the film, down to the bit part of the nurse who bursts into the room with her one line, "It's a fucking miracle!" Marshall made the actress do the scene fifty-two times because, "It's a difficult line to say, 'It's a *miracle*,' or '*It's* a miracle,' or. . . . It's clear [Marshall] was once an actress."[12]

The beauty, the skill, the rhythm of a heart-beat that carries this movie so compassionately home, dares the industry to now consider Penny Marshall's formidable talents with a seriousness she has not been granted before.

Male bonding movies aside, we are grateful for a talent like Penny Marshall's. And we are also grateful that she continues to get chances to work. "You take on another project so you can start worrying about that one instead of this one,"[13] she kibitzes. The day to look forward to is the one when women directors will be able to focus on how the content of their pieces affect the world, instead of if they'll ever get a chance to direct again.

PENNY MARSHALL

1986 Jumpin' Jack Flash
1988 Big
1991 Awakenings

· III ·

REEL WOMEN OF
THE AVANT-GARDE

Shirley Clarke

Maya Deren

Yvonne Rainer

PREVIEW

♦ ♦ ♦

The realm of the avant-garde, the experimental, is traditionally the place women have been able to make a captivating mark, and to prove without a shadow of a doubt that indeed there is a unique and an endemically "female gaze." This is because the films are generally self-financed. Commercial questions are tossed to the wind in favor of artistic concerns. These women never had to waste time climbing the studio ladders to prove their merit. They forged ahead, trusting their inner voice, thereby changing every one of our perceptions of seeing. Optical creativity did not commence with the electronic age or with MTV! The pioneers of these new terrains of visual perception were these women.

These women asked why a piece of film had to tell stories with linear beginnings, middles, and endings. They painted on film, scratched it, stretched it, shot images too close and too far back, moved the middle to the front and repeated it five times at the end. They made film feel like a deep, rare voyage into the soul, so that we were forced to question that mutable state we dare to call "reality."

Maya Deren (1917–1961)

It was extremely rare for a woman to become a director in the forties in America. No one had done it since **Dorothy Arzner** made her rare mark in Hollywood, and had then made the choice to leave because she no longer could bear the pressures in an all-male studio system.

Maya Deren may have been the first to create what is known as the independent film movement in this country. She won the first Guggenheim grant for creative work ever given in the field of motion pictures. Deren holds her own as the first American woman to use film in a nonlinear way. As related by **Anaïs Nin**, Deren was idolized by later male pioneers of her generation such as Kenneth Anger and Curtis Harrington. They "looked up to Maya as the pioneer, the American equivalent of Bunuel, Cocteau, Dali. She was older, bolder, fiercer than they were."[1]

Deren did have a predecessor in Paris, **Germaine Dulac** who was the first to translate the psychological mind into filmic language by making the woman protagonist's point of view also the point of view of the camera. From Dulac, Deren inherited the concept that the medium of film is first and foremost an artistic canvas.

Among those who venerate her short-lived but remarkable achievements, Maya Deren is fondly remembered as the Mother of the Underground Film. In 1943, she collaborated with the surrealist painters Marcel Duchamp and Matta on a piece intended to defy the normal relationships of time and space. That film was never completed. But it was to set a precedent for what would be her aesthetic: film as poetry and not as prose. She would adapt this philosophy into the fifteen-minute film that would make her name. MESHES IN THE AFTERNOON (1943), continues to be a cult classic, and fascinates anyone interested in visual depictions of the workings of the mind. The *New York Times* said of the film on the occasion of Deren's death in 1961:

> From the early 1940's until her death in 1961, Maya Deren both evoked and exemplified the American avant-garde movement virtually by herself. She was unmistakably a woman with a cause [one of the first] to achieve recognition for the personal films [she made: films seen] as the magical creation of the solitary artist. Her first film, MESHES IN THE AFTERNOON, set the tone for the decade and linked the movement to the older European avant-garde films of Cocteau and Buñuel.[2]

Film critic Parker Tyler wrote of the film: "We see there is the magical . . . built in the vertical dimensions of dream to become complicated metaphors, an ideogram, or word structured by an aggregate of images." Her films became described as trances, literally, picture languages all their own.

What Deren took from the surreal movement, an art movement she grew to maturity with, was the concept of traveling to the interior of the mind for inspiration. But since one of the surrealist's credos was to use "the woman as muse, as the inspiration for the male imagination," her associations with the surrealists stopped there. Deren didn't have time to be anyone's muse, she was much too busy following her own vision as an artist.

Some of Deren's films are described as poetic dances choreographing movements and rhythms of the Wu-Tang and Saolin schools of Chinese boxing and transforming them into their cinematic equivalents, or tragic picturizations of the emotions linked to the intensity of a girl's frustrated search for companionship in the real and unreal world in which she lives.

Like many women in film, Deren began with an early fascination in dance, and apprenticed herself to the modern pioneering choreographer **Katheryn Dunham**. Dance becomes the ritualistic mode that provides the interlocking rhythm in all her work.

The author, **Anaïs Nin**, appeared in several of Deren's films and describes her thus:

> Maya had a fascinating face. She was a Russian Jewess. Under the wealth of curly, wild hair, which she allowed to frame her face in a halo, she had pale blue eyes, and a primitive face. The mouth was wide and fleshy, the nose a touch of South-Sea-islander fullness.[3]
>
> She had a strong will and influence, which we all felt. . . . We were captivated by the images. . . . What a fighter she was for her films, for her ideas.[4]
>
> Last night we were excavating the Maya Deren mystery. We all sit in a circle and wonder why we do exactly what she commands us to do. We are subject to her will, her strong personality, yet at the same time we do not trust her or love her wholly. We recognize her talent. We talk of rebellion, of being forced, of tyranny, but we bow to her projects, make sacrifices.[5]

Nin alludes to Deren's nonconventional openness of sexuality, which allowed her to take a knife to the stereotypic male/female icons in movies up to her day.

She has a need to seduce everyone, from Duits to Marshall to Pablo, and even me. We all live breathlessly, hoping she will find someone to pacify her so that filming may go on. We may have to draw lots: Now you, Number nine, go to Maya and make love to her and make her happy, for the sake of the film.[6]

Maya Deren created six films, two books,[7] and no children. In the forties, it was acceptable to be artistic as a student. You could also be an artist later as a woman if you had children as well. The schism that Maya Deren felt around this issue is exemplified throughout all of her work. Her characters challenged ideas of "masculine" and "feminine." Her films defied the romantic notion of woman as a passive, inactive icon.

What Virginia Woolf did in attempting to capture the workings of the inner mind on paper Maya Deren succeeded in doing on film. She had set herself the infinitely more difficult task of finding the visual images that might replicate our dream state. She succeeded in pioneering a world visual wonderment that would transform thoughts about film forever.

As **Anaïs Nin** recalls:

At the Provincetown Playhouse, we gathered to see three films by Maya Deren. The crowd was dense, and some policemen thought he should investigate. He asked: "Is this a demonstration?" Someone answered: "It is not a demonstration, it is a revolution in film-making."[8]

MAYA DEREN

1943	Meshes in the Afternoon
1944	At Land (Conceived, Directed)
1945	Study in Choreography for Camera, A
	Visual Variations on Noguchi (Pas de Deux)
1946	Ritual in Transfigured Time (Conceived, Directed)
1948	Meditation on Violence
1952–59	Very Eye of Night, The—A Choreography for Camera

Shirley Clarke (1925–   )

"I was never 'underground,' " says **Shirley Clarke**, "I was never 'Hollywood.' There was no group I was part of. I always hoped there was a niche I could fit into, but I never did."[1]

Shirley Clarke's films never looked like anyone else's. Perhaps twenty years ahead of her time (and making no bones about it, "I set the styles. . . . I was uncomfortable, even slightly insulted, when I succeeded at being anonymous. I wondered where people had been that they shouldn't know me through my work."[2]) Shirley Clarke is a role model for filmmakers who want to understand how to remain true to their own vision and not get seduced by the lure of Hollywood. Her clarity about the advantages and the struggles of staying an independent were and still are illuminating.

Clarke began her artistic career as a dancer and began making short dance films with a camera given to her for her wedding. "I never studied film. . . . The first thing I did was to make a finished film . . . I started at the top and never descended. I knew that if I started at the bottom, I would never get farther than sweeping the floor."[3]

A DANCE IN THE SUN was completed in 1953. "I'd gotten $1,500 from my grandfather. . . . I was going to make three dance films, $500 each, and become the most famous dance filmmaker of all time. Well, to

begin with, I didn't even get one film finished for $1,500. The film stock alone was
more than that."[4]

She made several more innovative shorts
following. BRIDGES-GO-ROUND, in 1958,
depicted bridges choreographed through
superimpositions and a continuously moving camera. In 1959, Clarke codirected SKY-
SCRAPER, which won first prize at the Venice
Film Festival, was nominated for an Academy Award, and granted her the opportunity to do her first feature, THE CONNECTION
(1961). The film won the Critic's Prize at
Cannes. Clarke won a court case with the
film, and set a standard for censorship in
films throughout the United States.

"It's more than my just being a woman,"
says Clarke. "My subject matter was different, dangerous. Drug addiction and not
putting it down [THE CONNECTION.] Black
people, for real, done in Harlem, with real
locations, real people, real settings."[5]

The latter refers to THE COOL WORLD,
Clarke's second feature, which cost
$250,000 to make in 1963—one-fourth of
what it would have cost to make in Hollywood. The remarkable thing about THE
COOL WORLD was that it was a case of history catching up with the insights of Shirley
Clarke. She started filming in 1961. Within
two years, the civil rights revolution for
blacks in America was just beginning. Most
of her films, she has said, are messages to
other filmmakers about things they are
doing that Clarke questions. The clearest
example of this is PORTRAIT OF JASON
(1967), which was made:

> to show Ricky Leacock and Penny Penne-
> baker the flaws in thinking about cinema
> verité. If you take twelve days of shooting
> and edit only the climax points, you get
> crap. My theory was that you don't take
> out the boring parts—the way someone
> reaches those climaxes, or an idea or what-
> ever. JASON is two hours of real time, not
> film time. The film took four hours to make
> because we had to stop every ten minutes
> to load the cameras. . . . There is no real
> difference between a traditional fiction film

> and a documentary. I've never made a doc-
> umentary. There is no such trip.[6]

Through the notion of using real time,
Clarke became a forerunner to the pioneering filmmaker **Chantal Akerman** who
would later use similar techniques.

In New York, in avant-garde art circles,
Shirley Clarke became well known for her
stridently independent ideas:

> I chose independent filmmaking rather than
> studio filmmaking because I didn't want the
> studios to decide what people should see. I
> never thought about how hard it was to be
> an independent. My problem was to learn
> how to make films. I have never wanted to
> make a film that wasn't, for me, learning
> the next thing I wanted to find out about.[7]

It took a tremendous amount of guts to
make THE COOL WORLD, a film that Clarke
improvised with street kids in order, she
says, to portray the honesty of their experience. As Clarke herself has pointed out,
there are filmmakers who would like to
make a first film this way and use it to
go on to Hollywood. There are others
who make one film and find that it is just
too hard to make a second. Clarke never
thought about the Hollywood alternative
until she realize that in fact that *was* an
alternative. Reality struck home after she
had made two successful films, and she
found that she was unable to get the money
to do another.

> I never have any intention of making a film
> in Hollywood. Hollywood has precon-
> ceived ideas about what audiences want. . . .
> I went into video because there wasn't any
> way for me to continue making films. I
> couldn't find a producer who would accept
> my scripts as I wrote them. I don't seem to
> be serious in a certain way [for Holly-
> wood]. Financially, my films weren't block-
> busters.[8]

But in most instances, like the emperor's
new clothes, good box office is nothing
more than great promotion.

Any serious film buff would agree that Shirley Clarke was a major innovator for her time—and certainly one of the first women directors of the new generation. How did she feel about being one of the first?

Initially I was worried about having problems with male crews, but then I found that those who don't like working with a woman simply don't join up. Pretty soon we begin functioning as people, not as members of different sexes.[9]

On the subject of a "female gaze," as in everything else, Shirley Clarke has a strong opinion:

I hope that as women make films they will start to say something that is meaningful to women in an entirely different way. And I don't mean about how women have babies—but with the sensitivity of someone who has looked with double vision, as women have had to, as black people have

had to. They will give us greater understanding, not of men but of humanity, expressed much more broadly than we've been allowed to see.[10]

Shirley Clarke went on to become one of the earliest pioneers of video as an art form.

SHIRLEY CLARKE

1953 Dance in the Sun, A
1954 In Paris Parks
1955 Bullfight
1957 Moment in Love
1958 Bridges-Go-Round
      Brussels 'Loops'
1959 Skyscraper
1961 Connection, The
      Scary Time
1963 Cool World, The
1964 Robert Frost—A Love Letter To
      the World
1967 Man in the Polar Regions
      Portrait of Jason

Yvonne Rainer

E. Ann Kaplan has said that **Yvonne Rainer**'s LIVES OF PERFORMERS (1972) "preceded any coherent feminist film community in New York and any assertions of their voices by the female artists working in the male-dominated avant-gardes."[1] The voice she pioneered by way of a "female-gaze" aesthetic were inherently her own. She was not met with any sort of emotional or intellectual support for her interests—the machinations of sexual conflicts—until the midseventies.

Rainer is a self-reflective, avant-garde artist, one who, as Kaplan says, makes us aware that narratives in films are consciously constructed.

She shows her awareness that love relationships so easily fall into the clichés of dominant narratives (Hollywood melo-

drama, soap opera), which is partly why she tries to avoid narrative. . . . She wants to retain the validity of the emotions; in fact, she frees emotions from the trappings of dominant narrative forms.[2]

Her pioneering work in the field of dance in the midsixties incorporated influences of Merce Cunningham, John Cage, and Robert Rauschenberg, "with its combination of exaggerated focus on ordinary objects with art-historical quotation."[3]

When Yvonne Rainer won the American Film Institute's Maya Deren Award in 1988 the program notes said:

An attentive reckoning of the American independent cinema's post-1970 fortunes would place Yvonne Rainer close towards the center. . . . Rainer began making short films in 1967 as inserted components of live performance and dance pieces reconvened for film.[4]

In 1975, Ms. Rainer's FILM ABOUT A WOMAN WHO. . . . thwarted all expectations of the continuous narrative story line. You may ask—and many do—a woman who *what*?

This crafted, tightly structured film may reveal to the viewer a woman who can't reconcile various external circumstances with her own perfections of imperfections. It is a political, if ambiguous message, revealed through visual and sound-modulated strata as the film progresses. One viewer said, "It seems to say that speaking is like walking on volcanic silence." Language hovers between motion and stillness. Suspension is the soul of what is finally this visually beautiful film.

Rainer is among a group of filmmakers who, in the seventies, became aware of film's power to be used as a tool for social criticism. Filmmakers like **Shirley Clarke** turned somewhat earlier from introspective experiments to frank "cinema-verité style films that dealt with social realities instead of fictions."[5] The growing accessibility of 16mm in the seventies showed a remarkable increase of "women working in independent film, acutely aware of their own oppression by both society and society's idea of what they should be and determined to use film as a means of righting these wrongs through political statements."[6]

In an interview about her film, Rainer said:

I wanted to reveal some very painful realities, which I had suffered through or had observed others suffering through; and I could not think of any presentation of these realities that surpasses the impact of the written form. I had experimented with language in dance. Now, in this film, I was faced with the problem of creating a continuity through image and text without encouraging the anticipation of a contin-

uous story, and yet not subverting the content of such a story, which I wanted to reveal with as much clarity and nakedness as possible.[7]

Carol Wikarska, in an early *Women and Film* issue said of Rainer's film:

The very actions of the performers sometimes take on the parataxic feeling of the language. Characters, for example, would abruptly freeze in the middle of a movement, taking on the appearance of a photograph. ("I shall become still, feign death.") Or they would pretend slow motion, eliminating the violence of their contact between themselves. ("I can't behave as though you don't exist.")[8]

The film's message is conveyed through a structure that is not narrative, and which itself mirrors the complexities and difficulties with which we attempt to communicate to one another.

There are stills from PSYCHO (1960), as well as a reenactment of PANDORA'S BOX (1928) that several critics have pegged as Rainer's "concern with woman as a victim of male violence. . . . Rainer is reluctant to build this into a politics of global female oppression," according to E. Ann Kaplan.

My women will probably continue to vacillate between being fools, heroines, and yes, victims. Victims of their own expectations no less than those of the opposite sex, or of the prevailing social mores.[9]

Despite these resistances of feminist associations, the very questioning of woman as an object of violence and/or oppression are an important contribution to questions of a female sensibility.

By refusing to individualize her characters in an ongoing sense . . . Rainer leaves situations open for us to speculate about them. All is not neatly provided for us as in a Hollywood film; we have to construct the film for ourselves, and in so doing we can learn a lot about the way relationships function, especially from the female point of view.[10]

Yvonne Rainer follows in the footsteps of **Maya Deren** through her use of film as an alternative expression for the phenomenon we call, "being human."

YVONNE RAINER

1972	Lives of Performers
1975	Film about a Woman Who. . . .
1976	Kristina Talking Pictures
1980	Journeys from Berlin
1985	Man Who Envied Women, The
In Progress	Privilege

SHORT TAKES

◆ ◆ ◆

Marie Menken (1909–1970)

Like **Maya Deren**, **Marie Menken** began her pioneering journey into independent moviemaking in the midforties when she redeemed a pawn ticket for a movie camera. With it, she made VISUAL VARIATIONS ON NOGUCHI (1945), which made Isamu Noguchi's sculptures seem to "move" through light.

One viewer said,

It was the first film I had ever seen which not only admitted but capitalized on the fact that the camera was hand-held. She was at that time the purest disciple of Jean Cocteau's advice to young filmmakers to take advantage of the freedom of the hand-held camera. . . . It led me to begin questioning the entire 'reality' of the motion picture image as related to ways of seeing.[1]

Film pioneer, Stan Brackage, found much inspiration in the work of Menken calling her "the Open Sesame."[2]

As Jackson Pollack would make breakthroughs in the use of paint, so Marie Menken would liberate the uses of the camera. She freed it from its tripod and let it do its dance.

Along with new ways to use light and camera motion, Menken was one of the underground film movement's principal character actresses. She was often referred to as the poetess of the new cinema.

Sheldon Renen in *An Introduction to the American Underground Film,* said of her work, "But whether they are a moving picture postcard (BAGATELLE FOR WILLARD MAAS) or a stylized biography (ANDY WARHOL), whether they use camera motion (GO GO GO) they have in common a lyric lightness and a love for jolting visual rhythms."[3]

Twelve years after making, NOGUCHI, Menken pioneered, HURRY! HURRY! in 1957. The piece was described as "a microscopic investigation of human sperm cells lashing around in search of an egg, double-exposed over flames and a soundtrack of bombardment."[4]

Aside from her repertoire of some ten films, Menken did camera work on and acted in all the films of her husband, Willard Maas. She also performed in Andy Warhol's THE LIFE OF JUANITA CASTRO. A consummate painter and abstract artist, her paintings were exhibited at the Brooklyn Museum and the Baltimore Museum of Art. Menken supported her film work, which she was careful never to mix up with questions of survival, by working as an editor on the cable desk of *Time/Life Magazines.*

MARIE MENKEN

1945   Visual Variations on Noguchi
1957   Hurry! Hurry!
1959   Dwightiana
1960   Faucets
1961   Arabesque for Kenneth Anger
          Bagatelle for Willard Maas
          Eye Music in Red Major

1961–63   Mood Mondrian
1962   Moonplay (Unfinished)
          Zenscapes (Unfinished)
1962–63   Notebooks
1963   Go Go Go
1964   Wrestling
1965   Andy Warhol
          Drips in Strips
1966   Lights (Unfinished)
          Sidewalks (Unfinished)
1968   Excursion
1969   Watts with Eggs

Mary Ellen Bute (1909–   )

"What does **Mary Ellen Bute** seek through the film?" asked writer Gregory Markopoulos in *Film Comment,* "Nothing less than the harnessing of the supersonic harmonies of Silence taken from the transplanetary areas of space."[1]

She was one of the first abstract filmmakers in the United States. Between 1934 and 1953, Mary Ellen Bute made over a dozen films using mirrors, oscilloscopes, and three dimensional objects often set to classical music.

Bute differed from her contemporary underground filmmaking colleagues through a concern with areas of reality made available to the five senses by new technology, rather than by psychoanalysis.[2]

She began her career as a painter, but soon became fascinated with mathematics and numbers.

> For years I have tried to find a method for controlling a source of light to produce images in rhythm. It was particularly while I listened to music that I felt an overwhelming urge to translate my reactions and ideas into a visual form that would have the ordered sequence of music. I worked towards simulating this continuity in my paintings. Painting was not flexible enough and too confined within its frame.[3]

With numbers, she said, you could analyze what had been done and then by expanding or contracting you could get the most fabulous new material. "I started with it as an exercise and then did POLKA GRAPH."[4]

In the late twenties Bute went to the Taj Mahal in India where, "I looked into the gems and saw reflected the Taj Mahal, and the lake, and the whole thing appealed to me enormously . . . because it was romantic and because it was a kinetic, visual thing. I started entertaining myself by imagining these designs and patterns all in movement."[5]

Back in New York in 1929, she related this to Thomas Wilfred who had developed a color organ. She then apprenticed with Leon Theremin and his sound studio to learn more about composition and its relationship to a new kinetic, visual art form. "We submerged tiny mirrors in tubes of oil, connected [them] to an oscillator, and drew where these points of light were flying. The effect was thrilling for us—it was so pure."[6]

The experience so excited her she picked up a Bolex camera and tried her hand at film. The result was RHYTHM IN LIGHT (1936). "It was mostly three-dimensional animation. Pyramids, and ping pong balls, and all interrelated by light patterns—and

Mary Ellen Bute (with Ted Nemuth and Bill Nemuth)

I wasn't happy unless it all entered and exited as I had planned."[7]

Her film experience commenced in documentary work with Lewis Jacobs. She later codirected films with her husband, Ted Nemeth, using oscilloscope-generated and electronically created imagery.

Her films became electronically composed with beats of music synchronized to light patterns. Her interest in musical composition stretched far into collaborations on filmic innovations with composers like George Gershwin. Her interest, she said, was in creating "visual music."

Critic Parker Tyler described Bute's early work as that of a "purist; a choreographer of light and colour . . . obeying patterns of classical music . . . using film as colour ab-straction developed from painting."[8]

Arthur Knight described her work as "visual symphonies of commonplace objects . . . pins, buttons, collars . . . photographed through distorted lenses and animated to the music of the Danse Macabre or a Bach toccata and fugue."[9]

Her most ambitious project was in 1965 with the full-length, FINNEGAN'S WAKE.[10] "Entering, reentering, never once closing our eyes," says one *Film Comment* writer, "the colors of Mary Ellen Bute's films delight; they glissade upon the average film spectator through her complex ribbons of light, but they remain dissimilar to the forces heard in the accompanying musical tones of the adopted sound track."[11]

MARY ELLEN BUTE

1934	Synchronization (Codirected)
1936	Anitra's Dance
	Dada
	Rhythm in Light
	Synchrony No. 2
1937	Evening Star
1938	Parabola
1940	Escape
	Toccata and Fugue
1941	Spool Sport
	Tarantella
1953	Polka Graph
1953	Pastorale
1954	Abstronics
	Moon Contrast
1956	Boy Who Saw Through, The
1958	Color Rhapsody
	RCA
1964	Skin of Our Teeth, The
1965	Finnegan's Wake
1967	Passages from Finnegan's Wake

·IV·

REEL WOMEN
OF COLOR

Euzhan Palcy

Kathleen Collins

Maya Angelou

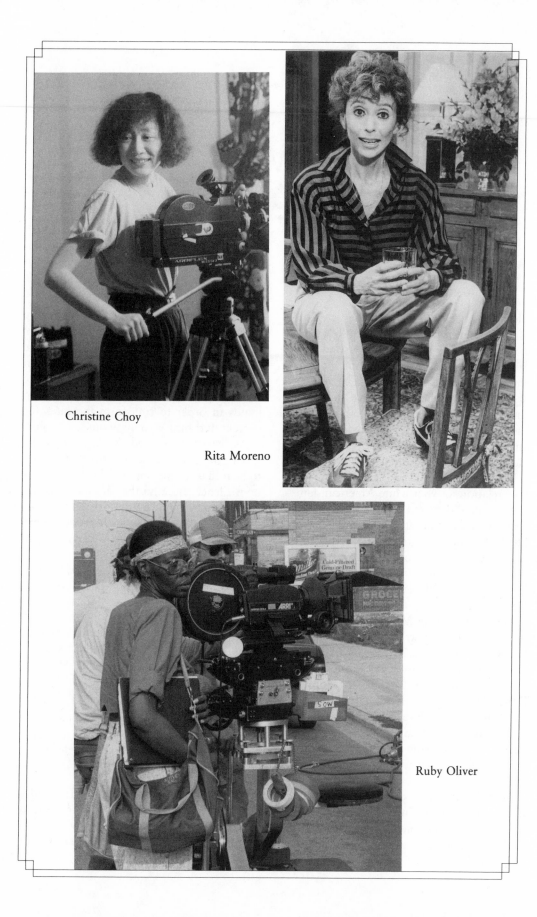

Christine Choy

Rita Moreno

Ruby Oliver

PREVIEW

◆ ◆ ◆

Silence has been the primary characteristic used to describe women behind the scenes in movies, although now we know that their presence there has been constant. For the filmmakers who also happen to be women of color, even when they have made attempts to break their silences, the culture has rarely responded. It is almost if the culture says, If we don't acknowledge you, then your experience cannot really exist.

But they do exist. And that existence has little relation to what white American filmmakers have depicted on the screen: The screen's many mindless "Mammys" or **Ethel Waters**, the first black American woman to star alone on a Broadway stage, shown as the strong, uneducated, endlessly forgiving maid, reduced to singing "Darkies Never Dream," in CABIN IN THE SKY (1943)[1]; and **Hattie McDaniel** and **Lousie Beavers**, "sexless matriarchs with no erotic life of their own."

And the ones who lived erotic screen lives, **Josephine Baker, Eartha Kitt, Dorothy Dandridge** were "black women as sex objects, often of the white man's desire." Their screen mythologies have "used rape as an excuse to continue the myth that only white men and black women are free [to have sex] in America."[2]

In the Hispanic arena, on the screen the incomparable **Rita Moreno** wasn't allowed to budge from her role as the little Spanish spitfire. This actress and dancer, exuding an endless supply of energy, won an Academy Award for her role in WEST SIDE STORY (1961), but couldn't escape the doom of the stereotype in which the white male film world had cast her. Today, she is taking the producing responsibilities into her own hands in order to transform the fates for current and future young women of color.

As every oppressed group eventually learns, the only way for the truth of history to be told is for the oppressed to break their own silence. Because the film industry has been primarily run by the privileged class, people of color—and women of color more particularly—have been ostracized from the means with which to speak.

"Of all the genres of film," said documentary filmmaker and poet **Michelle Parkerson,**

> dramatic features have remained staunchly white, the most staunchly male and the most expensive film format. The complexion of feature film directors is changing in Hollywood [witness a handful of black men] . . . And to some extent, the gender of the industry has made a transition [to] white women. . . . But the phenomenon of African-American women directing feature films still remains a phenomenon.[3]

This section is dotted with short profiles of women of color who are American filmmakers[4] even though they may not have finished full-length features. Currently they are doing important counter-white-culture screen work that is widening all our perspectives by telling the truth. Their truths. These women are pioneers by definition. They are breaking barriers, overcoming impossible odds, and somehow managing through all this to find and develop their own voices artistically. The tragically deceased film pioneer **Kathleen Collins** (1942–1988), described as "among the first generation of black female directors breaching the inner sanctum of feature film production,"[5] once provided us with this tip on how she survived:

> I don't spend a lot of time worrying about how I am perceived by other people. . . . The artist must be fundamentally honest. What you should get is his or her soul. If you get anything else, they have cheated themselves first, and they have cheated you second.[6]

The Mandarin Film Company

Ethnic film production seems to have begun in the United States with this company in 1917, and, according to the *Moving Picture World* of that same year, the Mandarin Film Company was the only Chinese producing concern in this country.[1]

It was based in Oakland, California, and boasted its own studio. The entire production entity was composed of Chinese participants. The company's woman president, **Marion E. Wong**, was also an actress. She and her sister took the principal female parts in their first production, THE CURSE OF QUON QWON (1917).[2] It is not clear whether this was their only completed production.

Kathleen Collins (1942–1988)

Here was an artistic model, someone who knew that excellence involved scrupulousness, that to practice a craft meant purging oneself against dishonesty.[1]

On October 18, 1988, **Kathleen Conwell Collins Prettyman** died of cancer, and the independent black film movement lost one of its leading role models. She was a playwright, a teacher, a mother as well as a filmmaker. In her twenty years as a writer— "I keep saying that I am more a writer than a filmmaker, and I think that's really true"[2]—Collins completed six plays, four screenplays, several short stories, and most of a novel. Her plays were produced in her lifetime at, among many other places, the American Place Theatre in New York.

As a writer/director, Kathleen Collins wrote and directed three films in her lifetime, THE CRUZ BROTHERS AND MISS MALLOY (1979), LOSING GROUND (1982), and GOULDTOWN: A MULATTO SETTLEMENT (1988). Her films were hard to categorize. CRUZ BROTHERS, for instance,

> is about three Puerto Rican brothers, their ghost-father, and an Irish women who hires the brothers to renovate her home. LOSING GROUND depicts the dilemma of a woman professor of philosophy in search of ecstasy and self-definition apart from her painter-husband and actress-mother.[3]

Her audiences asked her why she, a black woman, was making a film about Puerto Ricans. Or why in LOSING GROUND she would opt to show, in the critical eyes of some viewers, the more negative portraits of a black marriage.[4] In response, Collins replied:

I have a sense of going my own way, and I don't really think much about whether it's going against the grain. I don't really want to spend a lot of time worrying about how I am perceived by other people.[5]

Collins closely identifies with the sensibility of **Lorraine Hansberry**, whose essays she considered among the most insightful pieces of social criticism around. And of her plays Collins said:

The Sign in Sidney Brustein's Window [1965] . . . is a wonderful, absolutely brilliant play. [Hansberry knew that] anything in life was accessible for her to write about. [She didn't feel] that the Black experience was the only experience. And it is that breadth of vision that I have always sensed was ultimately my vision.[6]

Kathleen Collins hailed from Gouldtown, a long-established settlement of ancestors who had been there since 1623. "When *Roots* came out, I didn't get it in a way, because I've been able to trace every member of my family," she said.[7] Collins grew up in Jersey City, New Jersey. She graduated from Skidmore College and went on to do graduate work in Paris through Middlebury College. When she arrived back in the States, it was at a time that film was first becoming a respected medium in academia, and the colleges were looking for qualifed people to teach. Collins, who had done extensive film research and was also a film editor, was eminently qualified, but she wanted to make a movie. She took her new script, WOMEN, SISTERS, AND FRIENDS (never made) and went all about the country attempting to raise money. "This was 1971," she said later. "Forget it. It was ridiculous. . . . Nobody would give money to a black woman to direct a film."[8]

They all suggested she look for a "real" director and producer who could do the movie for her. Discouraged, she gave up her dream, moved to the country with her children, and went on writing plays.

In 1974 she took a job at City College in New York teaching production and screen writing. One of her students, Ronald Gray, wanted to know why someone who knew so much about making films wasn't making them. He kept after Collins, until pretty soon she was directing THE CRUZ BROTHERS AND MISS MALLOY on a five thousand dollar donation with Gray as producer. Said Collins:

It was awful doing a movie for five thousand dollars. It was like going down a terribly long tunnel. It was frightening. I was thirty-seven, not old, but it was not like I was twenty-one. And I had children and all that stuff. But we did it because Ronald and I were really good partners. . . . We both have an incredible tenacity.[9]

The film was well received and Collins felt a new, mature voice growing inside of her. They were "rolling," as Collins herself put it. Because of the first film, grant monies became easier for the second, LOSING GROUND (1982). But just at this time, Collins became ill.

My basic premise is that all illness is psychic disconnection of some kind. . . . The nature of illness and female success and the capacity of the female to acknowledge its own intelligence is a subject that interests me. . . . If there is any way in which women tend to be self-destructive it is in that area of creativity where they actually feel their own power and can't either acknowledge it or . . . go to the end of it. They get scared and retreat into illness or into having too many babies or destructive love affairs with men who run them ragged. Somewhere or other, they detour out of respect for their own creativity.[10]

Collins died of cancer just after finishing the forty-minute GOULDTOWN (1988) about her family and roots. It's been said that LOSING GROUND paved the way for dramatic work in cinema from the black female perspective. Black women filmmakers, said Collins, are "part of a larger redemptive process that black women have to achieve. The only residual softness that's possible in this culture, as far as I'm concerned, is in the hands of black women."[11]

Right before she died, Kathleen Collins was in the midst of working on a production about **Bessie Coleman**, the black aviatrix.[12]

KATHLEEN COLLINS

1979   Cruz Brothers and Miss Malloy, The
1982   Losing Ground
1988   Gouldtown: A Mulatto Settlement

Rita Moreno

I played all those roles the same way— barefoot with my nostrils flaring. . . . Hoop earrings, off-the-shoulder blouses, teeth gnashing—those were my trademark. The blouse and the earrings would get transferred from studio to studio and it became known as "THE RITA MORENO KIT.' "

—Rita Moreno interview with the author

You meet **Rita Moreno** and you can hardly believe it. Her energy sizzles like a blue laser. She bubbles about her new career. She's gone into producing. "I'm scared," she tells me, but really, it feeds her. "I'm excited. I feel like I'm starting my life all over again."[1] She deserves to. Laurels and options shouldn't arrive so late to such talent. Lucky for us she still has such roadrunner momentum. Among other things, she's working on a feature based on the making of the documentary, "Salt of the Earth," from 1953.

She wants to produce because like most women film pioneers she wants to set the record straight. She wants to tell the truth about Hispanic people, about people in general. After forty years on stage and screen and a career that is still very much in motion, she wants at last to be in the driver's seat. She wants to use her well-deserved influence to insure that no Hispanic woman will ever again have to play a "spitfire." She's played enough in her tumultuous career for every Hispanic woman in the world.

Rita Moreno speaks about all this with the contagious enthusiasm of a twenty-year-old. She's not twenty though, she's fifty-eight. And if I break the code of "ageism" here and make a point of it, it's because Rita does so herself. It's part of her nightclub act. She usually tells her age after a dance number that would compromise the physique of a woman half her years. And she's recently completed a low-impact exercise video.

"My agent had a heart attack the first time he heard me mention my age in public. I'm fifty-eight and I'm proud of it! I did the video because I felt that with my age and experience I had a lot to say that would be beneficial to women, particularly since I am a woman, as they say in Europe, of a 'certain' age."[2]

There's more to it than age, she points out. "When you are in control of your body, you find a way to control your life better. Your mental attitude improves."[3]

Whether or not her mental attitude that "people should go out and tackle life" is due to her physical health is not relevant in these pages. Our interest instead is in the *attitude*. It is one, as we will see, that nearly cost Moreno her life. And when she decided to transform her life dramatically she also irreversibly transformed the screen possibilities for Hispanic women everywhere.

Because Rita Moreno could sing and dance and act like the girl next door, she assumed she would also be accorded girl-next-door privileges. The problem was, she didn't *look* like the girl next door. Red, white, and blue did not mean Puerto Rican. The young seventeen-year-old-just-discovered-by-tinseltown was strikingly unprepared for the racist stereotype in store for her: the sexy, wildfire, nostrils flaring, Spanish "spitfire." "We all looked alike, or so they seemed to think," said Moreno. In a culture where being a Latina meant (and often still means) playing poor, brown-skinned princesses, it took a long time for Moreno to realize the problem was not hers alone.

"It took six years of therapy trying to get my 'ethnic' problems untangled," she told me. "I'd get to the point where I'd feel great, really sure of myself, and then audition for an important part only to have the producer say, 'Terrific. But really, honey, for this part we need a Mitzi Gaynor—we need an American.' "

And so, movie after forgetful B movie,[4] Rita Moreno finally *just said no*—like someone to a bad drug habit. What she didn't know then was how much she was benefiting all Latin women everywhere. For her own mental stability she made a brave decision to play only Latin women with integrity and dignity. No more wild, Chiquita Banana mamas who would get what was coming to them. No more fooling around with the leading lady's hunk only to get dumped. It was the time, as writer Arnold Bell has written, when ethnic in movies meant, "the other woman," and Rita Moreno was the fifties' answer to **Lupe Velez**.[5] No more of the Indian maidens of THE YELLOW TOMAHAWK (1954). No more LATIN LOVERS (1953) girls who said deathless things like "You Yonkee peeg, you rape my seester. I keel you!"

> The more I played those dusky innocents, the worst I felt inside. Once I was an Indian maiden in JIVARO [1954] with Rhonda Fleming. There she was in frills, all pink and blond and big-breasted. Right next to her, I had an ugly wig on, brown-shoe-polish make-up, and wore a tattered leopard skin. I felt ugly and stupid and more ashamed.[6]

The humiliation to herself, she decided, would end at last, even if that meant she'd never work again. As fate would cruelly have it, she did not work in films for eight years.

Her real name is **Rosita Dolores Alverio**. "Isn't that a beautiful name?" she asked me nostalgically. She was born in Humacao, Puerto Rico, near a famous rain forest in 1932, but grew up in the tough 180th Street and Amsterdam Avenue section of Spanish Harlem in New York. She made her Broadway debut at age thirteen in an Eli Wallach vehicle entitled, *Skydrift* (1944). And in typical Hollywood fashion, she was asked at age seventeen to abandon her beautiful name by Louis B. Mayer when she signed her MGM contract. He thought the name too corny, even for a Spanish spitfire. She did what he said, imagining he would make her into the next **Lana Turner**. Hollywood, however, had other plans. Which, as it turned out, were no plans at all.

> I was a terrified child who had no idea how cutthroat this business was. . . . It was the end of my first year on the lot, and I was bouncing around bombarding people with questions about my future, when this gruff casting executive scowled up out of his cigar smoke, "Star? Honey, you gotta be kiddin'." They're gonna drop you like a bad habit." . . . There I was, eighteen and a has-been.[7]

Their brains were too small. They didn't know what to do with her. They thought their only option for this bundle of talent was to type-cast her in Latina roles. And so, for the next ten years, she fed herself entirely by playing in B movies. She continued at MGM until she was twenty, and then was put under contract to Fox. For several more years she portrayed those sexy "señoritas," barefoot, dumb, born to play and lose. "It's funny now, but it wasn't then," she said with a generosity of spirit Hollywood doesn't deserve. "Can you imagine an early Rita Moreno Film Festival? Millions would click off their sets!"

Offscreen she was losing too. She was dating George Hormel of the Hormel meat industry family when he was booked on drug charges. The police harassed her. The headlines read, "Wildfire Lives up to Her Reputation." "My world," she said, "as far as I was concerned, had totally collapsed." She gulped down a bottle of sleeping pills. She now remembers the suicide attempt as a way to exorcise all her old demons.

The upshot of this period is that every step of the way Moreno made her living in her craft. "I can honestly say I never had to get a job outside show business," she says proudly. Not only would Rita Moreno finally break the mold for Hispanic women as Spanish spitfires, but she may well be the first actress in history who never had to wait on a single table!

Just once in her career did the Latin stereotyping come in handy. In 1961 Robert Wise cast her as Anita, a Puerto Rican, in WEST SIDE STORY. The supporting role won her the Oscar.

"I had just turned thirty and I thought I was *made* as an actress. I thought all the struggles were over. But I soon found out I was more typecast than ever! So in 1963, with the blessing of my therapist, I fled Hollywood."

It was a scary time for Moreno. She was tired of being Puerto Rican in a hostile country. She moved to New York, married a Jewish doctor, had a daughter, and settled down. Marlon Brando, with whom Moreno had an on-again, off-again love affair for nine years when she was in her twenties, said she was the only person he ever knew who made a complete right turn in life.

New York and Broadway turned out to be much kinder to Rita. Her luck changed. She was finally getting cast for her talent and not for her skin color. First was the role in Hal Prince's production of *She Loves Me* (1963), then the part in Lorraine Hansberry's *The Sign in Sidney Brustein's Window* (1965). The latter was her first real stage success. Success, failure; she loves me, she loves me not. "You have to develop a tough skin," says Moreno.

> You have to talk to yourself and say, "Okay, wait a minute, It's not me." It's the difference between being forty-four and being twenty. At twenty, the business destroys you. In your forties you say to yourself, "It's not really me. It's them with their Day-Glo minds."[8]

The years got progressively better, though it was never smooth sailing. Broadway continued to be sweet: *Last of the Red Hot Lovers* (1970) with James Coco. As Hollywood always lags ten years behind cultural consciousness, movies would continue to be tougher: THE NIGHT OF THE FOLLOWING DAY (1968) with Marlon Brando, came and went; POPI (1969), MARLOWE (1969), quickly disappeared too; a lucky bit in CARNAL KNOWLEDGE (1971). And just when she thought the hoops and earrings were a bad memory, along came a sparkling stage opportunity with *The Ritz* (1976) in which the indefatigable Moreno played the incredible Googie Gomez.

The part was different; the part *was* Rita Moreno.

Terrance McNally had seen Rita fooling around at a party in 1973 and wrote the play around her. The part for Moreno was something of a rebirth. It won her the Tony in 1975. As Arnold Bell wrote:

She doesn't die in the last reel, nor does she play the handmaiden to the wooden white goddess. The part is a travesty of all the ambitious, untalented, fifth-rate singers who have spent most of their lives playing fleabags. And [of course] the germ of the character came from Rita herself.[9]

Moreno said she would do it her way and win in the end, even if it killed her. It almost did. But today, you can open your *Guinness Book of World Records* and see this: Rita Moreno is the first woman in history to win all four major show-business awards: the Oscar, the Tony, the Grammy, and two Emmys.

Like her TV den mother character on the short-lived *Nine to Five* (executive-produced by **Jane Fonda**), Rita Moreno is the prototype female survivor. She knows the history of the women of her race. She knows the odds and how to play the game. Their way, *and* her way. If it is the last thing she does, she is determined to carve out a future for them that is altogether different.

RITA MORENO

1950	Pagan Love Song
	Toast of New Orleans
1952	Singin' in the Rain
1953	Latin Lovers
1954	Garden of Evil
	Jivaro
	Yellow Tomahawk
1955	Lieutenant Wore Skirts, The
	Seven Cities of God
	Untamed
1956	King and I, The
	Vagabond King, The
1957	Deerslayer, The
1960	This Rebel Breed
1961	Summer and Smoke
	West Side Story
1968	Night of the Following Day, The
1969	Marlowe
	Popi
1971	Carnal Knowledge
1976	Ritz, The

Maya Angelou

The headline of a *Los Angeles Examiner* article from May 1972 reads, "First Black Woman Director Readies Film." By 1976, the headlines had changed, "Finding Directing Assignment Tough for Multitalented Maya Angelou."

The title of this article from the *Hollywood Reporter* was misleading. **Maya Angelou** couldn't have found directing difficult for the simple reason that she was not allowed the chance to try. But more on that in a minute.

In the field of motion pictures she was a ground breaker for women of color. Maya Angelou was the first black woman to script and write the musical score for a produced motion picture, GEORGIA, GEORGIA, in

1972. Starring **Diana Sands**, the film concerned a black woman singer who tours Sweden. She becomes involved with American soldiers who defect from Vietnam to Sweden. This strong attraction to white society causes tremendous friction between Sands and a black woman companion.

Newsweek's Arthur Cooper said about the film in 1972: "GEORGIA, GEORGIA is admirable for the honesty with which it tries to get a psychic fix on the contemporary black woman."[1]

But Angelou did not so happily agree. "A Swedish man directed it and I think the essence of my work was lost. He had no understanding of black Americans, so he had no understanding of the romance in my script."[2] The frustrating experience of seeing her work diluted through another's vision inspired Angelou to want to direct. "I've not seen in any film what I think is an integral part of the black American life," she said in *Millimeter* magazine in 1974, "the rhythm of the life."

> If a person has to go downtown or uptown, whatever the city . . . as soon as that person leaves the black area, the rhythm changes. When they walk into a building with all whites there's a fractiousness about the rhythm. I'd like to show that with a camera. I haven't seen it done from an almost musical point of view. That's one of the things I'd like to try.[3]

She thought she was going to get the opportunity. When David Wolper hired Angelou for an acting part in the TV miniseries, *Roots,* she agreed to do the role with the stipulation that she'd later have a chance to direct something of her own. Wolper agreed, but then sold out his company. An option in 1972 for her book, *I Know Why the Caged Bird Sings* (1978), inspired hope in Angelou once again that she'd be allowed to direct her own project. At first, the producer agreed. Then he changed his mind.

Angelou bought her own script back. She had big dreams for what she hoped to do with it. In fact, she was almost optimistically naive. "Any film I do, I will write and direct," she said in 1974.

> The producers and I will agree in pre-production meetings and they will have nothing to do with it from then on. Those are definite conditions, or we don't make the film. I'm prepared to learn and share, cooperate and compromise in pre-production, but not once production begins. The only area in which I insist on control is direction.[4]

Maya Angelou holds membership in the Director's Guild of America. She's directed two plays for public television. She has published a five-volume epic biography of magnificence and beauty, has written books of verse, has scored numerous movies, and is a member of the board of trustees of the American Film Institute. In other words, Maya Angelou has paid her dues many times over. With her multiplicity of proven talents, she is a virtual one-woman creativity cult. And yet, she wasn't permitted to direct *I Know Why The Caged Bird Sings.*

By 1978 she felt defeated. She signed a contract with CBS that limited her production involvement with *Caged Bird* to coauthoring the script. She said in the *New York Times* in April of 1979:

> I wanted so badly to direct. But I realized that there is a difference between being convinced and being stubborn. I'm not certain what the difference is, but I do know that if you butt your head against a stone wall long enough, at some point you realize the wall is stone and that your head is flesh and bone. So I gave it up. Sometimes, because a particular piece of work is so sweet to us, we get so close that we indulge it and leave it without the wisdom of distance. I don't know now if I made the right decision. Maybe I will someday. I don't believe that control of black films must *always* be in a black person's hands. But any white person involved in a black story should be respectful of the black person's sensibilities on the subject.[5]

This artist with a wise inner voice, was defeated by a system that cuts its own throat by limiting its sources of creativity. What's worse, Angelou was now questioning her own best instincts. Was she, after all, the best person to direct her own piece of writing? She was confused and rankled.

> In the film business . . . when we take a meeting, it's very hard to get used to someone saying, "I don't think this works." I'm not sure my resistance is based on my ego or my instincts as a writer. I have to go

home and sort it all out at night. . . . I've thought about why I want to be in this kind of writer/producer position and very likely, what has attracted me is the power. I have to admit that.[6]

And why not? As Angelou herself says, "If you stick to your guns as a woman, you're stubborn. But if you stick to your guns as a man, you're persistent. *And* if you're black and female and six feet tall [as Angelou is]—PHEW!"[7]

Still and all, 1978 was a good year for Angelou. The *Hollywood Reporter* of November 6 said, "Maya Angelou is breaking the ice at Twentieth Century-Fox where she is the first black woman to be signed by a major production company to a writer-producer contract. She has a children's series set for CBS, a telefeature for NBC, and a sitcom in development."[8]

Angelou had received a request from CBS to develop the children's series mentioned above as a five-part program. The NBC project was *Sisters*, a telefeature that she wrote and coproduced. NBC's Peter Andrews called the film "Maya's black-Americanization of Chekhov." But the network was not yet ready for a black topic.

Sisters sat finished and waiting in the can for *four years* before it aired. By the time she left Los Angeles, Angelou was rightfully livid. She had coproduced and written a film that represented the first time any network or studio had risked a million and a half dollars in a black woman's hands. And yet

she was told that in order to get the director the executive producer wanted she would have to agree to share the coproducer title. She said okay, fine. Then suddenly, after the "answer print" came back on the series, the producer informed her that he wanted sole credit, "or they would take me to the Writers Guild so that he could have half of the writing credits. . . . I had written an entire screenplay by the time he came along."[9]

Angelou believes that Hollywood has some erroneous ideas about the black American. "The 'blaxploitation' films of the early seventies were not black films. They had nothing to do with being black. For the most part, they looked inside the black community, found the lowest elements and emboldened them. Distorted them! The result of that distortion has been a confirmation in the minds of most whites that our people are thugs and exploiters—loveless, lustful and shallow as hell."[10]

A true renaissance woman, Maya Angelou is an actress, composer, dancer, poet, novelist, screenwriter, and producer.

She was also the first black streetcar conductor in San Francisco.

MAYA ANGELOU

1972 Georgia, Georgia (Script, Score)
1978 I Know Why the Caged Bird Sings (TV)
1980 Sisters (TV)

Euzhan Palcy

Euzhan Palcy became the first black woman filmmaker to direct a feature-length film through the Hollywood system. The film, A DRY WHITE SEASON (1989), is, like Palcy herself, controversial, important, uncompromising.

Palcy knew from the age of ten that she

wanted to be a filmmaker. And if any aspiring director had reasons to believe all the odds were against her, it was Palcy. As a black woman born in Martinique, there was not only an absence of the film industry in her province, but the theater industry as well. The American films she saw bore no relationship or resemblance to the people she knew, either in color or in custom. By the age of fourteen, Palcy was angry. And the anger propelled her to become a filmmaker.

"I became a director out of rage. When I was very young, I was upset about the way black people were portrayed in American films."[1] She saw her task as no less than a mission: to tell the truth about her people on the screen.

"I don't stop," she said when I spoke with her in 1989, "I don't give up. I don't know what that means. I fight and I move, and at the end, when you do that relentlessly, you get something."

Although the indomitable Euzhan Palcy decided on her career early, her father, a supportive man whom she calls the first feminist she ever knew, made her promise to take a more secure route first and complete her baccalaureate. This she did, studying French literature, and later filmmaking at the Sorbonne.

But here we flash back to a nineteen-year-old Euzhan Palcy, still in Martinique. With no film industry to turn to, Palcy was instead writing poetry and songs. She showed enough promise to have the local TV station offer her a weekly poetry show. She had already released an album of children's songs that did well commercially.

"When I was still at the television station, I wrote this drama, *La Messangere*. I had no cinema training, you know. I bought some books from France. But I wrote it from my head and heart. I proposed to the station's director that we do this film. Well, there had never been a film made before in Martinique. The boss of the station didn't want to do it. After all, it was the first West Indian drama; no one knew what it was.

"But we did it anyway. Everybody paid for it. People were so excited, they worked on it for free. And finally when it was done, it brought a lot of attention to the station and the boss said, 'Great! I knew it was a good idea.'"

So after Palcy pioneered the first film-making venture ever undertaken in Martinique, she knew it was time to leave home for a real apprenticeship. "I knew I had to go to Paris. But I was so afraid. Paris was 5,000 kilometers away. So far!"

She took the very competitive examination to enter the Sorbonne, where only about twenty-five of every five hundred applicants are accepted, and majored in French literature. This was done mostly to appease her father. On the side, however, Palcy was getting her real education.

"Paris was the first opportunity I had to meet Africans. There was no cultural exchange between West Indians and Africans, you know. No relations."

Palcy worked as an assistant editor on films with young African directors who were shooting in France. She also spent her free moments writing, rewriting, and rewriting what would become SUGAR CANE ALLEY (1983), the first draft of which she wrote when she was seventeen.

In 1975 she met the man who would become her godfather—Palcy's own term—François Truffaut. Truffaut's daughter, Laura, had heard great things about this young, bright, ambitious woman who so boldly claimed that she wanted to be a director! Palcy had decided at age fourteen that she wanted to make a film based on the novel, *Black Shack Alley* (1974) by a Martinique author, Joseph Zobel. Laura told Palcy to give her the script. She promised that if she liked it she would pass it on to her father. The next thing Euzhan knew: "He called me! I couldn't believe it. *Truffaut* called *me*. I remember the man, with his intense small beady eyes. Both he and his assistant at the time, **Suzanne Shiffman**, were very kind. They loved my script. He showed me how to rework it."

Truffaut's encouragement gave Palcy the belief and determination she needed to go to battle. Even with his help, it would take three long years to raise the funds she needed to make LA RUE CASES NEGRES (*Sugar Cane Alley*).

The buoyant, beautiful, moving piece was completed with glory in 1983. It won a Silver Lion at the Venice Film Festival, and **Darling Legitimus**, the seventy-year-old actress who plays the grandmother, won a Best Actress Award. It was called

a simple, unpretentious, deeply human tale, one which . . . because of the hard circumstances behind its making, and the love and adulation it's inspired in its audiences, has become something of a legend.[2]

Palcy begins the film with the dedicatory words, "For all the Black Shack Alleys of the world." She explains that a black shack alley is the ghetto, the poorest section of the town, and insists, as she does with her latest film, A DRY WHITE SEASON, that "the film is universal . . . because there are many themes which have nothing to do with color. Dignity, passion, struggle, love."

After SUGAR CANE ALLEY Hollywood beckoned Euzhan Palcy.

"They called me," Palsy said, "and very few black women directors are called to Hollywood. But they wanted me to do their stories. I said, I appreciate your interest, but I am a black filmmaker. Your other white filmmakers can do those stories."

After SUGAR CANE ALLEY, Palcy decided she wanted to do something about apartheid. "I also knew that Hollywood would not do a film about black people unless the main character was a white man."

She chose as her second film a story based on a novel by André Brink. The protagonist, Ben Du Toit (played with sensitive skill by Donald Sutherland), is a wealthy, white South African, sheltered from the horrific realities going on just outside his fenced-in walls. He comes of age in the middle of his life when racial injustice shakes the very roots of his existence. For Palcy, such blatant racial injustice hit elsewhere.

"I knew as a black filmmaker I now needed to do something about apartheid. I also know that no one wants to put any

money into a film about black people. Black in Hollywood isn't commercial. Black in France was uncommercial until SUGAR CANE ALLEY came out and proved the contrary."

She found an ally in producer **Paula Weinstein**—daughter of the pioneer producer, **Hannah Weinstein**.

At first, they took the project to Warner Brothers. But they didn't see eye to eye. Despite the press coverage and the ensuing controversy, CRY FREEDOM (1987) had bombed at the box office. That experience chilled the studio's feelings toward making another movie about South Africa. Next, Palcy and Weinstein tried MGM where they found a sympathetic ear with Alan Ladd and the film had a home.

Marlon Brando thought the film so important that he ended a nine-year period of seclusion (since THE FORMULA in 1980). Palcy now finds herself in the unique position of being the only black woman ever to direct a feature of all-star caliber.

Although Palcy concedes that the film focuses on a white man's story, "without the black characters, the white characters do not exist. There is no story." For those who criticized the focus on white men in A DRY WHITE SEASON, Palcy vigilantly says:

I hate the idea that every time you talk about something like Vietnam, you have to have a white hero. But I want to scream to people who say this; they should write more, and they should join me and fight against those who have the money and the power to produce a movie.[3]

MGM did not have a clear vision on how to market the film. In the public's mind it rode in on the tails of the much less focused CRY FREEDOM. As a result, this skillful, moving film did not do well at the box office. But box-office results are not always an accurate barometer of a movie's worth.

Nevertheless, Euzhan Palcy has carved a place for herself as a director not to be ignored.

"I want to talk about the black struggle in my movies. But that doesn't mean my movies are only for black people. It also doesn't mean I won't have white characters in my scripts. I just want human beings, without any color."

Euzhan Palcy is a "fighter on a mission." We are fortunate, too, that she's made an early start. Euzhan Palcy may prove to be the first black woman filmmaker in the world to develop a body of work in feature films.

EUZHAN PALCY

1983 Sugar Cane Alley
1989 Dry White Season, A

Ruby Oliver

She was born in a ghetto of Chicago where, she said, money was never an obstacle. At the age of twenty-three after she was honorably discharged from the Navy, **Ruby Oliver** decided it was high time she did something crucial with her life. To this pioneer, it did not mean moviemaking. It meant taking the money she saved from working in a Chicago post office, going to the Small Business Administration for a three-thousand-dollar loan, and opening her first of what was to be five day-care facilities.

Much later, at the age of forty-eight, after twenty-three years in the day-care business, Ruby Oliver became the first black American woman to direct, write, produce, and sing in a 35mm feature. The movie is entitled LOVE YOUR MAMA (1990).[1]

"Everyone is always saying how hard it is to make a movie. The only thing I found hard was having to fire one crew and to hire another. It slowed down my shooting schedule."[2]

Ruby Oliver began as a pioneer in another field. She was one of the first students in the first day-care class taught at Kennedy King College, eventually becoming one of the best day-care operators in the business. Working as a businesswoman in day-care for the next twenty-three years gave Ruby credibility with business people, bankers, and investors; it made the raising of money just another routine problem of the kind Oliver was used to solving. The *real* problems in life as far as Ruby Oliver is concerned, have to do with day-care, with children, with raising the level of consciousness in this country so that young girls will avoid teenage pregnancy. Oliver has too much compassion and life experience to allow a town called Hollywood to dazzle her.

"Making a film is all right," says Ruby, "but I really feel that my contribution is in changing the educational system. If I gave something to help the day-care system, I'll feel like I really did something."

At the age of forty, Ruby Oliver went back to college. She went to a fine arts school in her home town, Columbia College in Chicago, where she majored in video and film directing with an emphasis in screen writing. She retired from full time day-care in 1986 and graduated eight years after she started at Columbia in June 1988—a year prior to completing the direction of her first feature.

LOVE YOUR MAMA (1990) focuses on the pregnancy of a teenage girl—a girl who has her own dreams of owning a day-care center someday, until a sudden pregnancy blights her dreams. "My film is a tribute to mothers," says Oliver, who at this writing (July 1990) is experiencing a typical problem for independent filmmakers—finding a distributor for the film.

"I've been told the most idiotic things by

people in high places like, 'Black people do not like films that don't include excessive sex, violence and vulgar language.' Isn't that the most ridiculous stereotype? What is wrong with this world? And if you look at the films that Hollywood puts out with black people in them, they only have sex, violence, and vulgar language. So they perpetuate this viscious cycle."

She goes on: "I've also been told that we'll have trouble getting the film out because it's not a black exploitation film. But my film isn't just for black people. It's about people with problems and problems don't have a color. They hit everyone! My thing is not necessarily writing about the black struggle. That's not what I do."

The pioneer **Kathleen Collins** had similar feelings of exasperation when her film LOSING GROUND (1982) was interpreted as critical of the black experience. Oliver had run into such criticism when some black viewers saw the villain of the film was the father who also happens to be a black male. But Oliver is not interested in dividing the world by showing our differences on the screen. Her goals, in fact, are quite the opposite. Oliver defends her piece:

"Any good screenplay must have a beginning, a middle, and an end. It must have a protagonist and a villain. Not everyone in the film is going to be seen in a positive light. You can't do this to please everyone. You just have to do your work and listen to yourself."

The ninety-minute film cost Oliver just under a million dollars to produce.

In a phone interview, Oliver said: "You can always get money if you have money. It doesn't matter what you look like or what you wear, banks will always let you borrow against assets. I walked into one bank I wanted to shoot in in Chicago and said, 'I have so much money running through here every month that I just bet you're gonna let me use this as a location to shoot.' He

looked up my account and said, 'I bet you're right.' I paid my dues businesswise. I had twenty years of business respect from the community. So there was really very little risk. I was luckier than those people who have to stop shooting because they run out of money. That wasn't the hard part."

The hard part, she said, was hiring a crew that would listen to her as they would listen to a director, which is what she was; a crew that wouldn't try and dupe her by taking twelve hours to set up a scene that should have taken three. Oliver had gone to the cameraman's union in search of a DP (director of photography). They assigned her someone who also brought along the rest of the crew.

"The problem was that they were a union crew trying to do a nonunion shoot. They were so negative. They treated me like I wasn't there. Finally, when they began to take forever to light an easy scene, they began to cost me money. I understand my pocketbook! And they just priced themselves right out of my movie."

Most likely, the crew remembered who the director of the film really was when they found themselves fired one morning.

With a new crew Ruby Oliver completed shooting on her movie in only six weeks.

"It's ironic," she says. "I'm beginning to get this press attention because I made a movie. What really excites me is holding a child in my arms who is thrilled because he just graduated from kindergarten. Our values are all screwed up."

And she adds: "We're going to stay planted right here in Hollywood until they open the doors and take my movie. And they will. I'll make it because I have staying power."

RUBY OLIVER

1990   Love Your Mama

Christine Choy

Christine Choy has made her name in America as a documentary filmmaker, and says that she doesn't really like to distinguish between documentary, nonfiction, and fiction. "To me what's important is not the form itself, it's how you tell a story and how you are either able to—with that particular story—influence people, raise a question, or change people's minds."[1]

She has apparently succeeded, if not in changing people's minds, then most definitely in raising poignant questions. Among the many films that Choy has made that focus on the Chinese-American question, her eighty-two minute documentary WHO KILLED VINCENT CHIN? (1988), made in conjunction with filmmaker Renée Tajima, was nominated for an Oscar. It focuses on the 1982 clubbing of a Chinese-American engineer, Vincent Chin, who was beaten to death with a baseball bat by a Caucasian Chrysler foreman, Ronald Ebens. Although Ebens pleaded guilty, he never spent a day in jail. The Asian-American community saw the case as a prime example of racial bigotry and violence.

This important film has been called RASHOMON in style.[2] The *New York Times* said the film "so successfully analyzed this sudden, sad, fatal confrontation that almost everything except the Big Mac becomes implicated in the events."[3]

In a comment you would most likely expect from a filmmaker who had made a fictional narrative, Choy said, "The film is not based on logic but on emotion. Once you respond to the emotion, we hope you'll find the logic."[4]

Christine Choy, who supports her filmmaking through teaching film at New York University, originally began in the world as **Chai Ming Huei**, daughter of a Korean father and a Chinese mother. In 1953, at the end of the Korean War, her father went back to Korea, leaving wife and daughter

in China. Christine would not see her father again for twelve years.

But in the meantime, her mother, out of necessity, learned about staunch independence. She passed the trait on to her daughter. At the onset of the Cultural Revolution in China in the midsixties, mother and daughter found their way to Korea, and it was there that Chai Ming Huei also found her way to the movies. A high score on a difficult international proficiency examination gave her the opportunity to study movies in America.

Cut to 1976, when Choy was first beginning to figure out that she might want to become a filmmaker. The problem was, she didn't know how she could learn about film. "I trained in film by watching other people make films. There was no money to go to film school. But while I was bouncing around about whether or not to be a filmmaker, someone suggested I join the organization, Newsreel. . . . When I joined [the sixties ultraradical organization that produced a film a week] in 1971 I was the first nonwhite in the entire group."[5] Not too long after, Choy would become executive director of Third World Newsreel.

Her breakthrough film, FROM SPIKES TO SPINDLES (1976), was about Chinese migration from the West Coast to the East Coast. Although she faced many obstacles in making the film, "I came at the right time as an Asian woman—I was the only person who did a film like that." The rights were swiftly sold to PBS, and to scores of companies all over the world.

> So from then on I just began to make films, and most films I make deal with social change. Some people classify me as a "political filmmaker"—and I'm not sure that's a correct label. I always get classified as either one category or another. It started with "immigrant," later on became

"Asian" later on became "woman of color" or "minority"[6]

About "political filmmaking" Choy says:

Sometimes [the term is] very much associated with documentary, because people in this country look at a documentary basically as propaganda. . . . In order to sell more seats in the narrative film, you better put down some other forms. I like documentary and I also like narrative. The documentary is accessible because I'm basically a self-taught filmmaker. . . . Throughout more and more shooting you become more confident in terms of how to tell a story.[7]

An associate professor at NYU's Tisch School of Arts, Choy has also been a visiting professor at Cornell University. Aside from being nominated for an Oscar, her previous films have won first prize in the International Black Film Festival as well as an award for best subject matter at the Ann Arbor Film Festival in 1982 for TO LOVE, HONOR, AND OBEY.

CHRISTINE CHOY

1971	Dead Earth, The (Editor, Animator)
1973	Nigeria, Nigeria One (Editor)
1974	Teach Our Children (Director, Cinematographer, Editor)
1975	Fresh Seeds in a Big Apple (Codirector, Editor, Sound)
	Generation of the Railroad Builder (Director, Editor)
	In the Event That Anyone Disappears (Editor)
1976	From Spikes to Spindles (Producer, Director)
1977	History of the Chinese Patriot Movement in the U.S. (Director, Editor)

	North Country Tour (Director, Sound Recordist)
1978	Inside Women Inside (Executive Producer, Director, Cinematographer)
	Loose Pages Bound (Producer, Director)
	Dream Is What You Wake up From, A (Executive Producer)
1979	People's Firehouse Number 1 (Executive Producer)
	Percussion, Impression & Reality (Executive Producer)
1980	To Love Honor and Obey (Director, Cinematographer)
1981	American Writer's Congress, The (Unit Director)
	Bittersweet Survival (Producer, Director, Second Camera)
	Boy and Tarzan Appear in a Clearing (Unit Director, Camera)
	White Flower Passing (Director)
1982	Go Between (Producer, Director)
1982–83	Mississippi Triangle (Producer, Director, Cinematographer, Researcher)
1983	Fei Tein, Goddess in Flight (Director)
1984	Chronicle of Hope: Nicaragua (Producer)
	Namibia, Independence Now (Director)
1985	Monkey King Looks West (Director, Cinematographer)
1986	Permanent Wave (Director)
1987	Audre Lorde Story (Producer, Cinematographer)
	Haitian Corner (Producer)
	Making of the Sun City (Unit Director)
	Korean War, The
1988	Homes Apart, Two Koreas (Producer, Cinematographer, Interviewer)

	Shanghai Lil's (Director, Producer)	Best Hotel on Skid Row (Producer, Cinematographer, Director)
	Who Killed Vincent Chin? (Director, Cinematographer)	Fortune Cookie: The Myth of the Model Minority (Producer, Director)
1989	China Today (Director, Producer)	

Julie Dash

Money for independents is hard to come by at any cost. Many filmmakers get worn down in the process, compromising and conforming their vision to that of their stockholders just to get a picture made.

Julie Dash says she has no intention of compromising for anyone. Watering down her vision for DAUGHTERS OF THE DUST, to make it digestible for white mainstream America, just isn't her style.

DAUGHTERS OF THE DUST, a feature in progress, is a turn-of-the-century tale about a fictional Gullah family. "Gullah" refers to the Georgia Sea Islands just off the coast of South Carolina. It will be Dash's first feature and her third film. Her FOUR WOMEN (1978) was a "choreopoem" based on the **Nina Simone** song of the same title. DIARY OF AN AFRICAN NUN (date unknown) was a film made from the **Alice Walker** short story, and ILLUSIONS (1982) was a ground-breaking half-hour short about a black woman executive in Hollywood passing for white in the 1940s.

Julie Dash was raised in the Queensridge Projects. She happily admits that she is a daydreamer. Her active imagination often won her nothing but trouble, such as being accused of plagiarism for a story she wrote in the third grade. Dash's mother stood up for her daughter and straightened out Julie's teacher. Such encouragement and faith, says Dash, were powerful contributors to her confident belief in the possibility of creating the impossible—such as a feature film where all the leading characters with the exception of one are black women.

Her inspiration to become a filmmaker began in 1971 at the Studio Museum in Harlem. Dash got her training by picking up the equipment and doing. Gary Tate of the *Village Voice* writes that

Dash's personal demeanor suggests both dreamy-eyed fabulist and focused professional. Her attitude on the set is casual but only because her preproduction work is meticulous. . . . Day charts detail the entire two-week shoot [her grant-monies only carrying her part way through production]. Once Dash sets up her shots, and sound and camera get rolling, the action plays until the takes sync with her vision. Her mood on the set is chillmaximus.[1]

The content of DAUGHTERS OF THE DUST is ground-breaking material for the screen as well.

The young adults of the Gullah family are preparing for a mass exodus north and a junking of their Gullah heritage in their diaspora to industrialized America.[2]

And, interspersed within the linear plot line,

there are several dream sequences. . . . Ancestral spirits visit the living to chase away their inner demons—an Africanist switch on conventional film. . . . There's also an offscreen rape which Dash uses symbolically to probe black women's wombs—investigating their powers of regeneration and the psychic scars left by forced miscegenation. Like [Tony] Morrison's novels, the script for DAUGHTERS . . . is a testimony to the secret celebrations and packed-away sorrows of African-American women.[3]

It's the sort of project to make every filmmaker pray that Dash will stick steadfast and oh-so-true to her vision.

To make a film is challenging enough. But to give oneself the added challenge of doing a period piece like DAUGHTERS OF THE DUST (with the huge expense it adds to the budget because of costumes, scenery, and period props) is enough to turn an already-pioneering spirit into a saint if she succeeds.

To date, Ms. Dash has received fifty thousand dollars in grant monies. Barely enough to do full-scale period production. The budget crunch requires Dash not only to play director, but wardrobe mistress and makeup artist as well. And she is not the only crew member pulling a triple load.

With the organizations that have the endowments to dole out the meaningful dollars to independents, Julie Dash hasn't had a lot of luck. The Corporation for Public Broadcasting said no, on the grounds that her script was "too mystical."[4] They suggested that her revisions be geared more toward what white Midwesterners could at least understand. The National Endowment for the Humanities, although it praised Dash's research and her endorsements from respected Gullah scholars, rejected her on the grounds that the film was too much an "intellectual exercise" and beyond the comprehension of prime-time viewers.[5]

Gary Tate has written, "What's really operating here is a fear of black people making political statements grounded in an autochthonous reading of black culture."[6]

Dash herself says,

The image of the black revolutionary was neutralized through caricature during the blaxploitation era. He was made to seem weak and a phony. Now there exists a fear of black people using our culture to make statements in code. It's the modern variation on the fear that led slaveholders to take our drums away.[7]

Tate goes on to comment: "What Dash has come up against here is an arrogance fortified by what appears to be the common belief that blacks' self-knowledge is like no knowledge at all."[8]

In typical pioneer fashion, Julie Dash doesn't know what the word *defeat* means. "I know I'm going to finish. I'm worried about other things, but not that piece of it."[9]

JULIE DASH

1978	Four Women
(Date unknown)	Diary of an African Nun
1982	Illusions
(Not yet released)	Daughters of the Dust

SHORT TAKES

♦ ♦ ♦

Peaches Jones (1952–1988)

Peaches Jones was one of the first black stuntwomen to be actively employed in Hollywood features. She began her career in 1968, around the same time as two other black stuntwomen, **Louise Johnson** and **Evelyn Coffee**.

According to **Jodie David**, a stuntwoman who began her career in 1971, who studied with Jones, and who is currently one of only four black stuntwomen in Hollywood, "Peaches won the respect of everybody in the business as a trained, competent professional. She deserves the title, 'pioneer,' hands down."[1]

The Pasadena-born Jones owed her unusual career to her father, Sam Jones, Sr. Mr. Jones was not a full-time stuntman, but he began working out with twenty-eight men and three women—a troupe that would later become the Black Stuntman's Association. Jones was sixteen at the time, tagged along, and made sure she was tossed around in every tumble. Soon, as an article in *Ebony* tells it, "She was daring falls off a high banister of a baseball diamond in Pasadena."[2]

"I'd climb up there and stand on the railing about forty feet up," said Jones, "and someone would pretend to shoot me off and I'd go flying to land on the mat below."[3] She claimed that her tomboy origins eliminated any fear she might have known.

Never once injured, she was "dragged by horses, thrown from horses, stomped on by horses, tossed from high buildings and beaten up in more stage fights than you can count."[4]

Jones studied exclusively with men and boys. Writer Walter Price Burrell says, "As might be expected, many a male ego has been deflated when she wound up doing a stunt better than he. In fact, boys have nearly busted their britches trying to outdo 'the girl.' "[5]

Ebony described her as a woman "with delicate skin, tapered fingers, an infectious smile, freckles, fetching hazel eyes, and a disarming naïveté. Jones appears at first to be anything but a daring, professional stuntwoman. But her inquisitive, willing-to-try-anything attitude is soon apparent." Sidney Poitier was so pleased with her work on BUCK AND THE PREACHER (1971) that he added stunts for her in the film, and gave her a small acting role.

Peaches Jones died tragically of an illness

at the young age of thirty-six. She leaves a proud legacy for other black women to follow. Current black women doing stunt work include **Jodie David, Kim Washington, Sharon Schaeffer**, and **Joy Hooper**.

PEACHES JONES

1969   Halls of Anger
1970   Strawberry Statement
1971   Buck and the Preacher

Michelle Parkerson

"Black people are so grounded in the reality of survival," says **Michelle Parkerson**, "we see through the glamour and the glitz."[1]

A filmmaker and poet committed to unearthing black women's history and immortalizing it for the screen, Parkerson has been one of the few black women filmmakers successful in getting her images out internationally. BUT THEN, SHE'S BETTY CARTER (1980), was featured in the 1981 Berlin Film Festival, and was aired on PBS. She turned to video for her next project, GOTTA MAKE THIS JOURNEY: SWEET HONEY IN THE ROCK (1983); it featured the radical black women's a cappella ensemble. It aired on PBS and won a blue ribbon at the prestigious American Film Festival. STORMÉ: THE LADY OF THE JEWEL BOX (1987) featured the multiracial female impersonators of the Jewel Box Revue.

> What black women are doing is rendering voices or visions that [have] been invisible or mutilated. We are unearthing a lot of history. Many of us are about the business of documenting black women's experience. . . . There has been a recognition—not large, and not in proportion to the talent of black women filmmakers—but I think there is beginning to be a recognition of our presences behind the camera.[2]

A self-identified lesbian, Parkerson called STORMÉ a coming-out film for herself.

> My other films have dealt with personalities, some of whom were lesbian women, but that was not an overt theme. This time, it is the foundation.[3]

Michelle Parkerson

Her most recent film-in-progress is a documentary about the poet, **Audre Lorde**, whom Parkerson calls "the beacon of black lesbian feminist thought."[4]

Parkerson serves as cochair for the National Coalition of Black Lesbians in Washington, DC, where she makes her home. She is a visiting instructor in the Women's Studies Department of the University of Delaware, as well as at Temple University's School of Communications. She also teaches at Howard University's Department of Radio/TV/Film.

Early in her filmmaking career, 1975–82, Parkerson supported her independent endeavors by working as a video engineer for NBC-TV in Washington. She was the 1989 recipient of the Mayor's Art Award for excellence in an artistic discipline.

Dubbing herself "a filmmaker of alternative vision," she says,

I don't subscribe to the word "minority." Black identity is the foundation of my work . . . but I want to highlight the diversity of black people, black women.[5]

MICHELLE PARKERSON

Ayoka Chenzira

I'm not much into digestive cinema where you sit down and digest your dinner. I want people to be on their feet testifying.
—Ayoka Chenzira

A dancer who also came up through the ranks of still photography, **Ayoka Chenzira** says she took to film and video because of a natural inclination to want "her photographs to move." She found herself enrolled in New York University Film School where "most of the people in my class were white men whose fathers were union cameramen. . . . People tried to pigeonhole me into editing because, you know, women are supposedly good with their hands."[1]

But Chenzira would have none of it. She became "a one-woman show," researching, writing, directing, editing, and marketing her own work. One interviewer, astounded by her capacities said, "I'm almost afraid to ask how you do all those things." "I'm poor," remarked Chenzira. And yet she said that learning how to do all film's varied crafts proved an invaluable training ground. At this writing she is in the midst of a feature where she is looking forward to the division of labor that will free her up to work solely on directing.

Chenzira is probably best known for a short, humorous visual treasure entitled HAIRPIECE: A FILM FOR NAPPY-HEADED PEOPLE (1982).

I was very concerned with the question of black women in this country and self-image aesthetics. If you look at all the commercials that come out and tell you how to fix yourself, they are all based on the idea that there is something wrong with you. And so, having a child, these things became very glaring and I think that's a part of HAIRPIECE. HAIRPIECE is funny, but it comes from a position of real anger.[2]

The pioneer **Kathleen Collins** found HAIRPIECE important because of its redemptive nature—"important in that her desire to reclaim black women, in a sense, reaffirms black women of their own beauty."[3]

A later work, SECRET SOUNDS SCREAMING: THE SEXUAL ABUSE OF CHILDREN (1982), a thirty-minute video piece, had people standing in the doorways and aisles at the Chicago Women in the Director's Chair festival. The idea for the piece arose when she was working at a hospital and met a four-year-old child who had gonorrhea of the mouth and throat.

My own child was six months old, and it scared me so bad I knew if I didn't find a way to release this fear and this anger, I would be real hard to deal with. So the sex-abuse piece came out of a desire to know this was not going to happen to my child.[4]

Once black women actually make their movies, distribution usually becomes a major problem. Chenzira was asked if Hollywood came knocking, would she go?

It depends on who knocked and what they wanted. I never really had a strong desire to work in Hollywood, because I always saw it as a world where everyone was a municipal employee. However, I am very interested in Hollywood distribution because when I go to fourteen countries in Africa and all they know about black people in America is what they get through Hollywood-distributed films, you've got to look twice at that.[5]

AYOKA CHENZIRA

1979 Syvilla: They Dance to Her Drum
1982 Hairpiece: A Film for Nappy-Headed People
Secret Sounds Screaming: The Sexual Abuse of Children
Flamboyant Ladies Speak Out
1986 5 out of 5
1988 Lure and the Lore, The
1989 Zajota and the Boogie Spirit

Saundra Sharp

I had heard that people are either fanatically video people or fanatically film people, and rarely in between. Once I got into film, I understood it. I am a film person. I want to pick it up. I want to touch it. I want to lay it over there and look at it and move it over here. And then get up and get a glass of water and come back and walk around the room and look at it and think about it. And then put it back on the Movieola.
—Saundra Sharp
Black Film Review

Saundra Sharp

Originally an actress, **Saundra Sharp** decided to enroll in Los Angeles City College to sharpen her knowledge of video. Instead, the result was that she became fanatical about filmmaking. Her five-minute film, BACK INSIDE HERSELF, won first prize at the 1984 Black American Cinema Society Competition. It features a made-up, bewigged woman who, by the end of the piece, rejects all images thrust at her from the outside.

Sharp then set about using the funds she had won from her first film for her second. She raised enough money to shoot the film, but faced real problems when the acting money she usually counted on dried up. (And it dried up because of her involvement with the Black Anti-Defamation Coalition, which she helped form in 1980 to protest the NBC miniseries *Beulahland*.)

As an actress, there were certain roles she would not accept. For the 1984 movie CALAMITY JANE she rushed down to read for the script, but when she got there she found it was a "mammy" role. "I just sat there and cried," Sharp said. . . . For the next year I concentrated on my film work."[1]

She did manage to finish her short film LIFE IS A SAXOPHONE (1985). All the money she raised, Sharp said, came from black people. No grant money found its way into the film. She managed to do the entire film on a twenty-five-thousand-dollar budget. As **Ayoka Chenzira** once pointed out, "It is politically very dangerous to believe that the only way to make films is to have a huge budget. That kind of thinking is pushing blacks out of the market."[2] SAXOPHONE has won awards from festivals worldwide.

Sharp says that in her work she wants to continue the message that black women have incredible power, yet

> very often we are talked into subverting it, or concealing it, in order not to offend our men, . . . or white folks, or whatever. In order to protect our children. And I feel that through film we lay out some road maps to move beyond that.[3]

PICKING TRIBES (1988) deals with "a daughter of the forties struggling to find an identity between her Black American and Native American heritages."[4] The film had its world premiere at the National Black Arts Festival's Black Cinematheque in Atlanta in November 1988, was shown at the Women in Film Festival in Cretil, France in March 1988, won First Prize in the Black Talkies on Parade festival in Los Angeles, and won the Paul Robeson Award in the Animation category of the Newark Black Film Festival.

Historian Tom Stempel says, "Technically and artistically it's a real jump ahead for Saundra, and should lay to rest any lingering doubts that either women and/or women of color cannot handle technically and artistically sophisticated films."[5]

SAUNDRA SHARP

1984   Back Inside Herself
1985   Life is a Saxophone
1988   Picking Tribes

Alile Sharon Larkin

Alile Sharon Larkin has made several films. Among them, YOUR CHILDREN COME BACK TO YOU (1979) depicts a little girl torn between Western and African values, and A DIFFERENT IMAGE (1981) about the destructive aspects of sexism.

> I am part of the independent black cinema movement. I believe it is important for black people to control their own image. . . . It is important that progressive and aware black people keep a check on Hollywood, but we must continue to build our own institutions.[1]

"There seem to be two schools among independents," says Larkin.

> Wait until you have all the money or shoot what you can and when you can. I shoot when I can. I apply for grants as a yearly and painful ritual.
>
> I must work full-time outside film to support not only myself but my film work as well. . . . I also fund my films through loans, small grants, community raffles, awards, in-kind services, and family support.[2]

ALILE SHARON LARKIN

1979   Your Children Come Back to You
1981   Different Image, A

Madeline Anderson

In the 1960s, **Madeline Anderson** was one of a select handful of women of color to become a film editor and then move on to directing. Her film on hospital workers, I AM SOMEBODY (1965), "was an award-winning prototype for labor organizing."[1]

Anderson directed many episodes for *Sesame Street*, and *The Electric Company*, and was the first black female producer at NET (National Educational Television, prior to PBS), as a part of the "Black Journal" documentary team.

Forgotten pioneers like Anderson were responsible for paving the way for women of color to begin seeing themselves in their own image.

Eloice Gist

Although there were small, all-black film companies that flourished in the silent days and in the 1920s such as the studio of Oscar Micheaux, it is tough to find a woman among the lot. This is probably due to the fact that although film was a wide-open medium before it codified into a profit-making industry, it was still basically a playground for the white middle class. With all the other chores that society loaded onto black women, filmmaking was unfortunately not one of them.

Thanks to **Michelle Parkerson**, **Eloice Gist** has been unearthed and brought to light. Gist, according to Parkerson, was a traveling evangelist in the rural South during the Depression. She scripted, produced, and "exhibited her self-style revivalist films to stir the faithful."[1]

Frances Williams

In 1943 **Frances Williams** became the first black woman to attend film school in the United States at the University of Southern California. She was lucky enough to tour the USSR and be inspired by the work of Eisenstein, and **Esther Shub**. Said Carroll Parrott Blue,

> Frances Williams . . . was a strong force in finishing SALT OF THE EARTH, in 1952. She now appears on *Frank's Place*, and television commercials to make a living. When Frances sees us [other black women filmmakers], her eyes sparkle, jumping out of her old and crippled body. She greets all of us equally with her, "Hello there, my little babies." I meet the courageous eyes of **Euzhan** [**Palcy**] and realize now that Frances greets herself in meeting all our eyes. Our heritage makes us a real family.[1]

·V·

REEL WOMEN
PRODUCERS

It took longer to make one of Mary's contracts than it
did to make one of her pictures.
                    —Sam Goldwyn on **Mary Pickford**

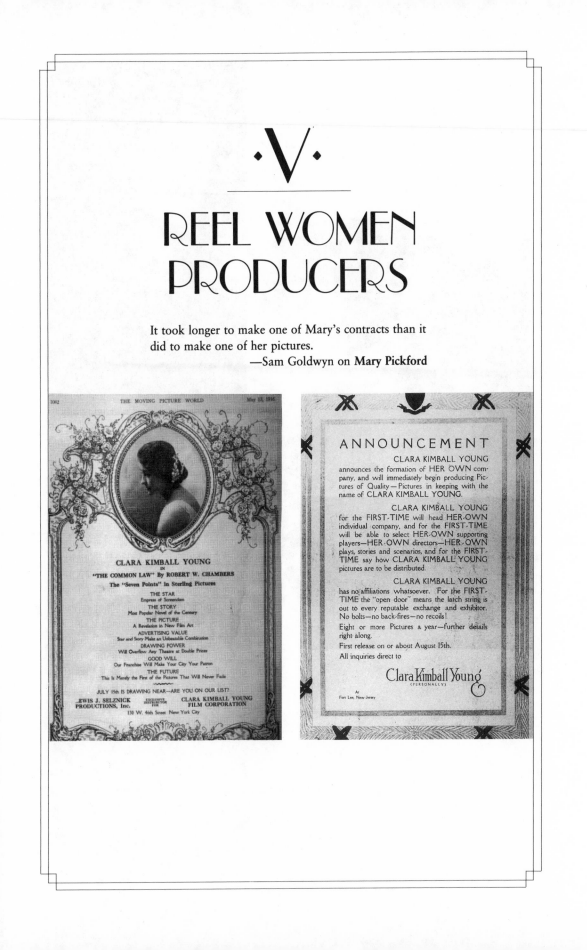

Sherry Lansing

Virginia Van Upp

Dawn Steel

PREVIEW

◆ ◆ ◆

Producing is one of those ambiguous umbrella terms that no one ever seems to know what it means. Producing is problem solving, plain and simple. How do you get from A to B within budget?

There are two kinds of producers. Depending on the size of the production, this may turn out to be one and the same person. The *executive producer* is the one who oversees the raising of the funds. This is either a person with multifaceted connections to money, or a wealthy benefactor who puts out the cash from her or his own pocket.

The *line producer* is the organizer, the person who takes care of the day-to-day obstacles that invariably come up in production—making sure the crew is there on time, making sure the director has everything she or he needs—the person to whom everyone else can turn with his/her problems for an authoritative decision.

Since consistent screen credit was not instituted until the twenties, and likewise the delineation of the individual crafts, it is hard to know exactly how many women producers actually existed in the early days of cinema.

As the first international star, and the first performer who consciously made a business (more like a multimillion-dollar enterprise) through the craft of acting, **Mary Pickford** was without a doubt among the first successful producers in history. She controlled the creative output of all of her pictures after 1919. **Clara Kimball Young, Alla Nazimova,** and a slew of other successful actresses followed suit, and reaped the benefit of their lucrative stance by opening their own studios and running the show.

After World War I the story changed considerably. The major studios swiftly put the little independents out of business. The flapper for all her daring independence was subtly encouraged not to carry it too far. She could be wild and free as long as she was still at home and financially dependent. Her main role in society's eyes was as material consumer.

All of the great female producer/directors were now outrightly denied their leverage. **Alice Guy Blaché** lost her studio and went back to France where, after making three hundred films, she was unable to find employment. **Lois Weber** went bankrupt, and ended her days testing starlets and playing script doctor. Many other women, like producer **Marion Fairfax,** simply disappeared from the industry and likewise from history.

By the midforties, Hollywood had solidly sunk into the philosophy that its raison d'être was as a business first and foremost. Artistic considerations came second and existed only as they pertained to box-office receipts. Even the broadminded generosity of Carl Laemmle's token intentions toward women at Universal were now but a memory. "Historic amnesia" had struck the movie industry with a heavy thud. It was a rare she-bird who made any kind of distinctive or authoritative dent in mainstream film between the twenties and the forties.

But early in 1945, **Virginia Van Upp** was made executive producer for Columbia pictures. Forgetting that only two decades before, women like **Lois Weber** and **Mary Pickford** had run their own studios and controlled the bulk of their own product, the *Los Angeles Times* of January 21, 1945, reported, "Virginia Van Upp has been granted more power over more films than any woman in cinema history."[1] The same article mistakenly declared **Lois Weber** as "the first woman director"—a typical example of how the power of print distorts and abuses fact. The unusually powerful and talented Van Upp was writing films like TOGETHER AGAIN (1944) and SHE WOULDN'T SAY YES (1945) (starring **Irene Dunne** and **Rosalind Russell** respectively), where the female role models were nothing less than full-fledged doctors and mayors of respected communities.

In the era when women on the screen were at the height of their ultimate goddess powers (who can forget the self-assured presences of **Roz Russell, Bette Davis, Eve Arden, Kate Hepburn**?) it is odd, somehow, that Van Upp was the only woman able to *be* one of those goddess behind the scenes in real life.

Not until 1975, when **Marcia Nasatir** became vice president of production at United Artists (**Paula Weinstein** was given the same title at Warner Bros.), and five years later, when **Sherry Lansing** took over the presidency at Twentieth Century-Fox, would women be allowed such awesome power again.

By 1989 Columbia's president, **Dawn Steel** was being called "the most powerful woman Hollywood has ever known."[2] Her name was, according to an article in *New York* magazine, "synonymous with brutality and terror."[3] Here was a woman who was better than the boys at their own game. But by 1990, **Dawn Steel** was out of her post.

A December 1990 article in the *Los Angeles Times* reported that women hold twenty-two vice presidential titles out of sixty-two presidential and vice presidential positions in the city's eight most influential studios.[4] Not one of those women, however, has the power to "green light" a project. And, as journalist Sharon Bernstein says, "as vice presidents, they are all working to find material to suit the taste of their bosses."[5] Hence, "of forty-five films released by the same eight studios during the four month period from June to September of [1990], only one . . . had female leads and told a woman's story."[6]

There is disagreement as to whether or not there is a correlation between the number of top female executives and the number of female-driven scripts that get produced. According to Bernstein for instance, Alan Ladd, Jr. has encouraged more women-centered vehicles (JULIA, AN UNMARRIED WOMAN), than either **Dawn Steel** or **Sherry Lansing**. Says Bernstein, "some women who have been vice presidents say they have had as much luck pushing women's stories with male bosses as with the rare female boss."[7] Could that be because the rare female boss, described as better than the boys at their own game, has arrived at where she is because she has also learned to *think* like one of the boys?

The likelihood of this correlation increases dramatically when one considers that the majority of women-centered films that actually get made in Hollywood are produced by women outside the studios (if not completely independently), and are only brought in "full-blown"—with script, star, and director all attached—to the studio late in the game. "Men are telling their stories from their perspective," says Marcy Kelly, the 1990 president of Los Angeles Women

In Film, "and women's voices are not being heard, period."[8]

Lucy Fisher, executive vice president of production at Warner Bros. as of 1990, has the highest rank of any current female vice president, and has the longest tenure of any woman in a similar position in the business. Fisher agrees that women executives "should foster relationships with women directors." She has said that "even though there is no woman at the top at Warner Bros., the presence of three female vice presidents has fostered an atmosphere of acceptance for films made by women."[9] On the con side of the issue, Roger Birnbaum, the 1990 president of production at Twentieth Century-Fox, said that he believes it is up to women to produce and write their own vehicals if they feel they want more women-oriented projects developed. "If an actress of the stature of **Meryl Streep** feels there are not enough good roles, she should develop some for herself," he said.[10]

As an author who has spent over five years unearthing the more-often-than-not unrecorded stories of women's lives in the movie industry, I have to agree with Birnbaum. Just as women have had to rewrite their own histories in order for the truth to be told, we can no longer wait and pray that "the other" will take care of our projected and imagined screen lives. Easy enough to say, but the point is, who will foot the bill?

"Ten years ago it would have made no difference [to have more women in decision-making positions]," says director **Martha Coolidge,** who spent five years trying but failing to get RAMBLING ROSE made in Hollywood. The coming-of-age story about a young woman finally ended up produced independently and will be released sometime in 1991. "But today," Coolidge continued, "it would make a big difference. Women are changing. Women in power are changing. The relationships they can rely on, and their attitude toward the future has changed."[11]

The issue is quality, not quantity. It isn't how many women in top-slotted jobs, but what exactly goes on in the minds of the women who have those jobs. Films like **Sherry Lansing's** BLACK RAIN cannot be credited as a great advancement in culturally projected images of women.

Even with all the years of experience of women at the helm, the question for women film producers and executives still remains, If a woman is given the ultimate power of a man, does that mean she also has to act like one?

Virginia Van Upp (1902–1970)

Virginia Van Upp was unusual for the era in which she was working. She was one of the very few women of the forties who was actually incorporating the gutsy, self-determined image of the woman on the screen into her own life. Never once did she deny or attempt to mask her gender as a public figure in the industry.

A description of her in the *Los Angeles Times* gives a good picture of the kind of pervasive, sexist societal attitudes she was up against.

Even sitting upright behind the imposing desk she inherited from Sidney Buchman, her predecessor, she seemed very small and feminine. Light-rimmed specs imparted the secretarial touch, so that for a moment you got the impression she was just waiting for the boss to return.[1]

The title of the article was, "Small Girl Makes Good in Big Film Job."

When the writer of the piece, Philip K. Scheuer, quotes her directly, he places her in a stance of defensiveness, with Scheuer, the "unbiased" journalist, as the innocent speaker of the facts.

> Mention the "woman's angle," and you put her on the defensive . . . "As for women not understanding how men react, [says Van Upp] that's nonsense. Why—it's a woman's job, learning how men react!" The nicest compliment I ever had was from Gene Kelly. We sent him my script of COVER GIRL, because he was dubious about a woman having been able to write one. Later he admitted to me that he couldn't tell it from the work of a man."[2]

Van Upp began as a child actress at the age of seven in Chicago, under the direction of **Lois Weber** at Universal, and of Thomas Ince. Her first role in about 1915 was in a vehicle starring William Desmond entitled SUDDEN GENTLEMAN. From that moment, and for the next thirty years, Virginia Van Upp went off salary only once, to give birth to a daughter, Gay.

Van Upp apprenticed herself in movies first as an actress, then as assistant casting director on BEN HUR (1926), assistant director on H. C. Witwer's FIGHTING BLOOD (1926) series, an actor's agent, a reader, cutter, writer/producer, to her eventual pinnacle post as executive producer with Columbia Pictures.

But mainly, she worked her way up as a writer, who had accrued her credits by collaborating with already-established names: J. P. McEvoy on THE PURSUIT OF HAPPINESS (1934), and Oscar Hammerstein II on SWING HIGH, SWING LOW (1937). By 1939, Van Upp was writing entirely on her own, and working with her favorite editor on pictures, **Eda Warren.**

By 1941, she had amassed a good many writing credits, placing her at the center of the film community. In 1944, her life would change dramatically. The president of Columbia Pictures, Harry Cohn, gave the go-ahead to Van Upp's script, COVER GIRL, a piece that seemed to be tailor-made to a contract player named **Rita Hayworth.**

With choreography by Gene Kelly, a score by Jerome Kern, and a script by Van Upp, the film spelled magic.

> It was GILDA that placed Rita in the uppermost ranks of film stars. The story was fashioned to her talents by Virginia Van Upp. Costarring was Glenn Ford, newly returned from the Marines. The combination was electric. Rita's principal number in which she simulated a striptease to 'Put the Blame on Mame,' was a miracle of sexual provocation.[3]

Hollywood had not dared such bold sexuality on the screen since the production code, and the film made Hayworth into a star. This bold move by Van Upp would single-handedly change the possibilities of what we would see on the screen from then on. America was not even *speaking* the "S-E-X" word as yet in the midforties. And here, Van Upp was showing it!

Watching Irene Dunne in Van Upp's TOGETHER AGAIN (1944) in the nineties, I thought at first that I had made a feminist archeological find! Dunne plays a small-town mayor who has taken over the duties from her five-years-deceased husband. She is the very model of groundedness, independence, and autonomy. Here is her soliloquy from the opening dialogue:

> FATHER-IN-LAW:
> It seems you're a big shot in your office and a nonentity in your own home. It isn't normal for a beautiful, young woman to have her sense of duty all swollen up like yours is. It isn't becoming.
> DUNNE
> Darling, you amuse me. You can't bear to see a woman alone and liking it. No man can. Instinctively, it terrifies them. You're a vanishing race and you know it. And the minute you lose your hold over us emotionally—Wow!
> So naturally, your platform must be "Husbands Are Necessary." And they're not really.

So stop bothering your nice old head about me because I'm *not* frustrated, I'm *not* to be pitied, I'm not anything but perfectly happy.

Hear, hear, Van Upp! Yet as the story went on, I lost courage. It seemed that this was formula Van Upp for formula letdown, with a message that goes something like: "If a woman labors under the assumption that she can function autonomously without a man for any extended period of time, she is deluding herself." Not to fear, the father figure, along with the help of Prince Charming, will assist her to see the error of her ways. After all, it is for her own good. She doesn't even know how unhappy she is! But *Fate* (or divine intervention), will do its classic intrusion to make sure that everything turns out "like it's supposed to."

So, "fatefully," she bumps into the prince who just happens to be a confirmed bachelor (until he meets her), unattached, available, and *determined* to win her heart. *Will she submit or no?* She usually gives a definite 'NO,' but that is the obstacle in the narrative.

Prince Charming and the father figure conspire to set some kind of trap until the woman feels (as in **Irene Dunne's** actual words): "I'm perfectly helpless." She has no choice but to succumb to her new fate—wife, mother, anonymous homebody figure, who must now give up her worldly responsibilities in order to fulfill her destinies as a woman.

Of course, secretly, she's ecstatic about it. After all, she has been "saved" from the necessity of having to create her own life.

In SHE WOULDN'T SAY YES (1945), **Rosalind Russell** is actually tricked into a marriage ceremony. In the Dunne film, she says to Charles Boyer as she is falling in love with him:

DUNNE
I can't look at you.
BOYER
Why not?

DUNNE
Because when I do, the most ridiculous thing happens to me—I stop thinking completely. And in my position, [as mayor] I can't afford to do that.

What she is saying is that, once she becomes truly a "woman" (and hence, a wife and mother), she is incapable of also maintaining her powers of rational thought and logical function in the outside world. These two energies are apparently biologically incompatible. As a woman, one can either think and be a "success" in the world (and be a eunuch), or one can be a whole, fulfilled (anonymous) human being as wife and mother. But in order to win this blessed state, she must abdicate her powers of reason.

We know which one she ultimately chooses, and she is more than thrilled to sacrifice her life. The fact that she feels this decision is out of her control—well, all the better. "I wouldn't want the responsibility of daring the supernatural," says Dunne near the end of the film. "I'll resign [as mayor] immediately! I'm free! I'm free!"

Ironically, in her own life, Virginia Van Upp was living a much more liberated existence than any of her creations. Happily married and with a child, Van Upp found herself in the executive dining room one day at lunch with Harry Cohn, the then president of Columbia Pictures and ten male producers. Bob Thomas tells the story:

One of the producers mentioned that a prominent producer had left his studio and hence might be available for the second-in-command at Columbia.

"Not interested," said Cohn. "I've made my choice."

"No kidding, Harry," said one of the men. "Can you tell us who it is?"

"Yes," answered Cohn. "It's Virginia."

The news was received in astonished silence.

That night, Cohn phoned Virginia to ask her who out of the crowd had wished her congratulations. One producer had. The next day, Cohn fired the other nine producers, and moved Virginia into a refurbished office next to his own. . . . She was the only second-in-command ever to have such proximity to Harry Cohn.

In 1946, Orson Welles found himself unable to direct, produce, author, and star in THE LADY OF SHANGHAI, and Cohn suggested Van Upp to produce and help to doctor the script.[4] Although not a commercial success, the film is considered one of Welles's great classics.

Interestingly, the studios would not allow a female force as powerful as Virginia Van Upp to invade their pearly gates again for another thirty-one years—not until 1975, when **Marcia Nasatir** would take over as vice president of production at United Artists.

VIRGINIA VAN UPP

1934	Pursuit of Happiness, The
1936	My American Wife
	Poppy
	Timothy's Quest
	Too Many Parents
1937	Swing High, Swing Low
1938	You and Me
1939	Honeymoon in Bali
1941	Come Live with Me
	One Night in Lisbon
	Virginia
1944	Cover Girl
	Impatient Years, The
	Together Again
1945	She Wouldn't Say Yes
1946	Gilda
1951	Here Comes the Groom
1952	Affair in Trinidad

Sherry Lansing

The plot line goes like this: Beautiful and smart, the young ingenue majors in theater at an impressive Midwestern college, marries a doctor, then suddenly escapes to Hollywood where she wants to try out her talent in the movies. She doesn't wait on tables like the other girls, she's got her standards to live up to, and so she decides instead to take a job as a substitute math teacher in the inner city where she's really needed.

She's only twenty-four, and just when her career is rising to a pinnacle, her marriage in tinseltown goes on the rocks. She divorces her young doctor and almost instantly becomes "The Max Factor Girl." Then the invariable TV and movie parts follow. Pretty soon—can you believe it?—she's playing the girl who walks off with John Wayne into the sunset.

But something is wrong. Her life is empty. She doesn't feel fulfilled. To everyone's surprise, she leaves her rising career behind and takes a job as a five-dollar-an-hour script reader. But once again, her new career rise is nearly meteoric. By 1975, she's an executive story editor at MGM. By 1977 she's senior vice president of production for Paramount. And by 1980, our ingenue, who is now thirty-five, is crowned the first woman president at the helm of a major studio in Hollywood history. Perhaps the last woman to fill these shoes was **Mary Pickford** in 1920 with United Artists—but that doesn't compare. That was, after all, her own company.

Sound like a good scenario for a Frank Capra movie? Maybe. But this is no celluloid adventure. This is real life. And it's the one that belongs to **Sherry Lansing**.

> When I got my first acting job, I walked on the set and I looked around and I said, I

don't want to be an actress. What everyone else is doing is so much more interesting. There were script supervisors and directors and cameramen that seemed to be having a lot more fun than I was. They seemed to be using their minds and their emotions in a way I was comfortable with. . . . Besides, I was a terrible actress.[1]

In 1977, when Sherry Lansing first ran into Michael Douglas in a studio meeting for THE CHINA SYNDROME, Meryl Gordon reported that the casting-couch mentality was still very much in evidence. Douglas's first thought was, "Who did [Lansing] sleep with to get into this room?" When [Lansing] proceeded to give her opinions about the script, Douglas quickly realized how good she was. "And she's pretty and sexy too," he is said to have thought. But even with the evidence of her talent, said Gordon, Douglas continued to keep Lansing in her place.[2]

Sherry Lansing is now an independent producer with her partner, Stanley Jaffe (KRAMER VS. KRAMER [1979], TAPS [1981]), and in spite of a sunshine image she, in the words of Swifty Lazar, "gets pictures done, people like to do business with her."[3] The movies she now independently sees to fruition are, in large measure, those that support sex, violence, and sins against women.

The $156-million box-office grossing FATAL ATTRACTION (1987) reinforces the image of woman-as-wicked-witch. Lansing's viewpoint, "I was trying to do a sympathetic movie about what happens if you lose your identity because someone left you. . . . Anyone could experience it."[4] THE ACCUSED (1988) skates a thin line of rape-as-exploitation. "It's a fine line, with this rape we show, between not being exploitive but also being brutally honest about the horror of a rape. I think we got it."[5] The film won an Academy Award for its star **Jodie Foster.**

Lansing insists that as far as she has come,

she has never been witness to signs of discrimination in the movie business.

> It would be very easy for me when I am frustrated about not being able to get a movie that I care desperately to get made to say, "Oh well, it's because they're prejudiced against women." In fact, it has nothing to do with it. I've never ever thought that my failures had anything to do with me being a woman. . . . If you have the passion, and the conviction and you really believe in something, eventually you will get it done.[6]

She responds to claims that not many women are directing in Hollywood by saying that it's equally difficult for the men in the guild (the Director's Guild). She attributes the lack of women technicians, notably camerawomen, to the fact that once women decide to enter the field and try to break into the union they will succeed.

> In order to improve the ratio of [female] cameramen . . . which there aren't a lot of at the moment, you have to have women who will consistently try to get into the union. . . .
>
> As more women become skilled in that area, they'll break down that barrier as well. . . .
>
> I've always believed that in this business there is only one God, and that God is talent, and that nobody will ever refuse a talented person.[7]

Lansing's Pollyanna view—if you work hard and you stick to it, you'll make it to the top, no matter what gender, color, or species you are—surprises many of the industry's women, such as **Brianne Murphy,** the first and still one of the only women directors of photography who has succeeded in becoming a member of the feature's union. Murphy's story about breaking the union barrier is becoming legendary.

Perhaps Lansing persists with her vision because of her own unusual meteoric rise.

Her reputation in the industry is rated by some as: "She doesn't want you not to like her."[8] She has been described by her friend, mentor, and twice-boss David Melnick (ROXANNE) as having "a unique ability to be both intelligent and unthreatening."[9] And if you are genderless and unthreatening in a studio system that has no desire to be challenged, is it any wonder Lansing has never run into discrimination?

Is she, like **Anita Loos** before her, another example of the rare, prolific woman who is happy just to be working and has no desire to rock the boat by using her power to transform the image of women on the screen? Like **Anita Loos** who perpetuated the stereotype of The Dumb Blond, Lansing sees no holes in the way the system is running where women are concerned.

In her vehicles, she too is doing her bit to perpetuate the worst of the stereotypes about women: woman-as-witch, or the well-she-asked-for-it girl. She does not threaten the system with a consciousness of transformation. For one thing, she does not believe that men and women see the world differently.

> I've always felt strongly that we are people. As people we're the product of our upbringing and environment. . . . And those are what make your sensibility. And I may be attuned to a man in responding to a script, or a woman. But I'm me, with my own taste. So Stanley and I don't have male/female, but Lansing and Jaffe sensibilities.[10]

Still, as a first, you're going to be subject to many arrows flying in the air. She is bright and talented at finding a "good" script (although the consciousness and politics in defining a "good" script over a "bad" script will vary widely), she showed great bravery in carving out the stance of role model when she had none of her own to follow:

"Everything I did as studio chief was accepted because there was nobody else to point to as a role model. I think that was really a great benefit as compared to trying to emulate somebody else and constantly trying not to be yourself . . . trying to adapt your own personality to what you think is proper.

"There's a quote I once gave to *Life* magazine. They asked me if I thought there would ever be a female president of a studio. And I said, Absolutely not. There never will be such a thing, but it's okay because we're very lucky to be doing the jobs that we are.

"Fortunately I had to eat those words. It was one of the times in life that I was happy to be wrong."[11]

Lansing paved the way for **Dawn Steel**, once called the most powerful woman Hollywood ever knew. As an inevitable target at the top, she has graciously smiled away the darts and criticisms that have been shot at her. And yet as writer Meryl Gordon put it, "Sherry Lansing, again on her way up in the male-dominated world of Hollywood, has proven that nice girls can finish first."[12] What she fails to say is, But only if Daddy thinks they're nice.

SHERRY LANSING

1984	Firstborn
	Racing with the Moon
1987	Fatal Attraction
1988	Accused, The
1989	Black Rain

Dawn Steel

Once they were known as "geishas." Pretty, unthreatening women, who may be in visible positions of power in Hollywood, but really they are allowed to be there because they serve up the wishes and desires of the men. "Their job is to look pretty, do script notes, provide men with the ability to be smart at meetings," says Lynda Obst,

> and when the tough stuff comes, leave it to them. Dawn was the first woman who defied that stereotype. She was not someone's daughter. She came up through merchandising—a man's route.[1]

As president of Columbia Pictures in 1987, **Dawn Steel** became the first woman in history to head a motion picture corporation, and the second woman after **Sherry Lansing** to hold such a powerful position in tinseltown. She was in charge of production, marketing, and distribution of not only all of Columbia Pictures product, but also their merger company, Tri-Star. Unlike **Sherry Lansing,** Dawn Steel was known as anything but a geisha. She was rough. She was nasty. She volleyed with the boys better than the boys at their own game. "If she was any more aggressive," said producer David Melnick (producer of FOOTLOOSE [1984], ROXANNE [1987]), "they would have to lock her up." Melnick nicknamed Steel "The Tank" because "she would just lower her head and charge through all of the red tape and bureaucracy. She's the most determined woman in the business."[2]

Why that kind of press draws bad marks for women when it's still fully acceptable for men is one of those mystifying cultural phenomena we have to live with.

After all, the "Steely Dawn" tales match with equal fervor those of the mythologized moguls of yesteryear—Louis B. Mayer, Sam Goldwyn, and the worst terrorist of all, Columbia's Harry Cohn.

Part of the hoopla was what Dawn herself created from her own mythology. She was a girl from a rich neighborhood in Long Island whose family didn't always have the means to keep up with the Joneses. She was motivated young. Motivated, like the industrious Jews who made Hollywood from cloth, Steel was following in well-carved footsteps. Her grandparents were Russian Jews who came over with so little they couldn't afford a berth on the steamer—and, in Steel's family joke, had to stand the whole trip over.[3] The family's original name was Speilberg, but her father changed it to Steel. Dawn still prods him that her career would have been easier if they had held on to *Speilberg*.

She *worked* for her designer Pappagallos since the age of sixteen, whereas other girls got them for Christmas from Santa Claus Daddy. Her "poor girl in a rich town" saga served her well. Like the best of her lineage, the young Steel was always fascinated at how and what and whereby a product was marketed to the public for consumption and thus miraculously transformed. She majored in marketing at Boston University, but dropped out for—what else—lack of funds.

A small jump into the future finds her doing research for a sports-digest book company, for whom the management of Yankee Stadium built her a private turret of an auxiliary press box because the male sportswriters wouldn't let a woman into theirs. Her first bout with batting in a boy's game.

Again, cut to Dawn as merchandising director for *Penthouse* magazine where she comes up with a brainchild she is convinced is the next pet-rock. She stamps the "Gucci" name (her boss's name was Bob Guccione) on toilet paper for the then-fledgling yuppie market. Then, innocently noticing one day how phallic is the amaryllis, Steel promoted the plant as a *Penthouse* phenomenon with the tag, "Grow your own.... All it takes is $6.98 and a lot of love." She didn't know it at the time, but she was priming for Hollywood. She was sued by the *real* Guccis, which for a marketing genius is exactly the kind of press you want ("More on the Toilet Paper Caper"), and next on her rung, she moves on to Paramount in Los Angeles to market movies. At that time (1979) Paramount was run by Barry Diller. "Diller operated the studio on the advocacy system, meaning that the individual who argued the most strenuously ... was the one whose projects got approved."[4] The studio at the time was described as a snake pit. "Anyone who emerged alive should be patted on the back. Can you imagine," said one independent producer working there at the time, "being a woman in that atmosphere? She had to be nastier than them."[5] And so she was. Survivor turned mogul, Dawn Steel was learning her trade.

Linda Obst, a powerful producer herself, is a longtime friend of Steel's, as well as the woman who passed on a project she had been developing called FLASHDANCE (1983). Dawn at the time was only an underling executive at Paramount, but she pushed the project as though she were a vice president of production, which is what she became, once she persuaded the studio to move with that film. Her gut-reaction instincts for the movie were right on, and it helped make her name. FLASHDANCE grossed $95 million at the box office and who knows how much more in video rentals.

"FLASHDANCE really created Dawn's persona," said James Wiatt, president of International Creative Management.

[She] put it together at Paramount at a time when she was literally the only voice that wanted to make it.... It put her on the map as someone who would fight for projects she believed in and someone who had instincts for material and concepts for movies.[6]

With a new title at Paramount, every man whom Dawn Steel dated wanted a production deal. She was given credit for bringing such movies to light as FATAL ATTRACTION and THE ACCUSED (both projects belonging to independent producer **Sherry Lansing** with her partner, Stan Jaffe). Although Steel's "made-of-steel" demeanor in the business was the mirror image of women, like Lansing (she actually *became* one of the boys and didn't just play nicely with them). Her lack of consciousness about the image of women in the films she promoted seems to match that of other women in the seats of Hollywood power.

As marketing director for Paramount at a time when production progress on STAR TREK was a mess, Steel, with no product to show potential investors, put on a party at Paramount where both she and William Shatner were "beamed" onto the stage. It was deemed such an enterprising coup that a year later she was made vice president of production. From marketing to production: here in a nutshell is a kind of microcosmic essence of the raison d'être of Hollywood.

By 1987, when Columbia Pictures was going through a series of crises, she was offered the job of running the studio. The last time a woman came even close to that offer was **Virginia Van Upp** as vice president under Harry Cohn in 1945. In that seat, Steel oversaw the marketing campaigns for WHEN HARRY MET SALLY (1989), and for Amy Heckerling's, LOOK WHO'S TALKING (1990). She also initiated the release of POSTCARDS FROM THE EDGE (1990), and Penny Marshall's AWAKENINGS (1991). By 1990, Dawn Steel was out of that seat. Sony bought Columbia Pictures, Guber/Peters became chairmen of the board, Dawn Steel was kicked downstairs, and life in Hollywood went on. Steel decided she didn't like the air downstairs and so was bought out of her contract. Thus freed, she reunited with her old Paramount cronies, and in association with Disney, she entered into an exclusive, long-term producing arrangement.

But as onetime president, her supporters in Hollywood were many. Some say she restored Columbia with "a philosophical approach about how to put a program of movies together." Steel herself said that she wanted "to get Columbia back to the days when it made great films that the public wanted to see."[7]

In tandem with her studio forefathers of yesteryear, Dawn Steel left behind her a legacy. Sam Goldwyn came to movies from selling gloves. Louis Mayer pushed junk. And now from the designer toilet-paper age (Steel called them, "logo tchotchkes") came Dawn Steel who, as Lynda Obst put it, came "completely self-invented. She invented herself whole out of cloth. She had no topos."[8]

Maybe you didn't like her style. "Dawn's not an individual who should be held up as a model for women in the film business. She has set us back,"[9] said one woman executive from another studio. Maybe it's not a good idea to have a role model whose name was synonymous with brutality and terror. But for others, "she served as the inspiration for all undereducated lower-middle-class girls fired with ambition. She was the proof that they too could reach the top. That it was possible without social connections or inherited wealth or even academic credentials to have it all in America."[10]

LeMaire, one of Hollywood's sought after hairdressers, who rose from similar roots, said about her client Steel, "She's able to be a wife and a mother and a business lady, and to be feminine on top of it! I look at her and it's like, 'Yeah. It can happen. It's the American dream!' "[11]

Steel was a first. And like her Jewish mogul forefathers before her (not to mention her foremothers, such as **Edith Head** who used Steel's very style), you have to give her credit for her chutzpah. I've a feeling we've not yet heard the final word on the Steel legacy. Steel is married to producer Charles Roven. They have a daughter, Rebecca, who was born in March of 1987, the same year Steel was crowned president of Columbia.

DAWN STEEL (Selected List)

1983	Flashdance
1984	Footloose
1986	Karate Kid, Part II, The
	Top Gun
1987	Beverly Hills Cop II
	Fatal Attraction
	Untouchables, The
1988	Accused, The
1989	Ghostbusters II
	Lawrence of Arabia (Restoration)
1990	Casualties of War

SHORT TAKES

• • •

Dorothy Davenport Reid (1895–1977)

Beginning as an actress with Biograph in 1909—by 1912 she was being hailed, "one of the youngest, classiest, most bewitching actresses of our time"[1]—**Dorothy Davenport Reid** turned her sights to producing in 1926. Her husband, superstar Wallace Reid, died of an overdose of narcotics, and as a direct result Dorothy Davenport Reid blossomed into a tireless crusader of the dramatic "antidrug" film, one of the very earliest to do so.

HUMAN WRECKAGE (1923), a film that Mrs. Reid produced and starred in, was the first near-biographic portrait of Wallace Reid's death. Depressing though its content was, it proved a huge success, and established Mrs. Reid (the name she preferred) as a major producer/writer/actress. Typical of her receptions as she traveled about the country with her films and her cause, were ones like her arrival in St. Louis, as Gerald Peary describes:

Five hundred banners announced her appearance. The health department contributed ambulances and wagons for Mrs. Reid's parade. The Mayor proclaimed Anti-Narcotics week and greeted her at the train station with two brass bands. The parade included twenty-five carloads of disabled veterans from the American Legion Hospital and eighty taxicabs with signs on their spare tires advertising the moviehouse showing of HUMAN WRECKAGE.[2]

Historian Kevin Brownlow recently located the original scenario to HUMAN WRECKAGE, which opened with this subtitle:

Dope is the gravest menace which today confronts the United States. Immense quantities of morphine, heroin and cocaine are yearly smuggled into America across the Canadian and Mexican borders. The Dope Ring is composed of rings within rings, the inner ring undoubtedly including men powerful in finance, politics and society. But the trail to the 'men higher up' is cunningly covered. No investigator has penetrated to the inner circle."[3]

Mrs. Reid formed her own production firm in 1925 to produce THE RED KIMONO (released in 1926). With an original story by **Adela Rogers St. Johns,** and a screenplay by **Dorothy Arzner,** this was virtually an all-woman production. Although she essentially directed all of her own pieces, she didn't officially take an on-screen credit until LINDA in 1929. She said in 1934:

Fanchon Royer

Dorothy Davenport Reid
(starring in HUMAN WRECKAGE,
1923, a film she also produced).

Marcia Nasatir

The first thing a woman producer must do is take the sex out of executive work. . . . Men are too polite and spare her the truth. . . . [A woman] can use the fact that she is a woman to motivate things. . . . She should use her feminine viewpoint for her *approach,* but she must go then to masculine attack and execution. Before this [she was, by this time, directing and writing for another studio] my experience has been with my own money. What I said had to go. Now I must work that much harder to convince that my slant is sound. I believe it takes a woman to believe in a woman's motives, and every story intended for the screen should have a woman working on it at some stage, to convince the audience of women. . . . A man and woman working together on the story can hit a better emotional angle. For instance, a man only knows that he gets fed up with a woman, but he doesn't know *why.* A woman writing the story has feminine vision into all the little irritations that caused it.[4]

The year of this comment, according to Anthony Slide, she directed two features, THE ROAD TO RUIN for True Life Photoplays and THE WOMAN CONDEMNED for Marcy Pictures. Of the former, *Film Daily* of 1934 said, "It is a frank presentation of the pitfalls of youth, and it whitewashes none of the characters. The results of their folly, ignorance, and carelessness are pointed graphically for the moral."[5] Apparently Lois Weber would not be the only filmmaker in history to mark a reputation with moralistic leanings.

By 1949, Mrs. Reid seemed to lose her confidence as a producer. She produced IMPACT, a piece she cowrote with Arthur Lubin, a man who was to become her longstanding writing collaborator, but when the assignment was completed, she seems to have lost faith and settled for a job as his gal Friday. In 1952 she said:

After years of training I feel that I am ready for the post of associate producer. . . . Women have a lot to give motion pictures,

but not in the capacity of producer. Men resent women in top executive positions in films as in any field of endeavor.[6]

It is hard to speculate what happened to Mrs. Reid in those later years. She had been very much in love with Wallace Reid and she never remarried. Work was all she had. In the beginning, it seemed to lighten her losses. But in her later years, she recalled her earlier feelings about work to Anthony Slide, "It wasn't arduous, it was just fun."[7]

Aside from producing, writing, and directing, Mrs. Reid established the Wallace Reid Foundation Sanitarium as a drug-addiction center, "for the cure of unfortunate addicts."[8] It was this that elicited an offer from Thomas Ince to produce and star in her first feature film.[9] She remained until the day she died "an astonishing woman. A leading lady during the cinema's infancy."[10] A woman who in 1933, after she had announced her retirement, was literally pulled out to "direct, produce, and write for a number of the poverty-row companies,"[11] because, "retiring is not so easy for a small dynamo with an idea per minute."[12]

DOROTHY DAVENPORT REID

1923	Human Wreckage
	Quicksands
1924	Broken Laws
1926	Earth Woman, The
	Red Kimono, The
1929	Linda
1933	Sucker Money (Codirector)
1934	Road to Ruin, The
	Woman Condemned, The
1935	Honeymoon Limited (Producer, Writer)
1949	Impact
1950–56	Francis (The Talking Mule) (Writer)

Fanchon Royer (1902–?)

In the midthirties, she was billed by Paramount Studios as "Hollywood's Only Woman Producer." Although cultural amnesia caused historians to discount the pioneering women of Hollywood's heyday, **Fanchon Royer** seems to be the first major woman figure in producing once the industry had made its radical transformation into the world of studio empires.

Famous in her day as merely, "Fanchon," she was born in Des Moines, Iowa, "started in the picture business as a player at the age of sixteen,"[1] and attended the University of Southern California for one year, long before it was fashionable for women to attend college.

Deciding that the best education was experience, Royer left USC to do extra work on productions, and to edit the trade publication, *Camera*. Her three years' experience on the magazine led her to meet every major figure in the motion-picture business. She swiftly moved on to publicity and agency work, until 1928 afforded her an opportunity to produce her first major studio picture, LIFE IS LIKE THAT. She continued with her agency business until 1930 when she instituted "Fanchon Royer Productions."

Under the new corporate heading, Royer produced seventeen features, including one in Spanish, all of which she distributed herself.[2] This led her to act in an advisory capacity for Mexican government picture production. She used the experience later in her life as inspiration for her novel *Padre Pro* (1954), the story of a Mexican priest who was executed by firing squad. Royer began producing for World Wide and for

Mayfair in 1931. What is perhaps most extraordinary about this woman is that she succeeded as the industry's lone woman producer while raising five children.

She briefly signed on to assist Nat Levine with his productions at Mascot, but left to start her own company, Fanchon Royer Features. She produced six feature titles under the new company heading. Paramount then adopted her proudly as its own mascot, "Fanchon," the trades said, "famous for her stage reviews, has become the only major woman motion picture producer in Hollywood. She has just completed her first picture for Paramount, TURN OFF THE MOON (1937)," and, "Fanchon, Hollywood's only woman producer, views production of Paramount's THRILL OF A LIFETIME (1937) [with Betty Grable, and Dorothy Lamour in a bit part], her second film since taking over production reins."[3] Both of these musicals were billed equally as, "Fanchon/Paramount Productions."

In 1939, Royer left her work in features and turned to 16mm educational film production. She was president of the Catholic Film and Radio Guild in 1943. Not much seems to be known about what became of "Fanchon." Like many women film pioneers who disappeared from history without a trace, *Variety Obits* makes no mention of her.

FANCHON ROYER

1928 Life Is Like That
1937 Thrill of a Lifetime
      Turn Off the Moon

Hannah Weinstein (1911–1984)

A good thirty years before **Marcia Nasatir** became vice president of production at Paramount in 1975, **Hannah Weinstein** ran her own studio outside of London.

Weinstein was a well-known political activist who was forced to leave this country during the McCarthy blacklisting because of her beliefs. She was known as an intrepid organizer and a savvy producer, her interest in film always beyond the monetary—a good enough reason to have left the United States even if there had been no blacklist.

A native New Yorker, Weinstein studied journalism, and spent her early career working for the *New York Herald Tribune*. She honed her political expertise at a young age as a speechwriter for Mayor Fiorello H. La Guardia. At the time of her death in 1984, Dale Pollock reported in the *Los Angeles Times* that "[Weinstein] organized artists and scientists in support of President Franklin D. Roosevelt, tried to elect Henry Wallace and Eugene McCarthy as President and organized a famous rally in Madison Square Garden to raise funds for the election of candidates opposed to the war in Vietnam."[1]

When she was forced in 1950 to move to London because of the blacklist—"My own belief," said her close friend **Lillian Hellman**, "is that she was the only person in the world Joe McCarthy was frightened of"— Weinstein was a divorced mother raising three children alone. Once abroad, her real career as a motion picture executive began. She produced several TV series, the main purpose of which was to employ blacklisted writers in the United States.

Although she did not have a long list of credits, Weinstein had an undeniably lasting impact on the world of movies. In 1972 she teamed up with James Earl Jones, Ossie Davis, and the late **Diana Sands** to form Third World Cinema, dedicated to making films about and with minorities.

Two of the films that came out of the effort were hers, CLAUDINE, with Jones and **Diahann Carroll** in 1974, and GREASED LIGHTNING in 1977. This last picture was Richard Pryor's first starring role, before he was able to command million-dollar film deals. Pollock said of these films, "They stood out as intelligent, well-crafted films in an era of violent and sexist black exploitation movies."[2]

She also obtained funding for a minority film-training academy (The Institute of New Cinema) and helped attain jobs for minority workers in film.

Actress **Jane Fonda** said of Weinstein, "Hannah taught me something very important: You can be successful and still be true to your values." **Lillian Hellman** observed: "In this shabby time, when either nobody believes in anything or has long given up hope, Hannah does believe, and she does carry out what she believes in. She has hope. Very few of us have hope any longer."[3]

Her last film, STIR CRAZY in 1980, was one of the most successful comedies to that time ever seen at the box office.

Hannah Weinstein's daughter, **Paula Weinstein**, has followed proudly in her mother's footsteps, as a producer in Hollywood who is known as an executive with a conscience.

The young Ms. Weinstein, who is quick to credit her inspirational, role-model mother most recently produced A DRY WHITE SEASON (1989), with **Euzhan Palcy** at the helm. So unusual was the piece in Hollywood (it's one of the few times that a major studio did a film with political content that goes far out on a limb), it has been called by many as "a fortunate mistake in the Hollywood system."

In 1975, when **Paula Weinstein** was made a vice president at Warner Bros., it was *so unusual* for the executive post to be held by a woman that her first day on the job she received dozens of phone calls from curious journalists. "There had never been a woman vice president before," Weinstein said, "and as soon as I had it, the janitor became the vice president of janitorial services. Everybody had a title."[4]

By the early eighties, Weinstein made her way to the top. As president of production for United Artists pictures she was one of the early catalysts for helping women executives who were once mere figureheads evolve into effective-change agents of the movies.

HANNAH WEINSTEIN (Selected List)

1974 Claudine
1977 Greased Lightning
1980 Stir Crazy

Marcia Nasatir

In 1974, **Marcia Nasatir** became the first woman executive of a major Hollywood studio since the days of **Virginia Van Upp.** "They offered me the job of story editor," Nasatir told me, "but I wouldn't take the job unless it was a vice presidency. That would break the deal, I was told. After all, no women held those jobs. Women read, men do. But titles are imperative. Don't let anyone tell you different. I knew that no one would negotiate with me seriously unless I was vice president. I stood firm."[1]

At the time, United Artists was facing big problems. They badly needed someone with Nasatir's skills. And so Nasatir got her title. Ironically, this same studio many incarnations previous, was the brainchild of another innovative woman, **Mary Pickford.** As vice president Nasatir helped to launch ONE FLEW OVER THE CUCKOO'S NEST (1975), and CARRIE (1976).

Today, every Hollywood studio has a legendary position known in homage as "the Marcia Nasatir job," or, vice president of production. It's a job that Nasatir has since risen above. First to president of Johnny Carson Productions, then senior vice president of production—east coast and London—for Twentieth Century-Fox, to her current job as president of her own independent production firm.

Nasatir was not unprepared for her seemingly meteoric rise in movies. She began in publishing and was the innovator of the "instant book," with the printing of *The Warren Commission Report on JFK's Assassination,* in eighty days.

"The reason so many women come to the film industry from publishing is simple," said Nasatir. "Women were always paid less than men, but they hung on. When the men moved on to higher-paying fields, the women got their jobs. Now, women dominate publishing."

Nasatir recalled, "For a long time at U.A. I was the only woman at the meeting. Many of the men had never taken meetings with a woman present before. They would use four-letter words, then suddenly turn to me and say, 'Oh Marcia, excuse us.' I'd say something banal like, 'I've heard that word before.'

"About three years into the job, another woman came into the meeting—a secretary who'd come in to take dictation. Someone used one of the four-letter words. And they turned to her and said, 'Rose, excuse us.' I realized they no longer saw me as a woman in the room. It was a great moment. I was very conscious of it."

Nasatir came from the generation where successful women were suspect. Men were the ones who were supposed to be successful.

"I remember going back to San Antonio where I was raised and going to visit this friend, a woman my mother's age, who was recently widowed. The next time I went back, she had gone into real estate. By my third visit, she had become the most successful realtor in town. This eerie notion entered my brain. 'In order to succeed as a woman, you have to kill your husband.' On the other hand, there's hope. My sister is a judge who is happily married to a doctor. So maybe things are changing."

Nasatir is the mother of two grown sons. She doesn't have much of a desire to marry again. "I spent ten years after my divorce looking for Mr. Right. Then you become successful in your career and you wonder how many men can handle your success. Or your hours! My job has never been nine to five. More like nine to midnight. As Lewis Carroll once said, 'It takes all the running you can do to stand in one spot.'"

As president of Carson Productions, Na-satir executive-produced THE BIG CHILL (1983)—"Every studio in town had turned it down twice," she says—before moving on to the presidency of Fox in 1983.

In her current job as independent producer, Nasatir has overseen the Vietnam film, HAMBURGER HILL (1987), and was executive producer of IRONWEED (1987), with Meryl Streep and Jack Nicholson.

"I can understand why the men kept us out for such a long time," says Nasatir. "They wanted to keep this to themselves. It's great to have a big job."

MARCIA NASATIR

1975	One Flew over the Cuckoo's Nest
1976	Carrie
1977	Annie Hall
1983	Big Chill, The
1987	Hamburger Hill
	Ironweed

·VI·

REEL WOMEN WRITERS

Of course, calling them "women writers" is their ruin.
They begin to think of themselves that way.
—Dorothy Parker

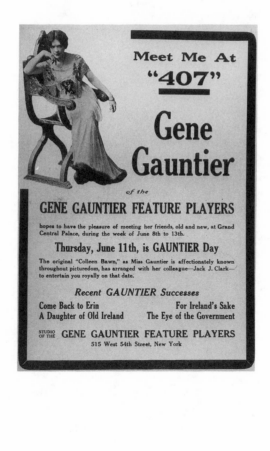

Meet Me At "407"

Gene Gauntier

of the

GENE GAUNTIER FEATURE PLAYERS

hopes to have the pleasure of meeting her friends, old and new, at Grand
Central Palace, during the week of June 8th to 13th.

Thursday, June 11th, is GAUNTIER Day

The original "Colleen Bawn," as Miss Gauntier is affectionately known
throughout picturedom, has arranged with her colleague—Jack J. Clark—
to entertain you royally on that date.

Recent GAUNTIER Successes

Come Back to Erin   For Ireland's Sake
A Daughter of Old Ireland   The Eye of the Government

STUDIO OF THE GENE GAUNTIER FEATURE PLAYERS
515 West 54th Street, New York

PREVIEW

◆ ◆ ◆

An important study done by the Writers Guild of America in 1987 tells us that from the turn of the century until the mid-1920s, women outnumbered men in the screenwriting trade ten to one.[1]

Why should this be so?

Perhaps it is because writers, like film editors, are a fairly anonymous breed. They do their work quietly hidden away, while their conceptions are realized in the outer world by the director—the person, in recent film history, who also typically claims all the creative credit.

Gary Carey's speculation about this surge of women in the screen trade is that "women were more attuned than men to turning out the kitsch melodramas and hot-house romances that dominated the run-of-the-mill Hollywood product of the period."[2]

Tom Stempel, author of *FrameWork* (1988), also suggests that beginning with the late teens and on, the producer was the power figure, while writers, editors, and even directors played a more "nurturing" role. And since they were aiming so many films at their main consumer audience, women, perhaps they thought it natural that women should also write those films.[3]

This theory concurs with the recent rise of women writers in dramatic television, since women make up the majority of television viewers. We also find the current number of women screenwriters slacking off in feature films. The trend in movies in recent years toward violent, action-packed thrillers, leads studio executives to blithely assume that women cannot write those kinds of movies. Cannot and do not want to are two different concepts.

All one has to do to blow these assumptions out of the water is to look at history. **Leigh Brackett** made her name by writing many of the great John Wayne "he-man" dramas. Ask any one of the pioneering scriptwriters whose successful careers began in the forties, **Leigh Brackett, Harriet Frank, Jr., Fay Kanin,** if there are subjects that are endemically male or female, and they turn beet red. Sheer nonsense. In fact, all three of these writers began their careers in the industry doing subjects that are considered typically "male." **Frank** and **Kanin** both started with fight films. **Brackett** began as a science-fiction and crime writer.

The point here is that uncontested assumptions are dangerous, and often damaging to people's careers—more often than not, these turn out to be women's careers. Critic Pat McGilligan in a review of Tom Stempel's *FrameWork* for *Film Quarterly*, irresponsibly, even maliciously, makes these uncalled-for remarks about women screenwriters:

Stempel tells us that **Jeanie Macpherson**, one of Cecil B. De Mille's corps, "had herself arrested and spent three days in a Detroit jail" in order to write MANSLAUGHTER in 1922. He notes, without further comment, "She later told friends she had tried to escape, but was caught." Stempel might have added that Macpherson was on De Mille's payroll seemingly forever because she served more amorous purposes.[4]

If Jeanie Macpherson *was* sleeping with De Mille, does it prove that she was not a good writer? Does it say anything about the twenty years' worth of box-office hits she turned out for De Mille? Does it comment about her being so talented as to be granted her own production unit as a director at Universal before she ever met De Mille? McGilligan accuses Stempel of noting, "without further comment," then goes ahead in the very next sentence, and is guilty of not backing up his own aspersions.

But wait. McGilligan is not yet through with denigrating the female race through his name-calling antics.

> The director George Cukor, a great admirer of writers (they were urged to be present while he filmed, and characteristically he adhered to every comma in their scripts) once stated that certain of the famous "lady writers"—Macpherson, June Mathis, Frances Marion—had in common the fact that they absolutely could not write. The writers who could not write!—they should be part of a history of Hollywood scriptwriting as well.

The undermining here is dangerous because it is subtle enough to pass unnoticed. The assumption we make instantly, without thinking twice, is that women screenwriters (these in particular and others in general) cannot write because a famous and influential man in the industry said so.

Responsible and substantiated research reveals the following:

1. By the time Cukor arrived in Hollywood, **June Mathis** was dead.
2. Cukor never worked with **Jeanie Mac-**

pherson. How would he know whether or not she could write except on hearsay?
3. **Frances Marion** cowrote two films for George Cukor, DINNER AT EIGHT (1933), and CAMILLE (1936). One wouldn't exactly call either of these "bombs." **Marion** went on to have a thirty-year, blockbuster career (with or without the permission of either George Cukor or Pat McGilligan) and came out with a filmography that reads like a best-hits list of the cinema.

All these women were older and more experienced than George Cukor. "The "bat that flew out of Cukor's mouth" (from a personal letter he wrote to Alex Tiers, which Mr. McGilligan did not have permission to quote from directly) says more about Cukor's feelings around women than it does about women as scriptwriters.

Unsubstantiated aspersions such as these by influential critics about historic women are as bad as the McCarthy days of "seeing Red." They tend to denigrate *all* women role models. They are as dangerous as Andrew Sarris's famous comment that the first two generations of women filmmakers were "little more than a ladies' auxiliary."[5]

The important thing to note here is that women writers have been numerous, active, and influential in the field since movies began. Writing is one area women have always been able to pursue, even when all other avenues to them have been sealed off.

Tony Slide, author of *Early Women Directors* (1977), said, "It strikes me in looking through a checklist of Selig [a studio from early Hollywood] releases from 1911–1914 that at least fifty percent, if not a higher percentage, are written by women."[6]

Did the woman screenwriter seek merely to be a part of the new industry, or did she hope to use her influence, to transform the female image on the screen? In a few instances, the mainstream Hollywood woman writer did envision possibilities for her sex, such as **Zoë Akins** who wrote many of **Dorothy Arzner's** scripts, but many more felt that in order to be accepted, they must present at all costs images that varied little from expected norms and standards of stereotyped female behavior—**Anita Loos's** "Loreli Lee" (from GENTLEMEN PREFER BLONDS [1928]), immediately springs to mind. Among the brave ones however were **Lois Weber, Cleo Madison, Dorothy Davenport Reid, Leigh Brackett,** and **Lillian Hellman.**

As long as there have been movies, there have been women writing them. And as long as there have been women writing movies, there have been male critics cavalierly dismissing their talent and contribution. But don't we have **Leigh Brackett** to thank for her contribution to making John Wayne into a timeless hero? **Frances Marion** gave us the immortal woman-child we came to know as "America's Sweetheart." And honestly, would movies be what they are today if not for the inimitable creations of **Mae West?**

Gene Gauntier

June Mathis (center).

Elinor Glyn

Grace Cunard

THE SILENTS

♦ ♦ ♦

Gene Gauntier (1891–1966)

"It was June 1906," says **Gene Gauntier**, "that I literally jumped into the moving pictures, being thrown into a river."[1] From that day forward, Gene Gauntier found herself connected with the "flickers" as actress, scenario writer, producer, and critic.

Professionally, Gene Gauntier worked in many crafts, but mainly she liked to write. Gauntier created the genre we now refer to as the "serial,"[2] replete with their daredevil stunts and those helpless "girls" tied to buzzsaws toward the episode's end.

As one of the early industry's most powerful and important writers she wrote more than five hundred films in which she also starred.

I wrote ADVENTURES OF THE GIRL SPY, which embodied all the difficult and dangerous stunts I could conjure up. I played a southern girl disguised as a boy of '61. It made a tremendous hit and exhibitors wrote in for more. Thus began the first series made in films. I kept them up for two years until, tired of sprains and bruises and with brains sucked dry of any more adventures for the intrepid young woman, I married her off and ended the [Civil] War. . . . I thought I was finished. But no! The demand for them still came back with one

called, "A Hitherto Unrelated Incident of the Girl Spy." There is always a way in pictures![3]

So why is such an important figure eclipsed from film history?

I suspect the true reason historians do not like her is that (1) she is a woman and (2) she is a screenwriter,

says Tom Stempel in *FrameWork*.[4]

Gauntier was a scenario writer and an actress in Hollywood in 1906, before the arrival of D. W. Griffith. A year later the Kalem Film Company was formed by Biograph's former business manager. That winter, Gauntier did her first acting assignment for the new company. By the summer, Sidney Olcott took over as the company's director, Gauntier immediately took a liking to him. A long creative partnership was formed.

Scenarios were needed frequently and desperately. Olcott asked Gauntier if she could write a screen version of *Tom Sawyer* that, according to Tom Stempel, "would include only as much as they could shoot in one day."

It was pretty dreadful, but it was what . . . Olcott wanted. And I had caught the knack. From henceforth I was the mainstay of the Kalem Scenario Department.

The woods were full of ideas. . . . All was grist that came to my mill. There was no copyright law [a statement that would later make her ears ring] to protect authors and I could, and did, infringe upon everything. . . . I sometimes wrote three complete scenarios, one-reelers of course, in one day. . . . That was when "inspiration burned."[5]

Initially, she was paid twenty dollars for one reel. Most directors of the day were paid ten. That fall at Kalem she was asked to do the screen's first adaptation of BEN HUR (1907), with two days notice (not to be confused with the later **June Mathis** version of 1926). Her dramatization must have proved authentic, because the novel's publisher recognized enough of the book's material to sue Kalem and win. This was the first such case, and it established copyright laws in the area of film rights.[6]

The example cost the company twenty-five thousand dollars in legal fees, making the film, as Tom Stempel said, the costliest one-reeler of the time.[7]

Gauntier upgraded her salary by going over to Biograph as a scenario writer and editor for forty dollars a week. While she was there, a young man named D. W. Griffith had just started working as an actor. When another young writer, Stanner E. Taylor, was given an opportunity to direct, Griffith said to Gauntier, "Why don't they give an actor a chance to direct? I wish I had Taylor's opportunity." Gauntier put in a good word to the higher-ups at Biograph, and the next thing he knew, D. W. Griffith was directing.[8]

After being with Biograph only a short time, Gauntier's bargaining power was heightened. She returned to Kalem the following year with a requirement of thirty dollars a week as their leading lady, with twenty dollars additional per script.

Regarding her stuntwork, she wrote:

Only youth and a strong constitution could have stood up under it. I was playing in two pictures a week, working in almost every scene, and writing two or three scenarios a week, in the effort to keep up with our production. My screen work was all strenuous, horseback riding for hours each day, water scenes in which I committed suicide or floated on spars in shark-infested waters, climbing trees, coming down on ropes from second-story windows, jumping from roofs or rolling down to be caught in blankets, overturning skiffs, paddling canoes, a hundred and one "stunts" thought out to give the action Kalem films demanded. I was terrified at each daring thing I had to do, but for some inexplicable reason I continued to write them. They never seemed so difficult when I was seated before the typewriter in the throes of creating them, but as the moment for performance drew near they assumed unwarranted aspects of terror. A "double" was never even thought of in those days![9]

When she had turned out enough plots to make her bosses fearful of losing her, they suggested she try directing one of her own scripts. She did so, with a film called, GRANDMOTHER. "The picture was successful, but," she says, "I did not care for directing."[10] Subsequently, she refused her bosses' offer to control a directing unit of her own—every director's dream in those days.

In 1909, Gauntier suggested an entrepreneurial idea for the time: why not go on location in Europe and make films there? So, off went Kalem (Gauntier, Olcott, and a camera person) to Germany and Ireland. She wrote three screenplays on the boat going over, all of which they filmed. Pictures were usually filmed as rapidly as Gauntier turned them out. It was on such a journey through Egypt two years later in 1911 that Gauntier conceived FROM THE MANGER TO THE CROSS (1912), the first truly major life of Christ ever to be conceived for the screen.

Filming began in Egypt then moved to the Holy Land. The locations were so breathtaking that they decided to expand the film from three to six reels. Olcott went to London to get additional actors, leaving Gauntier to supervise the building of the sets. In between, she turned out two travel scripts, which the company filmed in order to cover expenses.

In the film, Gauntier played the Virgin Mary, helped with the title sequences, and participated in the editing, as was customary for the time.[11]

The picture was an enormous success. Kalem, however, was not interested in crediting the individuals who made the film work, so Gauntier and Olcott left to form their own company, the Gene Gauntier Film Players.

The company lasted only a brief while. The majors were quickly encroaching on the livelihood of small companies. Ever survivors, Gauntier and Olcott, by now a famous directing/writing team, joined Universal in 1915.

Only three years later, Gauntier had her fill of it. She was savvy enough to see that the days of innocence in pictures were numbered. She retired to become a war correspondent in 1918.

GENE GAUNTIER

1907?	Tom Sawyer (Adaptation, Writer)
1907	Ben Hur (Adaptation, Writer)
1908–9	Hitherto Unrelated Incident of the Girl Spy, A (Serials) (Adaptation, Writer)
1909	Grandmother (Director, Writer)
1911	Captured by the Bedouins
	Fighting Dervishes of the Desert
	Down through the Ages
1912	From the Manger to the Cross

Grace Cunard (1893–1967)

If you're a fan of the soap opera idea, you can thank **Grace Cunard**. Even if you hate soap opera, you have to hand it to the person who made them popular. It was the now little remembered actress/director/stuntwoman/writer, Grace Cunard—no less talented for being barely remembered. The headline of an interview with her in the September 4, 1915, issue of *Moving Picture World*, read, "She Has Written Four Hundred Scenarios!" All of them, by the way, were produced. "Of course," reads the article,

every one who goes to a picture show knows Grace Cunard as a wonderfully appealing actress, capable of some of the biggest scenes ever recorded by the camera. But few persons know that Miss Cunard has made fully as big a success as a photoplaywright. Indeed, it is very doubtful if there is any author in America who has a

larger list of screen successes than those credited to Miss Cunard. . . . Many will be stunned to learn that she is also one of the most capable directors in the business.[1]

What she and Francis Ford excerpted from literature and then made popular on the screen were called *cliff-hangers*. The audiences would appear faithfully week after week with baited breath to see what became of the heroine tied to the railroad tracks the week before.

A former actress with Biograph, Bison, and Universal, she starred in the serial LUCILLE LOVE, GIRL OF MYSTERY (1914), her most famous acting role. She penned and directed many of the episodes herself for Universal. She must have loved danger for, as she said, she

was forced to take time off in the hospital on several occasions for injuries sustained on the set. Her courting of danger applied off the screen also, to driving her automobile. Said Cunard: "I am a perfect devotee of motoring, and simply must take time for a spin in my Lozier car. No speed is great enough to please me."[2]

A press release listed Cunard as having been born in Paris; actually she was Harriet Mildred Jeffries, born in Columbus, Ohio. In those days, the essence of filmmaking was the glamour of world travel and the lure of romantic and exotic places far across the sea. Thus, Harriet Jeffries chose her romantic stage name from the names of the two most famous ocean liner companies of the period: Grace and Cunard. Miss "Cunard" made her stage debut at the age of thirteen in a play called *Dora Thorne,* and performed with a traveling stock company before touring with Eddie Foy until 1909.

Hard up for work as a stage actress in 1910, she was forced to seek employment in the then much denigrated medium of moving pictures.

In 1916, Cunard entered a tremendously successful partnership with Francis Ford, older brother of director John. The team took turns writing and directing.

Their story could have been one classically written, as writer Eldon Everett has suggested,[3] for one of their own serials. They were given hundreds of thousands of dollars to play with very suddenly. They had facilities galore to access with which to create their wildest fantasies. Some of these included serial ideas like LADY RAFFLES (1914), in which Cunard played a lady jewel thief with a devil-may-care attitude. She escaped the good guys by galloping off on the back of an elephant. Although *how* one "gallops" on an elephant may be a pioneering feat in itself.

LUCILLE LOVE, GIRL OF MYSTERY was amazingly successful. You may fantasize silent comedies being done on tiny budgets with a cast of five or six people, but on the

1200-acre ranch where the "new" Universal City was beginning construction, a twenty-five-thousand-dollar bond brought three hundred natives from the Marquesas Islands. There they sat in a complete South Sea Island Village specially constructed on the new lot . . . an underground city inhabited by strange half-human, half-ape creatures, expensive costumes, with Grace conceiving all the plots they could pay for, while she was escaping on her elephant, Anna May (even then, about the only dupe dumb enough to work for peanuts).[4]

It has been speculated that the reason why the successful LUCILLE LOVE, GIRL OF MYSTERY is hardly recalled today is due to the awesome success of their second serial, THE BROKEN COIN (1915).[5]

Grace is described by Eldon K. Everett in *Classic Film Collector* as by

> no means a beautiful woman. Red hair, grey eyes, 5'4" and this hypnotic trace of insanity in her eyes—much like that of silent comedian Harry Langdon—which she realized and capitalized on in her film roles.[6]

As the popularity of the serials died down, so did the career of Grace Cunard. The Cunard-Ford team split up in 1917, at the time when the majors were eating tiny companies for breakfast. Cunard was by this time commanding $450 a week, plus 25 cents a foot of film over 1,500 feet, and 10 percent of the profits of the sale of the film. She had had it with the physical exertions that the serials demanded and wanted to spend more of her professional energies on features.

Cunard's career continued, mostly for Universal, well into the thirties. One of her last good roles was in 1929 in LAST MAN ON EARTH. Described as a "science-fiction comedy" (perhaps a genre in itself) she plays a lady gangster who kidnaps the only surviving male on the planet and holds him for ransom from the "all-girl" government.

Unlike the frenetic pace of her pictures, she lived quietly and died in the motion-picture home in Los Angeles. Her obituary in the *New York Times* said, "Like Pearl White, she helped build the popularity of serials in 1912 and remained a favorite nationwide through World War I."[7]

Cunard was married to actor Jack Shannon, and like many women who pioneered the film industry, she had no children. She died at age seventy-three.

GRACE CUNARD

1912	Dante's Inferno
	Duke's Plan, The
1913	Be Neutral
	Favorite Son, The
1914	Bride of Mystery
	In the Fall of '64
	Lady Raffles
	Lucille Love, Girl of Mystery (Serial)
	Madcap Queen of Gretzhoffen, The
	Mystery of the White Car, The
	Mysterious Hand, The
	Mysterious Leopard Lady, The
	Mysterious Rose, The
	Phantom of the Violin, The
	Washington at Valley Forge
1915	And They Called Him Hero
	Broken Coin, The (Serial)
	Campbells Are Coming, The
	Doorway of Destruction, The
	Hidden City, The
	Lumber Yard Gang, The
	Nabbed
	One Kind of a Friend
	3 Bad Men and a Girl
1916	Bandit's Wager, The
	Behind the Mask
	Brennon o' the Moor
	Born of the People
	Dumb Bandit, The (Story)

	Elusive Enemy, The
	Her Better Self
	Her Sister's Sin
	Heroine of San Juan, The
	His Majesty Dick Turpin
	Lady Raffles Returns
	Mad Hermit, The
	Madcap Queen of Crona, The
	Mr. Vampire (Story)
	Phantom Island
	Peg o' the Ring (Serial)
	Poisoned Lips (Story)
	Powder Trail, The
	Princely Bandit, The
	Purple Mask, The (Serial)
	Sham Reality, The
	Strong Arm Squad, The (Serial)
1917	Circus Sarah
	Her Western Adventure
	In Treason's Grasp
	Puzzle Woman, The
	Society's Driftwood
	True to their Colors
	Unmasked
1918	Hell's Crater
	Spawn, The
1919	After the War
	Elmo the Mighty (Serial)
1920	A Daughter of the Law
	Gasoline Buckaroo
	Man Hater, The
	Woman of Mystery, The
1921	Girl in the Taxi, The
1922	A Dangerous Adventure (Serial)
	Heart of Lincoln, The
1925	Kiss Barrier, The
	Outwitted
1926	Exclusive Rights
	Fighting with Buffalo Bill (Serial)
	Winking Idol, The (Serial)
1927	Blake of Scotland Yard (Serial)
	Denver Dude, The
	Return of the Riddle Rider, The (Serial)
	Rest Cure, The
1928	Haunted Island, The (Serial)
	Masked Angel, The
	Price of Fear, The

Scrappin' Ranger, The (Story)
1929 Ace of Scotland Yard, The
Last Man on Earth Untamed
1930 Lady Surrenders, A

1931 Ex-Bad Boy
Resurrection
1935 Bride of Frankenstein, The

June Mathis (1892–1927)

At the time of her sudden death at the age of thirty-five, **June Mathis** was the highest paid, and possibly the most powerful female voice in the studio system. Her credits are among the best-hits list in early cinema.

Mathis was able to demonstrate the advantage of screenwriters using their multi-faceted talents to full capacity, as a screenwriter, producer, actress, casting director, and editor—all with equal dexterity. She laid the groundwork for the later development in the Hollywood system of screenwriters becoming producers.

Mathis's film career began in the mid-teens when scenarios for films were begging for ingenuity. In order to support her mother after her father's death, she entered the movies playing in vaudeville and on stage as an actress. Although she had no experience as a writer, Mathis was determined this would be her course. Only seven years after her decision, Samuel Goldwyn would insure her life for $1,000,000, so valuable an asset had she become to the screen business.[1]

As a result of her talent with short stories, Metro employed her as a regular scenarist. Her true pioneering spirit showed through soon after, with the desire to convert Vicente Blasco Ibáñez's novel of war, *The Four Horsemen of the Apocalypse* (1918), into a vehicle for the screen. The novel had been considered by every major studio in the country as impossible to adapt. But Mathis was determined. Her persuasive powers won over Richard Rowland, head of Metro, who paid twenty thousand dollars for the rights in 1919. After a long and difficult birthing, the film was finally released in 1921. It became "one of the most commercial silent movies ever made, thanks largely to the efforts of June Mathis."[2] She was also adamant that Rex Ingram (who had only directed small films before) direct, and that an unknown player, one whom she had never met in person, and had only viewed in one picture, should be the film's star. The actor's name was Rudolph Valentino.[3]

Several people, including Rex Ingram, claimed credit for discovering Valentino, but it was Mathis who plucked him out of obscurity and made him a star in this vehicle. The film was a tremendous success, now ranked among the screen's classic silent epics. Jacob Lewis in *The Rise of the American Film* (1939), wrote that FOUR HORSEMEN was

distinguished by pictorial beauty and an uncommon exotic atmosphere. Many hail the film a magnificent work of art. . . . The symbolic sequences of the Four Horsemen—War, Plague, Famine, Death—galloping through clouds over a battle-torn world were reminiscent of Griffith; [so were] the spectacular mass scenes. . . . The whole was blended of exotic settings, striking compositions, dramatic lighting.[4]

According to Tom Stempel in *Framework*, Mathis left Metro in 1921 after a dispute, went to Famous Players, and then left there a year later. As Kevin Brownlow describes it she was "tempted over to Goldwyn by Frank Godsol's offer of an enormous salary and autonomous control."[5]

Her job at Goldwyn was running the

story division. She was with Goldwyn during the monumental merger of Metro-Goldwyn-Mayer, and was an integral part of that transition. At this time, she also worked on **Alla Nazimova**'s famous screen version of SALOME (1922). Previously, Mathis wrote several other **Nazimova** productions, the most famous of which was CAMILLE (1921).

Mathis later took THE SHIEK (1921) with her to Famous Players (Paramount) where Valentino would stay when she moved on. But what would firmly carve Valentino's name into motion-picture history was the Mathis script for another silent classic, BLOOD AND SAND (1922), a film that also assisted in catapulting the career of its editor, **Dorothy Arzner,** into directing.

Mathis was suddenly becoming known as the scenarist who specialized in epics.

In 1923, she was assigned the formidable task of rewriting, reediting, and reducing, Eric von Stroheim's GREED from twenty-four reels down to ten.

In 1925 the theatrical producers of *Ben Hur* (the play) were suspicious of movie people wanting to picturize it, since an illegal version had already been done by the Kalem Company. But June Mathis used her persuasive powers. Not only did the Goldwyn company acquire the rights, but Mathis was assured to be the only screenwriter who could do the task, as well as act as the on-location studio representative. Kevin Brownlow describes Mathis's zeal for the production:

A woman of indomitable strength and energy, Miss Mathis threw herself into this new task with an enthusiasm that ground to dust all obstacles and objections. Her word was law.[6]

The monumental film (1926) was, as Kevin Brownlow had said, one of the films that created the language of cinema:

feats of imagination of the legitimate stage, such as the chariot race of "Ben-Hur," with horses thundering on a treadmill while an orchestra crashed out "The Ride of the Valkyries" and a cyclorama of the stadium revolved behind . . .[7]

Mathis continued to develop epics for her creation, THE SHEIK. Her death at age thirty-five was unexpected, and a universally acknowledged loss to an industry she helped to transform.

JUNE MATHIS

1918   Eye for an Eye, An
       To Hell with the Kaiser
1919   Brat, The
       Out of the Fog
       Red Lantern, The
1920   Hearts Are Trumps
       Our Lady 31
       Polly with a Past
1921   Camille
       Conquering Power, The
       Four Horsemen of the Apocalypse, The
       Idle Rich, The
       Sheik, The
       Trip to Paradise, A
1922   Blood and Sand
       Hate
       Kisses
       Turn to the Right
       Young Rajah, The
1923   Greed
       In the Palace of the King
       Spanish Dancer, The
       Three Wise Fools
1925   Classified
       Desert Flower, The
       Sally
       We Moderns
1926   Ben Hur
       Greater Glory, The
       Irene
1927   Magic Flame, The
       Masked Woman, The

Elinor Glyn (1864–1943)

She was Jackie Collins, Ann Landers, Emily Post, Jacquelyn Susann, and producer Dawn Steel all rolled into one, with all of their collective, colossal influence and power. She was the ultimate dictate about style, sophistication, love, and class.

She can be summarized by one word, "*It*". *It* was a word that became synonomous with an entire era. IT (1927) turned **Clara Bow** into the hottest thing to happen to movies since **Mary Pickford.** IT was the brainchild of **Elinor Glyn,** who didn't even know what a "movie" was until the age of fifty-seven. But when she made the discovery, she proceeded to and succeeded in taking Hollywood by storm.

She was the uncontested goddess of exotic passion. What **Mae West** did on the screen, Elinor Glyn could do on paper, and with equal alacrity. Her characters never once disrobed or used profanity. Gliding on the heels of Victorian romanticism, and spicing it up with jazz-age innuendo, Elinor Glyn, a British woman, became one of the richest most influential writers in Hollywood's history.

She was born on the Jersey Islands off the English coast, and was at once raised by an old world, aristocratic grandmother. When Elinor was about age five her mother reentered the scene with a tyrannical, if unwelcomed stepfather. Wealthy but lonely in a severe, caged childhood, the young Elinor found her escape and her refuge in books— anything she could get her hands on. When she was fourteen she wrote,

> On my eighteenth birthday I will have five thousand [dollars] a year. . . . I have been pretty since I was born and have known it ever since I could understand what the word pretty meant, so I have given up all vanity on the subject.[1]

From an early age, she was aware of her own distinction. Indeed she was pretty. Her grandson, Anthony Glyn, describes her: "milk-white skin, flowing red hair, vivid green eyes. . . . Men were drawn to her like moths to a candle."[2]

Glyn was a quixotic figure. To the millions who would later see her films, they would envision Elinor Glyn as "a siren reclining on a tiger skin, smoking a purple, scented cigarette and sipping a liqueur." The image was garnered from her novel, *Three Weeks,* written in 1907, which told the story of an upstanding, rather prudish young Englishman who falls hopelessly in love with a mysterious older woman. "The Lady," as she is called, is revealed to be of royal lineage. The novel's sultriest scene takes place on a tiger skin, and created a huge scandal that assured the book a place in worldwide circulation a good twenty-five years after publication, with sales totaling more than five million. The following is an excerpt from the "unspeakable" *Three Weeks,*

> Between her red lips . . . was an almost scarlet rose. Paul bounded forward but she raised one hand to stop him. . . . With a lightning movement, she lay on her face, raised her elbows on the tiger's head, and supported her chin in her hands. . . . A rage of passion was racing through Paul, his incoherent thoughts were that he did not want to talk—only to kiss her—to devour her—to strangle her with love if necessary. He bit the rose.[3]

And this was as racy as Elinor Glyn ever got. In brief, this style captures the mood and vibrations of an entire decade. Glyn's heroines did 'undulate' on tiger skins and beds of roses, but that was about the closest Elinor came to frank descriptions of sex. The love-making, in most of her books, followed a set and definitely limited pattern. The man, passionate and strong, mastered the woman with the strength and intensity of his love. Then suddenly all the mastery was gone, and he was on his knees before her, offering worship and homage. Nevertheless, Elinor was abused and reviled by critics, called an immortal woman and a glorifier of adultery.

However, to her few privileged friends Elinor Glyn was nothing like the idealized mysterious women of her imagination. As Anthony Glyn told it,

> She was an intellectual equal, with whom one could sit at a corner table at the Ritz and talk affairs of state or wander in the woods discussing Greek art and philosophy. To her family she was a regal creature from another time, whose beauty was a legend and whose guiding principle was always "noblesse oblige."[4]

Perhaps it wouldn't be as soon as her eighteenth birthday, but one day Elinor Glyn would have far more than five thousand a year, and her life would at least equal the most intricate escapist fantasies of her novels. In true noblesse fashion, Glyn was raised to expect that she would marry wealthy. But the idea of spending her life in a Cinderella cottage was hardly her notion of a good time. From Glyn's perspective, the whole point of Cinderella's struggle was that she would end up living in a palace. And so, Elinor Glyn made sure she did exactly that.

The problem, however, was that when imagination met reality, Glyn found herself stuck in a palace in the middle of nowhere. Her marriage to country gentleman, and long-confirmed bachelor, Clayton Glyn, quickly dissolved of a short-lived passion. Divorce in those days was of course out of the question. Elinor began, once again, to find solace in novels, but now they were ones that she wrote herself.

Three Weeks was like a World War II bomb that fell thirty-five years before its time. It was responded to as such by an unsuspecting public. As fast as the publisher could print it, that's how fast it sold out. The little-known novelist Mrs. Glyn (or "Madam Glyn" as she insisted on being

called), was an overnight, international sensation. She was the Emily Post of romance, desire, and love. She wrote articles for magazines both in England and in America with such titles as, "How to Get and Keep Your Man." She became the unquestioned authority on such topics, even though her own personal love life was a dismal failure. Glyn would have a few short romances, but for the most part she got a vicarious thrill from the passionate creations of her mind.

Three Weeks obtained exactly the lightning-fast reputation for immorality that Glyn intended. It was banned in Boston, which turned into the ideal publicity scam. Twenty-five years later, as late as 1932, a Mickey Mouse cartoon was banned in Ohio because it showed a cow reclining in a field reading *Three Weeks*. "For the most part," said Anthony Glyn, "Elinor Glyn books were to be kept out of sight. But it was considered social illiteracy not to have read them."[5]

The pioneer in Elinor Glyn really emerged at age fifty-seven, when she suddenly found herself a widow. The year was 1920. She was already a world renowned novelist when an offer came from Hollywood producer Jesse Lasky. He suggested that Glyn move to Hollywood, study the technical problems of making a motion picture, write a scenario, and then supervise its production. Anthony Glyn tells of her courageous departure from her native England,

> For a long moment, she stood on the pier staring up at the grate [sic], smoking funnels of the liner, and for almost the first time in her life she was afraid. Then, she pulled her purple wool scarf quickly around her shoulders and marched up the gangplank.[6]

Someone said that when she stepped off the boat she looked just like the Chalk Cliffs of Dover. Nearly sixty years of age, this brave woman was uprooting herself from *all* of her familiarities: her family, her friends, her homeland. This was not merely a visit, but a move to a strange land six thousand miles away, *And* she was going to apprentice herself in an entirely new career. If anyone was characteristic of a pioneer, Elinor Glyn was "*It*".

In Hollywood, in 1920, Samuel Goldwyn came up with the truly brilliant idea of flying in "eminent authors" from all over the world to write for the movies. Although a few adapted well to the new and tricky business (it is well known that Hollywood contributed to the ruin of F. Scott Fitzgerald's life, not to mention his career), Elinor Glyn took to it like a fish to water. More accurately, in her case, the waters made way for the fish.

Goldwyn had gathered his authors in a prominent hotel, the Gotham in Los Angeles, which became the grapevine and the nerve center of the town. In it were housed such celebrities of the day as Somerset Maugham, Rupert Hughes (uncle to Howard), **Lenore Coffee** (another pioneering scriptwriter), and Sir Gilbert Parker.

In her book *Storyline,* Lenore Coffee tells of how Sir Gilbert Parker invited Madam Glyn up to his room for drinks. When he amorously attempted to take her into his arms, Glyn held out her hand with magnificent hauteur and said, "You may kiss my hand. All emotion begins at the wrist."[7]

Glyn, however, had a contrasting side which was revealed during the filming of her first book. She and a casting director were discussing some fifteen young men who were to form a Palace Guard. She discussed the physique she wished these men to have in great, unembarrassed detail adding, "You must remember they are going to wear those silk, skin-clinging tights, so make certain they are the correct size. There is nothing so obscene as a man's legs in wrinkled tights." She shuddered at the unpleasant thought. Just as the casting director was about to turn away she added, "And no jock-straps." The man stopped dead in his tracks. Never before had he heard such

audacity from a woman! He replied in a shaky voice, "But you said the tights were to be skin-clinging." "Of course," replied Madam Glyn, with perfect sangfroid, "That is why there are to be no jock-straps. I do not believe in interfering with Nature." As **Lenore Coffee** reported, "It was said that on the days of these tests the Gotham complained a lamentable shortage of knackwursts!"[8]

Elinor Glyn threw herself into her new life in America with the energy and alacrity of a twenty-year-old. She found a new friend in **Mary Pickford,** whose gracious qualities reminded Elinor of the old-world personalities she had known in the vanished courts of Europe. Glyn and Pickford found their admiration for each other refreshingly pure and thankfully devoid of the glitter and gloss associated with Hollywood. Glyn's happiest hours were spent in Pickford's haven of Pickfair.

On the business front however, Glyn's life was hardly a fairytale. She quickly discovered the dismal, encumbered, and frustrating maze of conditions so peculiar to Hollywood. How impossible it seemed for a story to reach the screen as the writer conceived it! Eminent literary personalities, such as Somerset Maugham, were always on hand like so many peacocks strutting their feathers—but Glyn soon found that it wasn't the literary abilities of these writers which were of value, it was their status. She wrote in her memoirs:

> The blatantly crude or utterly false psychology of the stories as finally shown upon the screen was on a par with the absurdity of the sets and clothes, but we were powerless to prevent this. All authors, living or dead, famous or obscure, shared the same fate. Their stories were rewritten and completely altered, either by the stenographers and continuity girls, or by the assistant director and his lovelady. . . . Even when at last, after infinite struggle, a scene was shot which bore some resemblance to the original story, it was certain to be left out in the cutting room, or pared away to such

an extent that all meaning which it might once have had was lost.[9]

When she was at last to see her dream of the filmming of *Three Weeks* come true in 1923, she hoped the hero would be allowed to play the final love scene in pajamas. The censors, however, would hear none of it. "In the approved version," reported one early film magazine, "the queen tiptoed away, wracked with sobs, leaving Paul asleep on a couch of rose petals, still in full evening dress, his hair smooth and his waistcoat uncrumpled."[10]

Nevertheless, *Three Weeks* was tauted a "colossal success," words rarely used even in Hollywood in the twenties. Metro Studio (later to become part of Metro-Goldwyn-Mayer), made a fortune, and its executives gave Elinor Glyn carte blanche to write whatever she next wanted for the moves. She chose *His Hour,* a vehicle that turned John Gilbert into a star.

By the time the phenomenal film IT did the same for the red-headed and charismatic **Clara Bow,** in the mind of the public it was hard to differentiate IT from its author. Glyn played a cameo of herself in the film, the unquestioned, world-renowned authority on etiquette. She, and only she, intrinsically knew what "it" was—a characteristic she determined for an entire Jazz Age generation.

As was to be for the next quarter of a century, the name Elinor Glyn became syn-onymous with everything that was gla-mourous, mysterious, and forbidden. A rhyme, which caused her much amusement, appeared soon after the release of the screen version of *Three Weeks,*

> Would you like to sin
> with Elinor Glyn
> on a tiger skin?
> Or would you prefer
> to err with her
> on some other fur?[11]

It contributed considerably toward her reputation as a scarlett woman.

Many wanted "*It,*" but few had it. "*It*" was harder to obtain than it looked. You really had to be there to know just what "*It*" was. But whatever it was, it was the heart, the blood, and the creation of a sixty-year-old British woman who set the pace and the trends for an entire American generation—the first real "liberated" generation that America would know. The name Elinor Glyn would become like that of Atlantis: something antiquated but frozen in time—a lost world—never to be duplicated, replicated, or forgotten.

ELINOR GLYN

1927	It (Writer)
1929	Knowing Men (Director)
(Date Unknown)	Price of Things, The (Director)

Anita Loos

Frances Marion (with Mary Pickford).

FROM THE SILENTS
TO THE SOUND ERA

◆ ◆ ◆

Frances Marion (1887–1973)

The Scarlet Letter (1850) was proclaimed an impossible story to adapt for the screen by many, including, indirectly, the author himself, Nathaniel Hawthorne. "My writings do not appeal to the broadest class of sympathies," he said, "and therefore will not obtain a wide popularity. The main narrative lacks sunshine."[1]

After two screen versions had bombed, the 1926 version starring **Lillian Gish** turned out to be, as Joe Franklin puts it in *Classics of the Silent Screen* (1959), "one of the screen's most skillful literary adaptations."

Here are other fragments of Franklin's description of the film. It was,

> made by the noted Swedish director, Victor Seastrom,

and,

> Hendrik Sartov's camerawork is magnificent throughout.

So what is wrong with this picture? Actually, the *picture* was a hit. It's the *re-counting* of the picture that presents a problem. Classically, the director and the cinematographer, both male, are touted by name for their genius. But the woman responsible for this most "successful adaptation" is unnamed and thus rendered invisible. She was the pioneering screenwriter with a fifty-year career, **Frances Marion.**

Frances Marion was considered during the twenties and the thirties to be "the Dean of Hollywood Screenwriters." Adela Rogers St. John called her "the greatest scriptwriter who ever lived." At the height of her career, she was bringing in a salary to the tune of seventeen thousand dollars a week.[2] Marion was among the first writers ever to work closely on the set in the actual making of motion pictures.

She began as a cub writer for the *San Francisco Reporter* at the age of nineteen. She distinguished herself early as the first woman war correspondent, commissioned by General John Pershing to cover World War I battles.

Her role was to write about women's war activities, but when the Armistice was signed, she scored a coup by getting a lift with a Red Cross truck into Coblenz on the Rhine, opposite Ehrenbreitstein, where the U.S. Army of occupation was to establish its headquarters.[3]

When Frances Marion arrived in Hollywood in 1913, the movies were still known as "flickers." It would be some time before film would be thought of as a respectable medium. In any case, actors were certainly not considered respectable tenants. Bad news for a young Marion who pursued acting briefly during her early tenure in Hollywood.

Her first real paying job, however, was working for **Lois Weber** as her protégée. Part of Marion's duties was stunting as a rider for **Weber's** leading actress, **Winifred Kingston.** Subsequently Marion, an excellent horsewoman, did all **Kingston's** riding scenes for the Bosworth studio.[4] She was described by Elsie Janis in her autobiography *So Far, So Good* as

a pretty blue-eyed girl very much in evidence around the studio. It was difficult to find what her job was, for she did a little of everything. She played in the picture one week, helped "cut" the next, wrote a story the next, and in her spare moments handled the publicity.... I told [the production head of Bosworth] that she'd be heard from someday.[5]

Indeed Janis's predictions were right on the money. Marion's first full-fledged job as a scenario writer was on a **Mary Pickford** film, THE FOUNDLING (1916)—a picture that would alter the course of her life.

From there, Marion became, as Gavin Lambert said, "as prolific as the silent screen itself."[6] She wrote many of **Mary Pickford's** most successful films, among them, REBECCA OF SUNNYBROOK FARM (1917), and POLLYANNA (1920). Buddy Rogers, **Mary Pickford's** second husband,

claims, "It was Frances [Marion] who was responsible for coining the multi-million dollar image of 'America's Sweetheart.' "[7]

Marion was responsible for writing two of **Lillian Gish's** films directed by Victor Seastrom THE WIND, (1927) and THE SCARLET LETTER (1926). She also wrote THE SON OF THE SHEIK (1926) for Rudolph Valentino.

In 1925 she formed "Frances Marion Pictures." By 1927 her roster for writing for the great stars was nearly as long as cinema itself: LOVE (1927) for **Greta Garbo,** TILLIE WAKES UP (1917) for **Marie Dressler,** THE LADY (1925) for **Norma Talmadge,** HE COMES UP SMILING (1918) for Douglas Fairbanks, and many more of the "romantic" Fairbanks classics. The list goes on and on. By the end of her journey, her films read like a best-hits list of the cinema's all-time great classics: CAMILLE (1936), ANNA CHRISTIE (**Garbo's** first talkie [1930]), MIN AND BILL (**Marie Dressler** won an Oscar for this one [1930]), DINNER AT EIGHT (1933), and STELLA DALLAS (1937).

The bulk of her pictures are, as Marjorie Rosen has said,

action dramas, glib and fast-paced, with gangsters and gun battles. THE SECRET SIX (1931), set among the Chicago stockyards and speakeasies, attacked bootlegging and organized crime, racketeers and corruption. THE BIG HOUSE (1930) depicted in harsh, unsentimental terms the horrors of penitentiary life. Marion's films were without romance and alarmingly naturalistic, exactly the antithesis of ... the archetypical "women's pictures."[8]

Marion won the second and third Oscars ever given for the craft of screen writing: THE BIG HOUSE, and THE CHAMP (1931), starring Wallace Beery, who also won an Oscar for his performance.

Altogether, Frances Marion wrote as many as 136 produced screenplays in her career. Prolific? Yes, but that fact is inconsequential when one considers the sheer quality of her accomplishment. First, it was difficult for anyone to make the tough transition from silents to talkies no matter what the craft. Marion made the transition effortlessly. But even more important, there are only perhaps three or four women in Hollywood today who have had more than three of their screenplays actually produced. The way the studio system now works, it is not at all uncommon for a writer to have a thriving career from writing screenplays that are commissioned but will never see the light of the silver screen.

In the 1930s Marion signed on as a contract writer for MGM. The idea of "assembly line" writing was then becoming common practice at the studios. "After you have spent years in a studio," she wrote in her autobiography, "you feel like one of the legs of a centipede, useful as a sort of insignificant modus operandi."[9] But by this time, she was an extremely *powerful* centipede at MGM. Writers who wanted more control over their own product launched themselves into directing . . . an urge that Marion satisfied years before in her youth under **Mary Pickford**'s reign.

Marion's professional compatibility with **Pickford** can not be overstated. "They had a remarkably happy union, one which benefited both careers mutually."[10] After a time Pickford entrusted Marion with anything she would have entrusted her own daughter with, had she had one. This included opportunities to direct a **Pickford** film: THE LOVE LIGHT (1921). Marion also directed a great many of **Marion Davies**'s films later on. But even with a modicum of success in the craft, directing was never really Marion's medium. It was one she felt best left to others.

Hollywood often remade foreign versions of American films in the late twenties and midthirties. It was in this way that Marion's screenplays found their way into German, French, and Spanish translations.

Unlike many of the cinema's female pioneers, Marion never felt she had to sacrifice a personal life to have a career. Classically, this is truer of writers than with women in any of the other allied film crafts. She was first married to an early cowboy of the movies, Fred Thomson, with whom she had two sons. After his death, she married director George Hill. Somehow she found spare time to write *How to Write and Sell Film Stories* (1937), several novels, an autobiography, *Off with Their Heads* (1973), and she also found time to paint. She believed in honing and actively pursuing her painting as a means of transcribing her visual sense to paper.

Buddy Rogers told me that Marion was sitting about one day with **Pickford** and several other friends. Someone was sketching designs for what would become the official statuette of the Academy Award. When Marion took a look at the sketch she said, "This looks just like my uncle Oscar!" And that became its familiar name. She may continue to be challenged for making this claim by historians,[11] as well as **Bette Davis,** who said *she* named it after the rear end of one of her husbands. But whether or not she'll be remembered as the woman who named the Oscar, Frances Marion can confidently claim her title as "First Lady" of screen writing.

FRANCES MARION

1915 Camille
       Daughter of the Sea, A
       Girl of Yesterday, A
       Wild Girl from the Hills, The
1916 All Man
       Battle of the Hearts, The
       Bought and Paid For
       Crucial Test, The
       Feast of Life, The
       Foundling, The
       Friday the 13th
       Gilded Cage, The
       Hidden Scar, The
       La Vie de Boheme

On Dangerous Ground
Revolt, The
Rise of Susan, The
Social Highwayman, The
Summer Girl, The
Tangled Fates
Then I'll Come Back to You
Woman's Way, A
Yellow Passport, The
1917 Amazons, The
As Man He Made Her
Beloved Adventuress, The
Crimson Dove, The
Darkest Russia
Divorce Game, The
Forget-Me-Not
Girl's Folly, A
Hungry Heart, The
Little Princess, A
Poor Little Rich Girl, A
Rebecca of Sunnybrook Farm
Social Leper, The
Square Deal, A
Stolen Paradise, The
Tillie Wakes Up
Web of Desire, The
Woman Alone, A
1918 Amarilly of Clothesline Alley
City of Dim Faces, The
Goat, The
He Comes up Smiling
How Could You, Jean?
Johanna Enlists
M'Liss
Stella Maris
Temple of Dusk, The
1919 Anne of Green Gables
Captain Kidd, Jr.
Misleading Widow, The
Regular Girl, A
1920 Cinema Murder, The
Flapper, The
Humoresque
Pollyanna
Restless Sex, The
World and His Wife, The
1921 Love Light, The
Straight Is the Way

1922 Back Pay
East Is West
Eternal Flame, The
Just around the Corner
Primitive Lover, The
Sonny
Toll of the Sea, The
1923 Famous Mrs. Fair, The
French Doll, The
Love Piker, The
Nth Commandment, The
Potash and Perlmutter
Voice from the Minaret, The
Within the Law
1924 Abraham Lincoln
Cytherea
In Hollywood with Potash and
    Perlmutter
Secrets
Song of Love, The
Sundown
Tarnish
Through the Dark
1925 Dark Angel, The
Flaming Forties, The
Graustark
His Supreme Moment
Lady, The
Lazybones
Lightnin'
Simon, the Jester
Thank You
Thief in Paradise, A
Zander the Great
1926 First Year, The
Paris at Midnight
Partners Again—Potash and
    Perlmutter
Scarlet Letter, The
Son of the Sheik, The
Winning of Barbara Worth, The
1927 Callahans and the Murphys, The
Love
Madame Pompadour
Red Mill, The
Wind, The
1928 Awakening, The
Bringing up Father

Anita Loos (1893–1981)

"Gentlemen might prefer blonds," quipped **Anita Loos** before her death at age eighty-eight, "but they marry brunettes."[1] She should know. This 4′ 11″ powerhouse of comedic talent, infamously renowned for her blond bombshell of a creation, GENTLEMEN PREFER BLONDS (1928), was a brunette herself. Anita Loos bravely launched her theories on what was an essentially brown-haired world until her book came out in 1925. Is it true blonds have more fun? Well, if they do now, we've only Loos to blame. It was her idea. By the time her blockbuster came to the stands, Loos had been a leading Hollywood scriptwriter for more than a decade.

Anita Loos's prolific contribution to the world of film is undeniable. She turned out 105 scripts between 1912 and 1915, only 4 of which went unproduced. She was the first to turn "title writing" on the silent screen into a wisecracking art form. Between 1919 and 1921 everyone tried to copy her wit, making the reading of screen titles nearly unbearable, for no one could quite match her humor. By the time her smash hit GENTLEMEN PREFER BLONDS was adapted for the screen from her novel, the

New York Times commented that Anita Loos's big triumph was to bring an element of maturity to an art form that was in danger of becoming infantile.

She popped on the film scene as a child prodigy. Said Loos, "The fact that movies were actually written instead of being ad-libbed on the set, and that one of the authors was young, and for a writer, rather toothsome, made me seem a sort of West Coast Aspasia."[2]

GENTLEMEN PREFER BLONDS was never *meant* to be a blockbuster. Originally, it wasn't even intended as a book. Loos had been writing a letter to amuse her friend, H. L. Mencken. It amused him so much he suggested she get it published. "Young lady," he warned, "you're the first American writer ever to make fun of sex! Why don't you send it to *Harper's Bazaar* where it'll get lost among the ads and won't offend the boobus americanus?"[3] She did. *Harper's*, a nice "ladies" publication in those days, suddenly found itself negotiating ads for men's apparel, cigars, sporting goods. Apparently not only the ladies liked Loos's story. The magazine's circulation immediately quadrupled. The book version ran through eighty-five editions, and was translated into fourteen languages including Chinese. *Gentlemen Prefer Blonds,* more than any other single American classic, made its author's name.

With Anita Loos, the question rises as to exactly how did women fit into the Hollywood machine? If movies reflect and, as some would argue, *create* our mores, how did women participate in establishing the status quo? As prolific and talented a dynamo as she was, Loos presented images that varied little from the expected norms and standard stereotypes of female behavior.

Loos's own youth and her predilection for relationships with dominant, controlling men appears to have taken precedence over her fine mind in dealing with female characterizations." How could a girl like Loos fail to write, in the more than two hundred screenplays of her career, material that would reflect this preference for subservience to her men?[4]

She didn't write about being a 4' 11" dynamically intelligent woman who thought she deceived the world by wearing deliciously girlish flapper garb. (P.S. Bobbed hair and sailor dresses were originally her idea.)[5]

She didn't tell us how it felt to get paid gobs of money for her work, when the culture was saying that women really weren't working at all. She never wrote a film about what it must have felt like to be told by a beau that she was some kind of a monster because she was a writer—and a highly successful one at that.

She wrote and made her name with Loreli Lee—a stereotyped caricature of woman as the dumb blond, a woman who was charming because the culture knew her well: tits, ass, and no brains.

Nonetheless George Santayana said of *Gentlemen* that it was the most important philosophical work ever written by an American; Oliver Wendell Holmes said it was "a shot heard around the world."[6]

In Montreal when a publication devoted entirely to women in film entitled *Take One,* asked Anita Loos to write an article in the early seventies, she wrote back:

It's been forty years since I worked in films. When I did I found my male bosses adorable. I don't like women very much. I don't like their films, so I pass them up. Throughout my career women have done me much more dirt than men. I just find them tiresome, if not vicious. So I don't think you'll find me any help for your project. Just the same, good luck!   Anita Loos.[7]

"I learned very early to keep my mouth shut about my literary life," said Anita Loos. "When I first mentioned it to a beau he thought I was lying. . . . A few letters of acceptance . . . caused an even more unfortunate reaction: My beau didn't want to believe I was an authoress; it turned me into some sort of monster, I no longer seemed a girl! So, I decided my literary life belonged to a secret world where I could be alone with my plots, and an unknown man named Griffith."[8]

She was often called the **Dorothy Parker** of the movies. Parker herself got her start in movies when she was hired by *director* **Lillian Gish** to pen titles for Gish's REMODELING HER HUSBAND in 1920. Anita Loos proceeded to write 150 more over the next thirty years. The only other writer to beat her record was **Frances Marion.** Gary Carey in his biography, *Anita Loos* (1988), calls her "extraordinarily disciplined, resilient, morally fastidious."

What is less well-known about Loos is her real claim to fame. Gary Carey tells it this way.

She was the first practitioner of the wisecrack for the screen. . . . At a time when the film had not yet found its voice, [she] singlehandedly introduced verbal humor, with special attention to the national argot that was then evolving, and made the *printed subtitle* as ubiquitous as the photographic image.[9]

Titles like "Proteus Prindle was a self-made man who adored his maker," made Anita Loos well loved. Her screen career began when the Lupin Company in March 1912, then Biograph a month later, purchased two of Loos's scenarios. The first of her scripts to be translated into celluloid, however, was THE NEW YORK HAT (1909), which D. W. Griffith purchased for twenty-five dollars as a vehicle for **Mary Pickford** (her last picture with Biograph) and Lionel Barrymore. Not a bad sale for a sixteen-year-old in 1909. Loos had signed her story, "A. Loos." When Griffith met the girl accompanied by her father, he naturally assumed the latter had penned the tale. . . .

THE NEW YORK HAT would be one of the few Loos scripts to be directed by Griffith, although she followed him from studio to studio from 1912–16. As Gary Carey points out:

> Comedy was not his forté. . . . Many of Griffith's films, even at the time of their creation, must have seemed a backward glance at a life fast fading, whereas Miss Loos' little stories prick the pulse of the times.[10]

When Loos's scripts were turned over to one of Triangle's secondary directors, John Emerson (later Loos's husband), the art of the subtitle was born. Emerson, Loos, and Douglas Fairbanks, Sr., in his first trial run with the duo, turned out HIS PICTURE IN THE PAPERS (1916). Griffith took one look at the subtitles and shelved it. He reasoned that if audiences wanted to read, they would stay at home with a book. But Carey explains:

> Only a booking crisis forced Triangle into releasing it. A sensational hit, it established Fairbanks as a film star and the printed title

as a part of film grammar. She would continue to write many of Fairbanks's successful films prior to his adventure period, and she would live to see Griffith eat his words. He later hired her to pen the titles for his masterpiece, INTOLERANCE [1916].[11]

By the time writing credits became the rage, Loos obtained her first one by penning an adaptation of MACBETH. The credits read, "By William Shakespeare and Anita Loos." Such was her wit in a nutshell.

Loos went on to turn out many great screen classics, among them SAN FRANCISCO (1936) and THE WOMEN (1939). The first she deemed her favorite, because she based Clark Gable's role on the great love of her life, the legendary bon vivant Wilson Mizner. She memorably sketched Mizner again in her book *Kiss Hollywood Goodbye* (1974).

From her earliest days, when she paved the way as her family's breadwinner by child acting, Loos surmised that domesticity would never be her game (though to her dying day, she was loath to call herself a feminist). Quite early, she decided her real calling was to follow in her father's footsteps (he was a California newspaperman) and become a writer. But later, her marriage to John Emerson seemed to prove out her early instincts that marriage in the old way was a bad idea.

> [Emerson] was unfaithful. . . . A hypochondriac, he took advantage of her in innumerable ways: it is hard to say exactly what combination of love, loyalty and misplaced guilt persuaded her to put up with him. Finally, one morning in 1937, he told her that they were about to lose all their money (untrue), and that she would "have to live on Campbell's soup," which was something he couldn't allow—at which point he stretched out his arm and tried to strangle her. She managed to push him aside and get him into a sanitarium the next day. He was diagnosed schizophrenic, and remained a patient there for the last twenty years of his life.[12]

The following description of the men in her life somewhat explains Loos's inability to conceive healthier female characters on the page. Rayne Adams was an architect, as well as John Emerson's best friend and widower of Emerson's ex-wife. Adams tried to steal Emerson's second girl away when he fell in love with Loos and asked her to marry him. Loos, however, would have none of Rayne Adams.

> The reasons why I couldn't fall in love with Rayne have become obvious; he gave me full devotion and required nothing in return, while John treated me in an offhand manner, appropriated earnings, and demanded from me all the services of a hired maid. How could a girl like I resist him?" Emerson often demanded his name on scripts as coauthor, when he had nothing whatsoever to do with them.[13]

With Emerson gone, it is possible that Loos grew even more prolific. She proved to be one of the few writers in the world who moved successfully from a career in script writing to other mediums. Generally, one finds that's done the other way around. She had a wide versatility that proved she could turn out plays, novels, and memoirs as facilely as movies. She was best when targeting movies for specific actors: Douglas Fairbanks, **Constance Talmadge.** But the best of these she fashioned for **Jean Harlow.** "Her wise-cracking dialogue was enhanced by Harlow's brilliantly natural timing and gold-digging glamour,"[14] says Gary Carey about Loos's RED-HEADED WOMAN (1932).

The *New York Times* once described her as "a child of ten chortling over a disaster."[15] Loos knew that to be wise meant to see the folly in how we live, not to take ourselves too seriously. In 1974, when she was eighty-one, she said to *Newsweek:*

> Helen Hayes, Paulette Goddard, Adele Astaire, we were kids together in New York. I was just a girl who had a writing job. Adele was dancing with her brother.

It never occurred to us we'd amount to anything. We were too busy having fun. Well, she giggled, I'm still doing that.[16]

Although as Carey says, "Her humor acts as a deflection of human foibles and hypocrisy, but with the lightest of touches,"[17] one wonders what amazements might have flourished from Anita Loos's pen had she written about her own experiences instead of primarily concerning herself so scrupulously with male regard.

ANITA LOOS

1912	Earl and the Tomboy, The
	He Was a College Boy
	New York Hat, The
	Power of the Camera, The
	Road to Plaindale, The
1913	All for Mabel
	All on Account of a Cold
	Binks Runs Away
	Bunch of Flowers, A
	Cure for Suffragettes, A
	Deacon's Whiskers, The
	Fall of Hicksville's Finest
	Fallen Hero, A
	Fatal Deception, The
	Fireman's Love, A
	For Her Father's Sins
	Gentlemen and Theives
	Great Motor Race, The
	Girl Like Mother, A
	Hicksville Epicure, A
	His Awful Vengeance
	His Hoodoo
	Horse on a Bill, A
	How the Day Was Saved
	Lady in Black, The
	Making of a Masher, The
	Mayor Elect, The
	Mother, The
	Narrow Escape, A
	Pa Says
	Path of True Love
	Queen of the Carnival

Saving Grace, The
Suicide Pact, The
Two Women
Unlucky Fim
Wall Flower, The
Wedding Gown, The
When a Woman Guides
Widow's Kids, The
Yiddish Love

1914 At the Tunnel's End
Balked Heredity, A
Blasted Romance, A
Chieftian's Daughter, The
Comer in Hats, A
Deceiver, The
Deadly Glass of Beer, The
Hicksville Reformer, A
Fatal Curve, The
Fatal Dress Suit, The
Flurry in Art, A
Girl in The Shack, The
His Hated Rival
His Rival
How They Met
Last Drink of Whiskey, The
Life and Death Affairs, A
Meal Ticket, The
Million-Dollar Bride, The
Mortimer's Millions
Nearly a Burglar's Bride
Nell's Eugenic Wedding
Nellie, The Female Villain
No Bull Spy, A
Saving Presence, The
School of Acting, The
Sensible Girl, The
Stolen Masterpiece, The
Style Accustomed, The
Suffering of Susan, The
Where the Roads Part
White Slave Catchers, The

1915 Burlesquers, The
Cost of a Bargain, The
Fatal Fingerprints, The
Fatal Fourth, The
Heart That Truly Loved
How to Keep a Husband
Little Liar, The

Mixed Values
Mountain Bred
Nellie, The Female Victim
Pennington's Choice
Sympathy Sal
Tear on the Page, The
Wards of Fate

1916 American Aristocracy
Calico Vampire
Comer in Cotton, A
French Milliner
Half-Breed, The
His Picture in the Papers
Intolerance
Laundry Liz
Manhattan Madness
Macbeth
Matrimaniac, The
Social Secretary, The
Stranded
Wharf Rat, The
Wild Girl of the Sierras

1917 Americano, The
Down to Earth
In Again, Out Again
Reaching for the Moon
Wild and Wooly

1918 Come on In
Goodbye Bill
Hit-the-Trail Holiday
Let's Get a Divorce

1919 Getting Mary Married
Isle of Conquest, The
Oh, You Women!
Temperamental Wife, A
Virtuous Vamp, A

1920 Branded Woman, The
In Search of a Sinner
Love Expert, The
Perfect Woman, The
Two Weeks

1921 Dangerous Business
Mama's Affair
Woman's Place, A

1922 Polly of the Follies
Red Hot Romance

1923 Dulcy

1924 Three Miles Out

1925	Learning to Love
1927	Publicity Madness
1928	Gentlemen Prefer Blonds
1931	Struggle, The
1932	Blondie of the Follies
	Red-Headed Woman
1933	Barbarian, The
	Hold Your Man
	Midnight Mary
1934	Biography of a Bachelor Girl
	Girl from Missouri, The
	Social Register

1935	Riffraff
1936	San Francisco
1937	Mama Steps Out
	Saratoga
1938	Alaska
	Great Canadian, The
1939	Women, The
1940	Susan and God
1941	Blossoms in the Dust
	They Met in Bombay
	When Ladies Meet
1942	I Married an Angel

THE SOUND ERA

◆ ◆ ◆

Mae West (1893–1980)

"Let her go, she's different," said Mae's mother to her father.

From the moment of her birth in August of 1893, she was an unqualified anomaly. It was **Mae West** and Mae West alone who helped bring S-E-X out of America's closet. And for all of our appearances of Victorian propriety, the American people must have liked it, because in 1934 she earned next to the largest salary in the United States—second only to publisher William Randolph Hearst.

But that's not why she wins my vote as a pioneer. In 1933, when Paramount was in serious financial hot water, they turned to Mae West, the playwright, for help. Her play *Diamond Lil* (1928) had been a huge success on Broadway. At first the Paramount attitude was, "We don't think Mae West's play would make a good picture. The period, the Gay Nineties, would be all wrong for the moviegoers who are college students, teenagers, and children."[1] As Jon Tuska has written, "Things were no different in 1933 Hollywood from what they are today—the fact that the stage play had enjoyed immense financial success impressed almost no one."[2] Which is probably how Paramount got itself into box-office hot water in the first place. Astutely Tuska points out, "It was the Hollywood pattern to secure a new property of seemingly unique interest, decide upon a mode of exploitation, pursue that mode until it was exhausted, and then again to secure a new property. Mae West is one of the few who beat them at their own game."[3]

And so, although her tenure on the screen was not long, her Diamond Lil creation from the stage had already made her infamous in America's mind. The studio brass had nothing to lose by jumping into what they wrongly anticipated to be another commercial flop.

What they hadn't counted on were the conditions. First Mae West said that she would have the final cut. And although she wouldn't require the screen credit, she'd have all creative control, including the choice of director. Second, she wanted to choose her own leading man. Okay, okay, they said, so who would you like this leading man to be? She didn't know exactly. But as she was walking with two producers on the Paramount lot, she spotted a "sensational-looking young man." "Him!" she said—to their shock and dismay. "What's his name? I want him for the lead."[4] With

Leigh Brackett

Lenore Coffee

Sonya Levien

Mae West

Lillian Hellman

Fay Kanin (right).

Dorothy Parker

Jay Presson Allen
(with director
Sidney Lumet).

anyone else, such whimsical insanity might have been the last straw, but Paramount chiefs were desperate. They ended up giving Mae everything she wanted, reticence be damned. Overnight, that unknown lead, Cary Grant, was launched into stardom in SHE DONE HIM WRONG (1933). Who said female intuition and business don't mix?

Similarly, she was right about her choice of Lowell Sherman as director. Sherman was a former actor from the legitimate stage with a "trained sense of the theatre and a knowledge of filmmaking that went back to D. W. Griffith in his heyday."[5]

What is not always instantaneously observed about West is that she was a *heck* of a writer. Certainly she was in a class all by herself as a performer. But without the witticisms of her innuendoes, she would have been just another studio puppet. First and foremost, Mae West was a writer. And a genius at that. She knew how to take the pulse of the times and translate it directly into comedy. Sex goddess par excellence, she never once disrobed or used profanity.

The question arises again and again with women writers along the decades of Hollywood's train, did she use her pen as a vehicle for endemically *female* transformation? Or did she merely seek to be a cog in the system and feel grateful to be working at all? Very clearly, Mae West spoke directly out of her instincts as a woman—*all* the time. As if she were born with unflagging confidence, she had little worry of pleasing anybody. "I don't read," she said in an inteview, "never have read and I guess I never will. I write in my books what I learned myself, from life."

"In many ways," writes Jon Tuska, "her material for the stage surpasses her films in brilliance. Her plays and stories . . . reveal a stylistic command of literary technique both rare and unusual, if undeservedly neglected."

From the very start, West wrote her own material. She began in vaudeville with her sister in an eighteen-minute original act. Already the critics were balking: "Unless Miss West can tone down her stage presence in every way she just might as well hop right out of vaudeville into burlesque."[6] That was it. Stock companies billed her as "The Baby Vamp." But it was her introduction of the "shimmy" to the stage that would begin her infamy.

> I was in Chi at the time, doin' vaudeville, a single. And after the show one night I goes to this jernt where spades have a cabaret, see? And I see them dancing the bump and the jelly roll and all them. Then a girl starts doin' a funny sort of dance and I asks, "What's that?" and the waiter says, "Oh Lady, that's shakin' the shimmy." Next night, I put it into my act and it like to tore the house down.[7]

Mae continued to do well with the "shimmy" despite the fearful hand of prudish critics. She played the Winter Garden in 1919. Soon she began to write musical comedy skits for piano accompaniment only.

By the midtwenties, "Mae's interest in the subject of sexuality and its dramatic potential for the stage began to consume her."[8] She read and absorbed everything she could about eroticism. The result was her play, *The Constant Sinner*.

> Anyone who reads Mae's *The Constant Sinner* will readily concede that the author was intimately informed on her subject. It tells of life in the dives, among prostitutes, the whole of predatory society. *Sex* (1926) would be the first of Mae's popular essays in carnal existence.[9]

Here's what *Billboard* said about *Sex* in 1926:

> The piece is not just low entertainment. It is not entertainment at all. Poorly written, poorly acted, horribly staged, *Sex* does not even contain anything for dirt seekers. The theme is trite and the lines are dull, while the action is simply disgusting.[10]

Apparently, the audience felt quite differently. *Sex* played 385 sold-out performances, and probably would have played longer had it not been raided, with West jailed for ten days. So much for critics. One of her headlines read, "Welfare Island Fails to Tame the Wild West." Speakeasies. Prohibition. West had her finger on the pulse of the moment. Her talent was in speaking on what the heart of all Americans kept silent on, but was longing to scream at the top of their lungs.

Before the raid on *Sex,* West wrote another play of "dubious morals" on male homosexuality called *The Drag.* She herself wrote about the play, "It stated that an intelligent understanding of the problems of all homosexuals by society could avert such social tragedies." The response? Even after the scandal of *Sex* (probably *especially* after the scandal of *Sex*), opening night was a sellout and packs were turned away. The play opened in New Jersey, and she was "warned" not to bring it to Broadway.

By the time of her success on the screen with Cary Grant in SHE DONE HIM WRONG (1933), her witticisms were becoming a national pastime. As West said, "It's better to be looked over than overlooked." The censors had their hackles up and audiences had their expectations up—they couldn't wait to see what she would do next. Next was an instant smash hit with her new, now not-so-unknown leading man, Cary Grant: I'M NO ANGEL (1933).

Three more pictures came from her pen, until 1936 saw the production of her play, *Klondike Annie* (1936). Many claim it was Mae's best. "No motion picture Mae West was ever in has caused so much controversy for all the wrong reasons."[11] It set William Randolph Hearst off, enough to encourage the Hays Office to clamp down. Censorship in Hollywood took away everyone's sense of humor—everyone, that is, except West. "All I have ever wanted to do is entertain people," she said, "make them laugh so hard they forget they'd like to cry."

From then on, the censors wouldn't leave her alone. It's been said that "genius is an infinite capacity for taking pains." And like most geniuses not understood in their times, hers would prove her downfall. She fooled her public into thinking she was an "R" rating when she was only a "PG." The rest of the "dirt" was the script the audiences penned in their own minds. Innuendoes and double entendres do not obscenity make. She was light-years ahead of her public in sophistication. Her genius was to be a sex symbol and a parody of her own image. Her leading men ranged also from sex symbol to parody: Cary Grant to W. C. Fields.

After the development of the Production Code (1934), West faced continued decline in popularity at the box office and became, as Jon Tuska points out, "a legend by *not* making movies." Did her personal life suffer? "I'm my own original creation," said West in an interview for *Playboy.* "I concentrate on myself most of the time; that's the only way a person can become a star in the true sense. I never wanted a love that meant surrender of my self-possession. I saw what it did to other people when they loved another person the way I loved myself, and I didn't want that problem."[12]

She never hid anything from the public—except the details of her private life. And what they didn't know kept her career afloat. "My basic style had never changed," she said. "I couldn't change it if I wanted to. I am a captive of myself. It or I created Mae West and neither of us could let the other go."[13]

The screen work of Mae West brought about unparalleled changes in the field of motion pictures. Her style changed America's views on sexuality. Mainly, it changed the views of women in general. She made a comeback at the age of seventy-eight in MYRA BRECKINRIDGE (1970) that was unspoiled by the failure of the film. How can you not respect a sex symbol who has the gall to make a comeback at seventy-eight? At the age of eighty-five, she returned lasciviously as the star of her own, SEXTETTE (1978).

MAE WEST

1933 I'm No Angel
       She Done Him Wrong
1934 Belle of the Nineties (Story,
       Screenplay)

1935 Goin' to Town (Screenplay,
       Dialogue)
1936 Go West, Young Man (Screenplay)
       Klondike Annie (Story, Screenplay)
1939 Every Day's a Holiday (Story,
       Screenplay)
1940 My Little Chickadee (Story,
       Screenplay)
1970 Myra Breckenridge
1978 Sextette

Dorothy Parker (1893–1967)

The soul of wit who was one of those writers not so much read as quoted, **Dorothy Parker** wisecracked everything from Calvin Coolidge's death ("How do they know?") to **Kate Hepburn**'s talents ("She runs the gamut of emotions from A to B"), and in doing so became a hallmark of her generation. She was also one of the highest-paid screenwriters at a time when the rest of the country, was suffering a Depression. In 1934, MGM hired her for $5,200 a week. The equivalent of that weekly figure today would easily be quadruple.

Although Dorothy Parker declared in 1927, "I attend no movies, for any motion picture theatre is an enlarged and a magnificently decorated lethal chamber to me,"[1] she managed to shift her views a bit for love (of a man, not of motion pictures) and for money. Only seven years hence, and throughout the forties, the inimitable queen of print-wit for the *New Yorker* (the one who signed her column, "Constant Reader"), was collaborating avidly as a writer for the screen. But Parker never attained a fondness for the medium that kept her.

> I can't talk about Hollywood. It was a horror to me when I was there and it's a horror to look back on. I can't imagine how I did it. When I got away from it I couldn't even refer to the place by name. "Out there," I

called it. You want to know what "Out there" means to me? Once I saw a Cadillac about a block long, and out of the side window was a wonderfully slink mink, and an arm, and at the end of the arm a hand in a white suede glove wrinkled around the wrist, and in the hand was a bagel with a bite out of it.[2]

When Parker was asked if she thought Hollywood destroys the artist's talent, she replied:

> No, no, no. I think nobody on earth writes down. Garbage though they turn out, Hollywood writers aren't writing down. That is their best. If you're going to write down, don't pretend to write down. It's going to be the best you can do and it's the fact that it's the best you can do that kills you. I want so much to write well, though I know I don't, and that I didn't make it.[3]

What ultimately got Parker down about Hollywood however, had nothing to do with the work, but:

> The people. Like the director who put his finger in Scott Fitzgerald's face and complained, "Pay *you!* Why you should pay us." It was terrible about Scott; if you'd seen him you'd have been sick. When he died no one went to the funeral, not a single soul came, or even sent a flower. I said,

"Poor son of a bitch," a quote right out of *The Great Gatsby,* and everyone thought it was another wisecrack. But it was said in dead seriousness.

It wasn't only the people, but also the indignity to which your ability was put.[4]

Dorothy Parker was described as "a small woman, her voice gentle, her tone often apologetic, but, when given the opportunity to comment on matters she felt strongly about, her voice rose almost harshly, and her sentences were punctuated with observations phrased with a lethal force." She was known to many as the "Guinevere" of the Algonquin Round Table,[5] that famous literary coterie of notables that included her good friend Alexander Woollcott, as well as George S. Kaufman, Ring Lardner, Robert Benchley (the humorist with whom she shared an office at *Vanity Fair*), and playwright Robert Sherwood. But at birth, she began in the world as Dorothy Rothchild from West End, New Jersey.

Perhaps her caustic wit was a way of getting back at the world for her cruel beginnings. She was a child whose Scotch mother died when Dorothy was still a baby, and whose Jewish father left the world when she was only in her teens. Not connected to the Rothchilds of money, the young Dorothy was left broke and got her first job only two years after her father's death as a captions writer for *Vogue*. She later moved up in the world of magazines by joining *Vanity Fair*. At age twenty-four, she married Edwin Parker II, but the marriage dissolved soon after. The Parker name, however, was to stay for life.

Mainly, Dorothy Parker wrote about women, and the women she wrote about were those who were saddened by the downsides of freedom. They were bored with the lovers they had, and frustrated by the lovers they didn't have. *Time* magazine noted at the time of her death that "it was always the dream, not the reality, that mattered most. Her best story is 'Big Blond,'

about a woman who falls apart because she has no dream of her own."[6] It was a prophecy that ended up being not far from her own end.

In 1933, at the age of forty, Parker found her dream lad in the form of a much younger, would-be actor and scenarist, twenty-eight-year-old Alan Campbell. Campbell rode on Parker's coattails to success. But it was all right. Not only did he adore her, but as Leonard Woolf did for **Virginia,**

> Alan had bought the food, done the cooking, done all of the interior decorating in their apartment, painted all the insides of the bureau drawers, cleaned up after the dogs, washed and dried the dishes, made the beds, told Dorothy to wear her coat on coat days, amused her, adored her . . . and otherwise created space and time in her life for her to write.[7]

Even their close friend noted that Campbell was not the sort of fellow to marry as an opportunist. He genuinely did love her. When they met one another, Campbell was facing up to the fact that he'd never make a success as an actor, but the two of them might survive all right on Dorothy's reputation. Parker had worked for high stakes in Hollywood before, but

> after some weeks, I ran away. I could not stand it any more. I just sat in a cell-like office and did nothing. The life was expensive and the thousands of people I met were impossible. They never seemed to behave naturally, as if all their money gave them a wonderful background they could never stop to marvel over. I would imagine the Klondike like that—a place where people rush for gold.[8]

Nevertheless, they needed the money, and so she let Alan traipse her off to la-la-land once again in 1933, and this is the part of her story when MGM hires them for that legendary enormous sum. It suited Alan Campbell just fine to be happy writing drivel for Hollywood. The life-style too made him happy, and because of his attitude and her talent the two of them prospered. Between 1933 and 1938 they cranked out fifteen films, one of them, A STAR IS BORN (1937) was nominated for an Academy Award.[9]

Perhaps because she knew she was "a real writer" Parker felt all during that time that she was employed "by cretins . . . and was oppressed by the feeling that she was giving a real gloss to false pearls."[10] She was also disgusted because many of the scripts that she and Alan got credit for on the screen were rewritten (as is the old Hollywood custom) by five, six, seven different writers.

Hollywood needed the intelligence of Dorothy Parker, and they paid her dearly for it to the end. But aside from the cash flow, she in no way needed Hollywood. "After Hollywood," she said, "you need a rest. It's true that they pay you a pretty penny, but . . . you write, write, write, and then they call in a collaborator and you throw that out and start again. That's the *biggest* trouble in Hollywood, collaboration. But I needed the money."[11]

And boy, did they make money. It enabled them to buy a house in Beverly Hills, and soon, when the royalty checks started pouring in, it enabled them to buy a farm in Pennsylvania. It was in this way that Hollywood became bearable to Dorothy Parker. She hated the place with a passion but was smart enough to know she should not bite the hand that fed her. At the farm they could catch the red-eye when they needed to attend story conferences, but they didn't have to live with them. "You buy a farm," she said in 1943, "and when it's your own you can't enjoy it because you have to leave it to make money to pay for it."[12]

Much to her dismay, Dorothy Parker discovered, like everything else in Hollywood, that even the money wasn't real. "It's congealed snow; it melts in your hand."[13]

In the forties Parker became a staunch advocate of left-wing causes. She was proud that Campbell had volunteered and became a lieutenant against the axis dictatorship.[14] And although she may be remembered as a woman beset by the lighter side of life, she couldn't blink a comic eye at the goings-on overseas.

She began to write articles that were no laughing matter. She wrote a piece for *Mademoiselle* entitled, "Are We Women or Are We Mice?" in which the serious Parker fighter came out. She insisted to her readers that "there *was* something intelligent and effective that upper-class women could do. They could take on all sorts of work that had been done by the men who had gone to war,"[15] and thereby encouraged the days of Rosie the Riveter. Aside from her writings about taking action, Parker presented herself to the army recruiting office for the Women's Army Corps, but was rejected because of her age; she had just turned fifty. Infuriated, she made an application of waiver. They still answered no.

Dorothy Parker divorced Alan Campbell in 1947, remarried him in 1950, only to lose him to death (his) in 1963. She had collaborated in 1953 on an unsuccessful play called *The Ladies of the Corridor*, about lonely women who live in a hotel. Ironically, she spent her last years isolated and alone in a hotel room in Manhattan.

Perhaps her success was due to her determination "not to write like a woman" as she herself once put it.[16] She loathed the chatty style of women gossip columnists like **Louella Parsons,** and was determined to make her career as a writer of serious note, even if it was through cutting others down with humor, even if it meant using her incisive brain like "one of the boys," and quipping with the best literary men instead of her female peers. **Anita Loos** shared Parker's sentiments on this subject precisely.

And even at the age of fifty, when she was saddened and embittered by the world, she was still quipping, "I claim all the funny [remarks] whether I said them or not." But by this time, as perhaps always, her laconic side was only masking a saddened heart. She died at the age of seventy-three, melancholy and alone, and just as her friend Alexander Woollcott once suggested she might, "wringing her hands at sundown beside some open grave and looking pensively into the middle distance at the receding figure of some golden lad."[17]

DOROTHY PARKER

1934 Here Is My Heart
1935 Big Broadcast Of 1936, The (Songs)
    Mary Burns Fugitive (Songs)

One Hour Late
Paris in Spring (Songs)
1936 Lady Be Careful
    Moon's Our Home, The (Additional Dialogue)
    Suzy
    Three Married Men
1937 Star Is Born, A
    Woman Chases Man
1938 Sweethearts
1939 Trade Winds
1941 Little Foxes, The (Additional Dialogue)
    Weekend For Three
1942 Saboteur
1947 Smash Up (Costory)
1949 Fan, The
1954 Star Is Born, A (Remake)

Sonya Levien (1895–1960)

The author of some seventy screenplays, **Sonya Levien,** along with **Anita Loos** and **Frances Marion,** is among the most prolific screenwriters in Hollywood's history. The number is impressive because, along with **Loos** and **Marion,** Levien worked without a collaborator.[1]

Levien was born in Russia on Christmas Day and came to America at an early age. Since she was from a long line of famous Russian revolutionaries, the idea of crashing into the industry as a woman never daunted her for a moment.

Levien first acquired her law degree and practiced with the New York bar for six months before turning her focus entirely to writing. She was active in the women's suffrage movement and wrote for their official publication, *Woman's Journal.*[2] For six years, she worked with Theodore Roosevelt, editing his copy for *Metropolitan Magazine.* They wrote quite a number of pieces together.

Levien's many short stories were published in the *Saturday Evening Post, Wom-*

an's Home Companion, Life and scores of other magazines, eventually attracting the attention of Jesse Lasky (head of Famous Players Studio) in 1921. He invited Levien out to Hollywood to make a scenario out of one of her short stories. After she adapted her story, "Cheated Love" (1921), for the screen, Lasky offered her a twenty-four-thousand-dollar contract, but Levien didn't wish to leave her husband and son in New York. Her husband, Carl Hovey, was soon offered a job as a story editor for Cecil B. De Mille at Paramount, and the family moved to Hollywood.[3]

The Fox Film Corporation in 1932 wrote a publicity background about Levien:

> She possesses all the Russian instincts of impractibility. She's seldom on time for anything. She frequently misses trains. She is a friend of George Bernard Shaw and other literary dignitaries. She quarrels with herself, but never with her friends. And she always wants to be doing something other than what she is doing. She possesses a

wonderful smile. She's a Russian Jewess, but looks more like an Irish Colleen . . . dark brown hair, blue eyes, fresh peach complexion, and wears horned rimmed glasses when she works.[4]

It didn't take long for Levien to get hooked on movies. She wrote scores of screenplays, either alone or in collaboration, for Fox and MGM from the twenties through the fifties. Her impressive lineup includes, REBECCA OF SUNNYBOOK FARM (1932), THE HUNCHBACK OF NOTRE DAME (1939), and OKLAHOMA! (1955).

By 1929, Levien's natural flair for the art of writing for motion pictures won her a long-term writing contract with Fox Film Corporation. Their confidence when they signed her on must have been high because her first assignment was to design a picture for Fox's most popular duo of the time, **Janet Gaynor** and Charles Farrell. The assignment was LUCKY STAR (1929). She continued with the terrifically successful, THEY HAD TO SEE PARIS (1929), Will Rogers's first talking picture and the one that placed him under a Fox contract.

Levien partnered for ten collaborations with playwright S. N. Behrman. Among the many successful literary properties they adapted together were DADDY LONG LEGS (1931), starring Janet Gaynor; TESS OF THE STORM COUNTRY (1932), the third film Levien wrote for **Janet Gaynor** and Charles Farrell,[5] and REBECCA OF SUNNYBROOK FARM (1932).

The thirties would prove triumph after triumph for Levien. THE HUNCHBACK OF NOTRE DAME (1939), criticized for taking "too many liberties with the novel,"[6] succeeded in becoming one of the most remembered movies of all times.

But Levien's interests more often focused on the unity of the American family. STATE FAIR (1933) is probably the most famous example. The film, which had the simplest of plots, a Midwestern farm family at the fair, united two of the most popular stars

of the day, **Janet Gaynor** and Will Rogers. It also won Levien her first of several Academy Award nominations. STATE FAIR also garnered a best picture nomination that year but, lost to another picture written by Levien, CAVALCADE (1933). In that year, one of the most important years of her career, Levien won against herself.

At a time when it was far from a popular thing to do, Levien bravely drew from her Jewish roots in her early work. SALOME OF THE TENEMENTS (1925), was about a young Jewish female immigrant who is courted by a non-Jewish social worker. The film deals with the conflicts that arise in the family from the match.[7] THE YOUNGER GENERATION (1929) is about the sadness that the first generation of Jewish immigrants experience when their children conform to "the new America" and leave their Jewish community.

Perhaps Levien's most surprising pioneering achievement occurred in 1941 with ZIEGFELD GIRL, starring a great trio, **Judy Garland, Hedy Lamarr,** and **Lana Turner.** Displaying the way a female screenwriter can indeed implement her "female gaze" into a piece, even when it is a traditional Hollywood-backed film, Edith Hurwitz wrote:

> The premise was hardly new to musicals, but Levien gave it a twist: instead of competing ruthlessly with one another for the same job and the same man, a common plot of backstage stories in the 1930's, these women helped one another through some unhappy experiences.[8]

Levien wrote her most well-remembered screenplay, OKLAHOMA!, in 1955. Rogers and Hammerstein had waited ten long years to bring their successful stage musical to the screen, then selected Levien and William Ludwig as the screenwriters to collaborate on the adaptation. By this time, Levien was a proven success story with some sixty-six movies under her belt. That same year, Levien would win her only Academy Award (after a number of nominations) for INTERRUPTED MELODY (1955). It was based on the true story of **Marjorie Lawrence,** an Australian opera singer, who was stricken with polio at the height of her career.[9]

Ironically, art would partly reflect Levien's own life story. She was stricken with cancer in 1960. Undaunted, she went on writing screenplays that got made into films up to her last year. PEPE was written and released in 1960. Levien died in March of that year.

SONYA LEVIEN

1919   Who Will Marry Me? (Story)
1921   Cheated Love (Story, Scenario)
1922   First Love (Story)
       Pink Gods (Adaptation)
       Top of New York, The (Story)
1923   Exciters, The (Scenario)
       Snow Bride, The (Story)
1925   Salome of the Tenements (Scenario)
1926   Christine of the Big Top (Story, Scenario)
       Love Toy, The (Scenario)
       Why Girls Go Back Home (Scenario)
1927   Harp in Hock, A (Scenario)
       Princess from Hoboken, The (Story, Scenario)
1928   Power of the Press (Adaptation)
       Ship Comes In, A (Scenario)
1929   Behind That Curtain (Scenario)
       Frozen Justice (Scenario)
       Lucky Star (Scenario)
       They Had to See Paris (Scenario)
       Trial Marriage (Scenario)
       Younger Generation, The (Scenario)
1930   Lightnin' (Screenplay, Dialogue, Adaptation)
       Liliom (Continuity)
       Song o' My Heart (Continuity)
       So This Is London (Scenario)

1931   Brat, The (Screenplay)
       Daddy Long Legs (Screenplay)
       Delicious (Screenplay)
       Surrender (Screenplay)
1932   After Tomorrow (Screenplay)
       Rebecca of Sunnybrook Farm (Screenplay)
       She Wanted a Millionaire (Story, Continuity)
       Tess of the Storm Country (Screenplay)
1933   As Husbands Go (Screenplay)
       Berkeley Square (Screenplay)
       Cavalcade (Continuity)
       Mr. Skitch (Adaptation)
       State Fair (Screenplay)
       Warrior's Husband (Adaptation)
1934   Change of Heart (Screenplay)
       White Parade, The (Screenplay)
1935   Here's to Romance (Story)
       Navy Wife (Screenplay)
1936   Country Doctor, The (Screenplay)
       Reunion (Screenplay)
1937   In Old Chicago (Screenplay)
1938   Cowboy and the Lady, The (Screenplay)
       Four Men and a Prayer (Screenplay)
       Kidnapped (Screenplay)
1939   Drums Along the Mohawk (Screenplay)
       Hunchback of Notre Dame, The (Screenplay)
1941   Ziegfeld Girl (Screenplay)
1943   Amazing Mrs. Holliday, The (Screenplay)
1945   Rhapsody in Blue (Screen story)
       Valley of Decision, The (Screenplay)
1946   Green Years, The (Screenplay)
1947   Cass Timberlane (Adaptation)
1948   Three Daring Daughters (Screen story, Screenplay)
1951   Great Caruso, The (Screen story, Screenplay)
       Quo Vadis (Screenplay)
1952   Merry Widow, The (Screenplay)
1954   Student Prince, The (Screenplay)

1955 Hit the Deck (Screen story, Screenplay)	1956 Bhowani Junction (Screenplay)
Interrupted Melody (Screen story)	1957 Jeanne Eagles (Screenplay)
Oklahoma! (Screenplay)	1960 Pepe (Screen story)
	1962 State Fair (Remake)

Lenore Coffee (1900–1984)

Lenore Coffee was the writer in the twenties and the thirties who could indisputably be depended upon to save a picture that was in trouble. Studio heads from De Mille to Thalberg to Louis B. Mayer didn't always like dealing with her, but they knew she would make them money.

In her autobiography, *Storyline: Reflections of a Hollywood Screenwriter* (1973), Coffee aptly sums up the industry's notions about her as filtered through Irving Thalberg.

I was in one of my interminable waits to see Thalberg, when his secretary told me they were having a very heated conference about a script which needed work: when the door opened I heard one of the men say, "Why don't you put Coffee on this? She's free now." Whereupon Irving replied, "For Christ's sake, don't give me a writer with any ideas! She'll have them and I'll *listen* to them—and we just haven't time!" Backhanded praise, but it amused me.[1]

Lenore Coffee was born in San Francisco at the turn of the century and grew up desperate to be an actress. She rebelled against her father's wishes that she be a writer by burning all of her poetry. Pop won out in the end, for in 1919, when the famed actress/producer **Clara Kimball Young** was opening her own studio, she was in urgent need of a new screen-story image. The result of Coffee's first script attempt, THE BETTER WIFE (1919), a story completely filmable as written. It so impressed Harry Garson, the head of Garson Studios, that he immediately hired her at a contract of fifty dollars a week to move to Hollywood and learn screen writing.

Her experiences working for Garson proved invaluable. She reedited, rescripted and "fixed" numerous projects, garnering a reputation as one of the best "script doctors" in the business. She could save any problematic project and save it fast.

She was several months pregnant when Sam Goldwyn called one day pleading for help on [THE NIGHT OF LOVE, 1927]. Set in medieval Spain, the film opened with a scene in which Ronald Colman dramatically kidnaps a just-married bride. But nobody could think of a motive for his doing so, and the picture was stuck. Coffee thought for a while and then remembered a ritual in which a Spanish feudal duke had the right to and choice of any bride on his estate on her wedding night. She then wrote the rest of the script in less than three weeks.[2]

As early as 1921, on the merit of only her second screenplay, THE FORBIDDEN WOMAN (1920), Coffee received an offer of $250 a week to work from Bayard Veiller at Metro, turning down a $200 offer from Irving Thalberg at Universal. It was a smart move. Her experiences with Veiller provided a venue for learning about dialogue writing years before sound.

Coffee ambitiously built her lucrative career on a very simple formula—a formula tailor-made for an industry that liked formulas. She took a premise and built a story around it. FOR ALIMONY ONLY (1926) and LONESOME LADIES (1927) are titles that can summarize the plots of entire pictures.

Coffee's idea was to become invaluable

to studio chiefs, and she accomplished this with varying degrees of success. Her best and most amicable association was with Cecil B. De Mille. From the time she helped him save a picture in 1925 (HELL'S HIGH-ROAD, 1925) De Mille called on Coffee frequently and often for collaborations on stories.

Yet as Thomas Slater tells it, her relationships with Thalberg and Mayer were at least as frequent if less popular:

> She was hired, fired, rehired at MGM throughout the twenties and thirties. . . . Coffee constructed a detailed outline of a story called STEPMOTHER, which she offered to the studio for five thousand dollars. Mayer was furious about her asking price and said she would either take half that amount or "get the hell out of the studio." Coffee replied, "Mr. Mayer, I couldn't take twenty-five *thousand* dollars like that." Mayer fired her, threatening that she would never work in pictures again. . . . She was back at the studio five years later. In the interim, she wrote two scripts for De Mille.[3]

In 1930, at a time when screenwriters were being hired only to write plots, and playwrights were paid to write the dialogue, Lenore Coffee wrote her first talking picture, convincing Thalberg that she could do both. THE BISHOP MURDER CASE (1930) was a success, and starred Basil Rathbone as Philo Vance, S. S. Van Dyne's famous detective. Thalberg was pleased with her work, and hired her again the next year to write a "change of pace" script for **Joan Crawford.** The result was POSSESSED (1931), a film that by 1930s' standards was seen as a bold treatment of illicit sex. Again, the film made Thalberg money.

And yet no matter what she seemed to do for MGM, Thalberg just didn't like her.

> Coffee was never treated well at MGM. She had returned in order to write for the best actors and actresses in the business, but was paid half what she had been receiving from De Mille and was shunted aside into a small, dingy office.[4]

But write for the best actors she did. **Crawford,** Lionel and John Barrymore, Ronald Colman, **Bette Davis, Claudette Colbert, Jean Harlow,** Cary Grant. Thalberg's bad mood wasn't about to ruin Coffee's good time.

With regards to Grant, Coffee saved MGM's rear end from a possible lawsuit in 1936.

> As part of their block booking policy, the studio had sold a movie starring Jean Harlow and Cary Grant. But Grant never signed a contract agreeing to such a picture. He was refusing to play his part in SUZY [1936]. He thought it was wrong for him. Coffee convinced him that the part would be a perfect springboard to international stardom. He accepted the part.[5]

In 1955 she pulled the same sort of coup for Columbia Pictures with THE END OF THE AFFAIR by convincing Stewart Granger that he should star. He agreed, but only with Coffee as screenwriter.

Lenore Coffee was married to the novelist/director, William J. Cowen, with whom she had two children. She had met Cowen through C. B. De Mille in 1924 during her work on THE VOLGA BOATMAN (1926). Thirty-seven years after her screenplay debut, Coffee wrote her first novel "to show my women friends that it is just as important to be a wife and mother as it is to be a career person."[6] An interesting, backward notion for the woman of 1950! "I tried to show that a woman can be a career woman with lots of brains and have absolutely no sense."[7]

Although it was never Lenore Coffee's goal to transform the image of women on the screen away from expected norms, she certainly did her part in changing the attitude of studio heads to women behind the scenes. She made her presence known and she did so by demanding respect for her abilities. She was good. She knew it. And she made the studios pay for the worth of her services. She may have been a thorn in Irving Thalberg's side, but he never forgot that a script by Lenore Coffee virtually guaranteed him a large return on his dollar.

LENORE COFFEE

1919 Better Wife, The (Story)
1920 Forbidden Woman, The (Story)
1921 Alias Ladyfingers (Adaptation)
1922 Face Between, The
  Light That Failed, The (Scenario)
  Sherlock Brown (Scenario)
1923 Age of Desire, The (Titles)
  Daytime Wives (Story)
  Temptation (Story)
  Thundering Dawn (Scenario)
  Six-Fifty, The (Scenario)
  Wandering Daughters (Titles)
1924 Bread (Titles)
  Fools' Highway (Scenario)
  Rose of Paris, The (Adaptation)
1925 East Lynne (Adaptation)
  Hell's Highroad (Adaptation)
1926 For Alimony Only (Story, Scenario)
  Volga Boatman, The (Adaptation)
1927 Angel of Broadway, The (Screenplay)
  Lonesome Ladies (Story)
  Night of Love, The (Adaptation)
1928 Chicago (Scenario)
1929 Desert Nights (Continuity)

1930 Bishop Murder Case, The (Adaptation)
  Mother's Cry
  Street of Chance (Dialogue)
1931 Possessed (Adaptation, Dialogue, Continuity)
  Squaw Man, The (Screenplay)
1932 Arsene Lupin (Screenplay)
  Night Court (Screenplay)
1933 Torch Singer (Screenplay)
1934 Evelyn Prentice (Screenplay)
  Four Frightened People (Screenplay)
1935 Age of Indiscretion (Story)
  Vanessa, Her Love Story (Screenplay)
1936 Suzy (Screenplay)
1938 Four Daughters (Screenplay)
1939 Good Girls Go to Paris (Story)
  Way of All Flesh, The (Screenplay)
1940 My Son, My Son (Screenplay)
1941 Great Lie, The (Screenplay)
1942 Gay Sisters, The (Screenplay)
1943 Old Acquaintance (Screenplay)
1944 Marriage Is a Private Affair (Screenplay)
  Till We Meet Again (Screenplay)
1946 Tomorrow is Forever (Screenplay)
1947 Guilt of Janet Ames, The (Screenplay)
1949 Beyond the Forest (Screenplay)
1951 Lightning Strikes Twice (Screenplay)
1952 Sudden Fear (Screenplay)
1955 End of the Affair, The (Screenplay)
  Footsteps in the Fog (Screenplay)
1960 Cash McCall (Screenplay)

Lillian Hellman (1905–1984)

Known as the playwright who woke up America with tough-minded dramas about dishonesty, a power-hungry world, and the corrosive effects of greed on society. **Lillian Hellman** was one of the most commercially successful dramatists of the American stage.

Only Eugene O'Neill and Tennessee Williams had more successes.[1] In 1934, when she was a script reader for producer/director Herman Shumlin, she wrote her first major hit, THE CHILDREN'S HOUR (1934)— an important drama about how a slanderous lie of lesbianism on the part of a child ruins the lives of two women. It was soon after this that Samuel Goldwyn contracted Hellman to write for the movies.

Hellman encapsulates Goldwyn perfectly in an anecdote about how he went about hiring her after she had been blacklisted for many years.

> My phone rang in Martha's Vineyard. Mr. Goldwyn's secretary . . . said he had been trying to reach me for two days to ask if I wanted to write *Porgy and Bess*. After a long wait Mr. Goldwyn's voice said, "Hello Lillian, hello. Nice of you to call me after all these years. How can I help you?"[2]

But long before McCarthyism, when Goldwyn was in his early fifties and Hellman was a young woman who didn't care much about the seduction of Hollywood fame,[3] Goldwyn hired Lillian Hellman,

> to write an old silly [film] . . . to be directed by Sidney Franklin, a famous man who had done many of the Norma Shearer pictures. It was then the custom to talk for weeks and months before the writer was allowed to touch the typewriter. Such conferences were called breaking the back of the story, and that is, indeed, an accurate description.[4]

Her infamous intolerable nature allowed her to take very little of this and she was soon on a plane back to New York. She phoned Goldwyn two days after his first inquiry call, and he promised her that if she flew back instantly she'd be allowed to go into a room by herself and begin writing. Also, he'd give her a raise. She promised him she'd think about it, which she didn't, and went off to Paris. Goldwyn tracked her down a week later and offered her a long-term contract and all the stories she really wanted to do.

> I had become valuable to Mr. Goldwyn because I had left him for reasons he didn't understand. For many years that made me an unattainable woman as desirable as such women are, in another context, for men who like them that way.[5]

She goes on:

> They were good years and most of the time I enjoyed Mr. Goldwyn. . . . But as in the theatre, I have few memories of the actual work I did in pictures, although I have sharp recollections of much that happened outside the work. And maybe, in the end, they are the same tale.[6]

"The actual work" boiled down to many important translations for the screen, now forgotten like most women's film accomplishments. Aside from her plays for the stage, *The Little Foxes* (1936), *Watch on the Rhine* (1940), *Toys in the Attic* (1959), Hellman adapted many of her own plays for the screen. THESE THREE (1936) and a 1961 remake titled, as originally, THE CHILDREN'S HOUR. In 1943 she was nominated for an Oscar for best original screenplay for THE NORTH STAR. That same year, Dashiell Hammett's screenplay for Hellman's WATCH ON THE RHINE was also nominated for a best screenplay adaptation Oscar, but lost to CASABLANCA.[7]

Hellman also cowrote THE DARK ANGEL (1935), as well as scripted Goldwyn's DEAD END (1937), directed by William Wyler. In 1966 she wrote THE CHASE for the all-star cast of Marlon Brando, Robert Redford, and **Jane Fonda** with whom she would reunite with years later for JULIA (1977), and with whom she would remain good friends throughout her old age.

When she was asked if ever she worried about Hollywood being a dead end for a serious writer she replied:

> Never. I wouldn't have written movies if I'd thought that. When I first went to Hollywood, I heard talk from writers about whoring. But you are not tempted to whore unless you want to be a whore.[8]

What most people don't know about Hellman is that were it not for McCarthyism, she might have turned into a producer/director as well.

> Shortly after the first blacklisting I was offered a contract by Columbia Pictures—a contract that I always wanted—to direct, produce, and write, all three or any. And a great, great deal of money. But it came at the time of the famous movie conference of top Hollywood producers. They met to face the attacks of the Red-baiters and to appease them down. A new clause went into the movie contracts. I no longer remember the legal phrases, but it was a lulu. I didn't sign the contract.[9]

This gifted woman of German-Jewish origin was born in New Orleans to a wealthy family, and attended NYU for three years before studying journalism at Columbia. Mostly during her life she developed a "stubborn, relentless, driving desire to be alone, as it came into conflict with the desire not to be alone when I wanted not to be."[10] Her lover and friend of many years, Dashiell Hammett, is once reported to have said, "The truth is you don't like the theater ex-

cept the times when you're in a room by yourself putting the play on paper."[11] A statement she worried over for a long time, but finally came to some peace with in her brilliant memoir, *An Unfinished Woman* (1969).

Hellman had a knack for pursuing in her work and in her life controversial, poignant, and sticky social topics (McCarthyism, the Spanish Civil War, lesbianism [in her work]). She made others uncomfortable in her relentless pursuit of the truth, a stance that ultimately participated in changing not only the face of the American theater, but of the world.

LILLIAN HELLMAN

1935	Dark Angel, The
1936	These Three
1937	Dead End
1941	Little Foxes, The
1943	The North Star (Armored Attack) (Story)
1946	Searching Wind, The
1966	Chase, The
1977	Julia

Leigh Brackett (1915–1978)

When **Leigh Brackett**'s first novel, *No Good From a Corpse*, was published in 1944, the hard-boiled style of her prose brought her to the attention of director Howard Hawks. "Leigh," said Hawks to Richard Schickel, "I thought was a man's name, and in walked this fresh-looking girl who wrote like a man."[1]

He hired Brackett on the spot to collaborate with William Faulkner on THE BIG SLEEP (1946), and thus began one of the most successful and unusual writer/director collaborations in film history. Brackett later wrote several of the great "male" genre pic-

tures for John Wayne—two of Hawks's greatest pictures—RIO BRAVO (1959), and HATARI! (1962). With Leigh Brackett comes the inevitable question, What kind of transformation occurs when a woman takes on a male genre? In 1972, Leigh Brackett was asked the very same question. The interviewer wanted to know why Howard Hawks, a person with an "intensely male" outlook on life, would give a woman a position of equality and even dominance in a genre that relegates women to being decorative, while the hero goes off to save the world. Brackett responded that she suspected it was probably because Hawks didn't like women in their negative aspect, and

> until he can accept a female character, as the hero must, as another man, or an asexual *human being* with the attributes he respects, he can't like her. . . .

That might be all well and good for Hawks. It is natural for him to value masculine virtues. But what about for Brackett?

> Well, there's a curious parallel there. A friend who read my science fiction once asked me, "Why do your heroines always come down out of the hills swinging their swords like Genghis Khan?" And I said, "I suppose it's because conventional heroines bore me." They [her characters] are all *people* with independent lives and thoughts of their own, capable of being comrades and mates but always of their own free choice and always as equals. . . . So the Hawksian woman fitted my typewriter very well.

But why, asked the interviewer, should that have been the case?

> Partly, I suppose, I was just born hatefully independent . . . my father died when I was a baby and I was womaned to death by my mother, grandmother, and a great-aunt . . . Far from feeling in the slightest degree inferior to men, they believed that Woman was a sacred and special creature, infinitely superior to the lower orders, such as males, who were put here simply to serve them.[2]

When Leigh Brackett met with William Faulkner to collaborate on the screenplay of Raymond Chandler's novel, *The Big Sleep,* Faulkner greeted Brackett, opened a copy of Chandler's novel, and assigned her alternate chapters to adapt. That was their first and last conference.

For many reasons, it's been said that it is difficult to discriminate between Brackett's contribution on THE BIG SLEEP and that of

her collaborator. But when Humphrey Bogart joined the project, he went to Brackett to discuss the lines he found too genteel, assuming she had penned them. When he learned that those lines were written by Faulkner, and that her lines were the "tough-guy" lines, he nicknamed Brackett "Butch." Thereafter, he consulted her each time he needed his character toughened up.[3]

Leigh Brackett began what she calls her "serious" writing career at the age of thirteen, jotting down sequels to current films (mainly, those of Douglas Fairbanks). Ray Bradbury, a school chum of Brackett's, encouraged her to concentrate her energies on science fiction. It became her favorite genre, and eventually, with her last screenplay, THE EMPIRE STRIKES BACK (1980—George Lucas was a great admirer of Brackett's science fiction) it became inextricably associated with her name.

"I've been fascinated with the old Celtic mythology, and the names carry such magic . . . I tend to use them in exotic interplanetary settings."[4]

Although she died in the middle of the George Lucas project, the Celtic names of her space heroes anticipated the unfuturistic names of the STAR WARS characters by nearly a decade.[5]

It has been said by those who knew her that Leigh Brackett's most remarkable trait was her ability to adapt material from one medium to another. She wrote a "Philip Marlowe" to suit Howard Hawks, and then another Marlowe thirty years later to suit Robert Altman (THE LONG GOODBYE, 1973).

In the middle of her career, Brackett's long association with Howard Hawks resulted in what is critically remembered as one of the most extraordinary and well-constructed post–World War II westerns ever written. RIO BRAVO, starring John Wayne, had little in common with classic westerns like HIGH NOON (1952). Instead of the central concentration focusing on American expansionism and "the new frontier,"

Brackett's story concentrated instead on the moral dilemma of the characters.

The John T. Chance character played by John Wayne is a typical prototype of Brackett's fantasy novels. He embodies a sense of duty and a determined desire to fulfill that duty that takes on larger-than-life, nearly epic, proportions. "Brackett's science-fiction work typically follows an estranged male through a hostile environment. Challenges to his personal skill and honor are overcome; as a sidelight, a personal goal is often achieved."[6] Leigh Brackett wrote numerous novels, mainly science fiction, and won the prestigious Jules Verne Award for fantasy.

Mostly, she is remembered in the industry as the woman who so adeptly wrote all those wonderful 1940s private-eye stories.

She died of cancer in Lancaster, California, at the age of sixty-three—as tough a survivor in a hostile environment as any of her own toughest he-man creations.

LEIGH BRACKETT

1945	Vampire's Ghost, The
1946	Big Sleep, The
	Crime Doctor's Man-hunt
1959	Rio Bravo
1961	Gold of the Seven Saints
1962	Hatari!
	13 West Street
1967	El Dorado
1970	Rio Lobo
1973	Long Goodbye, The
1980	Empire Strikes Back, The

Harriet Frank, Jr.

A firm believer that "talent has no gender,"[1] **Harriet Frank, Jr.** took on her first writing job in the industry to toughen up the dialogue on a Dane Clark boxing picture at Warner Brothers. "I had as muscular an approach to those subjects as a man," Frank told me in 1986. "As a matter of fact, without denigrating the original authors, those scripts were rather soft and I just felt at home doing masculine subjects." In collaboration with her husband Irving Ravetch, they continue the tradition of great wife/husband writing teams in the way of **Goodrich**/Hackett, and **Gordon**/Kanin.

Renowned for their skillful adaptations of such pieces as THE LONG, HOT SUMMER (1958), Frank and Ravetch have a long collaboration with director Martin Ritt, best known for NORMA RAE (1979), MURPHY'S ROMANCE (1985), and STANLEY & IRIS (1990).

Although they both attended UCLA, Frank and Ravetch didn't meet until they were both young writers at MGM in the forties. Ravetch was born in Newark, but Frank describes herself as "a Hollywood baby. Louis B. Mayer practically leaned over my cradle." Because the industry, according to Frank, was "almost entirely a masculine pursuit" when she began, the fact that her mother was a story editor at Metro made life a lot easier for an aspiring young woman who had a crazy idea of wanting to write for the movies.

"The industry at that time was very leery of women writers. There were very few of them. It took leverage of a particular kind to have entry into the studios."

Frank candidly admits that her form of "leverage" was "holding my mother's hand," pure and simple.

"She was called the Sheharazade of MGM because she was a great story teller. Most of the gentlemen didn't read in those days. And she told the stories. So when she told them she had a writer in tow, there was opportunity."

But once you got into the front gate, says

Frank, there was no competition and enormous opportunity because of the tremendous output of the studios. "It was like a country club. Metro-Goldwyn-Mayer was affluent, and they were making sixty, seventy, ninety movies a year. They had a sports club for men on the top floor of the building. It was oppulent . . . the fairy tale dream of what a Hollywood studio was like."

Although MGM instituted a program for young writers and included some women in those ranks, "I don't think it was hardheartedness on the part of any of the women involved, but women were isolated in their particular job at that time. There was not the concept of sisterhood, and I'm not sure there is now for all the conversation that goes on about it. I'm a firm believer in women being of assistance to each other in this business."

The young writer's program, according to Frank meant you "aspired endlessly until someone took you seriously." Ravetch apparently got taken seriously earlier than his wife-to-be as a writer of shorts for the *Crime Doesn't Pay* series. It was when Frank left the country-club life at MGM for Warners that her career really got off the ground. She wrote SILVER RIVER (1948) for Errol Flynn who "felt he had to seduce everything that wore a skirt." But as soon as Frank informed him she was happily married he said, "May I escort you to the door?"

This was not Frank's first incident of being hassled in the business as a woman striving to be taken seriously by her cohorts. "When I began in this business," she said, "I was sent into an office and the producer said to me, 'How dare they send a Tootsie Roll in here to do this job?' And I said, 'Wait a minute, I am not sleeping with the head of this studio! If you wish to have me discuss this script with you, I'm delighted. You can make a judgment on my gifts and talents alone.' And much to his credit he said, 'Go.' The next day, I had that job.

"The prejudice going at the time was that I was young, and he made immediate assumptions that were not true. But by and large women are judged in this business, or in any business, by their competence. And it may be true that you have to go around this sexual concept. But once you make it clear that you are there to do a specific job, and that you are competent to do that job, everything else falls by the wayside. You must present yourself as somebody who is capable. And from that point on prove yourself or fail."

By the time she had gone over to Warners, Irving Ravetch had asked Frank to marry him. Ravetch is fond of saying that Mayer underwrote their courtship as well as their screenplay training. Husband and wife wrote separately for ten years until they mutually fell in love with William Faulkner. His novel *The Hamlet* (1931) struck them as a good concept for folk comedy. Producer Jerry Wald thought so as well, and when they all met Martin Ritt, a lifelong collaboration began.

Frank said that she and Ravetch have a line-by-line collaboration. Often writers will split up different scenes and come together to piece the whole, but this team feels best sitting together and hacking it out. If you even hint at the subject of a woman writer being better at some subjects than others, Frank's hackles go up.

"A good collaboration is seamless. Each writer has strengths and weaknesses. I can't point to any particular contribution that I make as, quote, a woman. I mean, gender simply disappears. I could write the roughest male scene in the script and Irving, the tenderest female. We could reverse roles with equal comfort. So I can't say there's a specifical feminine mystique that takes place in the process of collaboration, because it's simply not so."

If there is a single consistent characteristic to their pictures, it's that nearly every one includes decisive and strong female characters.

"We made a point of it. HUD (1963) had a very strong figure in Alma, HOMBRE (1967) in the housekeeper. There's hardly been a script that my husband and I have done that does not have a strong female role. We did this purposefully, because both of us feel strongly that women function in society, and they should function likewise in film."

Since there were no ostensible models for women when Frank, or certainly her story-editor mother, began their careers, I wanted to know where the inspirations for these strong women came from.

"My ancestors were sodbusters, and it was the women who busted the sod. I've been drawn to that all my life. And you know, having lived through the Great Depression and having seen my mother go to work, of necessity, and seeing a great many women go to work of necessity, I've always felt this an extraordinary chapter in American history that needs to be seen and talked about."

Thus her model for NORMA RAE, a remarkable film for which she categorically denies the label of "a woman's picture." "It was about a working stiff; about someone who had to earn a living, which puts *most* of the women in the work force." Until NORMA RAE came to pass, it was a rare sight in movies to see a story about a male/female friendship that did not end in sexual consummation. This is perhaps one of the script's most innovative qualities: a man and a woman who function simply as people after a comon goal, and not without warm, emotional intimacy being present. Why did it take so long for two real-live people to emerge on the screen? And why so long for such a woman to be a film's protagonist? "It came into fashion, to be absolutely candid," says Frank.

"You know, there was a time when women were relegated to a certain role. It takes the opportunity, the right material coming along at the right time. It takes a receptive management. They backed us all

the way with NORMA RAE, which could have been a controversial film. So the climate has to be right commercially, it has to be right realistically in terms of management, and historically the moment comes."

Like the mythologic Nick and Nora Charles, Harriet and Irving seem the epitome of the perfectly matched pair. Their large, spacious house on the top of the Hollywood Hills is filled with an ever-expanding collection of antiques that Frank has been acquiring since the age of twelve.

Unlike Michael and **Fay Kanin** who decided to go their separate writing ways early in their mutual careers, Frank and Ravetch agree that their best work began with the collaboration. The secret, Harriet Frank, Jr., revealed is to "marry a liberated man. . . . I would say that he's contributed to my happiness and to my career in equal parts. His contribution has been enormous, not only in screen writing, but I've written two novels and he functioned as a very cool, sane, and discreet editor."

Academy Award–nominated writer (HUD) though she is, Harriet Frank, Jr., still has a few unrealized dreams.

"I think women need a break in American films. The role of women in films in this country hasn't been fully exploited. The American woman is extraordinary because she usually has two careers: she maintains the household and she has a thrusting role in the work force. According to recent studies, she also controls American money.

"I think they have to be shown for what they are, which is very hard-working, serious and committed, because, as they say, they work out of necessity. In order to be fair to the portrait of the American woman you have to see that as the truth."

And yet, if there are overriding characteristics of the Frank/Ravetch touch, it is a commitment to an egalitarian view among people. Humanitarian feelings run high.

"I don't care what profession you're in. A man gets cardiac arrest and gets ulcers the same as a woman has high blood pressure and tension from being in the working world. Period. We have common problems. We have to make common resolutions and we have to live and work together. So I don't think it's a war between the sexes. I think it really needs to be a proclaimed peace. And cooperative steps taken to get there."

Perhaps the most inspirational thing about meeting Harriet Frank is her clarity of vision. One has the feeling that she was crystal clear about her path from the day she began. And so, when she forthrightly says, "Talent has no gender, talent will surface" you know it is a hard-won self-confidence inherited from that long line of no-nonsense women. Women who had too

many obstacles in their way to waste time worrying if they had enough talent to get the job.

HARRIET FRANK, JR. and IRVING RAVETCH

1948	Silver River
1958	Long, Hot Summer, The
1959	Sound and the Fury, The
1963	Hud
1967	Hombre
1974	Conrack
1979	Norma Rae
1985	Murphy's Romance
1990	Stanley & Iris

Jay Presson Allen

At the age of eighteen she went from her hometown in Angelo, Texas, to New York City to become an actress. That career lasted, she says for about twenty-five minutes when she realized that she only liked rehearsals and the first week of performance. She also realized she would rather be "out there" where the decisions were being made.

Six of **Jay Presson Allen's** seven produced films from 1964 to 1980 are marked by their strong focus on eclectic, nonstereotypic female characters. From THE PRIME OF MISS JEAN BRODIE (1969), to CABARET (1972), which won her an Academy Award nomination, to FUNNY LADY (1975) with **Barbra Streisand,** Allen "began a series of screenplays dealing with women whose control of their lives . . . is not as total as they would have others believe."[1] Like **Harriet Frank, Jr.,** Jay Allen is most comfortable and adept at adaptation. Unlike **Frank,** she has written all of her material solo, with the exception of PRINCE OF THE CITY (1981, cowritten with Sidney Lumet). She was also

executive producer on this film, a title, she says, she will no longer do without.

Of her famous JEAN BRODIE adaptation, it has been written that

> Allen makes [Brodie] a larger-than-life figure who is more sympathetic and comic than twisted and complex. Miss Brodie commands the audience's interest and sympathy without incurring contempt.[2]

This is characteristic of Jay Allen's writing style.

> Taking a literary original, she streamlines and simplifies, adding such dramatic focal points as the movie's final confrontation between Miss Brodie and the girl she has underestimated. As a result, the novel and the issues on which it touches—repression, sexual awakening, education fascism—become accessible to a wider audience.[3]

Lillian Hellman, Allen says, encouraged her that JEAN BRODIE could be successfully turned into a play. She says it was written in three days "after a year of being blocked."[4]

Allen will think nothing of dashing off a play in three days, and claims that everything she's written has been done in a maximum of two months.[5] She considers that she didn't begin her serious writing until the age of forty-one. Although her long apprenticeship for the Philco Playhouse in the golden age of television, you can be sure, didn't hurt. Live television dramas made Allen a writer who thought on her feet.

Her second marriage to producer Lewis Allen in 1955 provided a sabbatical time for Jay Presson who wanted to raise her daughter, Brooke, full-time. When she emerged in the early sixties, it was as the gifted playwright of *The Prime of Miss Jean Brodie*. It ran hundreds of performances with **Vanessa Redgrave** in London, then in New York with **Zoe Caldwell**. The role was instrumental in making **Caldwell**'s career. "All the women who played Brodie got whatever prize was going around at that time. Vanessa did, Maggie [Smith] did. . . . But they were also the best actresses going around."[6] Her next play, *Forty Carats* (1969), earned **Julie Harris** a Tony, for her portrayal of a woman in love with a much younger man.

Alfred Hitchcock saw an advance script of the play, *The Prime of Miss Jean Brodie,*[7] and was convinced that Jay Allen was the writer he was seeking to work on MARNIE (1964). The experience with Hitchcock, recalls Allen, was extraordinary.

"He was a breathtaking teacher, and I'm still doing the things he taught me to do." Her working relationship with him did not add up to an entree into Hollywood proper. "I never saw anything but 'Hitch' and his wife, Alma [Reville, 1900–1982]—a wonderful woman who'd been a very big-time editor before Hitch hit it."

Hitchcock worked in his own tiny arena, said Allen. "You know, a little fiefdom inside Universal," a kind of compound. That was pretty much all I saw."

As for Hitchcock, he "loved working with women. He was an old Turk. If he had his way, he would have liked to make me a director. So the sex thing, it just didn't exist. And consequently, maybe because of that experience with him, it has just never been an issue for me, at least not [to the extent] that I was conscious of."

Allen says she found movies tougher to write for than the stage.

"It's tougher to make film audiences suspend belief than it is a stage audience. Although it is a 'live' medium, the stage is, oddly enough, more artificial. There's a barrier between the characters on one side of the proscenium and the audience on the other. In a film you have to be more realistic when the camera can zoom in on a flaring nostril."

From her first film employer, Hitchcock, Allen says she learned that craft is 90 percent of screen writing. A very large part of writing, she is convinced, is reading—reading everything. "I might have a good ear, but I also have a good eye, which is imperative."

She names TRAVELS WITH MY AUNT (1972) as her most problematic screenplay venture.

"It was one of those situations where the problems weren't anybody's fault. Some things just don't fit together right. There was somebody who did a lot of work on that script who never got a bit of credit for it—and that was **Katharine Hepburn**. Originally she was going to play the aunt, and she wanted to work on the script, and she did. She did some damned good work. And they filmed a lot of her work. A lot. But she got no credit."

Jay Presson Allen may write and executive-produce her material, but when Hitchcock asked her to direct, she told him no. She had good reason to refuse. "It seems perfectly clear to me that any project takes a minimum of a year to direct. I like to get things on and over with. . . . Did you ever hear the phrase, 'the lady proposes, the studio disposes'? I didn't make it up. So I would never propose myself as a director."

Like many women screenwriters in the seventies whose penchant for writing incisive characters and relationship-based dramas persuaded them to turn their talents toward television, so went Jay Allen. **Fay Kanin** called it the period when devils and vampires were taking over the screen. It was then that Allen created the acclaimed series, *Family,* which won actress **Sada Thompson** several Emmys as the warm, perceptive matriarch, and catapulted **Kristy McNichol** into stardom.

In the era of "the woman's picture," says Allen, it was the women who decided what movies they went to. Her explanation for the transition of women writers from film to television is that "they've frozen the female audience out.

"They've killed it. They don't have an adult movie anymore. I don't mean X-rated. Maybe with video cassettes, something interesting will happen. I haven't had a script presented to me in three years that I was excited about. You know, I don't write nerd movies. I don't want to write science fiction—at least, not the ones that have been offered to me.

"But suddenly, right now, I'm starting to get a lot of big-time and exciting subjects. And it's very interesting that this influx of material has occurred almost to the week when cassette profits are beginning to equal the box-office profits."

Jay Presson Allen may be adept at creating illuminating female portraits for the screen that elude the stereotype, but she has also proven her skillful handling of "male" subjects with PRINCE OF THE CITY, and DEATHTRAP (1982).

"Why have we never looked all these years for 'the sensibilities of men' who did something so singularly different from anything a woman could do? That subject never came up. . . . I have never seen a script that a woman couldn't do.

"I feel that I can write movies about men. I know I can. There are men who know they can write movies about women and do. I don't get it. I really don't."

"You write to please yourself," she says. "The only office where there's no superior is the office of the scribe."[8]

JAY PRESSON ALLEN

1964	Marnie
1969	Prime of Miss Jean Brodie, The
1972	Cabaret
	Travels with My Aunt
1975	Funny Lady
1980	It's My Turn
	Just Tell Me What You Want
1981	Prince of the City
1982	Deathtrap
1983	Never Cry Wolf

Fay Kanin

"Women have a proud history in the industry," said **Fay Kanin,** "but as you say, it just isn't well known."[1] As one of the women who made that history proud, Emmy Award–winning screenwriter Fay Kanin became the second woman to become president of the Motion Picture Academy of Arts and Science (which hands out

the Oscars) and to hold that post for four terms. The first woman was **Bette Davis,** who left after a month to do her bit for the war effort in 1941. Kanin was also the last president of the Screenwriters Guild before it amalgamated and became The Writers Guild of America-West.

Fay Kanin began early in her pioneering

career at the age of twelve when she won the New York State Spelling Bee. From there on, and for nearly a forty-five-year career that is still going on, her literary life has been all uphill. "No one ever told me I couldn't become anything I wanted to be."

What she wanted to be, always, was a writer for the movies. But where she grew up, in Elmira, New York, there wasn't a studio in sight. What there was, however, was Elmira College, the first college to give to women a degree equal to men's in the country.

Kanin spent three years at Elmira, but she wanted to finish at USC. She knew that Los Angeles was the place she really needed to be to realize her ambitions.

"I was an only child. My father was a clothing store manager. He was very supportive of my ambitions, and happily decided to come out to L.A. ahead of my mother and me to see if he could get a similar job out here. Which was very brave! So that's what we did. It was the ultimate kind of approval. Whatever self-confidence I mustered came from them."

A most unusual kind of parental encouragement and support. So although there weren't many women working in influential jobs when Kanin began, (at least not according to the press), she was ignorant of all but the notion that her options in the world were wide open.

She admits she might have been a bit cocky when she set out with her degree and some of her college themes to follow a lead someone had given her at Goldwyn. She assumed she would be swept up because of her talent. She had heard that Goldwyn wanted to do an adaptation of a novel called *Gone with the Wind,* and suggested to Sam Marx, the story editor at Goldwyn, that she was the writer for the job. "Much to his credit," said Kanin, "he kept a pretty straight face."[2] He tactfully explained to her that Mr. Goldwyn spent too much money on pictures to take a chance at hiring

a novice. "Youth in those days was not an asset as it is today," remarked Kanin. She thanked Marx for his kind suggestion that she come back when she was more experienced, and undaunted, went to see Robert Sparks, the story editor at RKO. He took one look at her work and suggested a producer on the lot who had a great deal of foresight where young talent was concerned. Three months after she graduated from college, Kanin had landed herself a job as a writer.

Her luck lasted three weeks, then she was bumped back to script reader when the head of the studio left and personnel was shifted around. But for the next two years in the story department, Kanin used the time as an opportunity to learn everything she could learn about movies.

"I invaded cutting rooms, snooped in the music department, made friends in publicity, learned about shooting scripts and how they were turned into movies. I walked onto live sets and dead sets."

If those sets were dead, they were still warm from the likes of Fred Astaire and Cary Grant, and **Kate Hepburn** whom Kanin would get to know later on after Hepburn's "box-office poison."

"Hepburn had a great deal to say about all the films she did. George Cukor would tell you, if he was alive, what he told us— she had input into every scene, every line, and had a strong impact on every one of her movies."

In the meantime, Kanin's own important input into movies was growing. A young writer fresh in from New York had come to RKO to work on his first screenplay. Michael and Fay Kanin were married a year later, and they began to collaborate.

But during World War II, while Michael was writing WOMAN OF THE YEAR (1942) with Ring Lardner, Jr., a screenplay that **Kate Hepburn** sold personally to MGM for the largest sum of money ever paid up to that time for an original screenplay, Fay came up with an idea to activate women in the general defense scheme. With the same self-confidence that got her a job at a studio so soon after college, she went to the top brass at NBC radio and in a month, *A Woman's Angle* was on the air as a biweekly show. Kanin wrote the scripts as well as performed the network commentary.

During the coming decades, Fay and Michael Kanin wrote a number of successes together, including TEACHER'S PET (1958), which won them an Academy Award and a Writers Guild nomination. A point came in the marriage, says Kanin, where she and Michael knew they had to choose between being collaborators and marriage partners. They decided to keep the marriage and pursue separate screen-writing careers.

Fay Kanin, who began calling herself "a very big feminist" back in 1948, is convinced that two people can't have a happy marriage unless both feel they are developing themselves to their complete potentials.

"In marriage, you shouldn't be 50 percent of the 100 percent; together you should come out to 200 percent, bringing your own 100 percent to the partnership."

The Kanins have been together now for nearly fifty years, proving the partnership theory a good one.

As a solo writer, Fay Kanin's triumphs are numerous. Her first try at a Broadway play, *Goodbye My Fancy,* in 1948 was a hit and ran for two years. Her first television movie, HEAT OF ANGER (1971), starred **Susan Hayward,** and Lee J. Cobb, and won the prestigious Gavel Award of the American Bar Association as "the best movie of 1972 devoted to the law." HUSTLING (1975), starring **Lee Remick,** earned her a Writers Guild Award as well as an Emmy nomination. FUN AND GAMES (1980), her coproduction with **Lillian Gallo,** was one of the first movies to address a woman's subjection to sexual harassment on the job, and starred **Valerie Harper.** At that time, 1980, the two women formed the only female producing team under exclusive contract to a network.

TELL ME WHERE IT HURTS (1974), her second television film, with **Maureen Stapleton** and Paul Sorvino won both Emmy and Christopher Awards. The film addressed consciousness raising before it was even a catch word in the culture.

"You didn't way that word, 'consciousness-raising.' That was the kiss of death. It was about women who didn't even know what consciousness raising was all about. They were housewives in a blue-collar neighborhood just beginning to talk to one another and take the first baby steps toward self-realization."

FRIENDLY FIRE (1979), perhaps her most controversial script, starred **Carol Burnett,** and was one of the first films to deal with the aftermath of the Vietnam War.

Kanin turned to writing for television after five produced feature films because, she says, she was discouraged by the devils and the vampires that were arriving on the big screen in droves. Her preference for relationship drama, for what she calls, "small, personal work," was a genre that was becoming more prevalent in television.

"I don't believe there is such a thing as 'a woman's story.' I resent it when men say that emotions are the precinct of women. The men I like best are the ones who show their emotions. Both sexes lose out when we are categorized this way."

Since starting in the business in the golden days of Hollywood, Fay Kanin has long been a tireless advocate for women's rights. "Really," she says, "all my strong protagonists have been women. I had two great role models that I grew up with, Eleanor Roosevelt and Margaret Mead. I never felt like a pioneer, I just felt very fortunate to be able to do the work I wanted to do.

"I insist on coproducing now. It allows me the close collaboration I enjoy. As a writer, I think it's better for the movie."

FAY KANIN

Screenplays with Michael Kanin
(1950?)	Sunday Punch
1952	My Pal Gus
1954	Rhapsody
1956	Opposite Sex, The
1958	Teacher's Pet

For Television (Solo)
1971	Heat of Anger
1974	Tell Me Where it Hurts
1975	Hustling
1979	Friendly Fire
1980	Fun and Games

SHORT TAKES—THE SILENTS

◆ ◆ ◆

Julia Crawford Ivers (?–1930)

She was given up by Anthony Slide in his book *Early Women Directors* as the "mystery woman director." Perhaps it was because, as Douglas J. Whitton said, "While everyone around her sought publicity and notoriety by every means possible, she shunned the limelight."[1]

Her pioneering claim? **Julia Crawford Ivers** was the only woman to be a general manager of a Hollywood studio—Bosworth—for several years, beginning in 1915.[2]

According to Whitton, she was in full charge of production, running the business, supervising many titles, directing several others herself, and writing scripts. The firm was originally incorporated to produce the film versions of Broadway productions, but soon branched out into Westerns and historic dramas copyrighted under the title, "Produced under the Direction of Julia Crawford Ivers."

Of her film THE CALL OF THE CUMBERLANDS (1915), one review said, "The Story is absolutely natural and due to excellent direction its effectiveness is most impressive and the photography is well nigh perfect."[3]

A prolific scriptwriter as well—she was under contract with Famous Players–Lasky—Ivers wrote many films for **Constance Talmadge** and almost everything for the later infamous Hollywood legend, William Desmond Taylor.[4] In 1923 she directed THE WHITE FLOWER, "a melodrama," as Anthony Slide says, "involving curses and volcanoes set in Hawaii."[5] Replete with a sorceress, the film had Adolph Zukor producing.

Her work life was curtailed mysteriously upon the murder of her friend, William Desmond Taylor. No one knows if the end of her career had anything to do with the mystery of Taylor's murder. But one thing is sure, her short-lived life in the movies was lucrative. In the midtwenties, the multitalented Ivers left the screen trade with a $310,000 estate.[6]

JULIA CRAWFORD IVERS

1915   Majesty of the Law, The
       Nearly a Lady
       Rugmaker's Daughter, The
       Call of the Cumberlands, The
1916   American Beauty, The
       Ben Blair
       He Fell in Love with His Wife

Heart of Paula, The
Intrigue, The
Parson of Panamint, The
Right Direction, The
Son of Erin, A
1917 Cook of Canyon Camp, The
Davy Crockett
Spirit of '17, The
Tom Sawyer
World Apart, The
1918 Good Night, Paul
His Majesty Bunker Bean
Huck and Tom
Up the Road with Sallie
Viviette
1919 Huckleberry Finn

More Deadly Than the Male
Veiled Adventure, The
1920 Easy To Get
Furnace, The
Jenny Be Good
Nurse Marjorie
Soul of Youth, The
1921 Beyond
Morals
Sacred and Profane Love
Wealth
Witching Hour, The
1922 Green Temptation, The
1923 White Flower, The
1924 Married Flirts
1927 In a Moment of Temptation

Jane Murfin (1893–1955)

Jane Murfin was the first woman supervisor at RKO in 1934, this after a long career as a Broadway playwright and a screenwriter who frequently directed her own scripts. Says Anthony Slide, "She co-directed one production, FLAPPER WIVES (1927), starring May Allison."[1]

She went back to writing and continued to add to her credits until 1944. Among the titles in sound films she is credited with are: WHAT PRICE HOLLYWOOD? (1932) (the first version of the story later told in A STAR IS BORN), ALICE ADAMS (1935), ROBERTA (1935), COME AND GET IT (1936), and PRIDE AND PREJUDICE (1940).

Among the stories about Jane Murfin is one about her purchase of a German police dog (who became "Strongheart") after his career in the German Red Cross. Murfin owned the dog and wrote a series of pictures in which the dog starred. This was two years before the popularity of Rin Tin Tin, and certainly long before Lassie. Strongheart stories began in 1922 and it was 1924 before Rin Tin Tin made his debut.

JANE MURFIN

1927 Flapper Wives (Co-director)
Love Master (Writer)
1932 What Price Hollywood? (Writer)
1935 Alice Adams (Writer)
Roberta (Writer)
1936 Come and Get It (Writer)
1940 Pride and Prejudice (Writer)

Jane Murfin

SHORT TAKES—THE SOUND ERA

◆ ◆ ◆

Frances Goodrich (1891–1984)

Like **Ruth Gordon** and Garson Kanin, **Jeanie Macpherson** and Cecil B. De Mille, and **Harriet Frank, Jr.,** and Irving Ravetch, **Frances Goodrich** and Albert Hackett created some of the most classically enduring screen dramas America has known. Less well-known, perhaps, than other writing teams, they nevertheless turned out screenplays close to the heart of the American experience: THE THIN MAN (1934), IT'S A WONDERFUL LIFE (1946), and THE DIARY OF ANNE FRANK (1959) all came from their collaborations.

It would be impossible to credit the achievements of one without noting the other, so enmeshed were they in their process.

> "Each of us writes the same scene," said Frances Goodrich. "Then each looks at what the other has done and we try to decide which of us has done the better. We advise each other and then go back at it again. We argue but we don't quarrel. When a scenario or play is finished, neither of us can recognize his own work."[1]

Both Goodrich and Hackett began their careers as actors. Frances Goodrich graduated from Vassar in 1912, made her Broadway debut in 1916, married once in 1917, married again in 1927 (with a divorce in between!) and divorced again in 1927, when she began her collaboration with Albert Hackett. Between 1933 and 1939, Goodrich and Hackett are credited with no less than thirteen produced films, many of which were box-office successes.

The Goodrich/Hackett trademark was their talent in creating witticisms and mannerisms particularly suited to the actors playing their scripts. The film that best exemplifies this was THE THIN MAN in 1934. Based on the Dashiell Hammet novel, THE THIN MAN shows some of the best screen writing in the thirties. Nick and Nora Charles might have been conceived by Hammett, but the equality of the marriage, the camaraderie, the gestures of the detail, and the fun were all the brainchildren of the screen-writing pair. Taken, no doubt, from close observation of their own collaboration.

By 1935 the team won its first Academy Award nomination for an adaptation of Eugene O'Neill's *Ah, Wilderness!* (1935). The forties brought them their most enduring

Francis Goodrich

Zoë Akins

Ruth Gordon

Eleanor Perry, June 1973

collaboration of all, IT'S A WONDERFUL LIFE (1946), with Frank Capra. But it wasn't until nearly their last effort in 1955 that the names of Goodrich and Hackett would become known at all to the public. Ironically, it was with a labor-of-love vehicle that originated far away from the headlights of Hollywood. *The Diary of Anne Frank,* said Hackett, "was a cause for us, not just a play."[2] Perhaps because it was a piece so closely linked to their hearts and not just another studio assignment that they received the Pulitzer Prize for the play (not the screenplay) in 1956.

Their last effort, FIVE FINGER EXERCISE was written in 1962. Goodrich and Hackett garnered six Academy nominations in their productive careers. Frances Goodrich died at the age of ninety-three.

FRANCES GOODRICH

1931 Up Pops the Devil
1933 Secret of Madame Blanche, The (Screenplay)
1934 Fugitive Lovers (Screenplay)
      Hide-Out (Screenplay)
      Thin Man, The (Screenplay)
1935 Ah Wilderness! (Screenplay)
      Naughty Marietta (Screenplay)

1936 After the Thin Man (Screenplay)
      Rose Marie (Screenplay)
      Small Town Girl (Screenplay)
1937 Firefly, The (Screenplay)
1938 Thanks for the Memory
1939 Another Thin Man (Screenplay)
      Penthouse (Screenplay)
      Society Lawyer
1944 Lady In the Dark (Screenplay)
      Hitler Gang, The (Screen story, Screenplay)
1946 It's a Wonderful Life (Screenplay)
      Virginian, The (Screenplay)
1948 Easter Parade (Screenplay)
      Pirate, The (Screenplay)
      Summer Holiday (Screenplay)
1949 In the Good Old Summertime (Screenplay)
1950 Father of the Bride (Screenplay)
1951 Father's Little Dividend (Screenplay, Screen story)
      Too Young to Kiss (Screenplay)
1954 Give a Girl a Break (Screenplay)
      Long, Long Trailer, The (Screenplay)
      Seven Brides for Seven Brothers (Screenplay)
1956 Gaby (Screenplay)
1958 Certain Smile, A (Screenplay)
1959 Diary of Anne Frank, The (Screenplay)
1962 Five Finger Exercise (Screenplay)

Zoë Akins (1886–1958)

She's remembered as the writer who wrote many of the great films for director **Dorothy Arzner**. **Zoë Akins** began her writing career with her first play at the age of twelve and never turned back. Her early poems, also from this prodigy period, were published by William Marion Reedy's *St. Louis Mirror,* a publication that later discovered the talents of Edgar Lee Masters and **Sara Teasdale**.

Akins was born in Missouri to a wealthy,

strongly Republican family. Her first play hit Broadway in 1919. *Declassée* starred the great **Ethel Barrymore**. As the historian Anthony Slide has said of this work, about a woman who commits the unpardonable sin of becoming involved with a man who cheats in cards. "This English society drama written by a lady from Missouri, has its origins not in the trashy romance magazines of the period, but in the writing of **Elinor Glyn** and in the short works of Saki."[1] After writing several more "overblown" melodramas that would later become her trademark, Akins received the Pulitzer Prize for drama in 1935 for her adaptation of Edith Wharton's *The Old Maid* (1939).

From the onset of the early twenties, the film studios were swiftly buying up stage properties for the screen. Akins's elitest yarns seemed tailor-made for the period. Nearly without apprenticeship in the new medium, she became a top-dollar screenwriter. Her 1933 play *Morning Glory*, produced by Paramount, gave its star **Katharine Hepburn** her first Academy Award.

After writing four films for Dorothy Arzner, Akins collaborated with writer Frances Marion and director George Cukor in 1936 for a great film event, CAMILLE.[2] This renowned masterpiece starring **Greta Garbo** and Robert Taylor, received widespread praise from critics for the natural dialogue. As screenwriter, Akins was praised for adhering closely to Alexandre Dumas's original story.[3]

After a couple more collaborations with Cukor (including PRIDE AND PREJUDICE [1940], in which Cukor was replaced by director Robert Leonard), Akins turned her talents back to the theater. Her screen work, so greatly typified by projects such as CAMILLE, are part of a frozen and lost golden age of cinema. An age in which female writers like Zoë Akins were the uncontested pioneers.

ZOË AKINS

1930	Anybody's Woman (Screenplay)
	Right to Love, The (Screenplay)
	Sarah and Son (Screenplay)
1931	Once a Lady (Screenplay)
	Working Girls (Screenplay)
	Women Love Once (Screenplay)
1933	Christopher Strong (Screenplay)
1934	Outcast Lady (Screenplay)
1936	Accused (Screenplay)
	Camille (Screenplay)
	Lady of Secrets (Screenplay)
1938	Toy Wife, The (Screenplay)
1939	Zaza (Screenplay)
1947	Desire Me (Screenplay)

Eleanor Perry (1915–1981)

Her career as a screenwriter covers only eleven years. But the **Eleanor Perry** decade was a remarkable one: DAVID AND LISA (1962), LAST SUMMER (1969), DIARY OF A MAD HOUSEWIFE (1970). All the films were made under the direction of her husband, Frank Perry.

The Eleanor Perry films, especially DIARY OF A MAD HOUSEWIFE, are a kind of pioneering breakthrough for women on the screen. For perhaps the first time a kind of search for a woman's personal identity was being explored. But not so surprisingly, Perry's stories for the screen were reflective of her struggle against the male domination of motion pictures in Hollywood. Her fight for more power led her to become one of the first producers among the "new pioneers" of the early seventies.

In 1973, when she was in her midfifties, the *New York Times* described her as "one of those Babe Paley types of women, stunning, silver-haired, the kind of woman who *does* get better as she gets older. 'Handsome,' you would probably call her, and charming and cerebral, and, an angry feminist."[1] At the time, all for good reason. A picture that she wrote and was "coproducing" with Martin Poll was taken completely out of her hands. Each time she wanted in on the creative decision making, Poll would tell her, "they don't want to work with a woman. They want to work with a man."[2] And in each instance, when

Perry went directly to the source, she discovered that Poll had been fibbing.

Born **Eleanor Rosenfeld** in Cleveland, Ohio, she received a masters degree in psychiatric social work from Western Reserve. It would prove an important base of personal research for her later great screenplay DAVID AND LISA. Along with her first husband, the lawyer Leo G. Bayer, the couple wrote mystery novels and plays under the pseudonym of Oliver Weld Bayer. When Eleanor traveled to New York in 1958 to see a production of their play, *Third Best Sport,* she met producer Frank Perry, and never returned to her life in Cleveland.

No Hollywood studio would finance the remarkable DAVID AND LISA script, leaving the Perrys to raise the money and finance the project themselves. By 1962, the film, which starred inexperienced actors and was written by a woman who had never before done a screenplay, was named best picture of the year by *Time* magazine.

The Perrys' last picture together was DIARY OF A MAD HOUSEWIFE. It was perhaps not a feminist picture, but certainly the initiation of another kind of thinking for women on the screen, and certainly a kind of breakthrough in thinking for Eleanor Perry. Frank Perry filed for divorce at the time of the picture. Three years later Eleanor said, "Now, I would write the ending differently. I would carry it one step further. I'd show Tina liberating herself, but not through a man. She'd get a job, or go back to school or whatever."[3]

Perry became an ardent spokesperson for women's need to obtain greater power in the movie business. She led a feminist protest at the Cannes Film Festival in 1972. Eight years after her divorce from Frank Perry she published *Blue Pages,* a novel about a woman screenwriter who is exploited by her director husband.

Perry subsequently wrote two screenplays that were psychological thrillers on her own after her divorce. She died of cancer in 1981, never to fulfill her potential as a screenwriter.

And yet with DIARY OF A MAD HOUSEWIFE (1970), Eleanor Perry set an irreversible trend for independent female characters on the screen. It was to be a transformation she would never see realized in her own lifetime.

Before her death, Perry commented both about the image of woman on the screen up until that time as well as about being a woman in the industry. Of the pictures made in the last decade, she said,

> Few of them are about women as human beings. They're about women who get hacked up and raped and knifed and cut and who make biscuits and stand behind everybody like squaws. Most of the pictures are male buddy-buddy friendship films or violence pictures. You wouldn't know women were part of the human race from most of the films.[4]

THE MAN WHO LOVED CAT DANCING (1973), was a property she found and Perry was made co-producer. Everything was fine, Perry said, until the real work on the film began.

> I saw the film as the AFRICAN QUEEN in the West, a relationship between a man and a woman but an unlikely combination about a liberated woman in the 1880's who had the guts to run away from her husband. I never wanted to show her cooking, making biscuits, heating coffee, getting raped. Well, all those things are indeed in the film.[5]

ELEANOR PERRY

1970	Diary of a Mad Housewife (Screenplay) Lady in the Car with Glasses and a Gun (Screenplay)		1971 1973	Deadly Trap, The (Screenplay) Man Who Loved Cat Dancing, The (Screenplay)

Ruth Gordon (1896–1985)

Pan me, don't give me the part, publish everybody's book but this one and I will still make it! Why? Because I believe I will. If you believe, it means you've got imagination . . . you don't face facts—what can stop you?

Autobiography of Ruth Gordon
[My Side]

Ruth Gordon had everything going against her: she had no looks, she was too short, and after one term at the American Academy of Dramatic Arts at the age of eighteen she was informed she had no talent and was asked to leave. She did, only to return fifty-three years later to accept an American Academy Award for achievement. Through all the years of discouragement, every time someone said no to her, she pretended not to hear them and just went on. The finest role model any human being could wish to have, Ruth Gordon knew that the secret of her success was simply her attitude. "I never face facts," she said. "I never listen to good advice. I'm a slow starter, but I get there."

Ruth Gordon became a cult figure as an actress. We remember her with awe in her Oscar-winning role at age seventy-two in ROSEMARY'S BABY (1968),[1] and in grateful joy and fondness in the inimitable HAROLD AND MAUDE (1972). But few of us think of the Ruth Gordon who attacked her writing career with the same persistence and dedicated fervor that she brought to her acting.

Gordon in collaboration with her second husband and beloved long friend, Garson Kanin, gave us the best of the Tracy-**Hepburn** sparring team: ADAM'S RIB

(1949), and PAT AND MIKE (1952). **Fay Kanin,** sister-in-law to Ruth, a screenwriter herself, points out that we shouldn't forget the Gordon who was equally adept as a screenwriter. She won three Oscar nominations for her efforts.[2]

Born a seaman's daughter, Ruth Gordon inherited conquest and inquisitive exploration in her blood. When she left home in Quincy, Massachusetts, for her first year in a New York drama school her father gave her one year's tuition, fifty dollars spending money, and an old spyglass. He told her to hock it if she ever needed money. He said that if she was going to be an actress, she'd be in and out of hockshops all her life. Gordon hocked plenty in her years, but *never* that spyglass.

Perhaps the glass gave her a kind of sixth sight. Perhaps it enabled her to see beyond all the times people would tell her she hadn't a stitch of talent, and thus gave her the courage and the stamina it took to keep going. For even after her first starring role on Broadway as Lola Pratt in Booth Tarkington's *Seventeen* in 1918 (she made her debut on Broadway in 1915 as Nibs in *Peter Pan*), Heywood Broun wrote in the *New York Tribune,* "Anyone who looks like that and acts like that must get off the stage."[3]

She continued working consistently and hard at her crafts. Bad reviews turned to good. In the thirties her efforts won her an opportunity to perform with England's Old Vic Company. She was the first American actress to be so honored.

She wed her soul mate and collaborator, Garson Kanin, in the early 1940s. It was a partnership that proved professionally fruitful as well as personally. "They were as close as two human beings could be," said **Fay Kanin**. "I rarely ever saw them apart."[4] Aside from the screenplay collaborations with her husband, Gordon wrote at least two successful hit plays on her own, *Over 21* (1944), and *Years Ago* (1947). The latter play was made into a film, THE ACTRESS (1953), starring Spencer Tracy and **Jean Simmons**. It was called "an endearing romantic comedy of adolescent longing, with all the unearthing of early Philip Barry and George Kelly."[5]

Up to the end of her life at age eighty-eight, she was working on a new play. Age was meaningless to Ruth Gordon. She believed the only obstacles one had were in one's head. In her last few days she was discussing her plans for a new movie with friends. Just the year before, at the age of eighty-seven, in the movie MAXIE (1985) with **Glenn Close,** she insisted on doing her own stunt work and rode a motorcycle for the first time in her life. "She had a great gift for living in the moment," said her co-worker, **Glenn Close**, "and it kept her ageless."[6]

This inspiring woman, who's career spanned seventy years, passed on her spyglass in the form of these words to a graduating class at the place that once told her she had no talent: "And on that awful day when someone says, 'you're not pretty, you're no good,' think of me and don't give up!"

RUTH GORDON

1945   Over 21 (Play basis only)
1947   Double Life, A (Screenwriting)
1949   Adam's Rib (Screenwriting)
1952   Pat and Mike (Screenwriting)
        The Marrying Kind
          (Screenwriting)
1953   Actress, The (Screenwriting)
1967   Rosie! (Adaptation)

·VII·

REEL WOMEN
EDITORS

People ask me, "Why do you sit in a dark room?" I
tell them, "I like living vicariously."

—Carol Littleton

Margaret Booth

Dede Allen

Susan E. Morse

Verna Fields (with
director Steven Spielberg).

PREVIEW

◆ ◆ ◆

Like the craft of screen writing, editing is an invisible and somewhat anonymous trade. The creative input divvied up between director and editor has always had ambiguous boundary lines. In a sense, women were perfect foils for the one job in a very visible industry that was late in giving credit for behind-the-scenes labor.

"A well-edited film," veteran editor **Carol Littleton** said to me, "is one where no one notices the editing because you've worked to make it invisible."

Invisibility may be a key word in describing the role of the editor as well as her craft. **Littleton**'s comment, "I consider myself the director's instrument, which doesn't mean that I can't be outspoken about what works and what doesn't,"[1] sounds very similar to the way a wife might talk about her husband. Perhaps this is the reason the field of editing has always been open to women. The kind of collaboration that has occurred traditionally between a male director who thinks he has the initial driving vision and then basks in all the glory, and the female editor, who takes that vision, gives it a shape, but stays unobtrusive in the background, parallels the husband/wife archetype in an uncanny way.

As early as the Lumière Brothers, when women editors were known as *monteurs* in France, women were pioneers in the editing trade. And yet, according to a 1974 *MS*

article, when **Dede Allen** asked her male coworkers how the generation of women editors before her broke through, they explained to her that they slept their way up.[2]

Quite the contrary. Martin F. Norden in his article, "Women in the Early Film Industry,"[3] speculates that women very early got a foothold in editing because it was originally seen as a menial job, requiring only that they follow the orders of men as to the duration of a sequence or the order of the shots. By the time filmmakers began to discover that film could be rearranged, shuffled, and cut in ways that would make the final effect much more powerful for an audience, women were technical masters.

When movies were still known as "flickers," there was no such thing as "the craft" of editing. Splicing the finished pieces of celuloid together was no more creative than work on an assembly line. And as the cheapest exploitive labor around, women were the most likely candidates for the job.

Rose Smith, Anne Bauchens, Viola Lawrence, and **Margaret Booth,** the first women editors in Hollywood, were all important innovators in the bringing of silents into the age of sound.

Rose Smith won early distinction as the chief editor of D. W. Griffith's INTOLERANCE (1916). This approximately $400,000 extravaganza dwarfed Griffith's previous effort THE BIRTH OF A NATION (1915), "in its mammoth ambition, cost, complexity, and length."[4]

Viola Lawrence cut BULLDOG DRUMMOND (1929), Goldwyn's very first sound film, and **Margaret Booth** edited BROADWAY MELODY (1929), also the very first sound film for MGM. Actually it was a kind of half-sound/half-silent hybrid—*sound* was still a wild animal no one yet knew how to tame. There were no manuals on how to pin sound to picture at the time. By sheer ingenuity and necessity, these pioneers sweated as their audiences watched the picture drift in and out of "synch." "Sound," said **Margaret Booth**, "was a period you just suffered through."[5] Because of her efforts, Booth was made supervising editor at MGM from 1936 to 1964, Hollywood's Golden Age, where no film left the studio without her approval. Along with Booth, **Dorothy Arzner** was another one of the most sought-after editors in a 1920s' Hollywood. After she edited the classic silent BLOOD AND SAND (1922), she had the gumption to do what many editors want to do but are often afraid to—demand that she be given a picture to direct.

Great women editors behind the great male directors throughout history have included **Alma Reville** (1900–1982), who worked as a script girl on Alfred Hitchcock's first film, THE PLEASURE GARDEN (1925). She married Hitchcock the next year. Subsequently, she cut many of his films as well as collaborated as a screenwriter with him as well as for other directors. Cecil B. De Mille had the only contract in history that included a guarantee for his editor, **Anne Bauchens**. He wouldn't make a move on a picture unless **Bauchens** was cutting it. **Thelma Schoonmaker** has had a long-standing career cutting the films of Martin Scorsese. Similarly, post–ANNIE HALL (1977), **Susan E. Morse** has edited all of Woody Allen's films.

Dede Allen's observation as to why the field of editing has always been open to women is that perhaps "women have always been good at little details, like sewing." Before there were "edge numbers" on a film frame, those tiny numbers that identify a particular shot for the editor, **Margaret Booth** told me she would sit for hours trying to determine whether **Lillian Gish** had her eyelid closed or open.

But her painstaking efforts paid off. Today, gifted and talented female hands, like those of **Carol Littleton**, are cutting many of the most well-crafted films in recent years. **Littleton**'s impressive filmography includes, BODY HEAT (1981), E.T. THE EXTRA-TERRESTRIAL (1982), THE BIG CHILL (1983), PLACES IN THE HEART (1984). When I asked her if she felt like a pioneer, she replied, "I hope I am carrying on a tradition of women editors. But I feel like the pioneering has gone on with those like **Margaret Booth** and **Dede Allen**."[6]

With her innovative cutting style of BONNIE AND CLYDE (1967), a picture that became one of the highest-grossing box-office sensations of the 1960s, **Dede Allen**, for the first time, won solo screen credit for the craft of editing. It is said that she is the highest-paid, most demanded film editor in the business.

Like screen writing, these entries of "pioneers" were perhaps the most difficult to choose. There are, and have been, many talented women working in the field; all of them would be included if not for time and space limitations. Perhaps **Carol Littleton** doesn't feel like a pioneer, but my own sentiments are closer to those of **Dede Allen** who said, when I asked her the same question, "Sure, we were pioneers. But the women today are pioneers in a whole new kind of industry."

Margaret Booth (1898–   )

If you were to write down every MGM film from the 1930s to the 1950s, give or take a very few, you'd come up with a listing of the credits of **Margaret Booth**. And the list would still be incomplete.

The fact is, Hollywood in its heyday needed and used up people like Booth, satisfied never to take a stitch of credit, in order that the commodity called movies reached the public in factory-ordered condition. And, to our great exasperation, Hollywood mostly succeeded. This is our loss of some of the great role models in movies, not the least of which is pioneering editor Margaret Booth.

"Do you see yourself as a pioneer?" I inquired of the shy Ms. Booth.

"Well," she answered, "I think I was one of the first, I really do."[1]

For women who pioneered their way in the early days, it was as simple and as complicated as that: Margaret Booth was one of the boys. She was treated by others as such, and that was also the way she accepted herself. Her manner is humble. She's full of humility. She'll state quite simply, "I had no power," and mean it.

But history tells us quite differently.

Although she doesn't like being referred to as "Booth" in interviews ("That would sound too masculine"), the paradox and the remarkable talent that is Margaret Booth staked her claim as the supervising editor at MGM from 1937 to 1968. For three decades, no film left that studio without her imprint.

In 1935, she received an Academy Award nomination for her editing of MUTINY ON THE BOUNTY, with Clark Gable and Charles Laughton. The winning picture of that year, MIDSUMMER NIGHT'S DREAM, she considers "a terrible picture." About MUTINY, she says, "When it first came out none of us thought it was very good. Now everyone hails it as a classic."

Margaret Booth began her career quite by accident. Her brother, Elmer, who worked for D. W. Griffith as an actor, died in a traffic accident, and the Booth family needed a new source of income. Griffith hired Margaret for ten dollars a week as one of the "girls" in the splicing room to be a "cutter." At the time, Margaret Booth had just graduated from Los Angeles High School.

Booth moved from under Griffith's wing to L. B. Mayer's old Mission Road studio. There, she worked under the guidance of the man to whom she attributes everything she currently knows about the art of film, John Stahl. "He taught me the value of a scene. When a scene drops or doesn't drop, and when it sustains. You have to feel this, intuitively, in your work." At the time, Irving Thalberg said that her eye was so good she really ought to consider directing. But Booth wasn't interested. She just wanted to be the best film editor there ever was. "Maybe that was foolish," she said later, at age eighty-two, in a way that you know she doesn't really believe it was foolish at all.

When Thalberg died, Mayer asked Margaret Booth to take over as supervising editor of the studio. "They liked me because I was fast. I was always very fast cutting everything I did. And boy, was I tough." She remained at MGM until the sixties, cutting such classics as THE BRIDGE OF SAN LUIS REY (1929), THE BARRETTS OF WIMPOLE STREET (1934), ROMEO AND JULIET (1936), and CAMILLE (1936).

She says that before the advent of "talkies" the titles would be cut in on the trolley ride to the theater. "The audiences used to wait until we'd finish splicing. They'd never do that now." With no manuals on the topic, Booth not only learned how to edit sound as she went along, but she created the early pioneering methods that others would follow.

In 1963 she met Ray Stark and obtained MGM's permission to work with him on one picture. "I was so scared of him," recalls Booth. "Whatever I did was all right with him. He never said no!" That film, A BOY TEN FEET TALL (1963), won a prize at the Cannes Film Festival.

Years hence, after she left MGM, she continued her supervisory capacity for Ray Stark overseeing such contemporary works as THE WAY WE WERE (1973), FUNNY LADY (1975), THE GOODBYE GIRL (1977), and ANNIE (1982). By the time Margaret Booth really retired in Los Angeles, she was eighty-five and a genuine legend in her own time. Ray Stark has said about Margaret Booth, "One doesn't 'hire' her, one is lucky to get her."

By 1990, the industry finally nodded in her direction as well. . . . The American Cinema Editors (ACE), a prestigious organization for Hollywood editors, awarded Booth a Lifetime Achievement Award for her broad contribution to the field.

Booth never married. And she's never seen her working life in films as a sacrifice to her personal life. "I loved it," she said. "I loved everything about it—the studio, the cutting room—everything. I'd work nights you know, and not get paid. I was a workaholic. I never felt I was mistreated. I was always happy about my work. I'd do it all again."

MARGARET BOOTH

1924	Husbands and Lovers
	Why Men Leave Home
1925	Fine Clothes
1926	Memory Lane
	Gay Deceiver, The
1927	Bringing Up Father
	Enemy, The
	In Old Kentucky
	Lovers
1928	Lady of Chance, A
	Mysterious Lady, The
	Telling the World
1929	Bridge of San Luis Rey, The
	Wise Girls
1930	Lady of Scandal, The
	Lady's Morals, A
	Redemption
	Rogue Song, The
	Strictly Unconventional
1931	Cuban Love Song, The
	Five and Ten
	It's a Wise Child
	New Moon
	Southernor, The
	Susan Lenox, Her Fall and Rise
1932	Smilin' Through
	Son-Daughter, The
	Strange Interlude
1933	Bombshell
	Dancing Lady
	Peg o' My Heart
	Storm at Daybreak
1934	Barretts of Wimpole Street, The
	Riptide
1935	Reckless
	Mutiny on the Bounty
1936	Camille
	Romeo and Juliet
1937	Yank at Oxford, A
1970	Owl and the Pussycat, The
1972	To Find a Man
	Fat City
1973	Way We Were, The
1975	Funny Lady
	Sunshine Boys
1976	Murder by Death
1977	Goodbye Girl, The
1978	California Suite
1979	Chapter Two
1982	Annie

Verna Fields (1918–1982)

She was known as the "Mother Cutter" turned Mother Mogul. She was that nice Jewish lady who said things like, "Call me Verna, not Mrs. Fields! Why stand on ceremony?" Had you passed her on the street, you would never suspect that from 1976, until her death in 1982, she was vice president of feature productions for Universal Pictures, and one of the most influential women in Hollywood. She gave George Lucas his start. She got Steve Spielberg out of more than one major jam. And she had an avid political consciousness that bore a history of involvement with blacklisted artists, making agitprop films before it was kitsch to do so.

Editor **Verna Fields** spun her cutting magic over more than thirty motion pictures, including WHAT'S UP, DOC? (1972), PAPER MOON (1973), DAISY MILLER (1974), and JAWS (1975) for which she won an Oscar. She supervised the ground-breaking AMERICAN GRAFFITI (1973). And she got into the business purely by a fluke.

"It was World War II and I was on canteen duty," she told film writer Gerald Peary. "My friend Margie Johnson and I were on our way to serve coffee to the GI's. Margie's boyfriend was an assistant editor, so she said, 'Come over to the studio first.' Well, this guy met us at the gate. He was cute. I started hanging out there to be with the cute guy."[1]

Meanwhile, Fritz Lang was wondering who this girl was, hanging around the studio. He hired her to be an apprentice on sound, without any knowledge or experience. Fields was not a complete stranger to the industry. Her father, Sam Hellman, was a onetime journalist who had moved his family to Hollywood in the thirties in order to pursue a career in screen writing. The results were LITTLE MISS MARKER (1934) and MY DARLING CLEMENTINE (1946), among others. It's clear that Verna inherited

a talent for the screen trade. "But I was totally ambitionless," she confessed.[2]

After working with Fritz Lang for four years and joining the union, Verna married "the cute guy," Sam Fields, had two children, and gave up working for eight years. She might have intended to give up working forever, but Sam Fields died suddenly in 1954, leaving Verna and her brood to survive by her wits. Aside from being talented, she was lucky. Those were the early days of television, when work was plentiful and sound editors were badly needed. Fields began to work on episodes of series like, *Death Valley Days, Sky King,* and *Fury.*

By 1960, she moved to full-length features with STUDS LONIGAN, directed by Irving Lerner, who became her mentor. From there her career rolled on with ease. For one, a classic piece of cinema verité called THE SAVAGE EYE (1960). In 1961 she received a Motion Picture Sound Editing Award for EL CID.

During LBJ's "Great Society," Verna went to work for the USIA ("I've always been interested in using film for social reform")[3] and took a one-year job teaching at USC where she hired a young student named George Lucas, and his future wife, **Marcia Griffin**. It wouldn't be long before Lucas would direct AMERICAN GRAFFITI (1973). **Marcia Lucas** did the first cut, with Verna coming in for the final edit. **Marcia Lucas** would go solo to edit STAR WARS (1977). Fields then went on to edit the twenty-three-year-old Steven Spielberg's first film, THE SUGARLAND EXPRESS (1974). It was at this time in her life that she honed a preference for working with young directors.

"The idea of an editor having control over the director's work is ludicrous," said Fields in a seminar at the Center for Advanced Film Studies in 1975. "I wish the word *editing* had never been invented; people feel there is some kind of friction between the director and the editor, because the word *editing* implies correcting, and it's not. In French, the word is *monteur,* which is what it is; you're mounting the film. . . . I'm enormously proud of a lot of pictures I've done. By God, I saved the picture, and I've been given credit for it. I don't think that my creative input has ever been denied by the fact that the director has complete control."[4]

One of the instances in which Fields "saved the picture" was on Steve Spielberg's JAWS.

> I was the liaison with the studio for Steven. When there was thought of ditching the picture because the shark wasn't working, I told them, "Keep doing it, even if you need to use miniatures."[5]

They did keep doing it, and they weren't sorry. The picture made a mint, and Verna won an Academy Award, plus a new job for herself as Universal's vice president in charge of feature productions.

She didn't have experience, she lacked ambition, she wasn't even looking for a job. The pioneering saga of mother editor

mogul, Verna Fields, is an inspirational testament—a nice Jewish lady without airs who turned a Hollywood lunch into a neighborhood deli.

VERNA FIELDS

1960	Savage Eye, The
	Studs Lonigan
1961	El Cid (Sound)
1963	Affair of the Skin, An
	Balcony, The (Sound)
	Cry of Battle
1964	Nothing But A Man
1965	Bus, The
1966	Country Boy
	Deathwatch
1967	Legend of the Boy and the Eagle
1968	Targets (Sound)
	Track of Thunder
	Wild Racers, The
1969	Medium Cool
1972	What's Up, Doc?
1973	American Graffiti
	Paper Moon
1974	Daisy Miller
	Sugarland Express, The
1975	Jaws

Dede Allen

To this day she is arguably the highest-paid, and, as most people will agree, one of the top five film editors in the business. No one will deny her influence in changing the course of editing with her legendary cutting of BONNIE AND CLYDE (1967)—among the top highest-grossing pictures of the 1960s.[1] As if all this weren't enough to set **Dede Allen** firmly into the shoes of a pioneer, she was the first editor to win a solo credit card on the screen titles for the craft of editing.

"You can't be careful," says Allen, "You can't be cautious. You can't worry, 'Does my cut match? Does it look good? What will the studio think?' If I worried about those things . . . well, it just wouldn't be *me*."[2] This woman who struggles to define the indomitable person she is harbors an impressive credit roster: THE HUSTLER (1961), AMERICA, AMERICA (1964), RACHEL, RACHEL (1968), ALICE'S RESTAURANT (1969), LITTLE BIG MAN (1970), SLAUGHTERHOUSE FIVE (1972), DOG DAY AFTERNOON (1975), REDS

(1981), and THE BREAKFAST CLUB (1985). The list is far from over.

Allen began as a messenger "girl" ("That's what they called us") in 1943. "I came out of a period that you just didn't take a job away from a man. You just didn't. It was a sin. They said, 'Girls will get married, and then they'll have children, and they won't be able to work.' I had to work as a messenger ten months before I could move up. When I finally pestered my way into the cutting room, I carried more film cans and swore more than anyone else. That way I proved myself. I felt the men accepted me."

Allen, and a later successful screenwriter, **Faith Hubley,** reorganized the entire messenger department at Columbia, in order to collect more spare minutes to learn about moviemaking. "When you're young, and not a threat," explained Allen, "people love to teach you."

She got a shot at sound editing, but got "bumped back to the bottom" when the boys came home from the war. About a year later, because of the war's residual alcohol problems and broken marriages, she was bumped right back to the top. "Women did have to work harder; they had to be better, be more exploitable to prove themselves."

In 1950, Dede Allen became disillusioned with Hollywood and moved to New York. "In truth of fact, I was blacklisted, and I didn't even know it. I had taken what they considered a bad stand during the Hollywood strike. Having been a messenger, I had to cross the picket line of story analysts. Well, I had a hell of a time getting my card back. It was SLAP SHOT (1977) that eventually got it back for me."

Coming from her cutting job at Columbia Pictures, she had no trouble landing a job editing commercials in New York. One day Carl Lerner, a respected editor and one of Allen's early teachers, recommended her to Robert Wise (once the much-respected editor for Orson Welles) for her first editing entrée, ODDS AGAINST TOMORROW (1959).

"In those days," says Allen, "editing was done primitively. We couldn't Scotch-tape film the way we do now. So every time I wanted to make a cut, I literally needed to melt a piece of film away. But the black slugs were distracting, so editors tried *not* to make too many changes if they could help it.

"But I kept reworking and reworking the scenes. I was terrified that Bob Wise would get angry. But he said, 'I see you're experimenting. I like that. Never be afraid to show me your mistakes.'"

It was this kind of nurturing encouragement that egged Allen on to do in editing what she does best: follow her gut about what is best for a picture. There was a kind of training in her early years she certainly *didn't* appreciate. "I had watched Carl Lerner, and I had learned that the thing to do was always try to stay one step ahead of the editor. Always anticipate their needs— Like an operating room. You know, 'Scalpel, scissors . . . blah, blah,' that kind of thing. I remember I was working as an assistant to a man who shall remain nameless, trying to anticipate what he might need next. I remember him turning around and saying, 'Young lady, would you mind *never, ever* looking over my shoulder!' So I said, 'Oh. Excuse me, Mr. so-and-so. I was only trying to—' He said, 'It's taken me a great many years to learn this craft and I don't intend to have young people like you come in and think you can learn it overnight.' I don't think I would have done the same thing with my life had I not had that experience. And that was one of the things that makes me very much involved with my apprentices. I believe whatever I've learned, I've learned from someone else, and it's up to me to pass it on—because we're here, and we're gone. I have a loyalty. People work very hard for you."

Allen's imaginative cutting of BONNIE AND CLYDE (1967) in the sixties made it one of the most talked about films of that decade. "If the editing broke new ground," says Allen, "It's because Arthur [Penn, the director] was saying, 'Forget match cuts! I want it faster faster faster!'" Jack Warner of Warner Brothers wasn't even inclined to finish a picture where the audience might have trouble telling the good guys from the bad guys. He wanted to throw Allen off the picture and replace her. Penn and star/producer Warren Beatty refused. Beatty paid the rest of Allen's salary out of his pocket. The rest is history. To date, BONNIE AND CLYDE has grossed nearly $22 million. No doubt Mr. Beatty has recouped his money. He also must have liked the way Allen worked—he hired her again later for REDS (1981).

A colleague of Allen's, fellow editor **Carol Littleton** has said, "The editors whose work I admire most are those whose style is totally compatible with the picture they're working on. The first who comes to mind, of course, is Dede Allen. With Dede, her style of editing never draws attention to itself."

Dede Allen feels blessed by working for so many talented directors who allowed her to trust her gut instinct. Of Robert Rossen (THE HUSTLER [1961]) she says, "He showed me that events in a story were not necessarily locked into continuity. Scenes could be moved around to reveal something about a character earlier than intended in the script—and still be within logic. Problems like this are not always clear from the written script."

Elia Kazan's AMERICA, AMERICA proved how underrated the editor's job is in the real creation of a picture. Contrary to some stereotyped beliefs, an editor does not simply wait for the all-creative director to command: "Splice here!" By the end of shooting AMERICA, AMERICA, Kazan was exhausted. He said he had total confidence in what Allen would do with the material and said he was going to take some time off. Allen took the raw footage and cut the first draft of the picture.

"I'm basically a coal miner. When you go into a cutting room, you come home—and you don't really want to go down the hall before you go home to wash your hands. You're so tired. You stick on your gloves in winter, and you go home. When you take your gloves off your hands are black. It takes a lot of patience in a relationship to put up with that kind of thing. Not to mention the hours."

In fact her husband Steve Fleischman—a writer and producer for television—has "put up" with it quite well. They have been happily married for many years and have two children.

Aside from fighting for, and attaining, recognition for the important contribution of the editor through solo screen credit, Dede Allen more often than not now shares in the film's profits.

As unsurpassed as any film editor's career could hope to be, Dede Allen has never even been nominated for an Academy Award. "I don't think it's because I'm a woman," says Allen. "I really don't. I think that Hollywood and it's politics turns its nose down on New York editors. . . . But, as a woman, I can tell you I had to work harder to prove I was equal."[3]

DEDE ALLEN

1948	Story of Life/Because of Eve, The
1957	Endowing Our Future
1958	Terror from the Year 5000
1959	Odds against Tomorrow
1961	Hustler, The
1964	America, America
1965	It's Always Now
1967	Bonnie and Clyde
1968	Rachel, Rachel
1969	Alice's Restaurant
1970	Little Big Man
1972	Slaughterhouse Five
1973	Visions of Eight

1974	Serpico	1981	Reds
1975	Dog Day Afternoon	1984	Harry and Son
	Night Moves		Mike's Murder
1976	Missouri Breaks, The	1985	Breakfast Club, The
1977	Slap Shot	1986	Off Beat
1978	Wiz, The	1988	Milagro Beanfield War, The

Thelma Schoonmaker

When she grew up, **Thelma Schoonmaker** wanted to be a diplomat. From the age of one to fifteen she lived in Aruba and North Africa where her father worked for an oil company. So it was natural, in a way, that she wanted to participate in foreign service when she came of age. But as an activist for Martin Luther King, and a believer in anti-Vietnam activities, she was told candidly by her interviewer, "This is not for you."

In a way, you could say that in becoming a film editor, Thelma Schoonmaker became the diplomat she always longed to be. Editors are perhaps the perfect diplomats between the director and the picture. And as the sole (and soul) right-hand editor for Martin Scorsese, she has served as the liaison for other important films and directors as well. Michael Wadleigh's WOODSTOCK (1970) won Schoonmaker her first Oscar nomination. The reputation she garnered from that led her to Paul McCartney and a concert film featuring Paul and his band *Wings,* for television. She cut films as diverse as the experimentalist **Mary Ellen Bute**'s PASSAGES FROM FINNEGAN'S WAKE (which she stepped into directly as a student from New York University), to a favorite part of her past—cutting documentaries in the radical sixties. "I loved being a maverick," she said nostalgically.

It meant that I could work on things I cared about. . . . I sometimes worked as a temporary rather than work on something I really didn't care about. Money didn't mean anything to me, but working with people who cared as deeply as someone like Marty [Scorsese] did about their films is very seductive—you never want to work any other way.[1]

Now, she is mainly Scorsese's cohort and has cut his most prolific works, from his first film WHO'S THAT KNOCKING AT MY DOOR (1968), to RAGING BULL (1980), for which she won an Academy Award, to THE KING OF COMEDY (1982), to THE LAST TEMPTATION OF CHRIST (1988). **Susan Morse** was associate editor on RAGING BULL.

Schoonmaker has a notion as to why Hollywood has always accepted women as editors while denying them places in film's other technical fields.

Maybe because the organizational aspects of a film are almost secretarial, especially at the beginning. In my experience, men are sort of baffled by that. And of course, editors weren't considered that important in the early days.[2]

And as to why the role of the editor is more important today than it was seventy years ago, she says:

In the old days, a director never went into the editing room, but then they only printed two takes or maybe one, so there were fewer options. Here, you'll sometimes have twenty takes of something, and you're working with an actor like De Niro who gives you such a wide variety of interpretations.[3]

All in all, Schoonmaker is deeply satisfied with this version of diplomat she has become.

> I like the creativity of it. You have tremendous control in editing. You're not dealing with a big set and hundreds of actors and huge crews, and you're not forced to make decisions under pressure and not get what you want and have to settle for something else.[4]

The only thing she regrets, she says, is the anonymity she lost when she garnered her Academy Award. If there is any trademark iron-branded to the film editor, it is anonymity with a capital *A*. Without it we have to wonder where film history's woman film editor would be today?

THELMA SCHOONMAKER
(Selected List)

1960	Passages from Finnegan's Wake
1968	Who's That Knocking at My Door
1970	Woodstock
1980	Raging Bull
1982	The King of Comedy
1985	After Hours
1988	Last Temptation of Christ, The

Carol Littleton

It's disheartening when people say, Oh, I loved the cuts! Then, I feel my work has failed. A well-edited film is one where no one notices the editing because you've worked to make it invisible.
—Carol Littleton
Interview with author

In a sense, the comment is one that also aptly describes **Carol Littleton** herself. Her manner is naturally unobtrusive, even when she is the subject of the interview. She is modest and kind and warm and quiet, her manner of dress utilitarian and unadorned. You get the feeling without even asking that her philosophy is "what is best is simple." Her blue eyes are sharp, intelligent, and focused with intensity on whatever she is speaking about, which, at the moment we were speaking, happened to be about her passion, film.

She told me that in the 1960s, when she was a Fulbright Scholar studying comparative literature in Paris, she saw a movie called THE BATTLE OF ALGIERS (1966). The experience changed her life. From that moment she knew what she had to do. She came back to the States and headed straight for Los Angeles with a determination to make her career in the movies.

But still in her soul was the French "film noir," and she submerged herself in the American film noir of the forties. The result of those powerful influences became transparent in the steamy, sensual BODY HEAT, Lawrence Kasdan's first film that she edited in 1981. She came to Kasdan after cutting LEGACY (1975) and THE MAFU CAGE (1978), both for **Karen Arthur,** and REMEMBER MY NAME (1978) for Alan Rudolph. What attracted her to Kasdan's film was the flip role-reversal of the protagonists, the manipulation of the man instead of the woman, with a kind of terse, no-nonsense dialogue reminiscent of the Bogart/**Bacall** movies.

What attracted Kasdan to Littleton is specifically that she was a woman. He wanted a feeling of eroticism vs. pornography that he felt a woman editor's sensibility could give. Kasdan had seen Littleton's cutting of **Karen Arthur's** THE MAFU CAGE and wanted to achieve that same lyric quality. He wanted an eroticism, a sensuality he felt only a woman editor could achieve. If a female sensibility is lodged in a male film director's vision, it is in BODY HEAT.

"There's really very little magic involved," says Littleton modestly, even after such impressive successes as THE BIG CHILL (1983), PLACES IN THE HEART (1984), and E.T. THE EXTRA-TERRESTRIAL (1982) for which she won an Oscar nomination. "We deal with the bits and pieces of film and manipulate them in such a way that they're the most powerful for an audience."[1] She speaks as though whatever imprint she has made on a movie happened by sheer accident. She believes that the most honed style of editing is one that blends seamlessly into the picture one is cutting.

If she has a notion of her power as an editor, it is a Zen Master's power in what she herself has called a Zen occupation: a tedious, exacting craft where one is alone in a dark room with the same material day after day for a long period of time.

Yet if Carol Littleton knows anything, she knows about the power of collaboration.

> People are always asking which was your decision and which was the director's? That's the kind of question I can't answer. When you sit in an editing room with the director it becomes a dialogue and you don't differentiate between whose idea is whose.[2]

This attitude toward her craft is one that has consistently made her one of the most sought after editors in recent years. It has also put her in a category of being choosey about the material she works on. She claims that she can't turn a poorly-shot film into a good one, and that she couldn't save a performance that is inadequate. "When the pieces are very good and when there is a concept behind the film, you can either misdirect it or bring it very close to what the director wants to achieve."[3]

The most difficult scenes to cut, she claims, are those with ensemble characters, like THE BIG CHILL, or the card-playing scene from PLACES IN THE HEART where all the emotion in the scene has to be conveyed underneath the words being spoken. Action scenes, she says are easy.

> People who don't really know what editing's about . . . talk more about the editing in action pictures. But films that focus on characters and ideas and conflicts are more challenging. BODY HEAT was just two characters in dark rooms. You have no recourse, nothing to cut away to.[4]

She says her confidence in her material must be such that she can get away from the notion "If someone's not talking, you have to cut." Sitcoms, she feels, have ruined film editing in this respect, in their habit of chopping back and forth with no feeling or rhythm or flow to the scene.

Does her mastery of "invisible" editing make her feel like a pioneer?

> No. I feel like I am carrying on a long tradition of women editors. But I don't feel like a pioneer. I feel like the pioneering has gone on through those like Margaret Booth and Dede Allen, who have more or less revolutionized the whole notion of film editing.[5]

Like a Zen Master, she passes along heady glory where it will not interfere with her task.

CAROL LITTLETON

1985	Silverado	1988	Accidental Tourist, The
1986	Brighton Beach Memoirs		Vibes
1987	Swimming to Cambodia	1990	White Palace

Susan E. Morse

Perhaps in no instance is the role of 'editor-as-collaborator' more crucial, than in the relationship between **Susan Morse** and Woody Allen. She has edited all of Allen's films since 1977. When the director's style is anecdotal and digressive, the trick is rhythm and cohesion, and the job of creating that belongs to Susan Morse. About Allen's RADIO DAYS (1987) Morse said:

> The challenge was to create a sense of a dramatic curve in a picture that didn't have a narrative line to it . . . to give a sort of forward momentum to a series of anecdotes. . . . You'd be amused if you saw the continuity list. . . . It goes from scene 72 to 94 to 10 to 58.[1]

It may sound more like a football call, but as with all non-linear genius, the seeming randomness has method in its madness. That method is what Susan (her friends call her Sandy) Morse helps Woody Allen find. Allen's vignette approach to moviemaking may stem from his stand-up comedy days, but whatever the reason, the style is one that demands that the editor virtually act as rewriter of the film in the edit room. "Free association was implicit in the way the script was written," says Morse about RADIO DAYS, "and we continued this free association in the editing room."[2]

Modest and soft-spoken, low-key and shy (a demeanor similar to Allen's own in his offscreen life), a twenty-four-year-old Sandy Morse got what she thought was a prank call on April Fools' Day in 1976. She was a graduate student in film at New York University (she had graduated from Yale as a history major), and the call was from Ralph Rosenblum asking her to

be his apprentice on a film. The apprenticeship led to a full-time job as Rosenblum's first assistant on Woody Allen's ANNIE HALL (1976). INTERIORS (1978) would be Rosenblum's last cutting assignment for Allen before he left to direct his own picture. Morse had been allowed to cut some of the scenes in INTERIORS and was asked by Allen to edit his next film, MANHATTAN (1979).

The two will closely collaborate behind closed doors about which scenes should stay in, which should go. When a large-cast opening scene of the scripted RADIO DAYS could not be shot because of weather, Morse and Allen together came up with the idea of beginning with the film's current opening scene of two burglars who pick up a ringing telephone in the house they're robbing and find themselves as contestants on a radio game show (scene 72 in the original script).

"I feel like Woody and I have grown up together, in a way, and that Ralph taught both of us how to edit," says Morse.[3]

Rosenblum, in his book *When the Shooting Stops the Cutting Begins* (1979), is a big advocate for a kind of public awareness of the intrinsic, vital role played by the too often uncredited editor. In the case of Susan Morse, who won an Academy Award nomination for her artful piecing together of HANNAH AND HER SISTERS (1986), that mythic invisibility of the editor as the silent roar behind the genius is unprecedented. Similar was the relationship between another great woman behind a great man, **Anne Bauchens** and Cecil B. De Mille. Thanks also to Morse's skillful editing, MANHATTAN (1979), ZELIG (1983), HANNAH AND HER SISTERS (1986), and RADIO DAYS

(1987) all garnered British Academy Award nominations. Perhaps in no other art form does such a crucial collaborator play so silent and invisible a role.

SUSAN E. MORSE

1979 Manhattan
      Warriors, The

1980 Raging Bull
      Stardust Memories
1981 Arthur
1982 Midsummer Night's Sex Comedy,
      A
1983 Zelig
1984 Broadway Danny Rose
1985 Purple Rose of Cairo, The
1986 Hannah and Her Sisters
1987 Radio Days
1991 Alice

Barbara McLean

Viola Lawrence

SHORT TAKES

♦ ♦ ♦

Viola Lawrence (1895–1973)

Viola Lawrence was one of Hollywood's first full-fledged female editors—a credit she shares with **Anne Bauchens,** editor for C. B. De Mille. Lawrence began her career in 1912 at the Brooklyn Vitagraph Studios as an errand "girl." Her first assignment as a cutter was for a three-reeler in 1915.

She circulated in several of the major studios, including First National, Columbia, and Goldwyn, where she learned how to pin sound to picture on Samuel Goldwyn's very first talkie, BULLDOG DRUMMOND (1929).

Her numerous accolades during her lifetime included two Academy Award nominations: PAL JOEY (1957), PEPE (1960), and the prestigious ACE (American Cinema Editors) Critics Award for THE EDDY DUCHIN STORY, in 1956.

She remained an editor highly in demand until her voluntary retirement in 1961, completing a career that stretched forty-five years from the silents through sound.

She edited films of John Ford, Howard Hawks and Orson Welles. She was also among **Dorothy Arzner's** favorite editors. She cut two of Arzner's best films, CRAIG'S WIFE (1936) with **Rosalind Russell,** and FIRST COMES COURAGE (1943) **Arzner's** last feature.

VIOLA LAWRENCE

1916	O'Henry
1917	Within the Law
1919	Alabaster Box, An
	Heart of Humanity, The
	His Divorced Wife
	Loot
1920	Once to Every Woman
	Virgin of Stamboul, The
1921	Man-Woman-Marriage
1925	Fighting the Flames
1926	Winning of Barbara Worth, The
1927	Devil Dancer, The
	Night of Love, The
	Magic Flame, The
1928	Awakening, The
	Queen Kelly
	Two Lovers
1929	Bulldog Drummond
	This is Heaven
1930	Great Parade, The
	Ladies Love Brutes
	What a Widow!
1931	Pagan's Lady
1932	Big Broadcast, The
1933	Man's Castle, A
	Midnight Club

	Sailor Be Good	1941	Bahama Passage
	Terror Abroad		One Night in Lisbon
1934	Lady By Choice		Virginia
	Lone Cowboy	1942	I Married a Witch
	No Greater Glory		Lady is Willing, The
	Party's Over, The	1943	China
	Whom the God's Destroy		First Comes Courage
1935	Car 99		Young and Willing
	Feather in Her Hat, A	1944	And the Angels Sing
	Love Me Forever		Hitler Gang, The
	Paris in the Spring	1945	Affairs of Susan, The
	Party Wire		You Came Along
	So Red the Rose	1946	California
	Whole Town's Talking, The	1947	Long Grey Line, The
1936	Anything Goes	1948	Alias Nick Beal
	Craig's Wife		Beyond Glory
	Forgotten Faces		Big Clock, The
	General Died at Dawn, The		Night Has a Thousand Eyes
	King Steps Out, The	1949	Red, Hot, and Blue
	Lady of Secrets	1950	Copper Canyon
	Lone Wolf Returns, The		Where Danger Lives
1937	Devil's Playground	1951	Darling How Could You
	Life Begins With Love		His Kind of Woman
	Mountain Music	1952	Son of Paleface
	Partners in Crime	1953	Pony Express
	She Married an Artist	1954	Secret of the Incas
	Speed to Spare		Strategic Air Command
	Swing High Swing Low	1955	At Gunpoint
1938	Big Broadcast of 1938	1956	Back From Eternity
	Booloo		Eddy Duchin Story, The
	City Streets		Johnny Concho
	I Am the Law		World Without End
	King of Alcatraz	1957	Pal Joey
	Penitentiary		Unholy Wife, The
	There's Always a Woman	1958	Hot Angel, The
	There's That Woman		St. Louis Blues, The
	Again	1959	John Paul Jones
1939	Amazing Mr. Williams, The		Wreck of the Mary Deare, The
1940	Rangers of Fortune	1960	One Foot in Hell
	Safari		Pepe

Barbara McLean (1909–   )

She was Darryl Zanuck's personal editor even before Zanuck formed Twentieth Century-Fox. In 1949, **Barbara McLean** became chief of the editing division at Fox, where she supervised all of Fox's features. It was a post that she would hold through the midsixties. *American* magazine wrote of her in 1949, "When Tyrone Power . . . gathers a lovely into his arms, the amount of film footage allowed them is largely in the scissored hands of Barbara McLean."[1]

In her then fifteen years as editor she had already seen nearly three million feet of film and was bringing in twenty-five thousand dollars a year—a large sum, especially for a woman at that time. In 1945, the *Los Angeles Times* listed her as one of eight women editors (out of Hollywood's three hundred editors) of the period.[2]

Barbara McLean was born in Palisades Park, New Jersey. During her summer vacations, she worked in a film laboratory owned by her father.

McLean arrived in Hollywood in 1924 hoping to be an actress. Instead she went to work for Sol Wurtzel, and soon after found herself editing COQUETTE (1929), one of **Mary Pickford**'s few roles playing a grown woman.

She edited thirty of Darryl Zanuck's personal productions. In 1955 she turned to coproducing with SEVEN CITIES OF GOLD, directed by her husband, Robert D. Webb. And in 1960 she was made head of the Fox Feature Editorial Division.

In 1970 McLean was interviewed by film historian Tom Stempel and spoke about being a woman in an all-male Hollywood of the 1940s. She was sitting with a group of male executives—in her words—"the only girl sitting there as usual," running a screen test for AN AMERICAN GUERRILLA IN THE PHILIPPINES (1950). Everyone in the room thought the actor was very good, except for McLean. In her words,

Henry King couldn't stand it any longer, so he said, "Well, Bobbie was the only one who didn't like him." Mr. Zanuck said, "What's the matter with you? Why don't you like him?" I said I thought he was a nice looking boy and everything else and it was a good test, but I didn't think he looked

like the American Guerrilla in the Philippines to me.

With typical forthrightness, McLean proceeded to tell the gentlemen that she thought the American Guerrilla in the Philippines would be a young fellow with a little ego and a little chip on his shoulder. They said that the girl in the mailroom thought this actor was great. "I don't care," said McLean, "I'm not Molly."

They just said, "Oh my God." And they never used him. Poor guy. They used Tyrone Power.[3]

McLean pointed out other advantages to being the only woman around the production house.

It was very funny, because I'd say I didn't like a dress. "I think that dress is horrible," and being the only woman, I'd get my way. Either that, or maybe they thought, "She knows a little something about clothes." I was just like the female audience.[4]

And when Zanuck made her a producer, McLean acted the same way, but now with an extra dose of self-confidence.

I'd just stick to my guns. I'd say, "I don't care. Don't ask me. If you're going to ask me, then listen to me." I can understand a woman's point of view could be a little different from a man's point of view.[5]

When editing a picture, remarked McLean, she always cut them first and foremost to please herself. If she didn't like something, she'd cut around it.

After twenty years in the industry, editing films with such personages as Billie Dove and Corinne Griffith, and after garnering eight Academy Award nominations, Barbara McLean won an Academy Award for her superior cutting of WILSON (1944).

She was asked in 1945 if she would recommend film editing as a career for other women.

"Oh yes," said McLean without hesitation. "The pay is very good. About $160 a week!"[6]

BARBARA MCLEAN

1929 Coquette
1933 Bowery, The
     Gallant Lady
1934 Affairs of Cellini, The
     House of Rothschild, The
     Mighty Barnum, The
1935 Clive of India
     Les Miserables
     Metropolitan
     Professional Soldier
1936 Country Doctor, The
     Lloyds of London
     Sing, Baby, Sing
     Sins of Man
1937 Seventh Heaven
     Love Under Fire
1938 Alexander's Ragtime Band
     Baroness and the Butler
     In Old Chicago
     Suez
1939 Jesse James
     Rains Came, The
     Stanley & Livingstone
1940 Chad Hanna
     Down Argentine Way
     Little Old New York
     Maryland
1941 Remember the Day
     Tobacco Road
     Yank in the RAF, A

1942 Black Swan, The
     Magnificent Dope, The
     Rings on Her Fingers
1943 Hello, Frisco, Hello
     Song of Bernadette, The
1944 Winged Victory
     Wilson
1945 Bell for Adano, A
     Dolly Sisters, The
1946 Margie
     Three Little Girls in Blue
1947 Captain from Castile
     Nightmare Alley
1948 Deep Waters
     When My Baby Smiles at Me
1949 Prince of Foxes
     Twelve O'clock High
1950 All about Eve
     Gunfighter, The
     No Way Out
1951 David and Bathsheba
     Follow the Sun
     I'd Climb the Highest Mountain
     People Will Talk
1952 Lure of the Wilderness
     O. Henry's Full House
     Snows of Kilimanjaro, The
     Viva Zapata
     Wait 'Til the Sun Shines, Nellie
1953 Desert Rats, The
     King of the Khyber Rifles
     Niagara
     Robe, The
1954 Egyptian, The
1955 Seven Cities of Gold (Co-
        producer)
     Untamed
1956 On the Threshold of Space (Asso-
        ciate Producer)

Adrienne Fazan (?–1965)

By the time **Adrienne Fazan** edited the Academy Award–winning AN AMERICAN IN PARIS in 1951, she had already been a con-

stantly requested editor at MGM for over twenty years.

Like the other two influential female editors at MGM during this period—Supervising Editor **Margaret Booth** and **Blanche Sewell**—Adrienne Fazan mentions nothing about her experiences as a woman in an all-male industry. The issue is never addressed because in neither her personal nor in the collective consciousness did it ever come up.

Not much is known about Adrienne Fazan's personal life, or her reasons for wanting to work in movies. The only thing that is absolutely clear is the evidence of her talent and her desire to work hard.

She began as an assistant editor in the late twenties for Alexander Hall in the **Colleen Moore** unit (Moore was a great star of the day). It was the confusing time when sound was entering motion pictures. For the theaters that did not yet own sound equipment a common studio practice was to provide sound pictures as silents so they could project them. As such, the films needed titles. This was how Fazan began, adding titles.

By 1930 she got herself a position at MGM cutting shorts. Awakening to a new foreign market, the studios at the time had adopted a practice of hiring foreign directors to remake some of the big pictures like THE BIG HOUSE (1930).[1] Fazan was fluent in several languages, especially German, and from then on she was regularly employed cutting features.

"There was overtime, but the studio made a rule that we could not work overtime without special permission. . . . So I said, "Oh, the hell with you." I worked the overtime, but I didn't put in for it, because I hate that business: 'You can't do that.' What the hell! I'm working on the picture for the picture, trying to do as good as possible. Then they tell me I can't work, I have to go home when I have work to do. I didn't go for that."[2]

Fazan confidently said, "It's easier to cut musicals than dramatic films. The dancers and the director take great pains to match action." But clearly she was being humble about her own skill. Director Don Weis

who had worked with Fazan on two projects comments:

> It is not more difficult to edit a musical or a dramatic film. Both are equally difficult. Some editors are simply more talented in one area than the other. Adrienne was obviously most effective with musicals.

He goes on to comment about her popularity around the studio.

> She was constantly being requested by many people, and it was more a matter of her availability—which accounts for the fact that she only did two pictures for me. She is a very strong-minded and forceful creator. We had a lot of noisy disagreements. She was known for that. She was in awe of the project she was working on—not of the personalities involved. She never withheld her opinion, and most of the time she was right.[3]

Laslo Benedek, who directed THE KISSING BANDIT (1948), with Fazan as editor, said, "I liked her very much. Working with Adrienne was always easy and pleasant, due to her easygoing personality and, perhaps more importantly, to her thorough knowledge of editing and her respect for the director's intentions."[4]

Director George Seaton said, "My film editor for years before was **Alma Mac-Crory,** but she was not available. She recommended Adrienne. We selected Adrienne because of her reputation. . . . She had an indomitable spirit. She refused to give in. I loved working with her."[5]

Her "indomitable spirit" fought a losing battle with cancer beginning in 1964. Fazan continued to do the work she loved best throughout the illness. She died as most behind-the-scenes giants do, without public recognition.

But she didn't care about that.

She would have edited for no pay. For years she edited for no credit. An Academy Award might have stroked the egos of some, but as Fazan said herself, "It was simply another indication of a job well done."[6]

ADRIENNE FAZAN

1933 Day of Reckoning
1937 Bride Wore Red, The
1938 You're Only Young Once
1944 Barbary Coast Gent
       Between Two Women
1945 Anchors Aweigh
       She Went to the Races
1946 Holiday in Mexico
       Secret Heart, The
1948 Kissing Bandit, The
       Three Darling Daughters
1949 In the Good Old Summertime
1950 Duchess of Idaho, The
       Nancy Goes to Rio
       Pagan Love Song, The
1951 American in Paris, An
       Texas Carnival
1952 Everything I Have Is Yours
       Singin' in the Rain
1953 Give a Girl a Break
       I Love Melvin

1954 Deep in My Heart
1955 It's Always Fair Weather
       Kismet
1956 Invitation to the Dance
       Lust for Life
1957 Designing Woman
       Don't Go Near the Water
1958 Gigi
       Reluctant Debutante, The
       Some Came Running
1959 Big Circus, The
       Gazebo, The
1960 Bells Are Ringing
1962 Four Horsemen of the Apocalypse, The
       Two Weeks in Another Town
1963 Courtship of Eddie's Father, The
       Prize, The
1964 Looking For Love
       36 Hours
1965 Billie
1966 This Property Is Condemned
1967 Who's Minding the Mint?
1968 Where Angels Go . . . Trouble Follows!
       With Six You Get Eggroll
1969 Comic, The
1970 Cheyenne Social Club, The

· VIII ·

REEL WOMEN
ANIMATORS

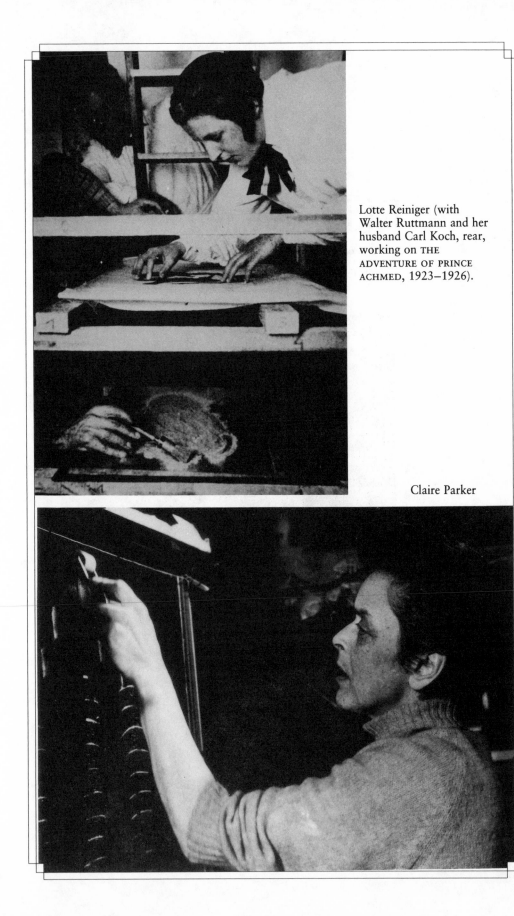

Lotte Reiniger (with
Walter Ruttmann and her
husband Carl Koch, rear,
working on THE
ADVENTURE OF PRINCE
ACHMED, 1923–1926).

Claire Parker

Lotte Reiniger (1899–1981)

She's the woman who beat out Walt Disney by ten years. **Lotte Reiniger** was the first person to create, and produce a fully animated feature from 1923 to 1926, using a technique that she pioneered known as "silhouette" animation.

Animation was in its infancy; there was just FELIX THE CAT,[1] Fleischer's cartoons, and Mickey Mouse was far away in the future. For the filmmakers of this period, those were the days: with each film we could make new discoveries, find new problems, new possibilities, technical and artistic. . . . The whole field was virgin soil and we had all the joys of explorers in an unknown country.[2]

The figures of silhouette are designed through freehand scissor cutting. The depth and delicate tones of the backgrounds are created from varying layers of tissue paper, and are photographed on a horizontal glass plate lit from below.[3] Different figures were made for close-ups and long shots, since the detail and silhouette in each case were subtly different.

The fascination of Reiniger's technique stems from our love of shadow plays. Because a silhouette bars showing detailed facial expressions, it is a perfect medium for archetypes and larger-than-life themes. Reiniger made her name doing exactly these. After World War II, she produced thirteen silhouette films based on traditional fairy tales.

Shadow theater had originally been introduced to Europe from the Orient. In the early twenties, Germany was showing an increasing interest in Oriental subjects, as is recognizable in the popularity of painters of the period such as Wassily Kandinsky. Franz Marc, another German painter, was reproducing pictures of Egyptian shadow-play figurines in *Der Blaue Reiter* magazine. The time was propitious for a film based on the shadow-play technique.[4]

The year was 1923. A banker saw Lotte Reiniger's cutouts for puppet shadow theater at a German museum. He commissioned her then and there to do a full-length film. Thus, THE ADVENTURES OF PRINCE ACHMED (finished in 1926), the first full-length animated feature in history, was born.

Reiniger and her husband, Carl Koch, hired leading animators of the day to collaborate on the project. The combined work of Reiniger, Walter Ruttmann, and Berthold Bartosch looks like a compendium of experimental techniques. The images were drawn from tales from the *Arabian Nights*. Reiniger's characters act out the story in pantomime, conveying emotion through a delicate shifting of gestures. Reiniger became a master at conveying feelings by shifting her paper figures to a certain pose through a delicate movement of the fingers.

In a film produced about her called THE ART OF LOTTE REINIGER, one gets an acute awareness of the endless patience required for the intensity of her skilled labor. **Pat Martin,** who worked with Reiniger on her later films, said:

When you see the work, you cannot really appreciate the hours and hours that painstakingly go into making each tiny sequence, of only ten or fifteen seconds: sitting in the dark, moving each little figure a fraction of an inch at a time before shooting. It's much harder than the beauty of the outcome could ever reveal.[5]

Born in Berlin, Reiniger studied briefly with Max Reinhardt. In 1918, she created hand-cut silhouette titles for Paul Wegener's film, THE PIED PIPER OF HAMELIN. She also "helped animate wooden rats in stop-motion, after Wegener's attempts with real rats and guinea pigs with false tails ended in total failure."[6]

"My life is a kind of Andersen's fairy tale," said Reiniger at one of her many international speaking engagements. She was eighty then. When she was only twenty years old, she organized a group of other young artistic filmmakers under the guidance of Dr. Hans Curlis and in 1919 made her first silhouette motion picture film, THE ORNAMENT OF THE LOVING HEART.

Reiniger's career may well be the longest in film history, extending from 1918 to her latest produced film in 1980. Her extensive filmography includes some sixty pictures. Jean Renoir, a close friend, who worked closely with Carl Koch and hired Reiniger to create a shadow-play sequence for his film LA MARSEILLAISE, has written:

> Lotte Reiniger is much above most animators. She is an artist and her work would be as good if instead of working with film she had been a painter or a musician. Artistically, I have to see her as a visual expression of Mozart's music. I have no stories to tell about her. She is of herself a fascinating story.[7]

She is one entirely self-made pioneer who at least in her own field has not gone unacknowledged. She has been rightly and widely praised as "one of the greatest artistic figures working in the cinema." Her film career is unrivaled for its duration, artistry, and originality. And most of all, she is unrivaled for her independence.

LOTTE REINIGER

1919	Ornament of the Loving Heart, The
1920	Love and the Steadfast Sweethearts
1921	Flying Coffer, The
	Star of Bethlehem, The
1922	Cinderella
	Sleeping Beauty
1923	Animated Sequence from Die Nibelungen
1923–26	Adventures of Prince Achmed, The
1927–28	Dr. Dolittle and His Animals
1929–30	Chase after Fortune, The
1931	Harlequin
1932	Sissi
1933	Carmen
	Don Quixote
1934	Puss in Boots
	Rolling Wheel, The
	Stolen Heart, The
1935	Galathea
	Little Chimney Sweep, The
	Papageno
1936	King's Breakfast, The
1937	Animated Sequence from La Marseillaise
	Tocher
1939	Dream Circus
	L'Elisir D'Amore
1944	Golden Goose, The
1949	Daughter, The
1951	Mary's Birthday
1953	Aladdin
	Magic Horse, The
	Snow White and Rose Red
	You've Asked for It
1954	Caliph Stork
1955	Hansel and Gretel
	Jack and the Beanstalk
	Thumbelina
1956	Star of Bethlehem, The
1957	La Belle Helene
1958	Seraglio, The
1975	Aucassin and Nicolette
1979	The Rose and the Ring

Claire Parker (1906–1981)

A pioneer animator born in Boston, **Claire Parker,** coinvented a technique of animation with the man who would later become her husband, Alexander Alexeieff, known as "pinboard." It is a means by which engravings may be brought to life.

According to an article written by Parker in 1961, "The pinboard is a black-and-white technique somewhat analogous to the half-tone process: the picture is made up of a very large number of very small black elements on a white ground. The darkness of a tone corresponds to the individual size of each black element on a given portion of the white ground. . . . The further forward a pin is pushed, the longer its shadow becomes. As there are a million pins on a board, we never consider the pins individually, but always as a group, like paint on a brush."[1]

Claire Parker studied art at Bryn Mawr, as well as in Austria and France. She met the Russian-born Alexeieff in Paris and requested that he give her lessons in engraving. They married in 1941 and moved to the United States. Here, at the request of their lifelong friend, Norman McLaren, they produced a film for the National Film Board of Canada entitled EN PASSANT (1942).

In 1932, they built the first model upon which they drew a now-classic film of animation, NIGHT ON BALD MOUNTAIN (1933). This film can be found in most film libraries in the Western world.

According to Cecile Starr of the Women's Independent Film Exchange in New York,

because she was an expert in reading scores, Claire Parker was also in charge of the relationship between music and image, no small task, especially in their first films which were made before music tracks could be transferred to tape. Even using sound tape, this work could be extremely complex, as in the ballroom scene of PICTURES AT AN EXHIBITION, in which as many as thirty-five loops of film were made in the camera, some of them on a second rotating pinscreen.[2]

In 1935, before what we know today as the "art film," Parker directed and produced RUBENS, based on an exhibition at Paris's Orangerie. In the thirties and the fifties Parker and Alexeieff developed original, inventive advertising films. A print of ETUDE SUR L'HARMONIE DES LIGNES (Exercise in line harmony) directed solely by Parker in 1934, has recently been found in Paris.

"If there had been no Claire Parker," said Alexeieff, "I would have never done animation. I would never have been capable of doing it alone."[3]

CLAIRE PARKER (Selected List)

1933 Night on Bald Mountain
1934 Etude sur L'Harmonie des Lignes
1935 Rubens
1942 En Passant
1963 Nose, The
1972 Pictures at an Exhibition
1980 Three Moods (Trois Thèmes)

·IX·

REEL
STUNT WOMEN

Pearl White (in THUNDER, her last serial).

Helen Gibson

Helen Holmes

PREVIEW

♦ ♦ ♦

Stunting is a field that has been more or less shut off to women. But before the days of unions, **Pearl White, Lillian Gish, Helen Holmes,** and other formative stars thought nothing of jumping atop a train racing at full speed if it was for the good of the picture.

Yet instead of noticing how few women have made their marks, why not celebrate the many great women who have? Although there haven't been large numbers of women in the field of stunt work, the ones that forged this terrain were truly inspiring.

It is important at the outset to clear up a standard, stereotypic misconception. Stunt work has never been any more physically difficult for women than it has for men. In the early days, actors and actresses stunted in equal numbers. Discrimination was an unknown denominator. In fact, if you wanted a particular role, and it called for a particular stunt, you either agreed to do it, or you didn't get the part. The same held true with costumes. You came dressed as your character to the audition—Heaven help your career if your wardrobe was skimpy!

Lillian Gish boasted about being her own double for Griffith. She did everything from putting her head in the guillotine to lying face down on ice floes. She did it before more sophisticated editing techniques made it possible to belie the identity of a certain

actor's actions to the camera. She did it for the betterment and for the authenticity of the picture.

But as unions became the rule rather than the exception, you were more likely to find a man dressed in women's clothing if any doubling was called for. Kathy Kelly, a writer who has done much research on women in stunting, told me, "You can always tell when a man is stunting for a woman. On a fall, a man will *always* protect his genitals first. A woman will always shield her breasts."

There were exceptions, of course, to men dressing up. **Helen Thurston** pioneered the forties, when stuntwomen were more or less unheard-of. Former rodeo rider, **Polly Berson** was no small potatoes a bit later on in the fifties through the seventies when she transferred herself from a racing horse to a racing train, doubling for **Betty Hutton.** TRUE GRIT (1969) was **Polly**'s claim to fame. **Lila Finn** is currently the oldest stuntwoman in the business and one who is still working.

The basic fee for stunting for women in the forties was about thirty-five dollars a day. Each woman negotiated individual deals, which were paid over and above the thirty-five dollars. Fees ranged from twenty-five dollars to as much as five hundred dollars.[1] The studios were well aware that the risks involved were worth far more than they were paying out and that they were getting off cheaply indeed. But then, if you weren't being exploited, you probably weren't in Hollywood.

Aline Goodwin was on call for one full year with GONE WITH THE WIND (1939), making herself a total of about $5,800 for one major fall. Remember Scarlett O'Hara's sprawling tumble down a long flight of stairs that cost her a baby? **Vivien Leigh** hardly felt a bruise, mainly because she was sitting on the sidelines watching Goodwin risk her neck. Thankfully, the skilled Goodwin wasn't bruised either.

Then, in 1943, Goodwin followed **Olivia de Havilland** to Washington, DC, to be her double in GOVERNMENT GIRL (1943). The job hiked her earnings that year to $6,700. "Stars get inflated notions about their own importance," said Goodwin in 1945.

> We don't. I got the break of my life when I lost out as an actress. When sound came in, my voice wasn't right. And am I glad! It's not the money stars earn that you look at, it's what they keep. Chances are, we keep much more.[2]

Jeanne Criswell once made a bargain for $150 to grab a bull by the tail and be dragged across a field while another woman rode the bull. Criswell padded herself thoroughly. A cow was stationed in the adjoining pasture to make certain the bull would run in the desired direction. The $150 would have been fine, except the other woman failed to remain astride the bull.

> They told me Kokomo, the bull, was nice and tame, but I was picking pebbles out of my anatomy for days. If I had bargained for a hundred and fifty a take, the studio would have got tired of paying me long before old Kokomo got tired of running.[3]

As it was, Kokomo ran on and on for miles. **Betty Danko** as well suffered serious injuries in stunting. She doubled the witch in THE WIZARD OF OZ (1939). When the tech

assistant used an overcharge of gunpowder the witch vanished in a cloud of smoke. Danko was severely burned. Another time, she was doubling **Patsy Kelly** in a scene with lions when she was clawed and bitten. Most stuntwomen of those days agreed that misfortunes were due to mechanical failures or careless assistants. They would much rather depend on their own quick thinking and nerve control. In 1945 the *Saturday Evening Post* reported that **Francis Miles** and **Jeanne Criswell** made a couple of thousand dollars each out of Samuel Goldwyn's THE NORTH STAR (1943), a mint for both male and female stunters.[4]

Francis Miles left Minneapolis for Hollywood in 1923, young and innocent. She dreamed of becoming a star like the Gish Sisters. Her first job was at Universal playing opposite Lon Chaney in the original HUNCHBACK OF NOTRE DAME (1923). The first day on the set, director Rupert Julian asked her if she was afraid of horses. She had never so much as curried one, but answered appropriately, "Oh, I love horses!" Next thing she knew, she was meandering alone in a field of about a hundred brood mares.

> It was rugged. I took a lot of pushing around, but my real fate in Hollywood was settled that day, although I didn't realize it then. I worked in fifty-two two-reel Westerns, and then graduated into five reelers with guys like Hoot Gibson, Jack Hoxie and Buck Jones. I've done all the falls, fights, chases you could ever think of. When Westerns began to go sissy with banjos, guitars and quartets, I branched out into features. I've doubled for lots of stars, but I wouldn't be one for love or money.[5]

Another Goldwyn bonanza was THE PRINCESS AND THE PIRATE (1944). You could just about guarantee that a pirate or battle film could make any stuntperson rich. **Helen Thurston** and **Betty Danko** received a pot of gold from RKO's RADIO SPANISH MAIN, and also received free fencing lessons to boot while training on the job. In the course of shooting THE MOON AND SIXPENCE (1942), **Francis Miles** threw a 235-pound professional wrestler over her shoulder.

In Cecil B. De Mille's day, actress **Betty Hutton** was informed that she'd play the trapeze artist in THE GREATEST SHOW ON EARTH (1952). Her joy quickly turned to alarm when she was told that she had to do all of her own stunts. When the film won an Academy Award, De Mille attributed the honor to the fact that Hutton did all her own stunt work which made the film more believable. But directors were never willing to allow Betty Hutton to risk her neck again.

Director Reeves (Breezy) Eason told a story in 1945 about the bravery of one of his stuntwomen, **Vivian Valdez.**

> These girls sometimes have more guts than any man. I remember a riding stunt I had to put on in the remake of BLOOD AND SAND (1941). It needed a girl, but I thought it was too dangerous, so I hired one of the best riders in the business. He had to gallop full tilt into a tree, grab a branch and hang on. The girl who thought she was going to pull off this trick was Vivian Valdez. She began to cry when she saw that I was having this man rider take her place.

Eason said he went over to cheer her, and she ended up convincing him that she was the woman for the job.

> In another way, it was not a mistake, because Vivian pulled off the job perfectly on her first try.[6]

But the fact that some director was compassionately looking out for a woman's welfare is not the main reason women were shunted out of stunting in droves. The decision was a financial one, pure and simple. Once the unions had solidified, insurance and budgetary considerations made it too risky to submit a main performer to possible injury. If **Kate Hepburn** was bitten while teasing the leopard in BRINGING UP BABY (1938), she would be laid up for weeks. The insurance people wouldn't stand for it, and it would mean thousands of crew hours and dollars. That is how **Helen Thurston** found herself in a new career.

In the fifties, **Mary Murphy** who also doubled as one of Paramount's rising stars, had to toss Bob Hope over her shoulder for a key scene in OFF LIMITS (1953)— a feat for which she had to enroll in jujitsu.

Certainly for black women and other minorities, the field did not begin to open up until the 1970s, and even then, the work was more than scarce. As poor as the numbers are for black women in stunting, other minority representations are even sadder. **Sammy Thurman** is an American Indian stuntwoman as well as a rodeo rider. **Simone Boisseree** is doing her piece for Oriental representation. And **Tonya Russell** seems to be a token in Hispanic doubling. Hollywood should hide its face in shame at the appalling numbers, as well as at the scarcity of vehicles these women can find work in.

Pearl White (1897–1938)

Here's what everyone was singing in 1914:

"Poor Pauline, I pity poor Pauline!
One night she's drifting out to sea,
Then they tie her to a tree,
I wonder what the end will be,

The suspense is awful!
Bing! Bang! Biff! They throw her o'er a cliff!

They dynamite her in a submarine
In the lion's den she sits with fright

The lion goes to take a bite—
Zip, goes fillum—Good night!
Poor Pauline!"[1]

She was the undisputed queen of the serials. THE PERILS OF PAULINE was one of the most successful films of the year 1914, and certainly one of the greatest sensations since movies were first made. It won for **Pearl White** a rather permanent place in American folklore. Whether tied to the railroad tracks before an oncoming locomotive, thrown to crocodiles, lashed to a whirring buzz saw, or pushed over a cliff—it was Pearl White who was the original hanger-on: the cliff-hanging Queen of Queens. In 1947 *Cue Magazine* named her "the original Blonde Bombshell of Flickers."[2]

The hottest films at the box office in 1914 were the serials that audiences would attend week after week to see what became of the heroine tied to the railroad tracks by "the villain" in the last episode. In the outbacks of Fort Lee, New Jersey, where filmmaking began in America, the incomparable Pearl White ran on rooftops, swung from clotheslines, was knocked down stairwells, and braved onrushing floods. In the meanwhile, **Kathlyn Williams** was rassling with lions in THE ADVENTURES OF KATHLYN (1913), **Grace Cunard** was fleeing Mexican outlaws in LUCILLE LOVE, GIRL OF MYSTERY (1914), and **Helen Holmes** was tied to another set of tracks in THE HAZARDS OF HELEN (1915).

But poor Pearl White was always struggling to beat off her attackers. And need I add, she always won. White's stock-in-trade was defending her own honor as well as the honor of women everywhere.

She was born in Greenridge, Missouri, the youngest of nine children. All of her female siblings were named after precious stones.

Although White insisted in interview after interview that she was of Irish and Italian ancestry, a combination she apparently found romantic, she actually descended from Puritan ancestry—the kind of stock that bred the Daughters of the American Revolution. "Her parents were as near being Americans as one can be without being Indian."[3]

Her mother died when Pearl was only three, leaving a large and hungry brood. One account of Pearl's life states that at age fifteen, in pursuit of free meals, the industrious young Pearl joined the circus. It was here that she learned the high wire and the trapeze, skills she found useful in her later career.[4] No doubt, it's a wonderful, romantic story! So in keeping with Pearl's nature that she encouraged it in interviews, as well as in her own biography.[5]

Another account, however, insists that she had no stage experience at all until the middle of her sophomore year in high school, when she began playing small parts for Diemer's Stock Company in Springfield. It was said that her father was so against a theatrical career that he spoke with a lawyer to see if he could prevent it.

But the stage was in her blood and after acting for a time, White married one Victor Sutherland, an actor in her stock company, on Columbus Day, 1907. It was just like Pearl to follow in the footsteps of a pioneer! Her autobiography ignores the existence of Sutherland entirely, and she divorced him in April 1914, just at the onset of her new career in serials.

Pearl White was ripe for this new genre called the *serial*, which was initiated by **Grace Cunard** and her partner Francis Ford. The arduous requirements listed for actors seemed to fit Pearl's dossier to a T and she was quickly cast. THE PERILS OF PAULINE was released in March 1914, and it was an immediate smash. Audiences would grip their seats in terror screaming, "Watch out, Pearl, he's behind you!"

Originally, the 5'6" Pearl, with her light skin, blue eyes, and red hair (under a blond wig for "better photographic effect") earned $250 a week—an incredible sum of money for the days when regular actors were pulling in $30.[6]

By nature she was not athletically inclined. In those days, however, before unions were there to protect them, it was part of the actor's job to do everything that was requested. The press agents of the day thought it a good stunt in itself to boast that Pearl White did all of her daredevil acts without the aid of a double. One article of the day was subtitled, "Behind-the-Scenes Adventures of Movie Heroine Who Loves Danger, Lives on Peril—and Doesn't Tolerate a Double Even When It Means Almost Certain Death." Certainly to a large part, this was true. Once she said to her director:

> Get a double for me in that scene. All I do is wallow around and drown out there which any fool can do. Now, if you will have somebody do that for me, I'll put on the hero's costume, ride off the dock and rescue her.[7]

This policy obviously had its risks. On one such publicity stunt in 1914, White was in a hot-air balloon that was mistakenly cut loose, sending her soaring some four thousand feet across the Manhattan skyline. She even survived a rainstorm! She finally landed safely, not without causing a great deal of excitement so desired by White's producing company. It was a great coup for ticket sales.

Pearl also descended a flight of stairs once and gained a spinal injury that was exacerbated over the years. Her producers realized all too soon that she was too valuable a commodity to put through such physical stress. Periodically from then on a prizefighter named Kelly put on a blond wig for the more hazardous routines.

Another time, she was lashed to a steel girder and

> was lifted to the twentieth story of the Bush Terminal Building on 42nd Street, all the while tossing down tiny American flags and recruiting circulars to the enthralled spectators below. On regaining the ground she is said to have said, "I've done my bit—

now you do yours." Wherewith she led the way to a recruiting booth, and thirty young men . . . signed up.[8]

The terrific success of THE PERILS OF PAULINE (it was rumored that her US audience ranged around the fifteen million mark) skyrocketed Pearl White's worth in no time to $2,500 with increases for each new serial.

The "new serials" included THE EXPLOITS OF ELAINE (1915), with Lionel Barrymore; THE IRON CLAW (1916), THE FATAL RING (1917), and THE HOUSE OF HATE (1918). The patriotic fever of World War I heralded PEARL OF THE ARMY (1916). By 1919, the serial days of THE PERILS OF PAULINE were coming to a close.

In 1922, a literal rags-to-riches Pearl White sailed to France on a vacation and was surprised to find herself an international sensation. Everywhere she docked, a parade was there to greet her. On arrival in France, she unexpectedly signed a three-picture deal. When this was completed she had a nervous breakdown. Wallace E. Davies reports that it was due to her "distress over the accidental death of a stuntman, John Stevenson, while doubling for her in PLUNDER, and the mysterious disappearance of her second husband, Wallace McCutcheon, who later turned up in a sanatorium."[9]

White settled down on her two million dollar savings, and was wise enough to retire when the going was still good. For a brief moment in 1932 she considered going back to pictures. "I am thinking of going into the talkies," she said.

> But I'm thinking of my friends and my fans. I would not make a flop for their sakes. . . . Nobody will have to "double" for me, and that helps. But I'm not sure I want to stage a comeback. There is one thing about the old stars of moviedom— we had to take our chances in the stunts and got many bruises.[10]

But a comeback was not in her cards. For one thing, her voice was all wrong. She had long suffered from throat trouble, and her voice was rough and hoarse. Not exactly the genteel background her image projected.

And although she was known as being warm, frank, friendly, given to practical jokes, and not at all temperamental to work with, it might be said that her visual image was a fake. The blond hair that identified her to the world was a wig. Once, upon its removal, she was asked what color her original hair had been. She replied, "I don't know. It's been dyed so often you'd have to say it's plaid."

Having endured one acrobatic stunt too many, Pearl White decided it was time to retire in style. She did try her hand at serious roles to see if she could do it between 1920 and 1922, but the efforts and the vehicles were undistinguished.

Older, richer, wiser, she married twice, divorced twice, and lived regally. "She owned an elegant town house," says Wallace Davies, "on the Avenue Henri Martin in the desirable Passy section in France, and a country villa at Rambouillet. . . . Toward the end of the twenties she acquired the Hotel de Paris, once a chateau of the Empress Eugenie."[11] She entertained lavishly, bought thirty-five race horses, and died young, age forty-nine, of a liver ailment.

A fellow player of the early days said about Pearl White, "She was a lady in every respect, but she got tough if you rubbed her the wrong way. Mainly she was kind. Beautiful, soft-spoken, and kind. She had respect for anyone who knew how to be respectful. She was always friendly with the extras. Never a snob."[12]

During her life, Pearl White traveled to nearly every corner of the globe. But she never made it to Hollywood.[13]

PEARL WHITE (Selected List)

1910	New Magdalene, The
1911	Lost Necklace, The
1912–14	Caught in the Act
	Dressmaker's Bill, The
	Girl Next Door, The
	Lady Doctor, The
	New Typist, The
	Oh Such a Night
	Pearl's Adventure
	Pearl as a Clairvoyant
	Pearl's Dilemma
	Pearl's Romance
	Pearl and the Tramp
	What Papa Got
1914	Perils of Pauline
1915	Exploits of Elaine, The
	Romance of Elaine, The
1916	Hazel Kirke
	Iron Claw, The
	King's Game, The
	Pearl of the Army
1917	Fatal Ring, The
	Mayblossom
1918	House of Hate, The
1919	Black Secret, The
	Lightning Raider, The
1920	Thief, The
	Tiger's Cub, The
	White Moll, The
1921	Beyond Price
	Know Your Men
	Mountain Woman, The
	Virgin Paradise, A
1922	Any Wife
	Broadway Peacock, The
	Without Fear
1923	Plunder
1924	Parisian Nights
	Perils of Paris
1925	Hooded Terror, The

Helen Holmes (1892–1950)

The basic model looked like this: She was tied to a locomotive piston. The villain said that she would never leave alive, that her death would be imminent as the engine picked up speed. Yet always, somehow, some way, she would outsmart the bandit, get out of the harrowing situation quite alive, and come out shining.

In the days when it was mysteriously customary for women on the screen to behave "like a man" in the most perilous circumstances, **Helen Holmes** (as well as the now-forgotten name of **Ruth Roland**) briefly rivaled **Pearl White** in popularity. Holmes began her career with Keystone and Mack Sennett, and made her specialty the "Queen of the Railroad." She made nine serials, beginning in 1914 with her most famous, THE HAZARDS OF HELEN.

Born in South Bend, Indiana, she was the daughter of an executive of the Great Northern Railroad. Tubercular as a child, she went West with her family where the air, in those days, was better. By a fluke, she met the picture star of Mack Sennett's Keystone Comedies, **Mabel Normand.** Normand told her, "I can get you work in the movies if you have enough money to get some good clothes."[1] In those days, actors

were cast with the appropriate costumes already on their backs. She borrowed the money. On Mabel's suggestion Mack Sennett cast Helen and her career had begun.

In a 1916 book entitled *Life Stories of the Movie Stars,* Holmes states, "She wishes it known that she can shoot, drive and train animals."[2] In fact, she was an avid race-car fanatic, and very often barred from participating in contests because women were not allowed to compete.

It was around 1916 that she married John Patrick MacGowan, the man who directed the HAZARDS OF HELEN series. Renting trains from local companies, the husband-and-wife team burned through an episode a week, forty in all, before they left the HAZARDS OF HELEN in the hands of others. The series continued and Holmes was replaced by a remarkable look-alike, **Helen (nee Rose) Gibson,** making HAZARDS OF HELEN the longest-running movie serial of all time.

Like Pearl White, Helen Holmes retired from serials when serials retired around 1919, and went to Universal, where she starred in pictures with such stalwarts as William Desmond, Jack Perrin, Ed Hearn, and Hoot Gibson.[3]

Helen Gibson (1894–1977)

She was described as "not a beautiful woman, and her rugged looks went hand in hand with her athletic skill."[1]

When she took over as the stunt "girl" for **Helen Holmes** in 1915, **Helen Gibson,** (often called an **Ethel Barrymore** look-alike), was making $50 a week.

So close was Helen Gibson to Helen Holmes, whom she replaced as a double in the great popular classic serial of the teens, THE HAZARDS OF HELEN (1914),

that many film historians still confuse the two.

Born **Rose Helen Wenger** to parents of Swiss-German heritage, she first saw the light of day in Cleveland, Ohio. As a young girl, Gibson made her name in the Miller Brothers 101 Ranch Wild West Show as a rodeo rider. When the show closed in Venice, California, Thomas Ince was present to sign them all up for his pictures. Paid the whopping sum of eight dollars a week, she used her horse as transportation from Venice to Topanga Canyon where the daily scenes were shot. For two years, she risked her life for meager wages.

Her luck improved in 1913 when she appeared with famous cowboy Tom Mix at Selig Studio. Her salary was raised to fifty dollars a week, quite a boost from the penny-pinching Ince! Her spirits were high, and romance was in the sky. She married "Hoot" Gibson in 1913.

Two years later she was having creative disagreements with Selig, and left them in the middle of a picture. At the right place at the right time, Gibson fit into Holmes's shoes perfectly, and she was fast on her way to becoming one of Kalem's biggest stars.

One hundred and nineteen episodes of THE HAZARDS OF HELEN later, Gibson was cast in an ill-fated serial, A DAUGHTER OF DARING. The idea, too close a clone of the first serial, didn't pan out, and was never released. Her best stunt, however, appeared in this serial. Traveling at full speed on a motorcycle going after a runaway freight train, Gibson rides through the open doors of a boxcar siding, her machine sailing through the air until it lands on a passing train's flatcar. The trick was to undercrank the camera. *And* execute it all with flawless timing. What could be simpler?

In 1917 Gibson was at Universal, again, risking her neck, but this time, earning $150 a week for her trouble. Only three years later, at Capital Film, she was making three hundred dollars for the same work she had performed on HAZARDS.

As many of the great women pioneers did in the early days, she had the power by now to form her own company. At Helen Gibson Productions she starred in five- and six-reel features, which were released through Associated Photoplays Corporation.

The year 1920, as many independents were finding out, was a bit late to start one's own firm. The majors were eating everyone alive. Shortly before she began, Gibson ran into financial trouble and the company went under. At this difficult time, her marriage to "Hoot" broke up too. Undaunted, Helen went to work in five-reel features on a $450-a-week salary. Not bad for a failure—but the cards seemed to be stacked against her. A ruptured appendix cost her the job.

She returned to Westerns after her recovery. The call of the circus led her to Ringling Brothers as a trick rider in 1924.

In later years, as women's double work slowly became the domain of men, Gibson hung in there, stunting for stars like **Marie Dressler, Edna May Oliver** and **Ethel Barrymore.** Her last film appearance was in THE MAN WHO SHOT LIBERTY VALANCE (1962) with John Wayne and Jimmy Stewart. Gibson wouldn't quit until she reached a fifty-year tenure in motion pictures.

"I got thirty-five dollars a day for driving a team of horses," she said in 1962. "The only real 'Hazard' in my life these days is the confusion that still persists over my marriage to the late 'Hoot' Gibson, the celebrated cowboy star. We were divorced in 1920. He then married *another* Helen [Holmes]. I'm still forwarding her mail."[2]

Helen Thurston (1916–?)

Growing up as a full-fledged tomboy in a minister's family in Redding, California, she was a swimming, diving, and aquaplaning champ by age thirteen. By sixteen she joined a traveling acrobatic troupe. By seventeen, she married an acrobat. She mothered a son

by eighteen, saw Europe and the US from a trapeze bar, and finally settled down to what she thought would be a quiet life in Los Angeles. Being in the movies was the last thing on **Helen Thurston**'s mind.

Then one day, someone asked her if she

was afraid of wild animals. She said she guessed not. "That's good," the person said, "because you are just **Katharine Hepburn**'s height, and the studio is looking for a girl to tease the leopard for her in BRINGING UP BABY."[1] That was Helen Thurston's apprenticeship in 1938, and she was a stuntwoman from that day on.

Helen Thurston doubled dozens of stars including **Bette Davis, Joan Bennett,** and **Lucille Ball.** She did everything from treehopping the jungle as Tarzan's mate to brawling in a bar for **Marlene Dietrich** in DESTRY RIDES AGAIN (1939). The movie set a precedent for pictures featuring fistic brawls involving women. Thurston became a prime favorite of "stunt girls" who could strew the floor in torn spangles without getting so much as a nick.

Not that she didn't put her life in danger over and over. There was the time in the San Fernando Valley when a crew waited two hours for a fast freight train to head out of the Glendale yards. With the locomotive speeding toward the cameraman at thirty miles an hour at night, Thurston dashed across the tracks barely in time to miss being hit. She had literally a split second to perform the stunt. Thurston crouched to peer under the train—part of the scene—when the engineer thought she had been hurt, stopped the train, and spoiled the shot. They were forced to shoot it all over. Thurston ended up making two hundred dollars for the day instead of her expected one hundred dollars.[2] The basic fee for stunting for women in the forties was about thirty-five dollars a day.

Helen Thurston once whirled the 230-pound Lou Costello in an airplane spin before splashing him into a pool ten feet away. From that experience, Thurston put together a one-woman act that she took to show the boys overseas. It involved a donnybrook in which she threw a dozen or so stalwart males over her shoulder.

·X·

"BEHIND EVERY GREAT MAN…"

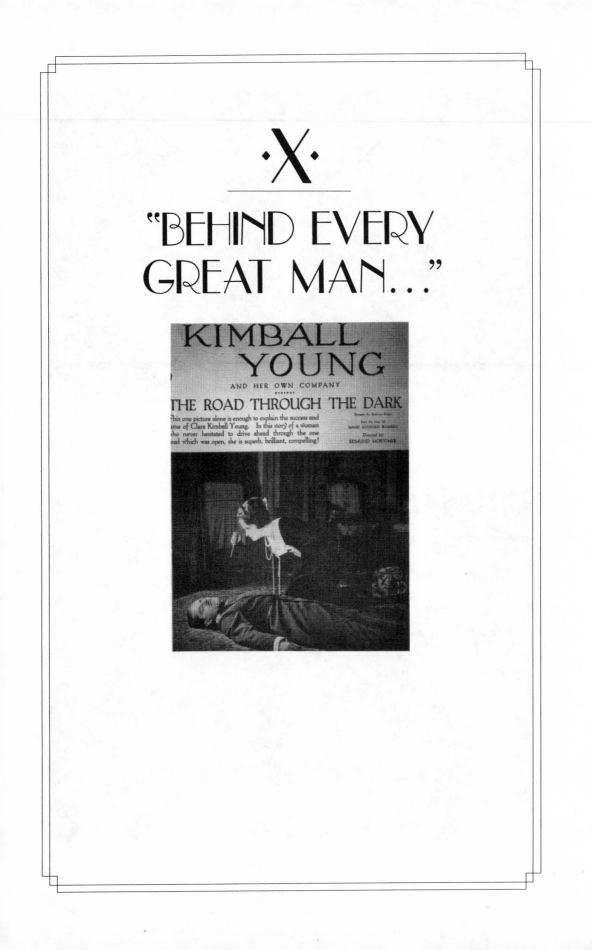

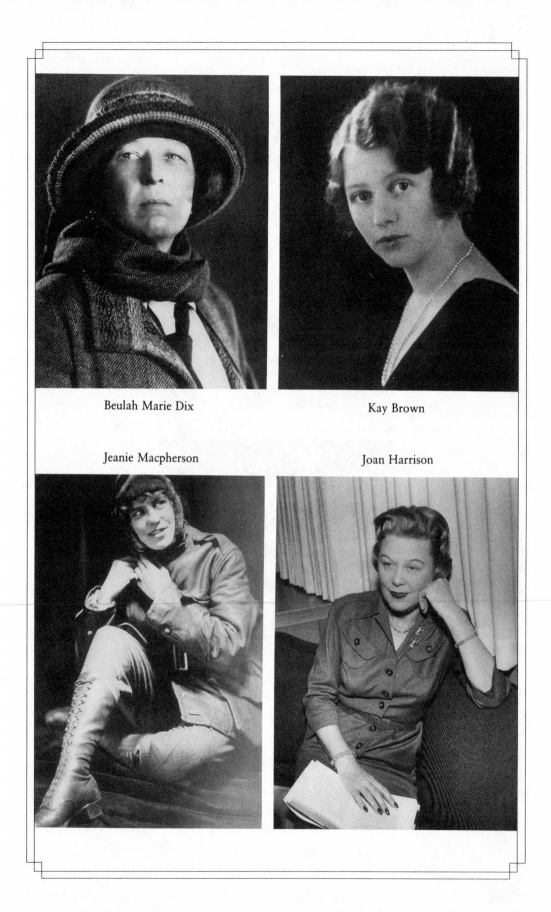

Beulah Marie Dix

Kay Brown

Jeanie Macpherson

Joan Harrison

Claire West, right (with director C. B. De Mille and Pauline Garon)

Clara Berenger

Anne Bauchens

PREVIEW

◆ ◆ ◆

The old saying goes that "behind every great man stands a great woman." If this is true, then Cecil B. De Mille must have been the greatest man who ever lived, for every important creative production staff job was "woman-ed" (it would hardly be appropriate to say "manned").

In *C. B. De Mille, a Guide to References and Sources,* author Sumiko Higashi writes:

> De Mille's contradictory attitudes toward women surfaced in his personal and professional relationships with them. About his wife he simply declared in his autobiography that he was incapable of discussing her. . . . Not content with a loyal spouse and his share of mistresses, De Mille surrounded himself with a contingent of professional women including his scenarist, **Jeanie Macpherson,** his editor, **Anne Bauchens,** his secretary, **Gladys Rossen,** and his researchers. All of these women never married, remained fiercely loyal to "the Chief," and spent day and night working at the studio or at the mansion. De Mille's professional association with women . . . was compromised by his tendency to convert his female staff into a peculiar version of a harem.[1]

To be added to this list of female exemplaries is **Claire West** who designed the costumes for De Mille's great masterworks.

Not to be forgotten is the indispensable **Gladys Rossen,** De Mille's faithful secretary for practically his entire career who took care of his tiniest whim, and with great worry. Cecil didn't make a move without telling **Gladys.** The two of them were as close as it was possible for two people to be who weren't married.

Cecil's brother, William De Mille, is responsible for recognizing the burgeoning talent of the young **Dorothy Arzner,** who began typing his scripts before moving into editing and then into directing, as well as the writer and eventual studio owner, **Marion Fairfax.**

William De Mille would also lure **Clara Beranger** away from a prolific writing life at other great studios to work for him at Paramount. The professional association became one of the great screen director/writer partnerships of all time, not to mention one of the greatest, most gossipy scandals of Hollywood romances. Both had to leave quite visibly established marriages. The press at the time softened the then-taboo decision of divorce by supporting the couple with a silver-screen metaphor:

> If the sophistry of a Lubitsch flicker couple was ever realized in reality, it was here. . . . Miss Beranger met Mr. De Mille at a dinner party given by a mutual Hol-

lywood friend. It was a case of "clicking" at first sight. This romance is one of the most curious ever to develop within motion picture circles. . . . Miss Beranger became the director's scenarist and remained so until he left Famous Players. They are in love, but both Mr. De Mille and Miss Beranger hesitated to take steps that would prove injurious to their families, or that would shadow their love for each other.[2]

Any romance that was at all associated with a Lubitsch flicker was accepted by the Hollywood press.

Included in this section too are some surprising female forces behind the likes of Hitchcock and Selznick as well. **Joan Harrison** and **Kay Brown** were not exactly hidden in their day, but they were later forgotten due to historic amnesia.

Jeanie Macpherson (1897–1946)

Descended from "The Fighting Scottish Macphersons," and named after "Jeanie Macpherson, the Scotch Joan of Arc," this **Jeanie Macpherson** was primed early for her role as a pioneer. Before she was C. B. De Mille's better half, she was the youngest director in motion-picture history.[1]

Originally a dancer, Macpherson became an actress for D. W. Griffith prior to becoming a leading lady for Universal. Before long, she was given her own directing unit. Caroline Lowrey explains:

She literally sat on a [dance] manager's doorstep until sheer admiration for her pluck secured an engagement. The same indomitable spirit took her to the office of D. W. Griffith whom she did not know. Here, her frankness made such an appeal that she was called the following morning. This engagement marked the beginning of an apprenticeship that led to a world of achievement.[2]

From Griffith's doors she entered the newly formed "Universal" company where she became their leading lady. While there she also directed, wrote, and starred in a number of films, but suddenly she was fired for being, in essence, too conscientious. What she did was to take seven days to complete one assignment—unduly leisurely for those early days of movies! The pressure of those years caused Macpherson to suffer a nervous breakdown in her prime.

And yet, during her tenure at Universal, Macpherson directed THE TARANTULA (1916), which, according to an early important film publication, "was for a time the most popular and profitable film the company had produced."[3]

C. B. De Mille came to her rescue by making Macpherson his main screenwriter. As it turned out, she more than likely was the rescue for De Mille. She contributed greatly to the writing of most of his classics.

Macpherson and De Mille held a common belief which would be the basis for every screenplay on which they collaborated: they despised weakness in men and women. . . . Their belief the men and women could change if they learned from experience and corrected their flaws is demonstrated in their early 1920's social dramas. . . . Their twenty-seven-year working relationship would rest on these principles.[4]

A good example of their collaboration in action was Macpherson's classic screenplay for Joan of Arc that was filmed as JOAN THE WOMAN (1916).

While De Mille created the huge frame around the French girl's life with his grandiose settings and hundreds of extras, Macpherson fashioned a human drama with which the audience could identify. Thus, while Joan of Arc may be part of a spectacular event, she is revealed as a frightened young girl driven by her spiritual beliefs. The picture's title was Macpherson's idea, as was the view of Joan as a human being rather than an indestructible saint.[5]

A fine example of how an early woman writer used her *female gaze* to transform the medium of movies.

For her hobby, Macpherson took up flying, and became the only woman who piloted the late Lieutenant Locklear, the world's greatest stunt flyer, while he performed his hazardous feats.

JEANIE MACPHERSON

1915	Captive, The (Scenario)
	Chimmie Fadden out West (Scenario)
	Unafraid, The (Scenario)
1916	Dream Girl, The (Scenario)
	Golden Chance, The (Scenario)
	Heart of Nora Flynn, The (Scenario)
	Joan the Woman (Scenario)
	Trail of the Lonesome Pine, The (Scenario)
1917	Devil Stone, The (Adaptation)
	Little American, The (Story)
	Romance of the Redwoods, A (Story)
	Woman God Forgot, The (Story)
1918	Don't Change Your Husband (Story)
	Old Wives for New (Scenario)
	Whispering Chorus (Scenario)
1919	For Better, for Worse (Scenario)
	Male and Female (Scenario)
1920	Something to Think About (Story)
1921	Affairs of Anatol, The (Scenario)
	Forbidden Fruit (Story)
	Saturday Night (Story, Scenario)
1922	Manslaughter (Adaptation, Scenario)
1923	Adam's Rib (Story, Adaptation)
	Ten Commandments, The (Story, Adaptation)
1924	Triumph (Adaptation)
1925	Golden Bed, The (Screenplay)
	Road to Yesterday, The (Adaptation)
1927	King of Kings, The (Story, Screenplay)
1929	Dynamite (Screenplay, Dialogue)
	Godless Girl, The (Story, Continuity, Dialogue)
1930	Madam Salan (Screenplay)
1933	Fra Diavolo (Devil's Brother, The) (Adaptation)
1938	Buccaneer, The (Adaptation)

Anne Bauchens (1882–1967)

She was called "Trojan Annie" around the Paramount lot because she could handle so much work. In a 1957 article, **Anne Bauchens** said, "These fourteen hour days are nothing compared with the eighteen hour stints Mr. De Mille and I would chalk up in the twenties."[1]

Beginning with WE CAN'T HAVE EVERY-THING (1919), and TILL I COME BACK TO YOU (1918), which she also helped him direct just prior to World War I, Bauchens was the only person, other than Cecil B. De Mille himself, who ever edited one of his pictures.

About editor Bauchens, De Mille wrote in his autobiography,

"Annie B." has edited every one of my pictures . . . and she will edit every one the Lord gives us time to make in the future. I believe she is the only film editor whose name is written into a producer's contract. There is a reason for that. Like myself, Annie is no longer as young as when she came wide-eyed to the screening of THE SQUAW MAN. I know those economy waves that sweep over studios, and the professional rivalries that smolder and sometimes flair. In every contract I sign to produce a picture one essential clause is that Anne Bauchens will be its editor. That is not sentiment, or at least not only sentiment. She is still the best film editor I know.[2]

In the days when women wore high-button shoes, and the men were singing "Pity the Poor Working Girl," Anne was braving the streets of New York looking for an acting career. With the good fortune of meeting William De Mille, she ended up crossing the country instead to become Hollywood's first script supervisor, one of the world's first film editors, and possibly the world's first woman film editor—a spot she shares with **Viola Lawrence.**

Beginning with a secretary's salary of forty dollars per month, Bauchens learned editing from William De Mille when he began his directing career. One day, sitting in the "cutting room," a magnet for Bauchens in her spare time, she said to William's younger brother Cecil, "Some day I'm going to cut your pictures." "No one," insisted De Mille with a huff, "will ever cut a picture of mine, except me!"[3] Two months later he sent for her to replace an absent assistant director. From that picture, WE CAN'T HAVE EVERYTHING in 1919, until the monumental, THE TEN COMMANDMENTS, De Mille's seventieth picture, in 1956, Bauchens cut every one of his pictures.

I made suggestions [on WE CAN'T HAVE EVERYTHING] when they occurred to me. Evidently, Mr. De Mille liked them, for he said that maybe I would like to try cutting. I cut his next picture and stayed on the job. And stayed and stayed. We've worked together so long, I'm almost like a habit to him.[4]

By the time of THE TEN COMMANDMENTS (1956), Bauchens was saying:

Now I work with Mr. De Mille very closely from the very inception of the story to the final finish of a picture. To me, each De Mille production is a chapter in hard work and concentration that completes itself when it comes to a close. I am busy, thoroughly busy, throughout. My hours are long, from eight to eight. When I'm not actually editing, I'm on the set observing. Mr. De Mille likes me to be there to get the feel of the scenes and to understand what he wants when I work on them.[5]

There was a legend that went, "You can't say NO to C. B. D Mille." But Bauchens did, many times, which is probably why they worked together so long. According to Charles West, a onetime head of Paramount's editing division,

Annie and De Mille did not always see eye to eye. They usually went through about five weeks of disagreement and out of it came good pictures. Annie, as everyone knew, was very strongminded and stubborn. So was De Mille. One of them always had to bring the other around because neither of them would give in.[6]

So much for editor as silent technician. One of the things Bauchens insisted upon was a female assistant, **Gladys M. Carley.**

Anne Bauchens was a serene, silver-haired woman with gentle brown eyes and a gracious, warm smile by the time she ended her forty-year editing career. "I'm more tired idling than when I work," she said at age sixty.

In fact, I feel in one hundred percent better health when I'm active and on the job rather than reclining back at home. Friends tell me it's much later than I think and shouldn't I have some fun out of life? Fun! Listen, it's never too late when you're interested. And I've always been interested in what I've been doing. . . . I expect to report to my editing room even when I'm a doddering old gal in a wheelchair![7]

Anne Bauchens was the first recipient of the Life Achievement Award given by the American Cinema Editors. Cecil B. De Mille said of Anne Bauchens:

She has contributed greatly to the motion picture art during the forty years she has been with me. THE TEN COMMANDMENTS, as far as I know, is the most monumental, ambitious picture ever to hit the screen of motion picture history. It is a great testament to Miss Bauchens.[8]

Anne Bauchens, one of De Mille's faithful "harem," never married. She lived with a cocker spaniel, Gyppy, and a housekeeper—"a wonderful woman who lives with me, and takes care of my every need"[9]—until the day she died.

ANNE BAUCHENS

1918	Squaw Man, The
	Till I Come Back to You
1919	Don't Change Your Husband
	For Better, or Worse
	Male and Female
	We Can't Have Everything
1920	Something to Think About
	Why Change Your Wife
1921	Affairs of Anatol, The
	Fool's Paradise
	Forbidden Fruit
1922	Manslaughter
	Saturday Night
1923	Adam's Rib
	Ten Commandments, The
1924	Feet of Clay
	Triumph
1925	Golden Bed, The
	Road to Yesterday, The
1927	King of Kings, The
1928	Chicago
	Craig's Wife

1929	Dynamite
	Godless Girl, The
	Ned McCobb's Daughter
	Noisy Neighbors
1930	Lord Byron of Broadway
	Madam Satan
	This Mad World
1931	Great Meadow, The
	Guilty Hands
	Squaw Man, The
1932	Beast of the City
	Sign of the Cross, The
	Wet Parade, The
1933	Cradle Song
	This Day and Age
1934	Cleopatra
	Four Frightened People
	Menace
	One Late Hour
1935	Crusades, The
1937	Plainsman, The
	This Way Please
1938	Buccaneer, The
	Bulldog Drummond in Africa
	Hunted Men
	Sons of the Legion
1939	Television Spy
	Union Pacific
1940	Northwest Mounted Police
	Women without Names
1942	Commandos Strike at Dawn
	Mrs. Wiggs of the Cabbage Patch
	Reap the Wild Wind
1944	Story of Dr. Wassell, The
	Tomorrow, the World!
1945	Love Letters
1947	Unconquered
1949	Samson and Delilah
1952	Greatest Show on Earth, The
1956	Ten Commandments, The

Claire West (1893–1980)

Claire West was one of those rare women fortunate enough to graduate from college in the 1910s. While she was still in high school she was already selling her sketches to women's magazines.

Later, in what appears to be a charmed

existence, she was sent off to Paris to study the various fashion lines; she became one of a group of successful fashion artists. For her first engagement, she started at the top. Her assignment was to design the costumes for D. W. Griffith's INTOLERANCE (1916), whose famous scenes in Babylon demanded broad ingenuity and showed off West's re-markable skill with the kind of instant port-folio that is every designer's dream.

By the time she reached Cecil B. De Mille she was a pro. Studio designing was still, in those days, a relatively new concept. Ac-cording to the *Woman's Home Companion* of May 1921, "Stars like **Norma** and **Con-stance Talmadge**, **Alice Brady**, **Pearl White**, and **Nazimova** usually dress their own roles . . . but many other stars . . . find in the studio designer a service which saves time and conserves strength."[1]

An interesting note is that many actresses who came to auditions appropriately dressed for the part usually *got* the part. Their wardrobe was a vital factor in casting decisions. Claire West was dressing three pictures a year for De Mille, spending many hours in conference with him and scenarist **Jeanie Macpherson** to determine just the right "feel," clothingwise, for the picture. It should be noted that Claire West's arrival on the design scene for women preceded **Edith Head** by nearly ten years.

CLAIRE WEST

1915	Birth of a Nation
1916	Intolerance
1919	Male and Female
1921	Affairs of Anatol, The
1922	Saturday Night
1923	Adam's Rib
	Bella Donna
1924	Flirting with Love
	For Sale
	Goldfish, The
	Lady, The
	Sherlock, Jr.
	Ten Commandments, The
1925	Golden Bed, The
	Merry Widow, The

Clara Beranger (1886–1956)

Born in Baltimore and educated at Goucher College, **Clara Beranger** spent the early part of her career writing for magazines and newspapers. She began her screen-writing career as a free-lancer for Edison, Vita-graph, and Kalem, as both an originals and continuities staff writer for Fox before it became Twentieth Century-Fox. There, she was the adaptor of A TALE OF TWO CITIES (1917) for the screen.

While working for Pathe Studio, Beran-ger wrote extensively for the then-famous "Baby Marie Osborne."

In his autobiography, William De Mille wrote, "In April of 1928, I had just finished my forty-fifth production and was working on CRAIG'S WIFE—with Clara Beranger, who had written the screenplays of all of my pictures for seven years and continued to do so even after our marriage."

CLARA BERANGER

1921	Exit the Vamp
	Gilded Lily, The
	Heart to Let, A
	Miss Lulu Bett
	Sheltered Daughters
	Wonderful Thing, The
1922	Bought and Paid For
	Clarence

Beulah Marie Dix (1876–1970)

A Phi Beta Kappa from Radcliffe in 1890 and the first woman to win Harvard's Sohier Literary Prize,[1] **Beulah Marie Dix** was destined early for the life of a pioneer.

When she arrived in Hollywood, Dix was already a successful playwright and novelist. She wrote historical romances, and was quite fussy about the accuracy of her facts, thus also becoming a noted historian. She was received in Hollywood as a mini-lioness. Anna De Mille (William's wife) threw her a "tea"[2]—Beatrice De Mille was a fellow author and Dix's friend. Dix arrived in good company. Count Tolstoy, son of Leo, attended the tea, whom Dix, in appropriate literary-New-York-nose-up-in-the-air style dismissed instantly as "an amiable enthusiast."[3]

If Dix became greatly successful as a screenwriter, it's because she decided she would be. "If I stay [in Hollywood]" she wrote early on, "I work only with William De Mille, who is a dramatist of equal standing with myself, so I lose no professional prestige."[4] Few published authors actually lived in Hollywood of 1916, so Dix began with a distinct advantage. One major advantage was that her children could call one of the De Mille brothers "Uncle Cecil."[5]

William started Beulah off in her new career as a continuity writer. In those days, that meant following the camera and the actors around and writing the dialogue that appeared on the screen.

"One learned quite quickly what could and couldn't be done with a camera," reports Dix in Kevin Brownlow's *The Parade's Gone By*. . . . "For instance, one did not write in the script: "Scene 40—the supply train is blown up." C. B. vowed that was the description of one episode that was handed to him. He developed it into fifteen scenes and took two days to shoot them. It was all very informal in those early days. Anybody on the set did anything he or she was called upon to do. I've walked on as an extra, I've tended lights—and anybody not doing anything else wrote down the director's notes on the script. I also spent a good deal of time in the cutting room."[6]

But as the industry traded art for commerce, the "eros" of the movies was lost. Brownlow points out that such casual and all-encompassing training was ideal for scenario writers in particular, who would later use this practical knowledge in their scripting.

Dix was soon scripting much original material, including THE CALL OF THE EAST (1922) for the Japanese actor, Sessue Hayakawa, the remake of THE SQUAW MAN (1931), and THE ROAD TO YESTERDAY, in 1925, in collaboration with C. B. De Mille's head writer, **Jeanie Macpherson.** Her last film was THE LIFE OF JIMMY DOLAN in 1933, adapted from her play of the same name.[7]

For all of her Radcliffe literary snobbery, Dix found her rebellious soul in the days of the censors. At a time when Hollywood was sure it could absorb women in droves "like coins in a slot machine,"[8] and ended up instead turning them toward disappointed lives of poverty and often depravity, Dix's Bostonian friends felt sure she was a prostitute. A prostitute for the *screen,* that is,[9] but in those days, it might as well have been the same thing. Dix had had a tangle with the censors with her film ACROSS THE BORDER (1922) when her characters said such vile and inexcusable things as, "By God!" and, "Damn your soul!" They labeled the character the "Man Who Curses!"[10] As her daughter Evelyn explained, in 1922 Dix rebelled against the censors in her titles,

> which the Boards required to be pure. As a strong pejorative, she dredged up the word *scut.* ("You scut! You knew the franchise belonged to Marna's brother!") *Webster's* gives *scut*'s second meaning as "dregs, as of beer . . . a contemptible fellow." The first meaning, though, is "short erect tail of an animal." Had the censors glanced at *Webster* they would have found this, too, very horrid. Mother hated censorship.[11]

BEULAH MARIE DIX

1921 Easy Road, The
Fool's Paradise
1922 Across the Border
Borderland
Call of the East, The
Crimson Challenge, The
Daughter of Luxury, A
For the Defense
Ordeal, The
1923 Children of Jazz
Nobody's Money
Spanish Dancer, The
1924 Feet of Clay
1925 Road to Yesterday, The
1926 Risky Business
Silence
Sunny Side Up
1927 Country Doctor, The
Fighting Love
1928 Leopard Lady, The
1929 Black Magic
Girls Gone Wild
Godless Girl, The
Ned McCobb's Daughter
Trent's Last Case
1930 Conspiracy
Girl of the Port
Midnight Mystery
1931 Squaw Man, The
1933 Life of Jimmy Dolan, The

Kay Brown (1903–   )

She read *Gone with the Wind,* in advance of its publication and thought it might make a terrific movie. By that time, **Kay Brown** was thirty-three, and head of Selznick International Pictures office in New York. She wired her boss about the material, who replied, "A Civil War story won't go." Bad timing. He was having his own problems with THE GARDEN OF ALLAH (1936). Un-

daunted, Brown, who never doubted her own good instincts, urged Selznick's partner, Jack Whitney, to buy the rights. Impressed with her strategy, Selznick reportedly offered fifty thousand dollars for the book.

But by the time she was eighty-three, Kay Brown was sick and tired of only being recalled for that one incident.

I've had a long and distinguished career. Sixty-two years. But you people only want to know about GONE WITH THE WIND, and everyone's bored with that.[1]

And so we will tout her other "broad" accomplishments. She is responsible for the American careers of both **Ingrid Bergman** and Alfred Hitchcock. Without Kay Brown, **Vivien Leigh** might never have played **Scarlett O'Hara,** and **Anne Baxter** would never have been a star. After quitting Selznick, Brown became one of Hollywood's most powerful agents—known as "the most tenacious agent in the business"[2]—and represented the likes of Arthur Miller and **Isak Dinesen.** A colleague of Brown's said about her at the age of eighty-three in 1986, while she was living in Manhattan, "As they used to say about King Kong, she's still holding that island in a grip of deadly fear."[3]

Her brilliant career began when she was still only a senior at Wellesley College, class of 1924. She got a job at an outdoor acting theater in Peterborough, New Hampshire, as a reader. Soon, the theater made its way into the fledgling film industry by buying a company called the Film Booking Office in 1925. Kay went along with the company that was transmuted into RKO one year later. With the title of story editor,

I had a little office in New York and a big initiation in the picture business. RKO needed stories. So I read everything from railroad magazines to great literature.[4]

Her first literary coup was hardly GONE WITH THE WIND, but CIMARRON in 1931.

We heard a lot about the book before it was published, but no one could get their hands on a copy. Leland Hayward, the agent, said he could steal me one. Of course, Miss [Edna] Ferber knew nothing about this. I loved what I read, and RKO

gave me the go-ahead to buy. How do you buy the rights to a purloined book? Leland and I, we did it.[5]

Her reputation from *this* coup is what won her the attention of David O. Selznick. When the whiz-kid producer left RKO to form his own company, he asked Kay (who was by now married to James Barrett, and the mother of two girls), to head his New York office. She rarely left New York, but became one of the most powerful figures in Hollywood.

I never felt like a pioneer or like the only woman in a man's world. All I can say is that it was the Depression, and I was happy to have a job. Not to mention a job I loved.[6]

On a tip that she should watch a Swedish film called INTERMEZZO (1938), Kay Brown discovered a young, beautiful actress named **Ingrid Bergman.** Selznick gave Brown the go-ahead to whisk off to Stockholm and bring her back to the States. Although Bergman was eight months pregnant, Brown convinced her, and thus Bergman became known in America. A similar story ensued with Alfred Hitchcock.

I thought it shrewd to befriend Hitch on his home turf in London first, to show that we would go to him instead of waiting for him to come to us. . . . But I'm given far too much credit for Hitch and not enough for [Vivien] Leigh. Hitch was well known and only required my diplomacy, Leigh was a real discovery.[7]

During World War II, Brown decided to switch to agenting. Her first clients were an impressive roster of all the talent she discovered from working with Selznick: **Anne Baxter, Ingrid Bergman,** Alfred Hitchcock, **Vivien Leigh** and her husband, Laurence Olivier, Alex Guinness, John Gielgud, and **Lillian Hellman.** In representing Isak Dinesen, Brown said, "I adored her work. But I couldn't get anyone to listen to me about *Out of Africa* [1952]."[8]

Brown admits that her preference in a story line is "not Trollope, mind you, but for a movie, give me a woman overcoming adversity every time."[9] A telling self-description for this great woman who realized her talents from behind the shadow of a great man.

KAY BROWN
(Selected List of Acquisitions)

1931   Cimarron
1939   Gone with the Wind

Joan Harrison (1911–   )

Known as Alfred Hitchcock's "valuable idea woman," **Joan Harrison** became one of the few successful women producers of the forties. When asked how she came to be in this vied-for position, she remarked, "Because I was the world's worst secretary."

Her tale begins in 1934 in England when a friend spread the news that Alfred Hitchcock was in search of a "gal Friday." She spanned the thirty miles to London like lightning, bluffed her way past twelve other applicants, and won out over forty others whom Hitch had already interviewed.

Because Hitchcock hated to read, Harrison began feeding him story ideas orally. Soon, the legend goes, she was improving on the originals, and soon became invaluable to Hitchcock. Brown did her first screen writing for Hitch with THE GIRL WAS YOUNG in 1937 (YOUNG AND INNOCENT in Britain). With JAMAICA INN (1939), Harrison won her first solo script-writing credit.

By the time Hitchcock found his way to America in 1939, thanks to the powerful **Kay Brown,** Joan Harrison was the most esteemed member of his creative team.

Two years after her arrival in America in 1941, Kay Brown was desperate. Smart, savvy, and electric with ideas, she was too much under the shadow of a famous man to see many of her ideas flourish. She left Hitchcock and free-lanced until 1943.

In 1944, she produced her first feature, the classic PHANTOM LADY for Universal Pictures.

In 1945 *Parade Magazine* did a profile on Joan Harrison. "As a top producer today," the piece said, "Joan has a number of qualifications to keep her there. She is beautiful with 'ah-inspiring' legs."[1] But aside from a fit anatomy, Harrison was educated at the Sorbonne and at Oxford before she did her tenure with Hitchcock.

Time magazine reported a year before this that when they asked Harrison in what respect she differed from other Hollywood producers, she "tilts one blond eyebrow, grins, and replies, 'I use my sex.' " That may have been true in more ways than she meant it. From her first solo producing venture, Harrison's producing methods were decidedly original. On PHANTOM LADY she lined up the art director before anyone else in order to lay down the tone of the picture. Then she came to the director. She did the casting down to the last bit player, and sank sixty thousand dollars into Franchot Tone on the theory that "unusual casting brings a different flavor."[2] She also persuaded Alan Curtis to play his role with no makeup. "on the equally startling theory that a hero looks more heroic if he looks like a human being."

She was better aware than most Hollywoodians of the value of silence—a good half of PHANTOM LADY is without the benefit of either talk or music.[3]

Joan Harrison proceeded to design the costumes as well.

Her follow-up ideas were to do "a film made entirely by women,"[4] a revolutionary concept that the Hollywood of the 1940s was not, and still is not, quite evolved enough to realize.

JOAN HARRISON (Selected List)

1937 Girl Was Young, The (Screenplay)
1939 Jamaica Inn (Screenplay)
1944 Phantom Lady (Producer)

·XI·

ONE-OF-A-KIND
REEL WOMEN

I think I had advantages because no one thought I
was really going to do anything with this information.
—**Brianne Murphy,** First woman director of
photography in Hollywood

Brianne Murphy

Edith Head (with Elizabeth Taylor).

DELIVERANCE, 1919
Helen Keller producer.

Natalie Kalmus

PREVIEW

◆ ◆ ◆

What can you say about the unclassifiable? Women who leapt beyond the boundaries of their gender, and in at least one case, of their humanness, to achieve what no one before had ever set out to do? They not only went against the grain of a world that said no to them as women, but they broke uncharted ground where few if anyone, female or male, had gone before.

ITEM:
A true example of how blindness may aid in one seeing more clearly and prophetically, **Helen Keller** foresaw the potential of the new medium of film to hold hundreds of eyes, ears, and hearts captive in one sitting. And so, in 1918, she became the first deaf-and-blind person to produce and star in a movie, as well as to do all her own stunt work.

ITEM:
At a time when color film was but a concept in filmmaking, **Natalie Kalmus** was on the board of a new company, called Technicolor, which she devised with her husband. She dreamed up a package deal to make the far-out idea not so far-out for movie producers.

ITEM:
The cameramen whom she asked out to lunch thought she was flirting as she grilled them relentlessly about their secretive craft. Where they would have been competitively silent to a male colleague, they ruffled their feathers and strutted their stuff to "Bree." The result was that **Brianne Murphy** became the first woman permitted to enter the Hollywood features union as a director of photography. Why? Well, as Bree herself put it, "No one thought I was really going to do anything with that information."

ITEM:
Among costume designers there might have been before and there might be again, there will never be another **Edith Head.** Through sheer perseverance, and a brilliant internal sense of public relations, she succeeded in taking a job that was nearly invisible and raising it to the level of high art. She succeeded in designing costumes for every major talent of her day, and as her creations turned into worldwide fashion phenomena, Edith Head became as famous as the stars that she costumed.

These are women who refused to be defined by preexisting standards. They often chose discomfort in the name of the new. Demanding that they self-define, they bravely won the lone title of "One-of-a-kind."

Helen Keller (1880–1968)

A woman way ahead of her age in a wide arena of venues, the deaf-and-blind **Helen Keller** spied early on the wide possibilities of film. What more powerful way to persuade the hearts of a large circle so quickly? What better method to educate the world about blindness?

"One of the most amazing of the early film companies headed by a woman was the Helen Keller Film Corporation," writes Marc Wanamaker.

> Her company was formed as an independent filmmaking corporation and space was rented at the Brunton Studios in Hollywood. **Mary Pickford, Bessie Barriscale, Anita Stewart** and other women producer/actresses were also using the lot at the time that the Helen Keller Corporation was gearing up for their film, DELIVERANCE.[1]

DELIVERANCE (1918) told the story of Helen Keller's life in the fashion of a docudrama. A unique and innovative genre for the time, the film moves in a chronological fashion, depicting Helen as a little girl (portrayed by a young actress) up through the triumph as Keller (playing herself!) gets her college degree.

Her teacher, **Annie Mae Sullivan**, who acts in the film along with Keller, helped in the formation of the company. It was a brave, difficult, and courageous task in 1918 just to make a film, not to mention the added obstacles Keller brought to bear! As Marc Wanamaker points out,

> Just twenty years before, the blind and deaf person was considered a hopeless burden on society, and doomed to die an early neglected death. . . . This must have been one of the most unique experiences for anyone who ever worked on a motion picture.[2]

Yet with director George Foster Platt at the helm, make the film they did. For those familiar with William Gibson's THE MIRACLE WORKER (1979), to see DELIVERANCE is truly an illuminating experience. It seems evident upon viewing the film that Gibson *must* have had the opportunity to see this production, for scene by scene the only visible difference between the two was Gibson's added dialogue and length.

In 1918, reporter Grace Kingsley wrote about the making of DELIVERANCE:

> Helen Keller . . . is making a picturization of a tale that will be partly the story of her own life and partly a historical tale written for her . . .

The theme of the film is the struggle of humanity to achieve success despite a handicap. In her article, Kingsley insisted that the film was not propaganda.

As the production proceeded with great ease, Kingsley watched with delight and awe.

> The director taps his foot lightly on the floor and Miss Keller is instantly alert. The stamp of the foot is a part of the signal system between star and director, and is possible because of Miss Keller's unbelievable sensitivity to vibration. He gives one tap of his foot when he wants the scene to begin, and two taps when it is finished.
>
> "And she never makes a mistake," said Platt, "No matter how many people may be walking about the stage, she recognizes my step."
>
> They say that in her emotional scenes, she is just as wonderful, just as effective, as any of the famous players in the moving pictures.

Kingsley then queried Helen Keller about her process.

"Do you visualize the scenes?" I asked.

"Yes," she answered. "And, oh, there are colors it seems to me in everything around me. If it were not for colors, I couldn't bear the darkness sometimes. I love the pale blues and pinks. They make me happy."

After a single rehearsal, the picture was ready to take. "Action! Camera! Lights!" shouted Mr. Platt, with that tap of his foot, and though Miss Keller couldn't see nor hear, she went unerringly through the scene. I understand that there has never been a single re-take of any scene in which Miss Keller appeared.

And because of Miss Keller's new found talent for producing, even President Wilson has agreed to take a bit part in the movie![3]

Which indeed he did as you will see if you ever treat yourself to the rare and marvelous opportunity of seeing this archival piece of work. Miraculously and luckily DELIVERANCE is one of the few, well-preserved productions from this era. It can be seen by anyone who is passing through Washington, DC, in the Library of Congress's motion-picture division.

The last scene of the film (in the typical corny fashion for this highly stylized era) has Keller astride a great white horse, wearing a Knight of Shining Armor helmet, carrying a torch of triumph, and riding victoriously into the sunset.

DELIVERANCE is a must-see for any serious film buff.

HELEN KELLER

1918   Deliverance (Producer/Actress)

Edith Head (1907–1981)

"Chutzpah" was her middle name. **Edith Head** is well regarded as Hollywood's best-known and most successful designer. "Best-known," because she participated avidly in her own publicity. Most successful, because she won an unprecedented eight Oscars, more than any other designer in Hollywood's history, and costumed most of the great stars of her day: **Audrey** and **Kate Hepburn,** Hope, Crosby, **Grace Kelly** and even Elvis!

She dressed the thousands of extras in THE MAN WHO WOULD BE KING (1975). She even dressed the elephants in THE GREATEST SHOW ON EARTH (1952), which gratefully ate their festooned garlands of flowers on their lunch break.

In the midtwenties, a young and restless Edith Head was bored with teaching art to schoolchildren. She didn't know a thing about movies, but, deciding it was best to keep this to herself, she bluffed her way into the Paramount wardrobe department by "borrowing" sketches from drawing schoolmates at the Chouinard Art Institute.[1] It would be a no-no she would later confess, but it was a practice typical of her that she would continue to keep her long career in motion.

She began by "hanging garlands on elephants and other animals for De Mille epics."[2] But life would improve for Head, and quickly. She wasn't at Paramount long when she landed her big break on a picture written and produced by **Mae West**—SHE DONE HIM WRONG (1933). She would dress **West** in her first, as well as her last picture (SEXTETTE [1978]).

Increasingly ambitious with her talent, she soon found herself chief costume designer for Paramount. Thereby, Edith Head set out to make herself as much a household name as any of the stars she dressed—a virtual "Who's Who" list of the all-time motion-picture greats.

Her "look" for a film often translated

into an American fashion sensation: "The Latin Look," for **Barbara Stanwyck** in THE LADY EVE (1941); her trend-setting "sarong" for **Dorothy Lamour** in THE JUNGLE PRINCESS (1936); the unforgettable peacock train for **Hedy Lamarr** in SAMSON AND DELILAH (1949), one of the most famous costumes in Hollywood's history. Each of the thousands of authentic feathers were gathered by hand from Cecil B. De Mille's ranch.

Head kept her name in the public eye by writing articles for magazines like *Photoplay* and *Screenland,* giving fashion suggestions from her latest screen designs for **Veronica Lake,** or whoever played her current chic. She expanded her nonmoviegoing constituency by writing books like *The Dress Doctor* (1969), and *How to Dress for Success* (1983). *The Dress Doctor* went into six printings and was translated into as many languages. She even "played" dress doctor on programs like Art Linkletter's *House Party,* where she would prescribe remedies and diagnose the "ills" of a guest. "If you have a large bust, don't put on clothes so tight you suggest a sausage," she once said. "To her home audience," said Carrie Rickey,

Head dictated trompe l'oeil strategies to make women appear ideally proportioned. For her stars, Head did the reverse: she made them special by exaggerating disproportions. Statuesque **Ingrid Bergman** wore a square-neck, zebra-patterned midriff blouse in NOTORIOUS, emphasizing her broad shoulders and ample bosom, baring her less-than-dainty waist. **Audrey Hepburn** of the swan neck, flat chest, and long waist donned a V-bodiced, off-the-shoulder princess in ROMAN HOLIDAY, making her look like an elongated highball, giving hope to legions of women during the C-cup decade.[3]

Remaining at the Paramount Studios longer than anyone else, except Adolph Zukor, Head adroitly hooked up with one or two stars of the prevailing decade: **Grace Kelly** in the fifties; **Natalie Wood** in the sixties; Newman and Redford in the seventies. When her contract was not renewed in 1967 after forty-four years, she went to Universal where, as Carrie Rickey tells us, "her bungalow was a stop on the studio tour."[4]

Head's personal life was not included in her publicity package of goodies. Charles Head, her first husband, was an alcoholic whom she divorced in 1938. A year later she married the well-known art director Wiard Ihnen (JANE EYRE [1944], BECKY SHARP [1935]). Wiard died in 1979.

When a young, aspiring woman designer would find her way onto the Paramount lot and under the tutelage of Edith Head, she would give them wise, if contradictory advice, "Dearie, you don't want to be a designer. The producers wouldn't really like it. They all like to work with men."[5]

Like **Frances Marion,** Edith Head's sixty-odd-year career spanned the history of film from the silents through the talkies. Steve Martin's DEAD MEN DON'T WEAR PLAID, in 1982, was her last picture.

In 1974 when she was sixty-seven, the Hollywood Chamber of Commerce awarded Edith Head a star on the boulevard. Sitting between "Alfred Hitchcock" and "James Cagney" she said in a *Los Angeles Times* interview, "My motto is never to be caught inactive, so figuring that it would be difficult to get all of my five feet one and a quarter inches in the same picture with the sidewalk, I stooped to polish the star with my Gucci scarf." This photograph ran in 350 newspapers around the world.

Edith Head. Ever the publicity monger. But why blame Head? She was merely performing the rite-of-passage taught to any young man aspiring to success.

So maybe Edith was bold, but no one could ever accuse her of being indiscreet. As **Lucille Ball** said of her old friend on the occasion of her death, "Edith knew the truth about all of us. She knew who had flat fannies and who didn't—but she never told."[6]

EDITH HEAD

1933 She Done Him Wrong
1936 Jungle Princess, The
1941 Lady Eve, The
1946 Notorious
1948 Emperor Waltz, The
1949 Heiress, The
     Samson and Delilah
1950 All About Eve
1951 Place in the Sun, A
1952 Carrie
     Greatest Show on Earth, The
1953 Roman Holiday
1954 Sabrina
1955 To Catch a Thief
     Rose Tattoo, The
1956 Ten Commandments, The
     Proud and the Profane, The
1957 Funny Face
1958 Buccaneer, The
1959 Career
     Five Pennies, The
1960 Facts of Life, The
     Pepe
1961 Pocketful of Miracles

1962 Man Who Shot Liberty Valance, The
     My Geisha
1963 Love With the Proper Stranger
     New Kind of Love, A
     Wives and Lovers
1964 House is Not a Home, A
     What a Way to Go
1965 Inside Daisy Clover
     Slender Thread, The
1966 Oscar, The
1969 Sweet Charity
1970 Airport
     Red Sky at Morning
1972 Hammersmith is Out
     Life and Times of Judge Roy Bean, The
     Pete 'n Tillie
1973 Ash Wednesday
     Divorce His, Divorce Hers (TV)
     Doll's House, A
     Don is Dead, The
     Sting, The
1974 Airport 1975
1975 Great Waldo Pepper, The
     Man Who Would Be King, The
     Rooster Cogburn
1978 Sextette
1982 Dead Men Don't Wear Plaid

Natalie Kalmus (1892–1965)

"My role was playing ringmaster to the rainbow,"[1] said **Natalie Kalmus**, who, along with her husband, developed the process we know today as "Technicolor."

"Technicolor consultant: Natalie Kalmus." That's how the credit read on all motion pictures done in color until 1949.[2] What in the world did those four words mean? Said one reviewer, "Those four magic words brusquely symbolized a whole

vari-colored, warm, enchanting world, which brought to cinema a new dimension." Kalmus was instrumental in evoking the most beautiful sequences in color in American cinema. Who can forget **Lana Turner** crowned by a green halo in THE THREE MUSKETEERS (1948)?

Kalmus was the creator of the marvelous *tones* of Technicolor's *color,* and she created them to precision. She was the first person ever truly to recognize that someday color would be standard in the industry, and it was therefore up to her to prepare Technicolor's future accordingly.

> Mrs. Kalmus became an indefatigable globetrotter, searching out business all over the world. She covered an average of forty thousand miles a year between this country and Europe for about a decade, conducting courses for art directors and technicians interested in learning the color process.[3]

What Herbert T. Kalmus didn't know about a young art student named Natalie Dunfee, who was a graduate of the Boston Art School and the Curry School of Expression, was that she would be integral and instrumental in a technological brainchild that would completely and *literally* transform the face of motion pictures. The couple married in 1902.

Ten years later, they formed an industrial research and development firm for the awakening field of motion pictures. One of the principals in the company, Daniel Comstock, had just come up with a new type of camera with the ability to photograph moving pictures in color. The year was 1915. All the kinks weren't worked out yet, but "Technicolor" technically found its name.

Only a year later, having found financial backing to improve an already ingenious idea, the governing board, of which Natalie was a member, decided to test their first script, THE GULF BETWEEN. Everyone on the governing board, was also a principal on the production team. The picture was shot in Florida, completed the summer of 1917, and screened in New York. "Some reviews agreed," reports Marc Wanamaker, "that the color was 'the finest natural color picture ever produced. But others weren't quite convinced.' "[4]

No one knew that the worst technical nightmares were right ahead of them. Nor would they be fully worked out until "three-strip" Technicolor in the mid-thirties. But

by about 1922, Kalmus and her cronies put their brains to use and found a way to interest Hollywood. Joseph M. Schenck agreed to coproduce (jointly with Technicolor) a film called THE TOLL OF THE SEA in 1922. By 1923, as Wanamaker says, "Technicolor was making color sequences for major Hollywood films."[5]

When color was introduced into the field, it was first done in "sequences"—some color cut in with mostly black and white. It wasn't until 1932 that Natalie Kalmus put together the first entrepreneurial business package that would make the scary process of "color" palatable to a timid Hollywood. The idea was that Technicolor would make available to studios the first camera designed to handle the "three-strip" color film process.

Along with this, a Technicolor "color consulting service" would be available to work with studios prior to and during production. The package deal whole and complete—take-it-or-leave-it—came with a Technicolor camera operator, art director, set director, designer, wardrobe and property masters, makeup artists, special requirements for studio lighting, and lab processing. This was Natalie's baby. She was a part of the color process since its inception, and it was she who was the chief consultant. She proved not only a good art consultant, but also a technical whiz, realizing that Technicolor was something, *someday,* that the motion-picture industry couldn't be without.

As the leading color consultant for Technicolor's formative years, Kalmus would lay out the entire color plans for a movie. "Until 1948," writes Wanamaker, "her name was required to appear as 'Color Consultant' on every motion picture made by the company."[6] Natalie Kalmus's face was the first official "model" for color testing, toward which Technicolor's cameras were pointed.

In his work on Kalmus Wanamaker goes on to explain that producers in the early days often thought they should flaunt the vivid colors before the viewer's eyes. But Natalie believed in simplicity and sought to eliminate the distracting focal points within scenes. "Natural colors and lights do not tax the eye nearly as much as man-made colors and artificial lights," she said. "Even when nature indulges in a riot of beautiful colors, there are subtle harmonies which justify these colors."[7]

As if to demonstrate her philosophy visually, she went on to develop a method of distinct "color separation." When one color is placed in front of or beside another, there must be enough difference in their hues to separate one from the other photographically. "If the colors are properly handled, it is possible to make it appear as though the actors are actually standing there in person, thus creating the illusion of a third dimension,"[8] she said. She introduced the art of modifying color, said Wanamaker, so that the eye would accept the desired shade.

"She discovered that under strong Technicolor lighting, white consistently changed the value and tone of the subject, picking up and absorbing the reflections of surrounding colors. When dyed a neutral grey, however, it would appear white on the film. Mrs. Kalmus was also a strong believer in the language of colors, and she often relied on it to establish mood."[9]

In later years, after color had become the standard, many studios resented the presence of Natalie Kalmus in the color package. It was like a deal their forefathers had made without realizing it would be the sons and daughters who would live to carry out the promises. Unhappily, Kalmus's presence became an intrusion and a joke on the set.

But a profile article in the forties in the *New York Times* once described her as "indispensable." "If she is indispensable today on a movie lot, where mistakes may cost many thousands, it is because she was diligent through the ordeal of selecting, rejecting, photographing, and projecting, through substitution of photographic equipment and of manifold types of film, of

discoveries of adaptable fabrics and forms, and of innumerable disappointments in finished products."[10] In short, in her day she was ruthless to a perfection.

In her reign, Kalmus supervised and guided the intricate color process on some of the great classics: GONE WITH THE WIND (1939), BECKY SHARP (1935), THE ADVENTURES OF ROBIN HOOD (1938), THE TEN COMMANDMENTS (1956), and perhaps the most artfully done picture in terms of color in motion pictures, THE WIZARD OF OZ (1939).

In her heyday in the forties she made sixty-five thousand dollars a year. For a woman to have such a responsible job in the forties was a kind of miracle unto itself.

In 1950, now divorced from her husband but advanced enough to write their business understanding into their divorce agreement—she was to remain an integral part of the company and a prime stockholder for life—she formed the Natalie Kalmus Television Company, which produced programs for the young medium.

If anyone asks you about the "ringmaster of the rainbow," tell them it was a woman who said at a time when women weren't allowed to have big jobs: "If you are properly devoted toward a career of any sort, you won't have to seek advice about it. No one is going to be able to stop you however hard they try."[11]

NATALIE KALMUS (Selected List)

1917	Gulf Between, The
1922	Toll of the Sea, The
1935	Becky Sharp
1938	Adventures of Robin Hood, The
1939	Gone with the Wind
	Wizard of Oz, The
1941	Blood and Sand
1948	Easter Parade, The
1956	Ten Commandments, The

Brianne Murphy

And the son-in-law also rises
—Anonymous

Brianne Murphy is holding her own in what is undoubtedly the last bastion of male supremacy in the movies. She was the first and only woman director of photography ("DP") in the Hollywod feature-film Union (IATSE). She is also a cofounder of NABET (the National Association of Broadcast Engineers and Technicians), the TV technicians' union. "Before 1920, there were only three women we know of who pioneered the world of the camera that are of note, **Dorothy Dunn, Grace Davison,** and **Margery Ordway.**"[1]

Through technical discourse with the camera, the DP is responsible for creating the mood, atmosphere, and visual style for every shot in a film—thereby giving the film its overall "look."

"No one wants to tell you what they used as a filter, or how they arrived at an exposure. It's hard to get that information for a male or a female. But I could take a cameraman out to lunch and ask him all kinds of questions. I think he felt flattered to talk about his work—whereas if a young man had taken him out and asked all these questions, he'd find some way to say "Go find out for yourself."[2]

Brianne, or Bri ("Bree") as she likes to be called, was born in England. But her mother moved the family to Bermuda to escape the air raids during World War II. She tells the story of how her career began. "One morning, I was having breakfast in the hotel restaurant and someone came over to me and said, 'You're Emily.' 'No,' my mother said, 'her name is Brianne.' 'No,' they insisted, 'She's definitely Emily.' " The person turned out to be a theatrical producer and the next thing Murphy knew, she was playing a character called "Emily" in a Broadway production of *Our Town* in New York.

After finishing college at Brown University, having been to twenty-three different schools in the process, she landed a job with a newspaper and an interview with Elia Kazan. He remembered her as "Emily" from her childhood days in the theater and asked her why she wasn't acting. "Next thing I knew, I was studying at the Neighborhood Playhouse with Sanford Meisner."

But acting really wasn't Bri's thing. "I just liked hanging around show people," she said. During her tenure as the starving actress, she played all the roles starving actresses are supposed to play.

"I did a brief stint as a dime-a-dance girl, where they give you a ticket, buy you drinks, and you're not supposed to go home with the patrons. The night the basketball team came in, I quit."

She then turned to trick riding in a rodeo, where she "did the liberty stand and rode under the belly of the horse. I was small enough." She's 5'2". What's a girl to do who's not sure what she wants to be when she grows up, but has enough chutzpah to try everything?

"Crash the circus. Barnum and Bailey came to town and I dressed up with a friend as a clown and we literally crashed the circus. The AP wire picked us up, and the next thing I knew, I was sitting in front of John Ringling North and a newsreel camera."

North asked her if she wanted to be a clown. "Oh no!" she said. And then she blurted out, "I want to be a photographer." She had no idea where that idea came from. She had never picked up a camera in her life. Before she knew it, she was shooting stills as a circus photographer and seeing the world.

While in New York, Murphy got the opportunity to watch Elia Kazan directing ON THE WATERFRONT (1954). Quickly assessing that she was in the presence of genius, she suddenly zoomed in on the man who was working the black box. And thought,

"That's the guy who really makes magic. I'm going to learn what he does before I slip into the directorial spot and grow up to be Elia Kazan."

Having heard as a "Brit" that America was all circus, rodeos, and movies, and having already tried the first two, Bri found her way to movieland—Hollywood. While there, an unusual opportunity came on a nonunion "quickie" entitled, MAN BEAST (1955). "I was hired to do makeup, props, and wardrobe—none of which I had ever done before, but I bluffed my way in for fifty dollars a week. I was hired because I was cheap. My advice to anyone who wants to get into the business is to be cheap and eager."

MAN BEAST, an abominable snowman pic, went on location to Arizona without the essential monster suit, which was in Hollywood being painted. When it arrived on set, it had shrunk too small for the intended actor. Short of changing the title of the film to BOY BEAST, they asked Bri to try on the suit. Luckily, unlike Cinderella's proverbial slipper, it was too small. The only one who really suited the suit was Vic Fisher, the film's cameraman.

"And Vic handed me his meter and said, 'Well, Bri will have to shoot if I get into the monster suit.' And that was my first break. . . . As soon as I started doing camerawork, I knew this is what I wanted to do."

So now she was qualified, willing, and able. She subsequently wrote and directed several of these quality masterfilms: VIRGINS FROM VENUS (1957), TEENAGE ZOMBIES (1958), etc. For a long time, Murphy *chose* not to pursue getting into the camera union. She knew that once she did, she'd no longer be able to work nonunion jobs. Her instincts told her that with all the competition, studios wouldn't exactly be on their knees to give a DP job to a woman.

"I did a lot of 'schlocky' stuff," says Murphy. "But I kept working. Eventually it became real clear to me that I'd never do any quality pictures until I was union. That's when I started hounding them. The union boss of IATSE told me point-blank that I'd get in over his dead body. He said, 'My wife don't drive a car, you ain't gonna operate a camera.' He simply wouldn't hear of a woman cameraman. He'd laugh at me. I just accepted that I would never get into the big boy's club. I accepted it as a way of life. I would use deception sometimes to get around male chauvinism. I'd be talking on the phone to a producer and I'd make the deal for Brian Murphy."

While in Chile doing what would turn out to be an award-winning film, MAGIC TIDE (1962) Murphy became the personal photographer for Allende in his 1963 campaign. Murphy's husband, a production manager who also worked on the Chilean film, died suddenly of a heart attack during this time.

"I had no impetus," Murphy confessed. "I came back to Hollywood to work. I guess what motivated me was poverty. I applied to the union again. The same guy who had said 'You'll get in over my dead body'—well, turned out he was dead. And right after his funeral, I got in."

Ironically, in 1979 Murphy was an alternate for a position on the executive board for IATSE.

Still, being in the union *hardly* guarantees work for anyone. "NBC needed a woman DP to shoot a documentary on breast cancer. They simply wouldn't let a man into the room to shoot this stuff. I was the only woman in the union."

The film was a hit. NBC kept her working for the next two years. "More than once," says Bri, "I was the cutaway for the other station's news stories."

By this time, she wanted to get into feature and dramatic work desperately. Award-winning cameraman Richard Glouner had to leave a job on a *Columbo* segment and recommended Bri for the job. "What!" they exclaimed. "A woman!" "But they couldn't *not* have me for the job," said Bri. "Richard insisted. 'What's the matter? You hate your mother?!' It was my first big break in major TV and I'll always be grateful to him."

Her first feature for television was for Alan Landsburg Productions. "On *Secrets of the Bermuda Triangle* (1976), there was a lot of boat-to-boat, air-to-air stuff. They said, 'It's not a woman's picture,' to my agent. I almost didn't get the job. But someone on the picture was someone who had worked with me before. It's a sad thing, but it's true—as a woman, you just have to be better."

With this credit, it became easier now for Bri to begin landing other TV work. But as sense would have it, her first major feature movie break would come from a woman. **Anne Bancroft,** who was directing the comedy, FATSO (1980), hired Murphy.

"She said to me quite frankly that she couldn't give orders to men. It was strictly because I was a woman and not fat that she chose me to shoot FATSO."

In the early 1980s Murphy joined Michael Landon's *Little House on the Prairie* series "because Ted Voigtlander, whom I knew from the ASC [American Society of Cinematographers] and with whom I went to video school, literally took my work over to Landon and sold me."

Brianne Murphy had proven that she was better than some of the guys at their own trade. Three times she has been nominated for an Emmy. In 1982 she won an Academy Scientific and Engineering Award for the design, concept, and manufacture of the MISI Camera Insert Car.

"I was brought up to be independent," she said. "We never had men around my house. My parents were divorced. I lived with my mother and sisters. Anything that needed fixing in the house, my mother would send us to the library to read up on it. There's nothing that can't be found out easily. When I lived on a ranch one Christmas, I always wanted to build fences, have my own land. My sister asked me what I wanted for Christmas. I told her power tools. I never had a man around as a copout, not to do it.

Murphy's philosophy about herself is this: "A lot of people expect me to be a leader. They think I should be out making speeches telling other women how to get jobs. I'm not the type to lead movements. I just wanted to make movies badly enough to pay the price to be kicked around, disappointed and unemployed. . . . It's all been worth it. This profession has been the greatest advantage to me. I've traveled all over the world with it. It's enriched my life in every way I can imagine."

BRIANNE MURPHY

1955 Man Beast (DP)
1957 Virgins from Venus (Director)
1958 Teenage Zombies (Director)
1960 Barrier, The
1961 Chivato
1962 Magic Tide (Director)
        Panchito y El Gringo
1972 Pago
1973 Pocket Filled with Dreams
1976 Secrets of the Bermuda Triangle
        (DP)
1978 Five Finger Discount (TV) (DP)
1980 Fatso (DP)
1981 Cheech and Chong's Nice Dreams
        (DP)

·XII·

A REEL
FEMALE GAZE/
SELECT FOREIGN
REEL WOMEN

PREVIEW

◆ ◆ ◆

Perhaps the most frequent question I am asked as I travel around the country speaking about women pioneers is "Do women filmmakers see differently than men when they are behind the camera? Is there an endemically *female* sensibility?" My answer is, "It depends. It depends on the woman, on her level of consciousness about the status of her gender in the world. It also depends on her technical facility and prowess with the variable possibilities of the camera."

Donna Deitch, director of DESERT HEARTS (1985), believes that women *do* have a distinctly female gaze.

I do think that women have a different perspective of the world that comes out in altered imagery. It's a different view of things than men have. I don't think that women always articulate that. It's an instinct, but that is often suppressed or repressed. . . . We live in a world that's so male-defined. Don't women dress, for the most part, to satisfy some idea in their minds about how they think men want them to look, or is fashion dictated by some instinct that women have themselves? So every time you go about doing art work or anything as a woman, you have to strive to follow some kind of instinct. Or if your motivation is unconscious you more than likely choose the male-influenced path of thinking.[1]

Women behind the scenes in film seem to come in two breeds: There are those simply happy to be working in the industry; their gender is insignificant and unrelated to their work. In fact they may even denigrate their status as women as being detrimental to their careers. And there are those whose films blatantly cry out with concern for what it means to be a woman in this world—what that experience consciously *feels* like. These are the filmmakers who make a deliberate decision through content to examine and transform the traditional images of women characters on the screen.

Of the first category, the startlingly prolific screenwriter, **Anita Loos,** springs to mind. Her most famous caricature, **Loreli Lee,** not only perpetuated the stereotype of the dumb blond, but Loos was initially instrumental in the creation of that stereotype.

Of the filmmakers in the second category, Barbara Quart presents a clear picture of how a female director's sensibility in film is categorically different than a man's. In observing a film by the German director **Margarethe von Trotta** she illustrates how a "female gaze" is implemented and defined:

At the heart of her first solo film, THE SECOND AWAKENING OF CHRISTA KLAGES (1977), von Trotta places a long highly charged look between two women, her heroine bank robber and the woman bank clerk whom Christa held up. It is almost as if von Trotta were directly responding to the issue of the famous Laura Mulvey male gaze. Everything hangs on this look, the whole film builds to it. Christa's future—freedom or imprisonment—depends on it. . . . If "the image of woman [has] always looked through the mediation of the male," according to Judith Mayne, in this scene the looking pointedly excludes and rejects the intrusive male intervention.[2]

It's almost as if von Trotta is knocking us over the head saying, "See! Women *do* *see* differently. We see other women. We see ourselves." It's a kind of tipping of the scales after so many generations of dijstortion and imbalance. Perhaps a more subtle and understated example in film of how women see differently than men, is the comparison between love scenes in John Sayles's LIANNA (1983), and **Donna Deitch**'s DESERT HEARTS (1985). In perhaps "the most sensitive, balanced, and sobering view of lesbians the movies will ever give us," as Rex Reed described it in 1983 (two years before DESERT HEARTS was released), Sales artfully paints the womens' first lovemaking experience together in lucious deep blues, while inaudible, sensuous, and dreamy whisperings fill the soundtrack. The camera gazing at the two women is distant. And for nearly the entire scene we view them from a wide-angle shot—voyeuristically, almost enviously watching an experience that even the filmmaker himself can never fully be involved in or understand.

But with Vivian and Cay's seduction in DESERT HEARTS, Deitch keeps us in intimate proximity. She uses close-ups generously, and those close-ups are of facial expressions, *emotions,* never anonymous body parts as is the case with so many erotic scenes directed by men.

In 1916 *Photoplay* gawked over the first "feminist filmmaker," **Cleo Madison**; "With the lovely but militant Cleo at their head, the suffragettes could capture the vote for their sex and smash down the opposi-

tion as easily as shooting fish in a bucket." But the writer felt compelled to reassure his readers, lest they become too distressed, that "Cleo Madison is a womanly woman, —if she were otherwise she couldn't play sympathetic emotional roles as she does."[3]

For a while, Madison stoically held the fort as the lone, suffragette, mainstream "directress," bravely spouting things to the press like,

> One of these days men are going to get over the fool idea that women have no brains, and quit getting insulted at the thought that a skirt-wearer can do their work quite as well as they can.[4]

and,

> Every play in which women appear needs the feminine touch. **Lois Weber**'s productions are phenomenally successful, partly because her women creations are true to the spirit of womanhood.[5]

The article from which the above was taken goes on to boost Madison's moral character as a "real" woman, by espousing her "domestic accomplishments" in great detail. "She enjoys nothing more than donning a big apron and setting to work to cook a real old-fashioned chicken dinner. . . . Can you imagine the temperamental Rethna of HER BITTER CUP [1916] concocting a plate of biscuits that simply melt in your mouth?"

In the end however, fighting a battle as a one-woman army in the industry got to her. She never made a "militant" picture again, and retired from the screen in 1921 because of a nervous breakdown.

Since that time, with only a few exceptions, the women filmmakers with this sort of conscious eye are doing their work outside Hollywood, and to a very large degree, on foreign terrain. When their work *is* done within the mighty, intimidating fortress, it is done so in spotty singular drips, like an accident that has to be wiped up. The appalling reception of **Barbra Streisand's** YENTL—otherwise remembered by some as "Barbra's folly" was one case in point. The fact that Streisand took the traditional form of the American musical, stood it on its head, and singlehandedly created what was essentially a new film genre was never addressed.

Women on foreign ground seem to have a much easier time not only declaring their interests and sensibilities, but in getting the support to see them realized. **Márta Mészáros** has always proudly asserted, "Ever since my first film, THE GIRL (1968) was made, I have with the obstinacy of a mule, pursued my attempt to study the characters of types of women with a strong personality and capable of forming decisions for themselves." Barbara Quart notes of **Mészáros's** films, "There's a constant, sometimes astonishing sense of the eye of a woman watching women in ways that we have not experienced before."[6]

And when first seen in 1977, "watching girls coming together after a summer apart," in **Diane Kurys's** PEPPERMINT SODA, "their joyful greetings to one another, their kissing and embracing, noticing this one's tan and that one's haircut, excited talk. For the woman spectator there was the stunned sense that one had never before seen a camera focus with this kind of attention, time, care, truth, affection and interest on young girls this way."[7]

Distinct uses of the camera; a focused eye and heart toward aspects of women's lives previously ignored or pooh-poohed by male cinema, because of a lack of shared experience—all this is what distinguishes a female gaze. The filmmakers in the upcoming section are pioneers. With a heightened awareness, and the courage to name a false representation of their own lives on the screen, they are succeeding in bursting open cultural archetypes, and in doing so, they are changing our lives forever.[8]

Germaine Dulac

Musidora in Louis Feuillade's LES VAMPIRES
(Third New York Film Festival, 1965).

THE SILENTS

* * *

Germaine Dulac (1882–1942)

The film world would ultimately crown her "the Heart of the Avant-Garde."[1] Between 1920 and 1930, when the American film industry was busy tallying up its box-office receipts, and suddenly realizing that the word *movie* could equal money, **Germaine Dulac,** the most important and most prolific filmmaker of the decade in France, was striving for what she called "a pure cinema"—a cinema as a viable and serious expression of art. This was at a time when films' archival importance was hardly recognized.

What she wanted was the best of art that cinema could provide—a cinema in which plot would all but be replaced by imagery, by a kind of visual music where, as she explained,

> objects would become symbols. The pure film we all dream of making is a visual symphony, composed of rhythmic images which the artist's feelings alone organize and project on the screen. A musician's writing is not always inspired by a story, most often it is through the inspiration of a feeling ... expressions of a soul's outpouring, a soul reacting. The only story is that which the soul experiences and thinks, and yet we are moved by it.[2]

Among the first feminist filmmakers the world would know—her film THE SMILING MADAME BEUDET in 1923 was the first film in history to tell a narrative tale from the psychological perspective of a woman protagonist—Dulac was described by her contemporaries as "intense, independent, indomitable, persevering."[3]

She was brought to artistic consciousness in the early twenties. By 1924, in his *Manifesto of Surrealism,* André Breton had laid down the common thoughts of his peers for a new art form. Woman, he stated, was a dream, the highest form of muse, the supreme inspiration for the male imagination.[4] But Dulac refused to be anyone's muse except her own.

Having done her first film in 1915, Dulac was making films before the surrealists, and continued after the other surrealists had stopped. She was incorporating elements of surrealism long before Breton ever wrote his theories down.

What interested her were elements that seem to be abstracted from surrealism: juxtaposing concrete images of reality with unexpected, generally nonassociated images; rearranging all notions of time and space on the screen, and then pulling from other sources that seemed to be antithetical to surrealism. Her camera work was most unembarrassedly from a female perspective, applying a seriousness of intent to her women characters that would have been way out of line with "the woman as muse."[5]

> Her 1923 film, THE SMILING MADAME BEUDET, could really be retitled, "The Original Diary of a Mad Housewife." It is one of the few films of the decade in which women are not fragmented, not shown as sexual freaks, not stripped in close-ups or through editing to reveal a bleeding mouth, bared breasts or buttocks. It is one of the few films of the decade in which a woman is the main character.[6]

Point-of-view shots, slow motion, trick photography, and wide-angle lens distortions were all incorporated stunningly by Dulac to convey the story of a housewife caught in a cage of domestic boredom that leads her close to madness.

Marjorie Baumgarten of the Museum of Modern Art called the film "one of the most underrated masterpieces of the silent cinema." Madame Beudet is a sort of Madame Bovary who seeks escape from her insipid, provincial life and the tyranny of her husband. Her suppressed life breaks into blossom through the use of visual fantasies, as Dulac brilliantly interposes superimpositions of Madame Beudet's imagined lovers.

In the last scene of the film, Mr. and Mrs. Beudet are walking down the street. Mr. Beudet tips his hat to a passerby. By the filmmaker's insightful angle of her camera, we wordlessly recognize with a chill that Madame Beudet is nothing more than an invisible appendage to her husband. She is his showpiece, no more and no less.

The fact that MADAME BEUDET is a feminist piece may be all the more reason for its blending into obscurity. As Marjorie Baumgarten points out, "Whereas the camerawork in Chaplin's story about the fate of a demimondaine and Murnau's tale of the eternal lover's triangle has been stu-

diously cited for its evocative subtleties, the camerawork in Dulac's story of a frustrated housewife's contempt for her husband has been referred to by some historians as 'excessive.' "[7]

Dulac began her career as a journalist for feminist French publications, first interviewing and writing portraits on famous women, and then as a drama critic. She left journalism in 1915 to form her own film production company with her husband of ten years, Albert Dulac, and her first scenarist, **Irene Hillel-Erlanger.** World War I provided a great opportunity for women to enter the film business.

Historians have found her difficult to categorize because Dulac was proficient in several genres: psychological realism, symbolism, elements of surrealism, straight documentary, even the episodic serial film.

AMES DE FOUS (1917) was one such episodic film. It incorporated Dulac's own trademark of an "impressionistism." The film was popular with the audience, but not with critics who complained that such "suggestive techniques" as shadows, backlighting, and silhouettes manipulated the viewer without the viewer's awareness. Like a true pioneering spirit, Dulac held steady and fast to her own voice that found no validation from the outside world:

> AMES DE FOUS made me understand that beyond precise facts and events, atmosphere is an element of emotion, that the emotional value of a film lies less in the action than in the subtitles it exudes, and that if the expression of an actor is obviously of value in itself, it can only attain its fullest intensity by a complimentary play of images coming in reaction to it. Lighting, camera placement, and editing all appeared to me as more essential elements than the production of a scene played according to dramatic laws.[8]

Soon, Dulac was to form an organization with filmmaker and writer Louis Delluc, called "Impressionists." They are often remembered as the first avant-garde. Their version of impressionism was to fuse the arts: painting, dramatics, poetry, and now, the cinema. The group included Dulac, Delluc, Abel Gance, and Jean Epstein.

Their fruitful collaboration brought about several filmic experiments, many of which were widely agreed upon as "revolutionary." LA FÊTE ESPAGNOLE (1919), for instance, attempted to capture the exoticism of the American Western through a quasi-documentary style—bold even for today. Louis Delluc's unexpected death in 1924 brought an end to all that. Dulac was again on her own.

At the time she was thirty-seven and this was her seventh film to his first. But the work with him is what made her ready for the breakthrough with THE SMILING MADAME BEUDET.

Although the film firmly established her as an artist, producers with an eye toward commercial considerations were reluctant to back her. Andre Daven describes Dulac at a time when she was a kind of infamy around the studios:

> Her fingers made up of rings, her wrists adorned with trinkets, an ankle circled with gold. A cane. She smokes, smokes. Her right hand twisting a cigarette, her left anchored in the pocket of her suit, give conviction to what she does. At the studio she ignores people, hours, meals. Smokes, smokes. Vehemently she rushes about. Lashes herself forward, and spurred on, gives orders. She is perfectly urbane ... and smokes, smokes.[9]

She tried her hand at being a studio director with a feature in 1924, with LE DIABLE DANS LA VILLE, about the fanaticism of the Middle Ages. The film was shot entirely with studio-built sets, including the exterior shots. Not liking the structures and conditions that the studio imposed, Dulac returned to independent production in 1925.

In 1927, after making a film that finally satisfied, as Charles Ford says, "commercial appeal with artistic efforts," Dulac made what William Van Wert has called, "the first truly Surrealistic film" in history, THE SEASHELL AND THE CLERGYMAN (1927). In this film, says Van Wert, she exploits the Freudian symbolism of her male colleagues. "She makes a film in their style," continues Van Wert, "in order to expose male fantasies. For this reason, the clear distinction between objective reality and subjective point-of-view shots that exist in THE SMILING MADAME BEUDET no longer exist in THE SEASHELL AND THE CLERGYMAN."[10]

The film was based on a screenplay by Antonin Artaud whose intent was that the film have no underlying psychoanalytic, metaphysic, or human meaning. He meant it to be a film of pure streams of images, as he said, "describing states of mind without any attempt at clarification or demonstration." Although Dulac's film was not radically different from Artaud's script, Artaud thought her interpretation too literal. A great uproar stirred between writer and director. At the screening, Artaud interrupted the film screaming, "Germaine Dulac is a cow!" Other protestors joined in vehemently opposing the "incoherence of images." Nonetheless, THE SEASHELL AND THE CLERGYMAN became a landmark classic in avant-garde cinema, and carved the name of Germaine Dulac firmly into pioneering film history.

"Instead of seeking inside ourselves," she said,

> having lost confidence, we look to the accomplishments of others, [over in America,] and try to conform to their standards. The time has come, I believe, to listen in silence to our own song, to try to express our own personal vision, to define our own sensibility, to make our own way. Let us learn to look, let us learn to see, let us learn to feel.[11]

Of the nearly thirty films made by Dulac in her lifetime, only two still currently exist in their entirety: THE SMILING MADAME

BEUDET and THE SEASHELL AND THE CLERGYMAN. "Due to the nature of their independent production and relative lack of distribution," says Marjorie Baumgarten, "as well as the difficulty in succinctly pigeonholing Dulac's varied career into a neat critical category, her work has slipped into the historical abyss."[12]

Germaine Dulac died of a long illness in 1942. Her biographer, Charles Ford, relates the difficulty that the French press had in printing her obituary:

> Bothered by Dulac's non-conformist ideas, disturbed by her impure origins, the censors had refused the article which, only after a vigorous protest by the editor-in-chief of the magazine, appeared three weeks late.[13]

Even dead, as Ford notes, Germaine Dulac still seemed dangerous.

GERMAINE DULAC

1915	Les Soeurs Ennemies
1916	Dans l'Ouragan de la Vie
	Geo Le Mysterieux
	Venus Victrix
1917	Ames de Fous
1918	Le Bonheur des Autres
1919	La Cigarette
	La Fête Espagnole
1920	La Belle Dame sans Merci
	Malencontre
1921	La Mort du Soleil
1922	Werther
1923	Gossette
	La Souriante Madame Beudet (Smiling Madame Beudet, The)
1924	Le Diable dans la Ville
1925	Ame d'Artiste
	La Folie des Vaillants
1926	Antoinette Sabrier
1927	La Coquille et Le Clergyman (The Seashell and the Clergyman)
	L'Invitation au Voyage
1928	Disque 927
	Germination d'un Haricot
	Mon Paris
	La Princesse Mandane
	Thèmes et Variations
1929	Étude Cinégraphique sur Une Arabesque
1930	Les 24 Heures du Mans
1932	Jaquelux
	Le Picador
1937	Le Cinéma au Service de l'Histoire

Musidora (1884–1957)

Riding the crest of the wave of surrealism in France, **Musidora** burst full-blown on the scene like the goddess Athena from the head of Zeus. The Parisian version of the vampire, she was an immediate sensation. The French adored her. Quite the opposite of an Arab Shiva, who would suck the blood from men and leave them dry, Musidora was androgynous, sexless. When she stole the heart of Paris in LES VAMPIRES (The vampires) in 1915, she wore a "simple form-fitting [mouthless] cloth. This vampire's teeth transcend[ed] the absence of the orifice. [Her] pull-away mask rendered Irma Vep's villainy almost genderless."[1]

The magic of Musidora's presence was largely due to her costume. The garment that made her nationally infamous was a single, full-bodied, black leotard. Thus garbed, this sprite—who would later direct some of the earliest surrealist films in history in collaboration with **Colette**—Musidora captured the heart of an era. Specifically, she captivated the souls of surrealists André Breton and Louis Aragon who wrote:

> A generation fell completely in love with Musidora in LES VAMPIRES. Those same passionate initiates found themselves, for

the first time, swept up by a grandiloquent and obvious problem, the intellectual problem of life . . . the same problem faced by all human beings: the impossibility of escaping the final catastrophe.[2]

She was born **Jeanne Roques** to a family of "freethinkers." Her father was a musician and a philosopher. Her mother was an educated woman who adored literature and became an ardent feminist in 1897 when she founded a journal *Le Vengeur*, dedicated to sociology, feminism, and art.[3] In a home with abundant love and artistic influence, Musidora's personality flourished in a bohemian life-style. She wrote:

At the age of three I wanted to be a painter. At five, I wanted to sell stamps behind the counter of the post office. By ten I wanted to manage a circus troupe . . . and at fifteen I wanted to be a school teacher in the country in a homey, ivy and rose-colored school house.[4]

She could have managed a schoolhouse or anything else she put her mind to. She was an exceptionally bright, precocious child, who was so quick to pass all her exams that she won a French endearment title of General![5]

She was accepted at the appropriate age into art school at the Jullian Academy of Fine Arts and the Schommer Studio. But painting and drawing proved too limiting for this outgoing spirit and she soon turned to the stage as a comedienne.

She first appeared in 1910 at the Star Theatre in vaudeville piece by Keroul and Barre, which led to an engagement with the Mount Parnasse acting troupe. Here, she appeared with her stage name, Musidora, for the first time. She adopted the name from the novel *Fortunio* (1870) by the late nineteenth-century decadent, Théophile Gautier. When Musidora undertook the role of *Claudine in Paris* (ghostwritten by **Colette** for her husband Willy), her future for greatness was foreshadowed.

In 1914 Musidora was recruited by Ra-

phael Clamour, a militant organizer and libertarian, to star in a didactic film vehicle, LES MISÈRES DE L'AIGUILLE (The sorrows of the needle), in which she, Musidora, portrayed a sewer worker exploited by her boss. This was only one film of many from the Society of the People Cinema produced for the purpose of furthering the cause of the working class. Such films came under attack by certain union factions in the belief that film was a medium used to stupefy the masses.

Musidora records seeing one such film of "a young woman who looked ready to shout; at first unmoving, she turns her head sweetly, bends down, then all of a sudden runs." It was an ephemeral image, most likely too personal and obscure for anyone except a potential filmmaker to understand. But in that moment, the splendiferous magic of cinema had captured Musidora's heart, and she knew she had found her model.

As Patrick Cazals notes, directing and producing a film was a privilege not afforded everyone in the France of 1916. **Alice Guy Blaché** had her opportunity because of her affiliation with Leon Gaumont. **Germaine Dulac** directed VENUS VICTRIX (1916) and LES SOEURS ENNEMIES (1915) because of her national reputation as a journalist. Likewise, Musidora's fame garnered from her appearance in Louis Feuillade's "masterful and delirious crime/horror serial, LES VAMPIRES in 1915, afforded her a similar opportunity."[6] The surrealist elements of Feuillade's series was striking.

Early on in the film, one sees a painted landscape, replete with sphinx, hanging on a bedroom wall. When the painting is moved, a familiar feature of the old-dark-house melodramas is uncovered: the secret passage. From the passage, pallid and black-eyed Musidora emerges. Her game is afoot, a playful yet murderous war of surrealist deceit hurled against a topical world. As a box-office attraction, Musidora triumphed.[7]

As Keith Patrick de Weese says, this vampire did not limit her teeth to the superficial clamping of men. She went for much bigger, socially redeeming stuff! She preyed on something hoarded by both sexes: wealth.

> In black leotards, cowl, and mask, she projected an androgynous presence that not only courted, but waged war on the complacent bourgeoisie.... Musidora's "Irma Vep"—proved to be a much greater threat to a "status in quo" already sapped by war [World War I] than the threat posed by the exotica of Arab Death.[8]

Having befriended **Colette**, Musidora chose to film the author's story, MINNE, or L'INGENUE LIBERTINE (1915). Not much is known about this first attempt except from what remains of a few production stills. Her second production, THE BLACK LEOTARD (1917), was written in collaboration with **Germaine Beaumont**. This short film premiered at the Theatre Saint-Denis in Paris on October 1, 1917. But it was with her third project, Colette's LA VAGABONDE (1917) that Musidora's talents as a director were widely applauded. Reports writer Patrick Casels:

> The film was received very favorably by Parisian film-goers and critics who at last realized that Musidora had other talents than those exhibited in black leotards.... This, despite some bad press by Colette's bitter ex-husband Willy.[9]

Colette assisted in the directing of this production, and in her own words, "It was a marvelous production! There was nothing else like it!" Musidora, of course, was the star. And an interesting footnote brought to light by Keith Patrick de Weese is that **Stacia de Napierkowska**, who costarred with Musidora in LES VAMPIRES, offered a camerawoman position to **Germaine Dulac** on CALIGULA in 1915. And so, the old-girl network was founded!

Musidora realized that the "handicap" of being a woman in a medium run by men

meant that she would need financial autonomy to complete her projects. She again linked her talents with **Colette**'s, and they created LA FLAMME CACHÉ (1918). This production was also the first time Musidora acted as executive producer of her own production company, La Societe des Film Musidora.

> In creating her own production company ... and in demanding a scenario from a renowned novelist, Musidora threw in quick succession two "bombs" in the world of film. Her example, which she strongly emphasized, was later followed by more illustrious stars, the first being Charlie Chaplin.[10]

But Casels, who wrote the above, is wrong. The first *star* who began to direct her own vehicles was **Mabel Normand**.

During the forties and fifties, long after the world had lost its innocence to war, Musidora continued delighting her public by directing stage productions, such as *La vie sentimental de George Sand* (1946). She directed and starred in her last vehicle LA MAGIQUE IMAGE in 1950. But the world was not yet ready to forget Musidora. Theatrical releases and telefilms, dedicated to keeping her image alive, flourished after her death in 1957. MUSIDORA was broadcast in 1973, documenting this remarkable woman's illustrious, colorful life. The New York Film Festival screened LES VAMPIRES in 1965. And a restored, six-hour version of the same closed the festival's twenty-fifth anniversary celebration.[11] The year 1990 marked the seventy-fifth anniversary of LES VAMPIRES, and as is well known, haunted spirits, especially pioneering ones, have ways of reappearing.

MUSIDORA

1913	Misères de l'aiguille, Les
1914	L'Autre Victoire
	Bout de Zan et L'Espion
	La Bouquetière des Catalans

Le Calvaire
Le Colonel Bontemps
Les Fiancés de 1914
Les Leçons de la Guerre
La Petite Réfugiée
Sainte Odile
Severo Torelli
Les Trois Rats
Tu N'Épousera Jamais un
    Avocat
L'Union Sacrée
La Ville de Madame Tango

1915   L'Autre Devoir
La Barrière
Bout de Zan et le Poilu
Celui Qui Reste
Le Collier de Perles
Le Coup du Fakir
Deux Françaises
Le Fer a Cheval
Fifi Tambour
Le Grand Souffle
L'Escapade de Filoche
Les Noces d'Argent
Une Page de Gloire
Le Roman de la Midinette
Le Sosie
Triple Entente
Le Trophée du Zouave
Une Page de Gloire

1915–16 Les Vampires
1916   Coeur Fragile
Débrouille-Toi
Les Fiançailles d'Agenor
Fille d'Éve
Les Fourberies de Pingouin
Jeunes Filles d'Hier et
    d'Aujourd'hui

Judex
Labourdette, Gentleman
    Cambrioleur
Les Mariés d'un Jour
Minne or l'ingenue libertine
    (Director, Producer)
Mon Oncle
La Peinte du Talion
Le Poète et sa Folle Amante
Si Vous ne m'Aimez Pas
Le Troisième Larron

1917   Les Chacals
Le Maillot Noir (Director,
    Producer)
La Vagabonda (Director,
    Producer)

1918   La Flamme Caché (Director,
    Producer)
La Geôle
La Jeune Fille la plus Méri-
    tante de France
Johannès Fils de Johannès
Mam'Zelle Chiffon

1919   Vicenta (Director, Producer)
1920   Pour Don Carlos (Director,
    Producer)
1922   Une Aventure de Musidors en
    Espagne (Director, Producer)
Soleil et Ombre (Director,
    Producer)

1924   La Tierra de los Toros
    (Director, Producer)
1925   Les Ombres du Passé
1950   La Magique Image (Director,
    Producer)

Chantal Akerman

Leni Riefenstahl

Margarethe von Trotta

Marguerite Duras

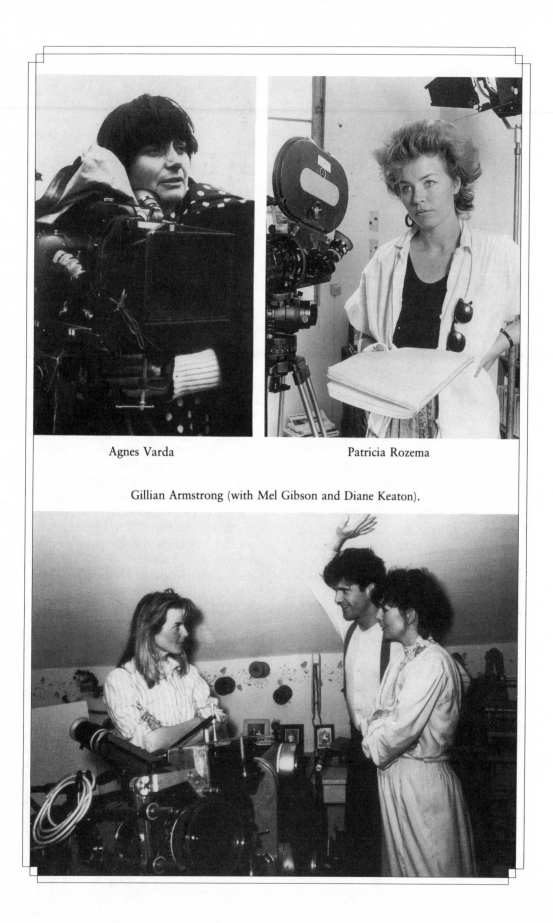

Agnes Varda

Patricia Rozema

Gillian Armstrong (with Mel Gibson and Diane Keaton).

THE SOUND ERA

◆ ◆ ◆

Leni Riefenstahl (1902–   )

"It's disgraceful," said film historian Kevin Brownlow. "Many feminists are guilty of it too. But the fact is that perhaps the greatest of all women filmmakers is constantly ignored because she worked for the wrong side. Her work was as good as Eisenstein's any day, but no one approves of her because she made films for the Third Reich."[1]

After viewing what I could of her films, and wading through the mass of written controversy, it was easy to conclude that Brownlow was right. **Leni Riefenstahl** was a gifted artist, interested only in the creation of film as a rhythmic, musical event. She wasn't interested in politics. She wasn't a propagandist, although she was persecuted for the rest of her life as though she were. She was interrogated by the United States Army throughout 1945 and 1946, and was released as "unchargeable." She was then taken to court in 1949 by the French but again was released with almost everything cleared. She was forever, it seemed, engaged in a struggle to clear her name of Nazi affiliation and to retrieve her films.

She was an ambitious, artist born in the wrong time and place, and of the wrong sex. Trying to pursue an artistic career was not an easy thing in the Germany of 1930.

Certainly, for a young woman with ambitions in a man's world anywhere in the thirties could not have been easy. And yet, after the war, she was denied her gift while other Nazi collaborators were able to assume their professional standings.

"Many many cineastes were shooting films," defends Riefenstahl, "and many others accepted commissions. But none of them were accused as I was. Why? Because I am a woman? Because the film was too successful? I don't know."[2]

Perhaps Riefenstahl tells the best version of her tale in an interview that appeared in *Cahiers du Cinema* in 1966. She speaks of her first independent film, THE BLUE LIGHT (1932), a film which she wrote, produced, choreographed, edited, and also starred in. It was completed by 1931.

The film tells of a young girl, Yunta, played by Riefenstahl, who in a sleepwalking travel, climbs at night towards a blue light at the summit of a certain mountain visible only when the moon is full. It is a metaphor in pictures, told through an exquisite use of light and mystical shadow, about the secret yearning in the heart of youth: a deep, mysterious longing toward an ideal. But when her secret is violated by the crowd—the townsfolk always being willing to burn her as a witch and a sorceress, a symbol of the loss of innocence—her heart is broken and she falls to her death.

It was a film of romanticism, made in the purity of youth. But as Riefenstahl said, in making this sort of film by instinct, she found herself expressing the path that would be purely her own. She played a child of nature who climbed to a blue light—an aspiration dreamed of. When her dream is destroyed, Yunta dies. In a way, this was to be Riefenstahl's own destiny, though she didn't know it at the time.

> For that is what was accomplished, much later for me after the war, when everything collapsed on us, when I was deprived of all possibility of creating. . . . My life became a tissue of rumors and accusations through which I had to beat a path; they all were revealed to be false, but for twenty years they deprived me of making films. I tried to write, but what I wanted to do was make films, but I couldn't. At that moment, I was dead.[3]

The life and work of Leni Riefenstahl is as classically mythic in scope as the story of the Phantom of the Opera. The mighty forces of dark and evil battle the angelic spirits of light and good. More than with any other filmmaker, the question of morality inevitably arises. Is it right to even include a woman who made films for the Nazis in a collection of women labeled pioneers?

Wading through the plethora of controversy surrounding her myth is a little like floating down a river with your feet on separate ice floes. Was she an artist or a propagandist? Is it possible to be both as a documentarian? Is it possible to be one to the exclusion of the other? Was Riefenstahl a committed Nazi or merely an artist submerged deeply in the love of her craft?

She is best remembered for two films, TRIUMPH OF THE WILL (1935) and OLYMPIA

(1938), both done under Hitler's regime and the first made at his request. Her reputation is a mixture of charged anger and high praise for her genius. As **Louise Heck-Rabi** said,

> The brief tenure of the Third Reich . . . encloses the era of Riefenstahl's best films, and the history of Germany during a dozen infamous years, 1933–1945, has integrated with Riefenstahl's private and public lives so inextricably that it has become nearly impossible to discuss her films as cinematic entities apart from an extremely emotional bias.[4]

Yet no matter whether you stand on the side that brands her a propagandist, or with those that say she couldn't have cared less for ideas but only for cinematic form, the fact of her artistry unanimously resounds among critics. Here are reports from various points of view:

Richard Meran Barsam—*Nonfiction Film: Theory and Criticism:*

> [TRIUMPH OF THE WILL] is a solemn, symbolic film, beautifully photographed and edited with a sense of structure and rhythm that make it a rival of its Russian masters. It should be studied not as propaganda only, but also as art of the highest order; no film has been more vilified for its subject matter, yet no film has been more misunderstood. TRIUMPH OF THE WILL, and OLYMPIA are among the greatest nonfiction films of all time.[5]

David Gunston in *Current Biography* adheres to the view that TRIUMPH OF THE WILL could not have been made "by anyone not fanatically at one with the events depicted," yet in the same breath he calls it a "historical document of utmost importance."[6] Robert Gardner vehemently disagrees:

> "Neither TRIUMPH nor OLYMPIA could have been made by a propagandist. . . . They are self-evidently the work of an art-

ist, even if an artist of an immensely naive political nature . . . There are virtually no ideas in her films. They state nothing, in a grandiloquent manner. Leni Riefenstahl does not care about ideas. . . . If she believed the Nazi myth it was because she thought it was a better road to health and physical fitness. Jim Card, head of the film collection at Eastman House, asserts that her OLYMPIA might be the best film ever made in history.[7]

Riefenstahl has always pleaded ignorance of Nazi intentions, and denied that she was a party member. She said she was someone who was well-known in Germany before Hitler came to power. Her company Leni Riefenstahl Studio Films was lucrative and well-established by 1931. She claims that she made more films before Hitler's rise than after, and that for her as a young girl it was impossible to foresee the nightmares of what that war was to bring.

TRIUMPH OF THE WILL brought me very hard troubles after the war. It was, effectively, a film made to order, proposed by Hitler. That was happening, you must remember in 1934. . . . At that period, Hitler had acquired a certain credit in the world, and he fascinated a certain number of people, among them Winston Churchill. And I, I alone, I should be able to foresee that one day things would change?[8]

At that time, said Reifenstahl, people believed in the promise of something beautiful; in construction, and peace. The worst was yet to come, but who knew it?

How could I have been better informed than Winston Churchill who was still declaring in '35–'36 that he envied Germany its Fuhrer? . . . Among other accusations brought at the beginning was this: I had been Hitler's mistress. There were many others. I deny all of them. All that anyone has been able to establish—and God knows after what research!—is that Hitler declared that I was talented. It happened that others also said so.[9]

Riefenstahl did not begin as a filmmaker. She was trained as a dancer and painter. She was gifted with an artist's touch. From the first, everything that she attempted brought her success, and often fame. As she says, "Dance and painting played a role in forming the style of composing and editing images that became mine."[10]

As a solo dancer she toured Germany, unable to fulfill the deluge of requests for performances. In 1923, she was seen by Max Reinhardt, who engaged her for his company in Berlin. But a knee injury put an end to her dance career, and she began acting in films. What attracted her, she says, was the exhilarating experience of making a film in geographically hazardous locations. Reifenstahl later explained. "Whatever is average, quotidian, doesn't interest me. Only the unusual, the specific, excites me."[11]

After a rigorous apprenticeship of acting and crewing on a rugged mountain film the idea for THE BLUE LIGHT came to her. As Glenn B. Infield tells in his book on Riefenstahl,

[In] her determination to direct and produce her own film . . . she was willing to go to practically any length . . . just as she was later, during the Third Reich, in an effort to fulfill her craving for recognition in the film world.[12]

But if Riefenstahl had ambitions it was for her craft and not for political power. The result of this first filmic attempt immediately established her name in the world of cinema.

Riefenstahl recalls that THE BLUE LIGHT was only a moderate success in Germany, but won a gold medal at the first Venice Festival in 1932, and enjoyed long runs in both London and Paris.

The period of Riefenstahl's entry into films coincided with the early birth of German cinema. She admits to limited influence by filmmakers from the world outside Germany (she is often compared with Eisenstein) for the simple reason that she did not have the opportunity to see many movies in Germany at that time. TRIUMPH OF THE WILL was a film heralded as a powerful masterpiece, even by those who berate its evil content, and this as well as everything she touched, was marked by her unique stamp and individuality of vision.

It is film-verité, she said of TRIUMPH. She claimed that the film was purely historical.

It reflects the truth that was then, in 1934, in history. It is therefore a documentary. Not a propaganda film.[13]

If a propaganda film consists of recreating certain events in order to illustrate a thesis then, Riefenstahl said with a tone of conviction, this is not the film that she created.

I found myself at the heart of an event which was the reality of a certain time and place.... It is difficult for me to think that in 1937, two years before the war, France would have awarded its *grand prix* to a propaganda film....[14]

Leni Riefenstahl went on to say that TRIUMPH OF THE WILL was very different in spirit and form from Eisenstein's POTEMKIN to which it has been compared.

My film is only a documentary. I showed what everyone was witness to or had heard about. Everyone was impressed by it. I am the one who fixed that impression, who registered it on film. And that is doubtless why people are angry with me: for having seized it, put it in a box. One saw things before the war out of different eyes than after.[15]

The idea for the filming of OLYMPIA, the coverage of the Olympic games in Munich, was to show "the transcendence of the human spirit over all physical obstacles."[16] Indeed, the massive obstacles in the sheer

filming of such an event was a transcendence in and of itself. Through the enormity of the filming, she pioneered, what she calls,

several improvisatory coups.... It wasn't pointed out how many things we discovered: the noiseless camera, made so as not to bother the athletes ... the camera for underwater shots ... the idea of digging trenches from which we might film the jumpers.[17]

Other ingenious filming innovations included mounting a camera in a cage that was moved along a track and placing the camera atop shock-resistant materials attached to a saddle. "For the ten meter dive," she said,

the cameraman dove with the diver, filmed him as he fell under the water and came with him to the surface.... Obviously, for every one hundred meters of exposed film, ninety-five were no good.[18]

Even to approach the enormous undertaking of such an event should explain the ambition of this pioneer, whose drive for her craft neared fanaticism. In *Film Culture* in 1973, Heinz von Jaworsky, one of Riefenstahl's crew members, describes working with her:

After a sixteen-hour day ... she would get the whole gang together.... We were all falling asleep. She had been with us all day long. But that woman was full of energy! She would assign you to your position.... She would go into minute detail.... And she would hear no contradictions, "you do this."[19]

Glenn Infield tells the tale of a top-notch cameraman assigned to THE BLUE LIGHT, who refused to use a green filter *along with* a red one. Riefenstahl insisted. He tried it. "The combination of filters resulted in the new, unexpected magical effect that made THE BLUE LIGHT so different."[20]

Louise Heck-Rabi looks at the odd entity a woman needed to be to succeed in a man's world in the thirties.

Her facile working relationships with men was a diamond-hard determination to attain perfection, plus a tireless propensity for improvisation and innovation. Suffuse these elements with Riefenstahl's hyper-energetic strength, an audacious intensity which remains incredulous, and a total submergence of self into the created object and one feels the fierce fire of her ambitions and an admiration for her quicksilver quality of getting whatever she wanted.[21]

Except, of course, in the end. All that Leni Riefenstahl wanted to get was a continuing chance to pursue her art. And in the end this was denied her. An interview with Richard Meran Barsam in the seventies revealed that she had no interest in the struggle for women's rights. Like most of the early women pioneers, her only desire was to work. When she worked, her awareness that she was the only woman doing what she was doing never dawned on her.

B. Ruby Rich analyzed Riefenstahl's politics:

Riefenstahl as a token Amazon accepted into the Nazi partriarchy because she adopted its values cannot be viewed as a feminist. She did not, could not, build a power base from which other women could rise to a position similar to her own.[22]

Riefenstahl was solicited to do other political films for the Nazis, but she refused, preferring instead to hark back to that most uninfected period of her purest art, the romantic phase of THE BLUE LIGHT. But no one was willing to fund these films, and like Orson Welles, Leni Riefenstahl could not raise the money. She made one more film, TIEFLAND, released in 1954, some twenty years after its initiation, and only to moderate success. For by this time, Leni Riefenstahl had become a kind of leper.

In 1949 she was imprisoned by the French as a Nazi sympathizer. A denazification court ruled that Leni was a follower, not an active member of the Nazi party, but still, as a filmmaker, she was blacklisted by the allies. The stigma against her would tarnish her career for the rest of her days.

Riefenstahl tried to complete a film on the Nubia tribe in Africa, but the footage was mysteriously destroyed. Undaunted and determined, she turned the project into a book of photography. Her exquisite images appeared in 1974. In 1976 a second book appeared; a photographic study of a people known as worshipers of beauty, *The People of Kau*. Still, Riefensathl was the bitter recipient of critical attacks that these visions were imbued with Nazi overtones— the perfection of the bodies of these African peoples. Bitterly she retorts, "I'd like to see the critics try to draw a parallel between the Third Reich and my next book—which will be on underwater photography!"[23]

At the age of seventy-one she learned to dive, desiring to capture on film the coral of the Caribbean. Her book *Coral Gardens* appeared in 1976, and coincided with a biography of her that continued her bad press.

"All lies," was her response. "I was fascinated by Hitler but took no political position. I have always been a romantic and loved beauty. People have been stoning me for years to destroy me. There is a Mafia-like international conspiracy against me."[24]

It is as though Leni Riefenstahl, by capturing a time and place on film that people would rather not remember, has become the scapegoat for the entire era. Like Yunta in THE BLUE LIGHT, in Richard Barsam's words, "She was destroyed by her naive disregard of the real world around her, the world she set out to avoid."[25]

Her reputation lies in four films. As Barsam ably describes them,

They are filled with a fanatically romantic vision of the good and simple life, of physical strength and spiritual purity. . . . From the crystal grotto of THE BLUE LIGHT, to the pure spectacle of human flight in . . . OLYMPIA, to the shepherd's victorious fight with the wolves in TIEFLAND, and finally to the primitive rituals of the Nubia tribe, Riefenstahl has transcended both time and space, as a visionary poet, to create a world of her own. TRIUMPH . . . is an aberration that will always stain her reputation, but it should not be allowed to obscure the beauty and strength of what remains her achievement.[26]

LENI RIEFENSTAHL

1932	Blue Light, The
1935	Day of Freedom
	Triumph of the Will
1938	Berchtesgaden Uber Salzburg
	Olympia: I and II
1954	Tiefland
1956	Schwarze Fracht

Marguerite Duras (1914–   )

When one thinks of **Marguerite Duras,** one almost hallucinates on a world of memory and desire. Eroticism, endless yearnings, love, solitude—all flow together in a cycle of memory and forgetting. The world of Marguerite Duras is a world of eternal return. She is best remembered by the film community for her ground-breaking script, HIROSHIMA, MON AMOUR (1960). "I didn't come to the cinema from nothing," she said. "I came from writing. . . . Literature comprises everything. The text contains the image, the performances, the readers, the spectators, everything."[1]

At the age of eight, in 1922, she still couldn't read or write, but in post–World War II Marguerite Duras would succeed in becoming one of the most crucial literary figures in the world. And along with **Germaine Dulac** and **Maya Deren,** she would succeed in becoming one of the first women in the world to burst many filmic constraints. For director/writer Duras, it was always "the primacy of text and atmosphere over camera technique and wizardry."[2]

Although she was associated with postmodern writers like **Nathalie Sarraute** and Alain Robbe-Grillet who revolutionized the French novel, Duras only shared their rebellious natures when it came to "literary rules." Where these writers were functioning theoretically, Duras functioned viscerally. She is remembered for her heart, not her head; for her passion, not her rationale.

Anne Desbaresdes, in Duras's breakthrough novel, *Moderato cantabile* (1959), is the typical Duras heroine. Once described as a contemporary Madame Bovary, she is a "brooding, young emotional woman who, neglected by her husband and trapped in bourgeois routine, dreams of escape and a love 'strong as death.' "[3]

A renegade for the time in her own social attitudes as well as in her revolutionary literary concepts, Duras once said that marriage was "the best situation yet invented for killing love." The obstacle of human communication was one of her major obsessions. Her themes circled around "the pain of all involvements, and the futility of trying to assuage loneliness through love."[4] It is unclear whether Duras ever married, although she lived with two men—the writer Robert Antelme and the political philosopher and critic Dionys Moscolo. Moscolo fathered her only son, Jean.

Duras was born in 1914 in French Indochina. Gia Dinh, just north of Saigon, is her hometown. The pen name of "Duras" came from a central village in France where her family owned property. Duras lost her father, a mathematics professor, when she was only four. Her mother and the three small siblings (two older brothers and Maguerite) moved back to France.

> My mother was very distracted and she forgot to send me to school. For two years I ran wild; it was probably the time in my life I came closest to complete happiness. At eight I still couldn't read or write.[5]

Many great thinkers, such as Virginia Woolf, had similar periods in their childhood where they were free from the bonds of formalized education.

A woman who must have been quite a free thinker herself, Duras's mother moved the family back to Indochina after only a few years. She couldn't manage to make a living for her family in France and so used all of her savings to purchase a section of land, sight unseen, near the Thai border. Her idea was to become a rice farmer. However, as Duras says, "It was salt, and we were ruined."

But somehow, the family got by. Money was scraped together to send Duras to the prestigious Lycée de Saigon. In 1932 she graduated, entering the University of Paris to study mathematics, politics, and law.

Some sources say that Duras was active in the Resistance movement during World War II. A onetime member of the French Communist Party, she left it "over a question of culture."

> We were told one day we should burn Sartre's books. So I said, Vive la liberte, and left. I wasn't even an admirer of Sartre! But the intrusion of political commitment into literary creation is for me the beginning of a moral position which is incompatible with literature.[6]

Duras's first two novels in the midforties were failures both critically and popularly, but they would introduce Duras to her own major theme of "the interplay of love and destruction."[7]

She continued with a slew of novels in the next decade, all exploring the eternal return to the self. "It, the writer-being, recounts the story of my life. . . . It modifies what was lived yesterday because of what was lived today. It classifies, closes certain chapters, opens others, leaves them open, waiting for what will be lived tomorrow." How this happens, according to Duras, "escapes all analysis."[8]

As did several well-known novelists in the fifties in France like Robbe-Grillet, Duras turned to filmmaking. Perhaps it was, as Judith Gollub suggests, because some new crisis with the novel form drove them to it.[9] For Duras, the camera was another extension of text. When she branched out on her own as a director after writing the script for Renais's HIROSHIMA, MON AMOUR, she claimed she would never let anyone direct her words again, wanting to see her own images on the screen.

In directing an adaptation of her novel *Le camion* (The truck), in 1977, she took her theories as far as they could go,

> by eliminating "such middlemen" [her words] as the director and the actors in order to preserve "textual obscurity."[10]

Starring Gerard Depardieu, "LE CAMION [1977] records a script-reading session, in which Miss Duras herself reads to the prospective leading player (Depardieu) the scenario for a motion picture about a truck driver and a mysterious female hitch-hiker. When the film was first shown at the Cannes Film Festival in 1977, the audience shouted insults at the screen, but reviewers found it to be . . . haunting and 'perversely transfixing.' "[11]

But Duras was never as interested in the reactions to her work as in the mind-inducing act of the process itself. She would pave the way for other French minimalist women filmmakers like **Chantal Akerman**.

At the age of seventy in 1984, Duras would have her greatest popular success with her novel, *The Lover,* which sold over 700,000 copies in hardcover in France. In 1985 when the book was published in America, Diane Johnson in the *New York Times Book Review* called it, "a perfect novel . . . with a felicitous and masterly balance between formalism and powerful emotional effect."[12]

It has been written that "her prose is cinematic, her films, literary, and her plays nontheatrical from a traditional point of view."[13] When seen in 1968, she was "small-boned, pale, with the olive and brown coloring of a Courbet portrait."[14]

Even in her appearance in life, Duras implemented the minimalist effect, preferring the *real* theater happening inside.

MARGUERITE DURAS

1960	Hiroshima, Mon Amour
1966	La musica
1969	*Détruire dit-elle* (Destroy, she said)
1971	Abahn Sabana David
1972	Nathalie Granger
1977	Le Camion

Agnes Varda

When she was only thirty years old she was internationally dubbed "grandmother of the new wave."[1] She was heralded in the early seventies as the figurehead of the Women's Movement in France. Today, she is in her sixties, and still describes herself as a fringe filmmaker radically outside the system. "There's a difference between Hollywood films and mine," says **Agnes Varda.**

> Hollywood is doing them because they will make money. Mine will make money too, but that is not my motivation. My pleasure is to show women in their totality—their joys, problems, potentials. And above all, the unique rhythms by which they live their lives.[2]

To make money in the industry and to work simultaneously towards such an enobled goal is something of a revolutionary achievement in itself.

For thirty years, since the midfifties, Varda has been making films, and in all them she has been astutely conscientious about relating women's experiences.

> I am a feminist, I am a filmmaker, I am a woman. That doesn't make me a feminist-

woman-filmmaker. Filmmaking is specific work. I do it. I try to do it well. But it includes the fact that my opinions as a woman, as a feminist, sometimes show up, sometimes are explicit, sometimes are implicit . . . But filmmaking is filmmaking.
> Do you ask a man who doesn't have hair if he considers himself a bald filmmaker? He's a man with no hair, and he's a filmmaker.[3]

Considering the world from which Varda emanated, the contemporaneity of the views held by the women in her work are startling and even astonishing. When these visions are scrutinized next to films made by other women in her same time period—**Lina Wertmuller, Ida Lupino,** and a bit later, **Elaine May**—she can easily be acknowledged as a *social* pioneer, as well as a film pioneer. As Barbara Quart has noted:

> For us in the United States with a film industry that is all compromise and box office, a director like Varda who works out of a larger vision of what filmmaking is about, that she has lived out all these years, with all the difficulties involved, in itself represents a most important kind of survival and triumph.[4]

Although Varda has been accused in her career, most notably by feminists, of misrepresenting women's concerns, she has always been quite clear that the ideas of the women in her films are strictly her own. The film that brought her mass-market acclaim in the United States in 1977, ONE SINGS, THE OTHER DOESN'T, was attacked because the woman "who sings" sings about her passion for babies. But the film, she argued, was about inner contradictions: about women's desire for self-reliance and the strong pull for family and a stable relationship. Most importantly in Varda's defense, she has always contended that "feminism must encompass all women, even those who choose to stay in home and in the kitchen and do their changes from there. At home is where they are most important. We need all kinds of women in films, because there are all kinds of women."[5] She has been a passionate and longtime activist for transforming the stereotypes of women on the screen. Indeed, her most powerful and successful moments in film, DOCUMENTEUR (1981) and THE VAGABOND (1985), concern "women outside domestic safety trying to maintain themselves." The dark conclusion is often that "she who is 'sans toit,' without a roof . . . is out in a very cold world indeed."[6]

Maybe I'm not conventional myself. I don't like so much the games and the roles that we have to supposedly play in society . . . I've been trying to escape that all my life, for myself, for my surroundings, for the people I live with. I'm very touched by the people not on the track, like VAGABOND . . . because they try so much just to go their own way, not to go where everybody goes, and most of the time they are not able to continue, or they die, or people hate them, or they're homeless and people refuse them.[7]

Varda's nonconventional outlook began as early as her first short film made in 1954. With LA POINTE-COURTE, made when she was only twenty-five, Varda instituted revolutionary techniques that critics regarded as landmarks in motion-picture development. The technique in LA POINTE-COURTE, Varda says, was arrived at by instinct, her technical film knowledge being severely limited at that stage. Her idea was to counterpoint characters against their environments. As the surrealists would juxtapose unlikely characters and objects next to one another so that they would associate but not necessarily intermingle, so Varda's people existed side by side with their unlikely backgrounds. The viewers, she theorized, would be free to make their own conclusions and associative connections.

Varda relied on symbolism to establish the relationship between her characters and objects: wood symbolizes the hero, and iron, the heroine. When their isolation from each other is at its height, objects are of first importance; those give way to their human counterparts as the relationship between hero and heroine becomes more personal.[8]

The experimental idea was not only successful filmically, it was also widely praised as revolutionary. What she learned was that the filmmaker must have as much associative freedom with the medium as the novelist. In this way, she came upon one of the leading theories of the French New Wave. Artists who would follow, such as Alain Renais, would acknowledge their debt to Varda. Renaise used her techniques in his master film, HIROSHIMA, MON AMOUR (1960), written by **Marguerite Duras.**

Not only, Renais said, did LA POINTE-COURTE technically and conceptually anticipate all the elements of the French "New Wave," but her unconventional methods of production were unheralded for the period. Varda made the film on only eighteen-thousand-dollars. She only had about one-quarter of that when she began, and so formed a cooperative with actors, technicians, and lab workers. In this way she established a nonpatriarchal, nonhierarchical way of working.

One of five children, Agnes Varda was born in Belgium in 1928 to a Greek engineer father and a French mother. At the end of World War II she took herself to Paris to study the classics at the Sorbonne. During a four-year course at the Ecole du Louvre, her passion turned to painting and sculpture, and she studied to become a museum curator.

> Suddenly I thought I would be spending my life in a little town filing things. Maybe there would be four or ten good paintings. The rest are in Leningrad and New York ... so I changed my mind and became a still photographer.[9]

She also took night courses at this time in photography. By 1951, when Jean Vilar founded the famous Theatre National Populaire, he appointed Varda the official photographer. It was a post she would hold for ten years.

In 1954, having seen only about five films in her life, including Disney's SNOW WHITE AND THE SEVEN DWARFS (1937), Agnes Varda sat down, "with a head full of movie images from a camera viewpoint," and made LA POINT-COURTE. In spite of its wide critical praise, Varda would have to wait seven years before she could find a producer to finance her next project.

Miraculously, one Georges de Beauregarde, a businessman who backed Jean-Luc Godard on BREATHLESS (1959), was looking around to finance other unknowns. Goddard suggested Jacques Demys, who in turn suggested his wife-to-be, Agnes Varda. The result was Varda's first feature that brought her wide international acclaim, CLEO FROM 5 TO 7 (1961). The film, "very much gender defined,"[10] is a study in the superficialities that made up the shallowness of women's lives to that point. The film traces two hours in the life of Cleo, a pop singer, as she awaits a confirmation of a cancer diagnosis. The pretty blond heroine submerged in a barrage of female concerns, makeup, mirrors, and facial masks that perpetuate the notion of woman as superficial creature, arrives at her own emancipation in the face of death. "Cleo's discontent, her growing dissatisfaction with the pretty facade as a major value, her acute awareness of mortality making everything else shallow and silly—is clearly at the center of the film.[11] Clearly too, for 1961, this kind of conscious focus and attention on a woman's locked-in predicament was extraordinary.

"Do you know any intelligent woman?" Varda countered when she was told that her viewpoint was different.

> Intelligent women exist, don't they? Why aren't they ever in films? There are always stories about virile male friendships, Brando and Nicholson, Newman and Redford, and so on, but not about friendship between women. The women are always motherly or tarty.[12]

In her own life with director Jacques Demys, Varda has lived as unconventionally as her characters. She maintains a separate residence from him and her two children when she is working.

> I'm a woman of tomorrow. I have children out of wedlock, advanced ideas, I work hard, all that, but I make my own clothes. . . .
> I like to sew a little, cook a little, garden a little, look after the baby a little, but just a little. It's got to be carefully rationed, not an institution. That's the trap for women. You say, I like to cook, I like children, and you're stuck with it and nothing else.[13]

For those who doubt that women directors have no eye for developing male characters, Varda's "advanced ideas" would unseat us once again with LE BONHEUR (1965). An ambiguous and transitional film for Varda, who was trying to test out her own beliefs, with little "sisterhood" support available at the time to help her, the film was nevertheless told entirely from a male point of view. Here, Varda continued as in CLEO her gaze of woman as sufferer and martyr. The film was denounced as reactionary for "celebrating bourgeois myths of women."[14]

Much was made in the film of "female deference to the guru male," and it was criticized for the blithe picture of happiness under the old patriarchal family structure that it painted. This might give one pause were it not for the filmmaker we are dealing with. The body of her work, the plethora of feminist statements in her interviews over the decades, points to valid reasons for suspicion. Would Agnes Varda be saying that life under the old domestic trappings was fine for women? As Barbara Quart points out a study of a scene from the film:

On a TV screen a patriarch-philosopher under a tree is exaggeratedly served by a pretty young thing who runs to bring him a drink and tell him how much she loves to hear him talk. He complies with a pronouncement that happiness may consist in submitting to the laws of nature, a statement that might be taken as the philosophic text of the film (and was by several critics of the time), were not the tone of the sequence so bristling with sardonic mockery.[15]

In all of her work, Varda has been more driven to ask questions than to answer them. She is fascinated by the relationships and the contradictions in people, and although her films are not autobiographical, they nonetheless embrace all her own contradictions as a filmmaker. Ten years later Varda said about the film:

It is true that I can now see my own films with a new vision because of things which have happened . . . because I did a kind of self-education on feminism . . . Things are clear now. But they weren't so clear ten years ago when I made LE BONHEUR.[16]

ONE SINGS, THE OTHER DOESN'T (1977) was perhaps Varda's most didactic film to date, in an era that needed the statement and welcomed its brashness. The movie, about two friends who must travel their separate ways and shape their own destinies, spoke from the Varda who believes the artist and the woman must fight to speak from her own voice, whatever the cost.

Varda is more successful in her films when she probes deeper—deeper into the darkness and pain of life that doesn't always have redeeming answers, as in the unforgettable, powerful, and sad VAGABOND (1985).

No matter how bleak, Varda has always dedicated her task to showing the concrete everydayness of life around her. Once she made a short film called, RUE DAGUERROTYPE about the block she lived on. There was one house on the block that was mauve with polka dots. Someone complained that "it wasn't a balanced picture of Paris." She replied, "Of course not, it isn't even the whole district or the whole street, but it is really how people talk to each other on my block."[17]

For Agnes Varda, the central impulse in her work is finding the truth and telling the truth—the truth about women's "inner contradictions," as she sees them. This small, husky-voiced woman, a bundle of voluble energy, with a **Louise Brooks** mass of hair sitting darkly on her head, has always known where she was headed without a moment's doubt of being able to arrive there. This at a time when no woman thought directing was a viable life option. Varda cinema is, at its base, transformational cinema. Like **von Trotta** and **Mészáros,** her contribution to the changed image of women on the screen is unmistakable, even if we don't always understand her reasoning.

I'm using my own sense of contradictions in no way to resolve them as a spring for my films. Most of my films have that contradiction. A live thing. It is *there*. The contradiction is there. You can feel it. One night of passion and maybe in some years you'll be dead. Oh, how nice to be romantic! How nice to be in love! How could you not understand the heavy contradiction?[18]

AGNES VARDA (Selected List)

1954	La Pointe-Courte
1957	O Saisons O Chateaux
1958	Du Côte de la Côte
	Opera Mouffle
1959	Cocotte d'Azur, La

1961	Cleo from 5 to 7
	Les Fiancés du Pont MacDonald
1963	Salut Les Cubains!
1965	La Bonheur
1966	Les Créatures
	Elsa
1967	Le Bonheur
	Oncle Janco
1969	Black Panthers
	Lion's Love
1977	One Sings, the Other Doesn't
1981	Documenteur
1982	Ulysses
1985	Vagabond, The
1989	Kung Fu Master!

Margarethe von Trotta

The way **Margarethe von Trotta** emerges from an elevator into an unknown space could be a metaphor for the way she shows herself in her films: immediate, unwavering eye contact, at once trusting and undefended. Here is an artist who embraces the moment at once, who fearlessly embraces change head-on without flinching. Here is a poet who trusts that the process of her own seeing must unfold in its own time, and feels safe in that unknowing.

In 1977 she burst onto the scene almost full-blown, like Athena, with THE SECOND AWAKENING OF CHRISTA KALGES, becoming the world's leading feminist filmmaker, a title she is still proud to claim. Yet it would be a mistake to limit her films by labeling them "feminist." The breadth of her characters and situations stretch far beyond the reaches of what any ideology could hold. She sympathizes with her male creations as deeply as her female. Her characters often behave in ways von Trotta herself admits she would never behave (the way Christa Klages resorts to violence as an alternative, something that von Trotta doesn't agree with). If she has any commitment to a "program" it is to develop her characters as far

as she can until they take charge of their own lives to go beyond her.

Von Trotta began as an actress for R. W. Fassbinder, and for her husband, director Volker Schlondorff (THE TIN DRUM [1979], THE HANDMAID'S TALE [1990]), but turned her attention to writing with Schlondorff in 1970. She says that although she wasn't always aware of when she began, acting was never her main goal but a backdoor entrance to directing. She never thought of being a director early on since before the New German Cinema women directors simply did not exist in Germany—not, that is, since **Leni Riefensthal**. She finally realized her latent dream to direct as a husband-wife collaboration with Schlondorff on THE LOST HONOR OF KATHARINA BLUM (1975).

But during that period in the mid-sixties before the New German Cinema, von Trotta found herself submerged and mesmerized for whole afternoons in Paris art-film houses, captivated by the films of Ingmar Bergman. She watched them over and over, she says, not so much in idolatry but in the realization she had found a soul mate. "People always ask me, Who is your idol? I never get what they mean. The first time I saw the films of Bergman I felt this unspoken connection. What he was showing up on the screen was something I had been thinking about already for years. Perhaps my whole life. I think you can only be influenced by those you already have an inner feeling for."

By 1978, despite her national reputation in Germany as an actress and not to mention her codirecting venture with Schlondorff in 1975, no one would bankroll von Trotta for her first directorial job. Unknown to her at the time, Schlondorff made a deal with German TV, guaranteeing the film if his wife's efforts failed.

> He knew I would have been furious and not accepted. So he didn't tell me about it until after I finished the film. Women still weren't allowed to direct.

1979 saw SISTERS, OR THE BALANCE OF HAPPINESS, which began a trilogy of films on the theme sister relationships. The follow-up was MARIANNE AND JULIANNE (1982), winner of the Grand Prix at the Venice Film Festival. The third in the series was also her first major attractor of an American audience, SHEER MADNESS in 1985. ROSA LUXEMBURG (1987), her ambitious and moving drama, is a film of epic proportions. As Barbara Quart aptly puts it, "It is moving simply to have an epic film built around a woman, an intellectual political heroine defined by intelligence, strength, courage, highly respected even to adulation."[1] And as Quart notes, von Trotta accomplishes this without a breath of sentimentality. As we will see, her contribution to unraveling the question of an endemically female gaze is unprecedented, undeniable, and direct. Says Quart,

> Her work is of special interest because it is a woman-centered and woman-affirming cinema of a kind still a rarity—women looked at with intensity and love by the woman behind the camera, by one another

on the screen, and by women like oneself in the audience, to whose eyes the whole is directed; and because of the visual and dramatic bounty of metaphors and ideas with which von Trotta turns this into art. Von Trotta is engaged in the immense task of creating a major women's/feminist cinema where so little that is helpful existed before by way of a model.[2]

Our debt to von Trotta's contribution is enormous. "I was born in a matriarchy," she has said. "My mother wasn't married when I was born, so I have my mother's last name and not my father's—the German painter, Alfred Roloff. I believe in the antihierarchy of matriarchies. In them, men and women are equal. Mother love is not conditional. It was in the patriarchy that the idea of the favorite son was introduced. He must earn his father's love through obedience and merit. That is the cornerstone of patriarchal thinking."[3]

Von Trotta's mother, a staunchly independent woman who refused to marry because she feared entrapment, was the first, and remains the primary model, that spurs on von Trotta's own powerful single-mindedness. Although she is currently married to Volker Schlondorff, the two of them often live in different countries as per the demands of their careers. She has a twenty-five-year-old son from a previous marriage whom she refuses to discuss.

> My mother always said that when a woman marries she is suppressed. I believed her. In my family there was no hierarchy of father first, *then* mother. There was only mother. She gave me great liberty of thinking.[4]

When confronted with von Trotta's body of work, we are aware at once of what a female gaze might mean, in a way that is unavailable to us in work done in the United States.[5]

As Barbara Quart points out, the numbers of self-identified feminist film directors in Germany at this juncture is unprecedented anywhere else in the world. The atmosphere of creative permissiveness for women filmmakers allows those who have broken through the male barriers—**von Trotta, Helka Sander, Helma Sanders-Brahms, Dorris Dorrie**[6]—to raise money with little resistance and, more importantly, to speak out of their own experiences as women.

I had the privilege of meeting Margarethe von Trotta in 1988 when she was in New York upon the completion of her film, LOVE AND FEAR, an updated version of Chekhov's *The Three Sisters* set in contemporary Italy. The subject of "sisters" comes close to an obsession for von Trotta. "Every artist has one theme," she says, "and all of her writings and makings are variations on that one note of internal conflict."

As an only child raised without the presence of her father, von Trotta first began to explore her deep longing for a sibling in SISTERS, OR THE BALANCE OF HAPPINESS. In an interview on German television after the film's release, she spoke about her mother, pointing out that she was unmarried at the time von Trotta was born. A woman wrote to her after the program with factual details about her mother that no stranger could possibly be familiar with. "Please," wrote von Trotta, "if you knew my mother, please tell me everything." The woman wrote back and revealed that she was really Margarethe's sister. It seems that the woman, Anna Radon, was given up at birth for adoption because von Trotta's mother was at that time too poor to care for her—too poor *and* too guilt-ridden.

"My mother had been an aristocrat. She could not admit pregnancy, much less poverty. What a shock! All my life, we were so close. I told my mother everything. Suddenly I realized that I never knew her. You can spend your whole life thinking you know someone, and yet you don't really. When I was a baby I was always saying to her, 'I wish I had a sister.' She never said anything. She must have felt so guilty, thinking about her first child. When I met

my sister she was like my mother's ghost. They looked exactly alike."

More amazing still was the fact that the names of the characters in von Trotta's film were—quite coincidentally—*also* the names of herself and her real-life sibling. Von Trotta felt urged, she said, to change the names during the filming, thinking they were too archaic and biblical—but something deeper compelled her not to.

To write about what is most sacred and close to one's heart is perhaps every artist's ultimate desire. And, because of its proximity to the self, it is also perhaps the ultimate taboo. As dramatic as the experience was, von Trotta says she has never been able to translate her life directly into art.

And yet, there are themes she handles of grave, personal importance that she may only obliquely acknowledge. Socialized child care, a theme in her first film, CHRISTA KLAGES, may be a reflection of deep yearning about her own impoverished youth, when her unmarried mother went off to work in an office, leaving her to beg in the streets.

No American woman filmmaker can rank on a par with Margarethe von Trotta's impressive body of filmmaking. Even at a juncture in her life when she has rung up success after success, and the producers are assured of making back their money, she is still faulted by German critics for having too narrow a scope. About the incomparable SHEER MADNESS one said, "Perhaps it is a woman's film. But it is not really a film." Yet the comments hardly faze her. She has struggled hard for the right to direct her own films, to decide what those films will talk about.

"It's not a program I have, I don't say, '*I do feminist films*!' It just comes from life. I don't go around with a banner or a weapon. I write my own scripts, so what comes up is my life's experience.

"And we are still so few women filmmakers in the world. If I have the opportunity to speak in films, why not speak about women's lives? There is so much to say about women. The real lives of women have been so taboo in cinema. I do feel that it's a task for me—even a duty."

From her first solo directing venture, through her epic ROSA LUXEMBURG, her female protagonists are constantly pulled by a main conflicted question: If you need to effect transformation in your life, a change that goes against the social order, how far should you go? When, if ever, should you resort to violence? Although von Trotta is a pacifist, she is committed to remaining an active and keen observer to see what her characters will choose for themselves. It's one of the ways she has learned to confront her own dualities.

She suggested to me that with the character of Rosa Luxemburg, she found her most unified self to date. For even though Luxemburg carries through her ideas for revolution, she is against the use of force. Her final conflict is also her ultimate revelation: true revolution cannot be achieved without bloodshed. "Every worm that's crushed underfoot on the road to revolution is a crime," says Rosa. Perhaps like von Trotta herself, Luxemburg is a woman caught between wanting to change the world and wishing to tend geese in the garden.

Yet von Trotta retains a great resolve to try and work out her conflicts and not just passively sit by. She knows how hard she herself had to work to raise her own consciousness. So many people in her life said, "You're in the perfect setup, you've got it made. You do the acting, and Volker does the directing. It's perfect." But it wasn't perfect. Von Trotta needed to struggle to realize a deeper self and she was completely alone in that struggle. She sees how hard all of us must work to do away with words like *postfeminism*—a term she finds dangerous in its absurd assumption that women's fight for their rights is somehow over.

Her active commitment to help raise the consciousness of younger generations is one way she has found to escape feelings of isolation and despair during what she believes is a conservative and reactionary time for women.

"It makes it seem like the whole women's movement was only a trend. Modes, after all, pass away like crazy ideas—you put on red clothes one year and brown the next. I see a lot of women ashamed to have called themselves feminists or call themselves that now because it's 'demondé'—not fashionable.

"Look at the younger women, **Dorris Dorrie** for instance, who had so much success with MEN. Now she gives interviews saying, 'Oh! There is no problem being a woman director. Men are on their knees to give money to women!' She doesn't see that she's able to do her films now because of what our generation fought for. By saying things like this in public, she undermines the generation of women who made success possible for her."

Von Trotta's last words to me on parting were, "Don't be afraid, eh?" It seemed out of context to anything we had been discussing. Still, it didn't strike me as odd. Her natural place of resting is in a space of deep, compassionate concern for anyone who crosses her path. In saying this to me, she was speaking to a younger self.

The upward lilt of her German accent made this comment sound almost like a question. The way she has of speaking is more than the mere inflection of a different language, it is a different way of seeing things altogether. It is Margarethe von Trotta's unique way of always soliciting something new that might enter her world and change her forever.

Virginia Woolf once wrote, "Life, what is it? Something you can ruffle with your breath." It is a view that sings throughout all von Trotta's work. Her films shy away from tight narrative structures, not because she is unable to tackle them (witness the tightly structured ROSA LUXEMBURG), but because they are too definite, and therefore, in her view, not quite truthful in their reflections of life.

It's a courageous vision in a world that sacrifices art in the name of three-picture deals. But what others view as courageous, von Trotta views much more simply as doing what she needs to do.

"So many women come up to me after seeing my films and say that I changed their lives. It's a fantastic thing if you have a voice and you can speak for others. My films are not only my voice, but the voice of those who don't have the possibility to speak. I take their voice and I make it mine."

MARGARETHE VON TROTTA

1975   Lost Honor of Katharina Blum, The
1977   Second Awakening of Christa Klages, The
1979   Sisters, or the Balance of Happiness
1982   Marianne and Julianne
1985   Sheer Madness
1987   Rosa Luxemburg

Gillian Armstrong

"I don't like being asked if I'm a feminist," said **Gillian Armstrong** in 1980, "but I hate women who are asked and say, No." This imaginative Australian director, who became the first woman in her country to direct a movie in forty years with MY BRILLIANT CAREER (1980), does not believe filmmaking is about making speeches.[1] And yet, her first full-length film, made when Armstrong was only twenty-eight, ends with a very definite and uncompromising final statement that a woman should have the option *not* to choose marriage.

> I wasn't saying that if Sybylla had married she could not have written that book. I was saying that in that time, that place, and with that man, it would have been difficult. I think women still have that problem today. . . . I see very sophisticated couples in which the woman has achieved some success and is still expected to perform traditional wifely chores and to support the man's creative pursuits, but he doesn't encourage her.[2]

The tremendous, worldwide attention garnered from this first effort made Armstrong the darling of the film world overnight. Hollywood came beckoning. And

initially, this rebellious spirit who once claimed *she* would never marry ("I don't believe in marriage. I suppose that's my one tiny rebellion in life")[3] turned down offers to direct the likes of **Glenda Jackson** in order to stay true to the independent spirit of filmmaking in Australia.[4] But just as she changed her mind about marriage when she married film editor John Pffefer and had his child in 1985, she also softened on the concept of American moviemaking. From an office on the MGM lot while directing MRS. SOFFEL (1985), with **Diane Keaton** and Mel Gibson, Armstrong declared that she was quite unprepared for the bureaucracy of Hollywood. Scott Rudin, producer of MRS. SOFFEL, spoke about this pioneer who was one of the few foreign women ever to direct a big-budget American feature:

> Gillian is very spirited. She felt if she didn't get her own way she could always go back to Australia and sleep in her own bed. It gave her a forthright, strong approach compared to an American director who needs the gig. She wasn't afraid to get bounced.[5]

STARSTRUCK (1983), described as the first Australian musical comedy, preceded MRS.

SOFFEL as Armstrong's second feature and had a two-million-dollar budget. Hollywood had enough confidence in the filmmaker to raise her next budget to thirteen million.

The mixed reviews and the loss of her naïveté about American studio politics sent Armstrong back to her homeland to make HIGH TIDE (1988). The film, which stars **Judy Davis,** of MY BRILLIANT CAREER, examines a woman of the "thirty something" generation as she becomes reacquainted with a daughter given up at birth. Armstrong explores the pain of denial and the difficult struggle to commit oneself to one's own life, making this perhaps her most risky and highly imaginative effort to date. HIGH TIDE, which takes place in Australia, continues Armstrong's deep commitment to create an endemically Australian cinema.

> A lot of Australian filmmakers . . . feel as I do that Australians ought to be offered a picture of their own heritage. You have to realize that the Australian film industry collapsed between the silent era and 1970. We were raised almost exclusively on American films. We know, from films, more about cowboys and Indians than about early Australia.[6]

Gillian considers her experience with discrimination in the industry to be minimal, and attributes her filmmaking success at a very early age to determination, talent, and, most of all, luck. She started in art school at the age of eighteen, and, like fellow Australian filmmaker Peter Weir, became interested in film at exactly the same time the government became interested in resurrecting a dying, if not already dead, film industry.

In her own country, Armstrong was attracting attention as a first-rate filmmaker long before the onset of her first feature. In 1971 she graduated from the Swinburne Institute of Advanced Education in Melbourne with a degree in film production. During her three-year tenure there, she turned out three shorts. After a brief waitressing stint, she moved to Sydney where she found work as a film editor. In Australia, as in most places in the world, Armstrong confirms that, "As a rule, there's very little discrimination for women in editing."[7]

By 1973 she was selected to enroll in a prestigious one-year director's training course in a newly established Film and Television School in Sydney. Again, Armstrong determinedly turned out three shorts. The first, 100 A DAY, garnered several prizes, among them the Australian Film Institute's Bronze Certificate for fiction. Her third film, GRETEL, became Australia's official entry into the International Festival of Short Films at Grenoble, France, in 1974. This was also the year that Armstrong worked as an art director on other people's projects, then as assistant director on **Margaret Fink**'s THE REMOVALISTS. Fink approached Armstrong to read Miles Franklin's book, *My Brilliant Career*. Armstrong said,

> She wanted my ideas and suggestions . . . She bought the book in 1965. . . . At the time, I'd only directed a few shorts, and *My Brilliant Career* seemed too expensive and important for me to handle.[8]

In 1975 Armstrong felt accomplished enough to try her hand at making a one-hour dramatic film, THE SINGER AND THE DANCER (1976), based on her own screenplay of Australian author Alan Marshall's book. It won an award for best dramatic short at the Sydney Film Festival, and was subsequently taken up by Columbia Pictures for commercial release.

> The years went by, and I became more sure of myself. When Margaret [Fink] came back . . . and asked whether I'd like to direct [MY BRILLIANT CAREER] I said I'd try. I started working with the writer on the script and soon got so involved I knew I had to direct it, no one else could.[9]

A standing ovation at Cannes for the film reinforced whatever doubts may have lingered. She is loath to label herself a "woman's director," and feels adamantly that her films must have strong women characters. "Sybylla [from MY BRILLIANT CAREER]," she said, "is certainly a strong character. She is sensitive, passionate, and rebellious. She knows she wants to do something with her life."[10] This description of her first widescreen heroine could be a prototype of another young rebellious woman, envisioning a great, nonconventional life for herself. It could be Gillian Armstrong.

GILLIAN ARMSTRONG

1976   Singer and the Dancer, The
1980   My Brilliant Career
1983   Starstruck
1985   Mrs. Soffel
1988   High Tide

Patricia Rozema

In 1987 **Patricia Rozema,** a brave young Canadian director took Woody Allen, stood him on his head, gave him a sex change, and transformed him from a larger-than-life buffoon who loses no matter which way he turns to a real-life underdog able to stand up for herself and in the end take control of her destiny. I'VE HEARD THE MERMAIDS SINGING (1987) is one woman's rebellious answer to a real woman's life on the screen.

> I wanted to take seriously someone you wouldn't talk to at a dinner party, to show respect for the internal universe of people. Polly represents any underdog, any individual or minority or country that has ever felt really secondary to those who are the movers and shakers. Everyone knows Polly; her emotions are a magnification of emotions all of us have felt; and Polly is very much me.[1]

Well, yes and no. For one, no one less than an ace mover and shaker could have gone from rough script to locked picture in eighteen months on a laughable $250,000 budget, and then boast a standing ovation at Cannes for her first effort. One can appreciate Rozema's sentiments in a kind of metaphoric way, but the awkward, bumbling, naive Polly, who daydreams away her life in black and white with fantasies of soaring above drab slabs of concrete to a fate of mystical beauty, can hardly have much in common with the woman who dared to bring her concretely and charmingly to life.

Rozema is one of the few woman feature directors to obtain recognition outside her Canadian borders; in lesser degrees are the talented three other Canadian directors known: **Sandy Wilson** with MY AMERICAN COUSIN (1985), **Anne Wheeler** with LOYALTIES (1986), and **Lea Pool** with ANNE TRISTER (date not available). Rozema was raised by strict Dutch immigrants in what she describes as a very religious environment. Perhaps it was significant that the first movie she saw at age sixteen was THE EXORCIST (1973). She attended college in America at Calvin College in Grand Rapids, Michigan, where she studied philosophy. "I'm frightened," she says, "by how hungry people are for gods, for leaders, for someone else to tell them how to be and how to dress and who to fight."[2]

This is the underlying theme of Rozema's first feature. Polly, a kind of lovable, goony amateur photographer in her twenties, who neither knows she's lovable or goony, and doesn't think of her hobby as "photography" but merely "taking pictures," gets a job as a receptionist in an art gallery, and takes as her goddess the curator for whom she works. Although Polly doesn't know it, she is at the place in her life where every artist wants to be. She "takes pictures" purely for the pleasure it brings her and pays no attention to the seductions of the outside world. In fact, until she gets her job at the chic gallery, she is naively unaware of the art world and its glimmering pretensions.

The curator, Gabrielle St. Pere (or in translation, Holy Father,[3]) is worldly, sophisticated, wealthy, and inhabits a part of the universe akin to Mount Olympus in Polly's view. As we are watching Polly objectively, and quite removed from her, so Polly watches the curator on a TV monitor that maintains a piercing gaze on the valuables in the inner gallery. One of the valuables is a secret the curator keeps—her love for a woman artist named Mary Joseph. The religious nom de plumes are no accident.

As the story unwinds, Polly moves from the stance of spectator to participant in the spotlight. One night the curator opens her heart to Polly and Polly is in ecstasy. Gabrielle reveals that she has done a piece of art that was rejected by a class of housewives as amateurish. She wishes, she says, that she had the talent to create. Polly finds the piece in question in the curator's house, and without the curator's knowledge, sends it to a local critic. He dubs it the work of a master talent, and the curator is an instant sensation. Needless to say, Gabrielle's arrogance soars beyond nausea, and Polly's contribution is quickly forgotten.

It occurs to Polly during this time that perhaps the curator would like her photographs. She wants to offer them up to her like a sacrifice, but is too shy to let her know they are her own creations. She decides instead to forward the photos to the curator anonymously as a gift. Gabrielle takes a quick glance at the pictures and throws them in the trash. Convinced she is worthless, Polly goes home and burns every last one of what in fact are extraordinary pieces,

all as unique as Polly herself. And, of course, this is precisely Rozema's point.

Very soon after, it is discovered that Gabrielle has lied. The art work that has caused a public sensation was not done by her at all, but by her closet lover, Mary Joseph. In Polly's eyes the curator quickly descends from her Olympian heights to the dregs of where mere mortals reside. No longer a spectator of life, Polly learns about self-empowerment, self-worth, about the only goddess entitled to the gift of her awe-filled worship, Polly herself.

Perhaps the bravest thing about this movie, is the way the lesbian theme is so blithely understated, as though it were simply one of the facts of the universe.

Patricia Rozema has been described as a cross between **Jane Fonda** and Ricky Schroder. Says Ron Graham who interviewed her in 1987, "[She] appears to be an incarnation of a *New York Review of Books* ad: Toronto; pretty, blond, intelligent, articulate, funny, free-minded, likes Woody Allen, Shakespeare, Fellini, Bergman, Laurie Anderson, Peter Gabriel, Dorothy Parker, Joyce Carol Oates."[4] As Rozema puts it:

> My theory of esthetics is that good art is what you like. I'm an artistic relativist, an anarchist that way.[5]

Anarchist or not, Rozema paid her dues through the ranks: first as an associate producer for a CBS public affairs show, and then as third or second director on a number of features including THE FLY (1986). She also wrote and produced her own half-hour film in 1985 during a five-week night course that gave her access to equipment. The piece, PASSION: A LETTER IN 16MM, won a number of awards and enabled her to raise the money for her first feature.

A report from the Canadian directors' guild shows that of 1,463 directors in 1987, 447 were women—a far higher percentage than we are dealing with in the United States.

But, as in America, only a handful of these women are actually working. "When film is considered an art form," says Rozema,

it's OK for women to be involved. When it's merely business, then you find a predominance of men. I never had trouble as a female—maintaining control on the set, or whatever—with a mostly male crew. My way is to never doubt that I have it.[6]

Rozema's view is that it's an asset to be a woman in this business because "anything that sets you apart from the herd helps."[7]

As for her model in doing a project as ambitious as a feature, Rozema took Polly who "has a simple relationship to her art."

It's not about angles or dollies, but emotions—and characters like Polly. I'm so proud of Polly. If I die tomorrow, at least I gave the world Polly![8]

This kind of ebullience is noticeably absent in filmmakers with strings attached to Hollywood. A personal relationship to their characters becomes lost to them when so many other hands have tampered with their creation.

The world of the female gaze is in this case one in which men are virtually nonexistent. We see life entirely through a woman's eyes, a woman who—among the few times in cinema—we might actually meet on the street. We are beginning to see real-life women characters vs. cultural fantasies more and more often in the works of foreign directors like **Margarethe von Trotta, Agnes Varda, Márta Mészáros.**

The endemic values of I'VE HEARD THE MERMAIDS SINGING are ones in which emotional integrity gets top billing. And, perhaps most importantly, it is a woman's coming-of-age story. Even proven women directors like **Lee Grant** with STAYING TOGETHER (1990) and **Penny Marshall** with BIG (1988) were offered male rites-of-passage stories for their subsequent works. With such a preponderance of boys-growing-up tales Rozema's contribution here cannot be overstated.

PATRICIA ROZEMA

1987   I've Heard the Mermaids Singing

Chantal Akerman

The enfant terrible of cinema—**Chantal Akerman**—made herself famous in feminist circles with JEANNE DIELMAN in 1975. This breakthrough piece of cinema is constructed around the chores traditionally assigned to women, played in real time vs. the "compressed" time capable in film. Imagine the frustrations, the anxieties, the desires that would arise as a viewer, if you watched a woman scrubbing a tub until it was spotless in the actual *time* it normally takes to do this!

Yet the film did everything that feminists had dreamed a woman's cinema would do. "To create a distinctly feminine film aes-

thetic, a political *and* pleasurable counter-cinema that would not reproduce the dominant male cinema's objectification of women."[1]

Of course this is Akerman's point and her overriding interest as a filmmaker: to elicit the angers, desires, and expectations inevitably aroused in her movies. It is the same construct Antonin Artaud was working with in the theater. Akerman's cinema is participatory cinema. Don't come to see her movies unless you are ready to experience your own humanness completely. Your boredom. Your expectations. Your embarrassments as you watch a love scene between two women that goes on and on past your comfort zone and beyond.

Here is a cinema that demands something of you, a cinema that asks you to become completely involved. Linda Williams, a writer for the *Chicago Reader,* recounts seeing JEANNE DIELMAN with a Parisian audience soon after it opened:

> The screening . . . became a shouting match between angry men, who eventually walked out, and fascinated women, who mostly yelled at the men to shut up. For the men the film's slow, detailed three and a half hour account of three days in the life of a Belgium housewife performing the precise, repetitive tasks of cooking, sewing, cleaning . . . was more than they could endure. . . . The drama . . . was for them a tempest in a teapot. For the same reasons the women in the audience were enthralled. Our eyes were opened wide to the time and space of a woman's material existence.[2]

If Belgium filmmaker Chantal Akerman is anything, she is what B. Ruby Rich has dubbed "a filmmaker's filmmaker." For, "Never before was the materiality of woman's time rendered so viscerally."[3]

> Akerman's work can be suggested through its themes. The excercise and repression of sexuality. Systems of desire. The nature of voyeurism. Explosions of repression. Hunger and appetite. Woman's isolation. Woman's exclusion from language. Housework. Mother-daughter bonds. Mother-son ties. The relation of woman to woman, and of woman to man. Travel.
>
> Outlining themes, however, even in such an epigrammatic fashion, is misleading. Akerman's films aren't really "about" any subject so much as they're about cinema itself.[4]

In not compromising her aesthetic fascinations, Chantal Akerman is not only a pioneering avant-gardist, but she is the first avant-gardist to move into big-budget production, and to continue her experimental considerations in the arena of features.

An exile from Belgium, where her Polish Jewish, concentration-camp survivor parents settled after the war, Akerman flew to the United States at the age of twenty-one. She was as yet unaware of the names Jonas Mekas, Stan Brakhage, Michael Snow— avant-garde filmmakers who were experimenting with the time, space, light continuum that would so occupy her imagination.

She had quit four months of film school in Belgium to come to the United States. She had come without a degree, without experience, and without anyone telling her that without these things a woman—especially a woman!—could not become a filmmaker. All she knew was that since she saw Jean-Luc Godard's PIERROT LE FOU (1965) at the age of fifteen, she knew what she would be doing with her life.

She acquired for herself the first job she could get in New York, a cashier for a porno movie house on 55th Street. Within the first few weeks, she told *Artforum Magazine,* she stole four thousand dollars and made LA CHAMBRE (1972) and HOTEL MONTEREY (1972).

Both these films are without conventional narratives. They explore Akerman's fascination with space, hotels, the transients they attract. Hotel guests move in and out of the frame of a stationary camera.

> This same sense of place, already there in the building, interior or space photographed but extracted and transformed into self-awareness by Akerman's framing, continues in JEANNE DIELMAN. You almost feel that her cinematic space, narrativeless in HOTEL MONTEREY, has gradually been peopled with characters, and also very gradually been given the outlines of a story. But the visual, the background, still remains an element that can at any moment take on independent life.[5]

In a review of JEANNE DIELMAN, J. Hoberman writes:

I feel like one of Kafka's messengers. The film is hardly an unknown master-piece. . . . Clearly it's a great film, a brilliant collaboration between director-writer Ak-erman, cinematographer **Babette Man-golte,** and actress **Delphine Seyrig.** . . .

Akerman, [was] only twenty-five when the film was made. . . . Her use of duration, repetition, and lights, invests the three and a half hour film with a monumentality that's as suggestive of filmmakers like Mi-chael Snow . . . as it is of . . . **Marguerite Duras.**[6]

"It's so weird," said Akerman, "to ex-press yourself without any rules. There is a convention, but you can say more about reality in an unrealistic way. I always liked that. It gives me pleasure. It's about pleasure and freedom."[7]

In JE . . . TU . . . IL . . . ELLE (1974), the camera opens on a naked woman (Aker-man) frantically eating sugar, and writing a letter (we don't know to whom). She then gets up and goes out. Next we see her hitch-hiking and accepting a ride from a truck driver. She gives him a hand job, but it is done off-camera. Finally, she arrives at her destination: her woman lover's house. The person she was writing the letter to? We are not informed. They make love. However, this is not what you would expect. . . . But then again, this is Akerman. Writer Lynne Tillman pointed out,

The love scene is compelling not just be-cause it explicitly shows a sexual encounter, but also because of Akerman's decision to keep the camera at a distance, from which it steadily records the lovers. The scene lasts so long that the pleasure of looking turns into unsatisfying and self-conscious voy-eurism. From the first image of glut-tony . . . Akerman brings us full circle by presenting a menu of appetites for sex, food, and life itself.[8]

Of course, the length of the overbearing love scene is a conscious choice for the film-maker. She has recently completed her first film in English, HISTOIRES D'AMERIQUE (1989). Akerman says about the film, "I have to say that my mother was in Ausch-witz and she didn't say one word about it. This is important to the making of the film . . . it fills a gap, a kind of hole. It's about something unconscious."[9]

There is a scene from JE . . . TU . . . IL . . . ELLE in which mother and daughter are snuggled up together in bed. Daughter is telling mother about an affair she is having with a woman whom the viewer never sees. Akerman's major mythological rewriting has these two women understanding one another through the gulf of generations, through different worlds—at least for this unusual, hopeful moment in time.

This wishful rewriting of the oedipal sce-nerio from the daughter's perspective takes on nothing less than the status of major mythography.[10]

An apt summation of Chantal Akerman's large filmic contribution.

As with all foreign women pioneers, the distribution of Akerman's work in America is much to be desired. Imagine not being able to see Godard, Fassbinder, or Truffaut in repertory and art-house movie theaters or in video stores. And when was the last time you remember seeing **von Trotta, Mészáros,** or **Akerman** advertised?

CHANTAL AKERMAN

1968   Saute Ma Ville (short)
1971   L'Enfant Aime (short)
1972   Hotel Monterey (short)
       La Chambre
1973   Le 15/8 (co-directed with Sammy
       Szlingerbaum)
1974   Je . . . Tu . . . Il . . . Elle
1975   Jeanne Dielman
1976   News From Home
1978   Les Rendezvous D'Anna
1983   Toute une Nuit
1989   Histoires d'Amerique

SHORT TAKES—THE SILENTS

◆ ◆ ◆

Leontine Sagan (1889–1974)

She was born **Leontine Schlesinger** in Vienna, Austria. Early in her life she was trained by Max Reinhardt and became a prominent actress and director of the stage. She moved to Johannesburg and married Dr. Victor Fleischer.

In 1931 **Leontine Sagan** took an extraordinary leap in her career. Although she had never made a film before, she decided to direct her first feature, MAEDCHEN IN UNIFORM, a look at the emotional pressures caused by authoritarian rule at an all-girls' boarding school. The film garnered international attention, caused worldwide upset, and was banned by Germany's Joseph Goebbels, who dubbed the film "unnatural" because of its frank depiction of a lesbian theme.

Nancy Scholar in *Sexual Strategems* said of the film:

[It] becomes even more remarkable when we consider the historical context in which it appeared. By 1931, Hitler was in the ascendency, and a wave of nationalism was spreading throughout the country; this was both reflected in and accelerated by the newsreels and films which were almost entirely nationalistic by this time. In this milieu, Sagan's film appeared overtly anti-nationalistic, anti-Prussian, anti-authori-

tarian. Not surprisingly, a separate ending, which was profascist, was shown in Germany, and eventually Goebbels had the film banned as unhealthy. Sagan and most of her cast exiled themselves from Germany after the film was released. . . .

Sagan's choice of location is an explicit indication of her intention, which is to juxtapose the Prussian values, against the humanitarian values. . . . The film departs radically from convention in its open presentation of the possibilities of love between two women. . . . Open is the key word here, since repressed homosexuality, undeclared and unexamined, would be a matter of course, as in the Nazi movement outside.[1]

The film was based on the stage play by a German woman playwright, **Christa Winsloe,** entitled, *Yesterday and Today* (1931). The most striking thing about this film by far, especially for the time in which it was made, is the absence of any male figures whatsoever, both in the performance, the production, and the direction of the film. The film was also the first in Germany to be produced cooperatively, meaning that the crew and the cast formed a cooperative film venture in which each member obtained shares vs. a salary.

Leontine Sagan

Lina Wertmuller

MAEDCHEN IN UNIFORM's controversy, mild by today's perspective,[2] attracted the attention of England's Alexander Korda who asked Sagan to come to the United Kingdom to direct. Although MEN OF TO-MORROW (1932), starring **Merle Oberon,** was an unsuccessful venture, Sagan was contacted by David Selznick in 1934 to come to work in America, but nothing ever came of the offer.

By 1939 Sagan had turned her pioneer-ing attentions back to the theater when she moved to South Africa and became co-founder of the National Theatre of Johannes-burg. But she never directed another film.

LEONTINE SAGAN

1931   Maedchen in Uniform
1932   Men of Tomorrow

Esther Shub (1894–1959)

In the Soviet Union, famous film editors are rare. Directors there usually edit their own pictures. **Esther Shub** was one great exception. She gained her reputation in the early twenties by recutting foreign productions.

Entirely on her own initiative, she helped to pioneer the "compilation film." She has been called "a genius for using all sorts of ill-considered oddments of footage as a painter uses his palette and as if it had been specially shot for her."[1]

For two films, THE GREAT ROAD, and, THE FALL OF THE ROMANOV DYNASTY, both re-leased in 1927, she scavenged every bit of old newsreel footage, closets of wartime cameramen, vaults, home footage shot by the imperial family—all with indefatigable determination. As writer Robert Dunbar tells it, "All of this was against the original reluctance of her studio to go ahead with these projects, and they refused to recognize her rights as author when she had finished the films."[2]

When sound came on the scene, Esther Shub changed her practices and anticipated the theories of cinema verité by about thirty years. She forged a new original style of "ultrarealism." She would purposely in-clude shots in which people looked directly into the lens, screwed up their eyes at the arc lamps, and stumbled in front of cameras and mikes quite visible in the shots. Her idea was to augment reality by reminding the viewer that the crew and apparatus were actually there, instead of pretending they were a part of some invisible, omnipotent eye.

Shub is remembered as an editor. But really she was a director who created her techniques almost solely in the editing room. One of the first in film industry his-tory to do so.

ESTHER SHUB

1927   Fall of the Romanov Dynasty, The
       Great Road, The
1928   Russia of Nikolai II and Lev Tol-
       stoy, The
1930   Today
1932   Komsomol
1934   Subway at Night, The
1937   Soviets' Land, The
1939   Spain
1940   20 Years of Soviet Cinema
1941   Face of the Enemy, The
1947   Sideways to Arax

SHORT TAKES—THE SOUND ERA

◆ ◆ ◆

Lina Wertmuller

Born of Swiss ancestry in the Rome of the 1930s **Lina Wertmuller** spent ten years of her life as a stage director before turning to film. In 1963 she landed a job as Federico Fellini's assistant on 8½, and has created patriarchal-applauded cinema ever since.

Still, Wertmuller was in that select group of women *allowed* to direct film in the sixties and seventies, preceded in recent history only by those like **Agnes Varda, Mai Zetterling,** and **Ida Lupino** in the late fifties and early sixties. As such, she provided an important cultural model for the women of her generation. Her films were among the first of the contemporary female voices to vibrate on the big screen and brashly so, before feminism in the early seventies would drastically transform the shape and content of those voices.

From her sparkling debut with THE LIZARDS (1963), about a young man who rebels against the social structure and fails, Wertmuller has consistently placed her camera behind male eyes. Her use of leftist politics in kitsch entanglements with what can only be called male sadomasochistic fantasies, some thought a cheap shot at a desire to attract a mass popular audience.

Among the best, most tightly structured films of her shining period are: LOVE AND ANARCHY (1973), about a naive young man ordered to assassinate Mussolini, but gets waylaid by a love affair with a prostitute. THE SEDUCTION OF MIMI (1974), is a round of sexual play with the Mafia. SEVEN BEAUTIES (1976), features the kinky perverseness of a Nazi concentration camp. The unreal power attributed a woman as commandant switches the male/female power structure in a way we sympathize with the "victimized" male. SWEPT AWAY (1975), displays the most conscious mass ridicule of the female, in which we learn that all any woman needs to straighten her out is a good fuck.

These story elements highlight,

> Wertmuller's detachment from her own femaleness, or her old-style sense of herself as Superwoman, allows her to treat women with more exaggerated scorn, even loathing, than most men would dare to. SWEPT AWAY's statement, particularly vile for a woman to be making, is finally that a woman . . . needs to be brought low, needs to be made submissive to the man by abuse, for her own happiness as well as his. That

astonishing kind of dancing to the master's tune makes Arzner's compliant endings, and even Lupino's full absorption of patriarchal values, look very mild by comparison.[1]

Nevertheless, Wertmuller's enormous skill as a filmmaker cannot be denied, no matter what one thinks of her politics. She was among the first women in the world to win great international respect and acclaim as a female director; thereby opening doors for other women to follow.

LINA WERTMULLER

1963	Lizards, The
1973	Love and Anarchy
1974	Seduction of Mimi, The
1975	Swept Away
1976	Seven Beauties

Liliana Cavani

A contemporary of **Wertmuller, Liliana Cavani** graduated from the Centro Speimentale in Rome in the 1960s, and began making documentaries for television.

In the early seventies she turned to dramatic features with THE YEAR OF THE CANNIBALS (1970), the story of two idealists trying to survive in a fascist regime. With THE NIGHT PORTER (1974), Cavani drew wide attention in America. In this sadomasochistic look at a love affair between a woman and her Nazi tormentor fifteen years after the war, the use of kinky fascist imagery was more difficult to bear than anything Wertmuller attempted in SEVEN BEAUTIES.

Cavani has always denied encountering any obstacles as a woman filmmaker. According to Sharon Smith in *Women Who Make Movies* (1975), if a woman comes from a free environment she won't necessarily bring any "special eye" to filmmaking. She does not, however, define what she means by a "free environment."

LILIANA CAVANI

Documentaries

1962–63	History of the Third Reich
1963	Age of Stalin, The
1964	House in Italy, The
1965	Day of Peace, The
	My Brother Jesus
	Philippe Pétain
	Women of the Resistance

Dramatic Features

1966	Francis of Assisi
1968	Galileo
1970	Year of the Cannibals, The
1971	Guest, The
1973–74	Milarepa
1974	Night Porter, The
1977	Beyond Good and Evil
1981	Skin, The
1982	Beyond the Door
1985	Berlin Affair, The

Mai Zetterling

A former actress, **Mai Zetterling** first appeared to American audiences in Ingmar Bergman's TORMENT (1944). Like **Marga**rethe von Trotta, she continued a prolific acting career, including roles in **Muriel Box's**[1] THE TRUTH ABOUT WOMEN (1958), until the early sixties when the disappointment she experienced in acting made her want to direct.

> As an actress, I had been horrified many times by directors who weren't careful with their jobs, people with vast reputations who never even bothered to do their homework. . . . Little by little, I began to realize that making films was what I wanted to do.[2]

After collaborating on several documentaries for British television with her husband, David Hughes, she turned to features with themes most notably on the issue of women's oppression. THE GIRLS (1968), (not to be confused with **Márta Mészáros's** THE GIRL [1968]), was one of the earliest explorations of women's coming to terms with their own lives. Three actresses on tour with the drama *Lysistrata* become immersed in their parts offstage, as the drama about women's oppression from the days of early Greece hauntingly begins to mirror their own.

In a viewpoint similar to that of **von Trotta**, whom she preceded in features by ten years, Zetterling said,

> There are many things I feel haven't been aired on the screen, haven't been looked at from a woman's viewpoint. So naturally I make films about women.[3]

Zetterling's first feature, LOVING COUPLES (1964), experimentally dealt with three pregnant mothers in the hospital. The moments their babies are born they are recounting their lives through a complex and sophisticated technique of flashbacks. It was an experimentation of the time/space continuum that stretched the boundaries of the medium boldly.

American film critics liked it. Judith Crist noted,

> The Swedish actress-turned-moviemaker has made an auspicious directorial debut with LOVING COUPLES . . . a study of three women and their society in beautiful bold terms . . . commercial though her premises may be, they are never cheap.[4]

Zetterling continued with NIGHT GAMES (1966), DOCTOR GLAS (1968), and THE GIRLS (1968).

Says Louise Heck-Rabi, "she admits . . . she hates the manners men have when reacting to female aggressiveness (hers). Zetterling pooh-poohs the notion that a woman loses her sensuality because she is in command."[5]

MAI ZETTERLING

1958	The Truth About Women
1960	Polite Invasion, The
1961	Lords of Little Egypt
1962	Presperity Race, The
	War Game, The
1963	Do-It-Yourself Democracy, The
1964	Loving Couples
1966	Night Games
1968	Doctor Glas
	Girls, The
1971	Van Gogh

Diane Kurys

The importance of **Diane Kurys** emergence on the film scene occurred with PEPPERMINT SODA in 1977. Ostensibly a "light movie," it was all the more startling to realize that rarely, if ever, had audiences been treated to such visual beauty on the screen before. Events such as the shy loving warmth of two teenage girls kissing each other after a summer apart delighted audiences and made this the largest-grossing film in France that year.

Kurys's contribution to filmmaking is substantial when we compare her choice of subject matter to that of women filmmakers of the past. If **Lina Wertmuller**, for example, had the chance to make a film about rites-of-passage issues, she did so through the eyes of young men.

Kurys's devotion to the oeuvre continued with COCKTAIL MOLOTOV (1980), a film about a trio of rebellious adolescents, then continued with her second important contribution, ENTRE NOUS (1983). This last film broke through into another rarified world for film—lesbian love. Although Kurys is careful not to be too explicit lest she alienate a wider market, she still explores a touchy subject in a charming, autobiographic light similar to PEPPERMINT SODA, and she does so with a distinguished and distinctly female eye.

In focusing on a relationship that goes beyond friendship into lesbian love, Kurys takes elements suggested in Mészáros's most intense films about two women, and von Trotta's as well, and pushes them fur-

ther . . . the shift to woman/woman intense involvement and importance . . . redirect[s] the flow of sexual energy.[1]

A MAN IN LOVE (1987), Kurys's most recent and unfocused effort, is disappointing in the way that **Susan Seidelman**'s successive films have been disappointing—"It appears to be a bid for commercial success."[2] Neither male nor female characterizations are entered or explored.

We have to hope that Kurys has her best work ahead of her. Certainly her contribution in portraying women's initiation rites with a unique, entertaining, and endemically female view, has earned her the right to fail in any terrain she wants to explore. We also have to hope that her risks in the future are for her own artistic curiosities and not for a box office she is trying to anticipate.

DIANE KURYS

1977 Peppermint Soda
1980 Cocktail Molotov
1983 Entre Nous
1987 A Man in Love

Márta Mészáros

This Hungarian filmmaker may be the most prolific living woman filmmaker in the world. With some twenty-five documentaries and fourteen feature films to her credit, **Márta Mészáros** has been consistently making movies for three decades, all of them with a conscious eye on women's lives.

Perhaps her most famous film in America, DIARY FOR MY CHILDREN (1984), suggests her most prevalent theme—orphans. It is a subject known intimately to Mészáros, whose own early orphaning put her on the forefront of this quest.

The search for Mother and Father is a determining experience in my life. The concept of the child left on its own or abandoned is something that has excited me in almost all of my films.[1]

Contentwise, Mészáros's commitment to "portray things from a woman's angle"[2] definitely places her work at the center of an oeuvre that defines a "female gaze." But the rhythm of her films is also worth a close study. As in THE GIRL (1968), their "rambling, almost improvisatory, open-ended inattention, even indifference, to the sort of tight seamless narrative that tries to create an illusion of verisimilitude,"[3] is a direct challenge to the rhythm of most male cinema. A romantic blending of a child's consciousness, the dreamworld of what it might be like in the fairy-tale existence in the arms of a real mother and father, suggests a kind of inner female rhythm that harks back to the much more open-ended structures of **Maya Deren.**

Feminist themes that might be difficult to express in other Eastern European countries are more possible in Hungary, where Mészáros made THE TWO OF THEM (1977), known in this country as WOMEN, where "domestic confinement is almost tantamount to imprisonment."[4] Several highly charged scenes between women characters momentarily perk up audience expectations, but they are then passed by with a sort of regret and denial on the part of Mészáros. She has commented that it has not been difficult to turn toward political subjects in Hungary, but that woman-to-woman eroticism has been off-limits. It is rumored that she has a lesbian love story in her hands that she wants to shoot. Judging from her long-standing commitment to the truth about women's lives on the screen, it is undoubtedly a venture to look forward to.

MÁRTA MÉSZÁROS

1968 Girl, The
1969 Binding Sentiments
1970 Don't Cry, Pretty Girls
1973 Riddance
1975 Adoption
1976 Nine Months
1977 Two of Them, The ("Women" in the US)
1978 Just Like at Home
1979 On the Move
1980 Heiress, The
1981 Mother and Daughter
1983 Land of Mirages, The
1984 Diary for My Children
1987 Diary for My Loves

·XIII·

SHORT TAKES
ON OTHER UNSUNG
REEL WOMEN

Marion Fairfax (1875–1970)

Marion Fairfax entered the industry as a writer for Lasky in 1915 at William De Mille's suggestion.[1] During the twenties, her success with Lasky was phenomenal. She wrote, edited, and supervised more than thirty produced features. Among them were THE BLACKLIST (1916), with William De Mille, and VALLEY OF THE GIANTS (1919), starring Wallace Reid, and directed by James Cruze, who would later direct the great Western classic, THE COVERED WAGON, edited by Dorothy Arzner.

In 1922 Fairfax formed her own company for the independent production of one feature on which she also acted as director. It was THE LYING FOOL from which the accompanying photograph was taken. Her production company's location on Santa Monica Boulevard was later the location of Francis Coppola's "Zoetrope Studio." The theme of THE LYING FOOL was drug addiction,[2] and seems to have beat Dorothy Davenport Reid's film on the same topic, HUMAN WRECKAGE, by about a year.

In 1921, at the instigation of her own powerful firm, Marion Fairfax told *Moving Picture World:*

I truly believe there is a specific place for the combination of literary achievement and stage presentation.

She also felt that

An author's place in the presentation of a motion picture, to my mind, is just as important to the screen as it is in the presentation of a play to the stage drama. It is my ambition to make my stories . . . human and clean, my characters natural; people that really exist in our own lives.[3]

An honorable goal that most films still haven't achieved!

Marion Fairfax continued to have a long, successful career, predominantly as a scenario writer.

MARION FAIRFAX

1921   Bob Hampton of Placer
       Lotus Eater, The
       Mad Marriage, The
       Through the Back Door
1922   Fools First
       Lying Fool, The
       Sherlock Holmes
1924   For Sale—A Lady of Quality
       Lillies of the Field
       Painted People
       So Big
       Woman on the Jury, The
1925   As Man Desires
       Clothes Make the Pirate
       Lost World, The
1926   Blonde Saint, The
       Old and New

Margaret J. Winkler

Carving her name in the virtually untrodden field of film distribution, Margaret Winkler (formerly secretary to Harry Warner in Warner Brothers' pioneering days in 1921), began her career with a single product, but it was the right one: the Felix the Cat cartoons. And with them, Winkler hit the jackpot.

Only three years later she was selling what she termed "Variety Packages" to theaters. These included KID KAPER COMEDIES, two-reelers based on the poems of Edgar Guest, and something called THE ALICE COMEDIES, a chance she took on a young unknown animator named Walt Disney.

All that any pioneering woman needs is a good intuitive eye. . . .

Louella Parsons (1893–1972)

She is more discussed than any star, more feared than any producer or director. You can hate her, you can jeer at her, you can respect her, you can love her. But if you are part of the movie business, you cannot possibly ignore her.

Isabella Taves, *Look*

Hollywood placed so much importance on her that she was the only columnist ever invited to place her hands and feet in the cement outside Grauman's Chinese Theatre.[1] This once-feared woman was also at one time the most controversial figure in Hollywood. **Louella Parsons** wrote the first movie gossip column in the country, and was the first columnist ever to cover Hollywood.[2]

If gossip columnists could make or break careers, it's because Hollywood practically begged them to. They had only the power given them by the people who put them in power. "Their columns were the first thing we looked at every morning," said Bob Hope, "to see what was going on."[3] What was "going on" ranged from a report by Parsons that HIGH NOON (1952) was a movie redeemed only by its music, to the news that **Doris Day** tied her own shoelaces.[4] Her reports, along with the other famous columnist of the day, **Hedda Hopper,** were often "whimsical, wrong, or both, but a thing like that didn't matter."[5] The point of gossip was to create more gossip—a little drama that could spill off the silver screen and change the plots of real lives.

Louella Parsons began as a story editor for the Essanay Movie Company in Chicago. She sold a story to Essanay for twenty-five dollars in 1910, and then was hired to read scripts at the same weekly rate. In her book, *The Gay Illiterate* (1944), she recalls how scripts would come to her on "pencil tablets, torn envelopes and even on bits of wallpaper. . . . I would distribute the stories

I selected indiscriminately down the line, and the directors made the stories I selected whether they liked them or not. Most of the time they didn't like them!"[6]

Parsons also appeared in several films, HOLLYWOOD HOTEL (1937), WITHOUT RESERVATIONS (1946), STARLIFT (1951). Her daughter, **Harriet Parsons,** followed in her mother's pioneering footsteps and became a producer for a number of features for RKO. Among Harriet's well-known features is I REMEMBER MAMA (1948) with **Irene Dunne.**

Feared for her ruthlessness, but always, always respected, Louella Parsons was trained in the tough old school of newspaper reporting reminiscent of Hildy Johnson. Those were also the days when it wasn't considered wise for a girl to let her brains show. In a fifties' milieu that encouraged a woman to be crafty by being manipulative, Louella would use her "feminine wiles"—bat her eyelashes, flirt, tell silly stories to demonstrate how flakey she was—but *always* be the first to scoop a hot story.

When Louella's big scoop on Ingrid Bergman's unexpected baby appeared, every newspaper and every columnist in Hollywood was hunting Joe Steele, Ingrid's press agent and close friend. They didn't find him, for Joe was sound asleep at Louella's house. . . . Louella had convinced Joe he was in bad nervous shape, tucked him safe in bed, safe from all competitors.[7]

Actress **Evelyn Keyes** said about Parson's world, "Women were supposed to be catty to each other. . . . I think their reputations came from that. It was our programming, like pink for girls. Gossip columnists were bitches—everybody knew that."[8]

Born of Irish and Jewish descent (the latter she kept very quiet in those days),[9] Louella Parsons might never have amounted to anything had she found early marital happiness. At the age of seventeen, just out of high school, she married John Parsons, who took her to Iowa from her beginnings in Freeport, Illinois. Because he didn't feel she was mature enough to run his household, even after she had a baby, Parsons placed his wife in a boarding home until her natural renegade fervor broke loose. She escaped with her baby daughter, **Harriet,** to an uncle in Montana. From there, she got a job with the early Essanay Movie Company and moved to Chicago. Before taking on tinseltown in 1926 at the age of forty-five, Louella wrote her first columns for newsprint in Chicago and New York.[10]

Parons had the "chutzpah" to demand $250 from William Randolph Hearst and got it. It was an unheard-of salary for a newspaper reporter in 1920. But Hearst knew good, raw talent when he saw it (besides, he liked what Louella wrote about **Marion Davies**), and soon, Parsons's column was syndicated to nearly a thousand papers worldwide.[11]

A burgeoning industry that above all else did promote itself well, Hollywood was ready for someone who knew how to spill all the dirt in print. Parsons was in the right place at the right time, and she filled her niche with a flair! If she obtained a reputation for being ruthless, two mouths to feed was her excuse and her motivation—and besides, the industry *asked* for it. **Liz Smith,** a contemporary columnist as near to the role that Louella played in her day recently said, "There's a whole different moral climate now about the gossip column trade. I don't take any moral position about whom people sleep with."[12]

By the 1950s Parsons was hosting *The*

Jergens-Woodbury Journal over the ABC radio network, and in a 1949 *Radio Mirror* poll, was voted best-beloved woman commentator. From radio, she was unstoppable. Aside from Hearst, she began writing for *Photoplay,* the number one fan magazine of the movie trade, and for *Modern Screen.* By 1944 her autobiography, *The Gay Illiterate* sold 150,000 copies.

In 1950, many moons before the days when reporters knew better than to write words like this, *Life* magazine summed up Parsons:

> Louella is no lady when she fights. She's plain female. She'll scream, she'll keep her claws out. She won't listen to explanations, no matter how reasonable.[13]

She had the power to make or break careers. She had the reputation by some of being a "hatchet woman." *Life* preferred to see her kinder side:

> She has, with shrewd and realistic advice, kept some Hollywood big names out of trouble. And, after trouble, she has frequently been generous in offering a friendly hand.[14]

Most likely that "friendly hand" depended upon which side of the bed Louella got out of that morning. But the most important single point to recall about Parsons is that she was not only a self-created woman—who out of sheer ingenuity fabricated an image of herself and successfully marketed it to the entire world—but she was the brainchild who created the "gossip column." And where in the world would Hollywood's promotion machine have been without that?

Hedda Hopper (1890–1966)

Hedda Hopper, gossip-columnist/actress, along with her famed rival **Louella Parsons,** had a combined readership of 75 million in a nation that claimed 160 million.[1] Once upon a time in Hollywood these two women were the most feared species walking the planet. Studio moguls deferred to them. Hopper had a Sunday morning ritual whereby the leading ladies of Hollywood called on her for breakfast.

Often both Hopper's and Parsons's information was wrong, certainly it was too often unnecessarily cruel. The actress **Joan Bennett** once sent Hopper a skunk in the mail, and Joseph Cotten actually kicked her in the ass.[2] It didn't matter; hate and fear is what enabled these two to live like the movie royalty they were. "That's the house that fear built," Hedda would laugh about her office/mansion near Benedict Canyon in Hollywood.

Hopper was born **Elda Furry** to Quaker parents in Hollidaysburg, Pennsylvania. The love of her life was DeWolf Hopper, whom she wed when she was twenty-eight. It was said that John Barrymore was incredibly jealous of this unlikely ladies' man and matinee idol. DeWolf was, after all, bald, and had "faintly blue skin." Married four times, he earned the title of "Husband of His Country."[3] The Hoppers moved to Hollywood with their newborn baby boy William in 1915, where DeWolf starred for the Triangle Company in such films as CASEY AT THE BAT (1916) and MACBETH (1916). Hedda too began to act, mostly as a vamp— an interesting portent of what she was later to become.

She divorced DeWolf in 1922 when she was thirty-seven. "I had legal permission to live with a star," she said about her husband. She then began a new career as social butterfly and supporting actress. Over a span of fifty years she appeared in scores of films, always wearing the multitudinous variety of hats she became famous for. She garnished so much fame as a gossip columnist that later in her career she appeared as herself in such classics as SUNSET BOULEVARD (1950).

In 1936 she initiated a chitchat radio hour, and two years later, at the age of forty-eight, began her twenty-eight year career as the infamous columnist who was to terrorize an industry.

> The nightmare in Hollywood was to be invited to Hedda's and Louella's on the same night. "That was a terrible thing to happen to you," [said photographer Murray Garrett]. "You knew you were going to make an enemy of one or the other of them. Some people would try to go to one and then duck out and slip into the other. It was tricky."[4]

In January 1966, Hopper contracted double pneumonia and died at the age of seventy-five. Louella had stopped writing only two years before because of a broken hip. The era when gossip columnists were more powerful than ambassadors had finally come to a close. By the midsixties, television put an end to the Golden Age of the studio system, which had ceased to maintain a roster of contracted stars under separate roofs. And from the world's viewpoint, news that was once "sensational" to a 1940s generation became blasé for the hippies of the sixties. World War II left us too shocked for anything formerly considered scandalous on celluloid. "It was not the real world," said writer Richard Lemon, "unless you lived in it."[5]

AFTERWORD

• ◆ •

In 1969, while I was a staff member of the American Film Institute, it was brought to my attention that women had a more important role in the history of the motion picture than I had realized. I am not just talking about women directors or actors who have been so visibly singled out in the media, but those who played important roles behind the scenes for many decades, and who are just now being recognized for their part in the formation and development of the industry.

By 1970, when I began to research the stories of the many motion-picture studios that existed in the United States for a book on the subject, I was constantly reminded of the women who had a great deal to do with the studios' history. At the American Film Institute, oral histories were being conducted and professional women who worked for years as editors, writers, directors, actors, agents, and others in many different jobs at the studios came to the sessions to be interviewed. I remember **Ida Lupino**'s arrival. Several friends mentioned that she had directed many of the *Have Gun Will Travel* episodes for television. Because the show was one of my favorites, I remember how unexpectedly the information struck me. I was stunned. The cowboys, the prairie dust, the guns, everything about it was as "male" as you could get. I began to wonder, did women see the same things as men when they directed films?

But the full impact of women's significance to the industry did not really sink in until several years of research had gone by on the studios book. As I continued to compile information, I couldn't help but notice that except for the camerapeople[1]—grips, electricians and other hands-on jobs, women had been there in every aspect of the studio organization! But it was those "special" women I researched—women like **Natalie Kalmus** who was on the board of Technicolor and became so instrumental in making color a fait accompli in the movies—who rose above the others and became famous in their day. Why had they been forgotten? Why had all the important women studio owners, producers, writers, directors, designers, etc., lost their place in history?

One of the most important of these women was **Alice Guy Blaché**. Not only was she a film director as early as 1896, but she built and operated her own studio in Fort Lee, New Jersey, where she produced and directed a slew of films from 1912 to 1917.

I began to travel extensively, looking for photographs and information on the studios, and everywhere I would turn there would be photographs of women—women working at the plants, women in decision-making positions, on location, in offices, sometimes the women outnumbering the men.

I began to collect photographs of women

doing everything and anything related to film. The result is what you see lovingly placed between these pages.

Women have always been around in films; indeed many of them made a lasting impact on the infant industry, but theirs was, and still is, a tough struggle for recognition. Although the famed director, **Dorothy Arzner,** once said in an interview, "I never had any obstacles put in my way by the men in the business . . . cameramen, assistants, property men, actors . . . everybody helped me." She never attained the "star" status that most of the successful male directors of the day received. Why not?

Information on women in the film industry is not easily found. So much depends on oral histories of those quickly dying out. One must cross-reference autobiographies of great male directors like De Mille to discover names like **Jeanie Macpherson,** his main writer, and **Anne Bauchens,** the only film editor up until that time written into a director's contract—De Mille wouldn't make a move without these indispensable women by his side. One must follow up the thinnest wisp of a lead in the hopes of unearthing another treasure. For depending upon traditional film sources for this sort of information is a little like looking for a diamond in a bowlful of crystals—if it doesn't hit you in the eye at once, you can more than likely bet you'll never find one.

Such is the case because no one thought of women as having any special role in the history of film while that history was being made; they were just "there," doing their job, making things possible, making things go smoothly and so were overlooked and not meticulously archived. When it came time later on for the story of the movies to be told, women were long forgotten, like the nannies who made our bedtime dreams a little sweeter when we were young. Many a male producer, C. B. De Mille and David Selznick among them, said it was their secretaries who were responsible for making their offices function efficiently; without them the studio would have been at a standstill. I believe that is still true today.

When it came to my attention that Ally Acker was interested in doing a film series and a book on this subject, I was happy that my research and photographs would at last find a home—the home where I've always known they rightfully belonged. That home is in the eyes of a public that shouldn't have gone so long without them; that home is the annals of a history of which they are so rightfully and indelibly a part. I hope this will inspire other researchers and writers to continue the digging. I can tell you now from long experience that the fruits of such dedicated labor are sweet.

Marc Wanamaker
The Bison Archives
Hollywood, California—1990

SELECT SOURCES

◆ ◆ ◆

Acker, Ally. "Lois Weber." *MS Magazine* (February 1988): 66–67.

Beranger, Clara. *Writing for the Screen.* New York: Little Brown & Co., 1950.

Betancourt, Jeanne. *Women in Focus.* Dayton, Ohio: Pflaum Publishing, 1974.

Brand, Ulricka. "Cinematic Pioneers: Filmmaker Ally Acker Seeks to Restore Lost Film Heritage." *Montage* (IFP West Publication October 1989): 8–10.

Brownlow, Kevin. *The Parade's Gone By . . .* New York: Ballantine Books, 1969. Excellent resource. Women in every facet of production are woven throughout.

Brownlow, Kevin, and John Kobal. *Hollywood: The Pioneers.* New York: Knopf, 1979.

Butler, Ivan. *Silent Magic—Rediscovering the Silent Film Era.* New York: Ungar, 1988.

Carey, Gary. "Written on the Screen: Anita Loos." *Film Comment* no. 6 and 4 (Winter 1970–71).

———. *Anita Loos.* New York: Knopf, 1988.

Coffee, Lenore. *Storyline: Reflections of a Hollywood Screenwriter.* London: Cassell, 1973.

Confino, Barbara. "An Interview with Agnes Varda." *Saturday Review* 55 (August 12, 1972): 35.

Corliss, Richard. "Calling Their Own Shots: Women Directors Are Starting to Make It in Hollywood." *Time* (March 24, 1986): 82–83.

Dictionary of Literary Biography. Volume 26, American Screenwriters. Detroit: Gale, 1984.

Erens, Patricia, ed. *Sexual Strategems: The World of Women in Film.* New York: Horizon, 1979. Excellent resource.

Fernley, Allison, and Paula Maloof. "Yentl." *Film Quarterly* (Spring 1985): 38–45.

Flitterman, Sandy. "Heart of the Avant-Garde: Some Biographical Notes on Germaine Dulac." *Women and Film* 1, no. 5–6 (1974): 58–61.

Ford, Charles. "The First Female Producer." (Alice Guy Blaché) *Films in Review* no. 15 (March 3, 1964).

Franklin, Joe. *Classics of the Silent Screen.* New York: Citadel, 1959.

Gauntier, Gene. "Blazing the Trail." *Woman's Home Companion* (October 1928).

Gibson, Helen. "In the Early Days." *Films in Review* no. 19 (January 1, 1968).

Gish, Lillian, with Ann Pinchot. *The Movies, Mr. Griffith and Me.* Englewood Cliffs, New Jersey: Prentice-Hall, 1969.

Glyn, Anthony. *Elinor Glyn.* Garden City, New York: Doubleday, 1955.

Haskell, Molly. *From Reverence to Rape: The Treatment of Women in the Movies.* New York: Holt, Rinehart, Winston, 1974, 1989. Excellent Resource.

Heck-Rabi, Louise. *Women Filmmakers: A Critical Reception.* Metuchen, New Jersey, and London: Scarecrow Press, 1984. Excellent resource.

Henshaw, Richard. "Women Directors: 150 Filmographies." *Film Comment* 8, no. 4 (November–December 1972): 33–36.

Higashi, Sumiko. *Virgins, Vamps, and Flappers—the American Silent Movie Heroine.* New York: Eden Press.

Johnston, Claire, ed. *The Work of Dorothy Arzner: Towards a Feminist Cinema.* London: British Film Institute, 1975.

Kaplan, E. Ann. *Women and Film: Both Sides of the Camera.* New York: Methuen, 1983.

Katz, Ephraim. *The Film Encyclopedia.* New York: Perigee Books, Putnam Publishing Group, 1979.

Kay, Karyn, and Gerald Peary, eds. *Women and the Cinema.* New York: Dutton, 1977.

Koszarski, Richard. "The Years Have Not Been Kind to Lois Weber." *Village Voice* (November 10, 1975): 40.

Koszarski, Richard. *Hollywood Directors 1914–1940.* New York: Oxford University Press, 1976.

Loos, Anita. *A Girl Like I.* New York: Viking Press, 1966.

Lupino, Ida. "Me, Mother Directress." *Action* 2, no. 3 (June 1967): 15.

Marion, Francis. *Off with Their Heads!* New York: Macmillan Co., 1973.

Norden, Martin F. "Women in the Early Film Industry." *Angle* 6, no. 3, 68–75.

Parker, Francine. "Discovering Ida Lupino." *Action* 2, (1967): 19.

Peary, Gerald. "Sanka, Pink Ladies, and Virginia Slims." *Women & Film* 1, no. 5–6 (1974): 82–84.

Pickford, Mary. *Sunshine and Shadow: The Autobiography of Mary Pickford.* New York: Doubleday & Co., 1955.

Quart, Barbara Koenig. *Women Directors: The Emergence of a New Cinema.* New York: Praeger, 1988.

Reininger, Lotte. *Shadow Theatre and Shadow Films.* New York: Watson-Guptil, 1970.

Rosen, Marjorie. *Popcorn Venus.* New York: Coward, McCann & Geoghegan, 1973. Excellent resource, with small chapter on early women directors at end.

Rosenberg, Jan. *Women's Reflections—the Feminist Film Movement.* Michigan: University of Michigan Research Press, no. 22.

Scheib, Ronnie. "Ida Lupino: Auteuress." *Film Comment* 16 (January 1980): 54–64.

Scott, Audrey. *I Was a Hollywood Stunt Girl.* Philadelphia: Dorrance, 1969.

Shipman, Nell. *The Silent Screen and My Talking Heart, an Autobiography.* Idaho: Boise State University Press, 1987.

Slide, Anthony. *Early Women Directors.* New York: A. S. Barnes, 1977. Good resource.

Slide, Anthony. *The Memoirs of Alice Guy-Blaché.* Metuchen, New Jersey, and London: Scarecrow Press, 1986.

Smith, Sharon. *Women Who Make Movies.* New York: Hopkinson and Blake, 1975. Good resource, despite being outdated.

Stempel, Tom. *FrameWork: A History of Screenwriting in the American Film.* New York: Continuum, 1988, 1991.

Stenn, David. *Clara Bow—Runnin' Wild.* New York: Doubleday, 1988.

Tuska, Jon. *The Films of Mae West,* Secaucus, New Jersey: Citadel Press, 1973.

West, Mae. *Goodness Had Nothing to Do with It.* Rev. ed. New York: Manor Books, 1970.

NOTES

◆ ◆ ◆

Introduction—The Feminization of Filmmaking

1. Anthony Slide, *Early Women Directors* (New York: A. S. Barnes, 1977), p. 9.
2. Betje Howell, "Janson Repeats His 2-Million-Volume Success," *Los Angeles Herald Examiner,* April 10, 1977, p. B-9.
3. In Barbara Koenig Quart's *Women Directors: The Emergence of a New Cinema* (New York: Praeger, 1988) p. 6, she describes a female vs. a male gaze thus: "Unlike the old Hollywood gaze of male control that rendered the woman merely an object to be observed, admired, desired, women in these films give the look and return it in an equity and reciprocity where no one is reduced to object and spectacle."
4. Karyn Kay and Gerald Peary, *Women and the Cinema* (New York: E. P. Dutton, 1977), p. 10.
5. Quart, *Women Directors,* p. 124.
6. Vito Russo, *The Celluloid Closet* (New York: Harper & Row, 1987), p. 275.
7. Ibid., pp. 293–94.
8. Marcia Pally, "Come Hither—but Slowly: Dessert with Diane Kurys," *Village Voice,* January 31, 1984.
9. Russo, p. 311.
10. Interview with Jim Brown for *The Today Show,* NBC, spring 1985.
11. Quart, p. 5.
12. Marjorie Rosen, *Popcorn Venus* (New York: Coward, McCann and Geoghegan, 1973), p. 389.
13. Peter Morris, "Nell Shipman in the Context of her Times," *The Silent Screen and My Talking Heart* by Nell Shipman (Idaho: Hemingway Western Studies Series, 1987), p. 213.
14. Ibid.
15. Louise Heck-Rabi, *Women Filmmakers: A Critical Reception* (Metuchen, NJ: Scarecrow Press, 1984), p. xiii.
16. Quart, p. 12.

Reel Women Directors—Preview

1. The poetry of Sylvia Plath and Anne Sexton were denigrated for years by the literary patriarchy on similar assumptions.
2. She did, in fact, give over her directing career in her second marriage to the pants in the family. Years later, her colleagues agreed that what Lupino regretted most was giving up her directing career during her marriage to Howard Duff, who apparently resented a family with two directors. Lupino harbored a great deal of bitterness in her later years at having been so blithely overlooked by the industry for her achievements.
3. Barbara Koenig Quart, *Women Directors: The Emergence of New Cinema* (New York: Praeger, 1988), p. 37.
4. Ibid., p. 93.
5. Ibid., p. 1.
6. Ulricka Brand, "Cinematic Pioneers," *Montage—An IFP Publication,* October 1989, p. 8.

Alice Guy Blaché

1. Revered film history sources such as William K. Everson's *American Silent Film* and Ben

jamin B. Hampton's *History of the Film Industry from its Beginnings to 1931* do not mention Blaché at all. Lewis Jacobs's vast study, *The Rise of the American Film*, mentions her in typical derogatory fashion, lumped within a list of names where she is all but lost: "There were . . . a number of minor directors of lesser talent who helped to consolidate the discoveries of Griffith and advance the industry. Among these were Francis Boggs, Alice and Herbert Blaché, Albert Capellani, Oscar Apfel, Romaine Fielding." etc., p. 127.

2. Susan Smith, *Women Who Make Movies* (New York: Hopkinson and Blake, 1975), p. 2.

3. Charles Ford, "The First Female Producer," *Films in Review* 15:3, March 1964, p. 142, Smith, p. 3.

4. Francis Lacassin, "Out of Oblivion: Alice Guy Blaché, *Sight and Sound* 40:3, summer, 1971, p. 154.

5. Ibid.

6. Ford, p. 141.

7. Louise Heck-Rabi, *Women Filmmakers: A Critical Reception* (Metuchen, NJ: Scarecrow Press, 1984), p. 2.

8. Ford, p. 141.

9. Heck-Rabi, p. 2.

10. Alice Guy Blaché, "Alice Guy: La naissance du cinema," *Image & Son* 283, April 1974, p. 42.

11. Smith, p. 5.

12. Ibid.

13. Richard Koszarski, *Hollywood Directors,* (New York: Oxford University Press, 1976), p. 7.

14. Ford, p. 142.

15. Lacassin, p. 152.

16. Ford, p. 142.

17. Heck-Rabi, p. 5.

18. Richard Henshaw, "Women Directors—150 Filmographies," *Film Comment* 8:4, Nov.–Dec. 1972, p. 33.

19. Lacassin, p. 153.

20. Karyn Kay and Gerald Peary, "Alice Guy Blaché: Czarina of the Silent Screen," in *Women and the Cinema* (New York: E. P. Dutton, 1977), p. 140.

21. Ibid., pp. 141–42.

22. Gerald Peary, "Czarina of the Silent Screen: Solax's Alice Blaché," *The Velvet Light Trap*, no. 6, Fall 1972, p. 35.

23. Louis Reeves Harrison, "Studio Saunterings," *Moving Picture World,* June 15, 1912, p. 1011.

24. Smith, p. 7.

25. Peary, *Women and the Cinema*, p. 143.

26. Alice Guy Blaché, "Woman's Place in Photoplay Production," *Moving Picture World,* July 11, 1914.

27. Ibid.

28. Peary, *Women and the Cinema*, p. 144.

29. Ibid.

30. Harrison, p. 1011.

31. Smith, p. 6.

32. Heck-Rabi, p. 16.

33. Ibid., 17.

34. Ibid.

35. Lacassin, p. 152.

36. Ibid.

37. Blaché, *Image & Son,* p. 47.

38. Ibid.

Lois Weber

1. This play was written by Gene Gauntier. See Gene Gauntier, "Blazing the Trail." *Women's Home Companion,* October 1928, p. 183.

2. Richard Koszarski, "The Years Have Not Been Kind to Lois Weber," *The Village Voice,* November 10, 1975, p. 40.

3. Anthony Slide, *Early Women Directors,* New York: A. S. Barnes, 1977, p. 38.

4. Ibid., p. 39.

5. Kevin Brownlow, notes on the manuscript of *Reel Women,* August 29, 1990.

6. Slide, p. 51.

7. [No author cited], "The Greatest Woman Director," *Moving Picture Stories,* July 7, 1916.

8. Aline Carter, "Muse of the Reel," *Motion Picture Magazine,* New York, March 1921.

9. Koszarski.

10. Ibid.

11. Carter.

12. Koszarski.

13. Ibid.

14. Her funeral expenses were paid by Hollywood's most famous writer, Frances Marion, who was indebted to Weber for her very first job in film, and the subsequent encouragement that made possible her own unprecedented fifty-year career.

15. *The International Dictionary of Films and*

Filmmakers, v. 2, Directors/Filmmakers, entry—Anthony Slide, editor, Christopher Lyon (Chicago: Macmillan Publishers St. James Press Inc., 1984), pp. 577–78.

Ida May Park

1. Lois Weber, Cleo Madison, Ruth Stonehouse, Lule Warrenton were others at Universal during this period.
2. Anthony Slide, *Early Women Directors* (New York: A. S. Barnes, 1977), p. 60. (Anthony Slide quotes *Motion Picture News,* June 5, 1920, p. 4646 for the source of information.)
3. Ibid.
4. Richard Koszarski, *Hollywood Directors 1914–1940.* (New York: Oxford University Press, 1976), p. 71.
5. Frances Denton, "Lights! Ready! Quiet! Camera! Shoot!" *Photoplay Magazine,* Feb. 1918.
6. Ida May Park, "The Motion Picture Director," *Careers for Women,* edited by Catharine Filene (Boston: Houghton, Mifflin, 1920).
7. Denton.
8. Koszarski, p. 71.

Ruth Ann Baldwin

1. Anthony Slide, *Early Women Directors* (New York: A. S. Barnes, 1977), p. 59.
2. Ibid.

Elizabeth Pickett

1. Anthony Slide, *Early Women Directors* (New York: A. S. Barnes, 1977), p. 115.
2. Ibid.
3. Ibid.
4. Ibid.

Marguerite Bertsch

1. Anthony Slide, *Early Women Directors* (New York: A. S. Barnes, 1977), p. 103.
2. Ibid.
3. Ibid.

Dorothy Arzner

1. Gerald Peary and Karyn Kay, "Interview with Dorothy Arzner," *Cinema,* no. 34, 1974, p. 25.

2. Jay Carr, "Director Arzner: A Mind of Her Own," *Boston Globe,* April 22, 1984, p. B-2.
3. Ida Lupino did the bulk of her films independently, as does Joan Micklin Silver today. Susan Seidelman is currently building a body of work. Only time will tell how "coherent" each turns out to be—whether indeed we will be able to decipher a distinct "Seidelman" voice, or if she will lose her style to the more homogenized churning of the mainstream.
4. Sharon Smith, *Women Who Make Movies* (New York: Hopkinson and Blake, 1975), p. 20.
5. Carr, p. B 2.
6. Parker, p. 4.
7. Peary and Kay, p. 19.
8. Carr, p. B 2.
9. Peary and Kay, p. 21.
10. Ibid., p. 22.
11. Ibid.
12. Ibid., p. 126.
13. Interview with Ally Acker, June 1989.
14. David Stenn, *Clara Bow, Runnin' Wild* (New York: Doubleday, 1988), p. 126.
15. Ibid.
16. [No author cited], "Feminine Director Depends on Reason, Discards Intuition," *New York Herald Tribune* June 26, 1932, sec. vii, p. 6.
17. Charles Higham, *Kate: The Life of Katharine Hepburn* (New York: Norton, 1975), p. 43.
18. Stenn, p. 127.
19. Ibid.
20. According to David Stenn, Bow was more than reticent to do a "talkie," and was terrified that audiences would stampede the theatre once they actually heard her speaking in films. *Clara Bow, Runnin' Wild,* p. 127.
21. Ibid., p. 160.
22. Ibid.
23. Ironically, as motion pictures became more codified, and it became more and more difficult for women to work in the industry, the American economy was waning. By the forties, it was not a matter of women *wanting* to work and not being allowed, it was the economic reality of families not being able to subsist on a single income. Most women simply *had* to work. By the time this

was a fact, motion pictures had closed down its patriarchal clamp, making work nearly impossible. One **Wanda Tuchock** co-directed a film called FINISHING SCHOOL at RKO in 1933, but seems to have disappeared soon after.

24. Smith, p. 20.
25. Interview with Ally Acker, 1988.
26. Marjorie Rosen, *Popcorn Venus.* (New York: Avon Books, 1974), p. 400.
27. "Feminine Director," p. 6.
28. Peary and Kay, p. 28.
29. Rosen, p. 400.
30. Ibid.
31. Guy Flatley, "At the Movies," *New York Times* (August 20, 1976), p.C-5.
32. Rosen, p. 398. "I wanted my pictures to stand on their own," Arzner said as if to expiate herself.
33. Ida Lupino's firm with Collier Young was independent of Hollywood.

Joan Tewkesbury

1. Susan Bravdy, "The Woman Behind Nashville" *MS Magazine,* July 1975, p. 22.
2. Jack Slater, "Out of the Doll's House," *Emmy,* May/June 1982, p. 20.
3. Ibid.
4. Ibid.
5. Ibid.
6. James Powers, "Dialogue on Film—Joan Tewkesbury," *American Film,* March 1979, pp. 40–41.
7. Slater, pp. 20–21.
8. "Dialogue," p. 44.
9. Ibid., p. 21.
10. Historically, the script supervisor (also called "script girl") who keeps track of new scenes, film continuity, action, dialogue, and any last-minute costume changes that might have to be "matched" in subsequent scenes, has usually been a woman.
11. "Dialogue," p. 35.
12. Joan Micklin Silver and Susan Seidelman are two notable exceptions to this rule for American women directors.
13. Slater.
14. "Dialogue," p. 46.
15. Ibid.

Claudia Weill

1. Susan Isaacs, "Sisterhood Isn't So Powerful in the Movies," *New York Times,* Arts & Leisure Section, January 14, 1990. As Isaacs points out, women's "buddy" films rarely succeed because men, among other distractions, get in the way. Male buddy movies, on the other hand, may have women in there as conversation pieces, but they are never tied in to the main driving plot line of the film. For the men, their *attainment* of women is not the main goal.
2. Beverly Gray, "A Conversation with Claudia Weill," *Performing Arts,* February 1981, p. 9.
3. Ibid.
4. Martha Coolidge interview with Ally Acker, summer 1986.
5. Donna Deitch (DESERT HEARTS) took two-and-a-half years to raise the hard cash to make her groundbreaking story of two women in love. "You can't continue that kind of pace. It just takes too much out of you. You bet I would take a three-picture deal with a studio now." Interview with Ally Acker, summer 1989.

Joan Micklin Silver

1. Barbara Koenig Quart notes in *Women Directors* (Praeger, 1988), that many contemporary women directors are Jewish—Susan Seidelman, Elaine May, Claudia Weill, Joyce Chopra, Amy Heckerling, Barbra Streisand—though only Silver and Streisand in YENTL, ever made their ethnicity a focal point for celebration in their movies.
2. "Dialogue on Film—Joan Micklin Silver," *American Film,* May 1989, p. 24.
3. Douglas W. Edwards, "Joan Micklin Silver/Between the Lines," *Advocate,* April 17, 1980, p. 38.
4. Quart, p. 51.
5. Ibid., p. 52.
6. "Dialogue," p. 22.
7. Nancy Mills, "Silver Has Lots of Company Now," *Los Angeles Times,* Calendar section, August 23, 1988, p. 4.
8. Ray Silver has since directed two films of his own—ON THE YARD, which Silver produced, and A WALK ON THE MOON.
9. Quart, p. 53.

Karen Arthur

1. Linda Gross, "Karen Arthur Dares to Do It All," *Los Angeles Times,* April 16, 1978, Calendar Section, p. 54.
2. "Dialogue on Film—Karen Arthur," *American Film,* October 1987, p. 13.
3. Tom Stempel's theory as to why trained dancers make good directors is as follows: "The dance training has given them the discipline and the physical strength they need to direct and the patience to keep knocking on the doors to get the money to do it. And being a choreographer like Karen Arthur was, gives them great experience at moving performers around, experience that's useful when moving the camera around. They develop strong feet and legs as well." (See Martha Coolidge's comment about the director's need for a good pair of shoes.) Comment made in Tom Stempel's notes to the author on the manuscript of *Reel Women,* August 1990.
4. Michael London, "From Australia to Hollywood, and Back—by Choice," *Los Angeles Times,* part 6, July 30, 1982, p. 12.
5. "Dialogue," p. 12.
6. Ibid., p. 13.

Martha Coolidge

1. Debby Birns, "Close Up," *American Premiere Magazine,* September 1985, p. 4.
2. "Dialogue on Film—Martha Coolidge," *American Film,* December 1988, p. 16.
3. What Coolidge never realized was that most people in the system, a good number of them women, have given up their moral values by the time they've gotten through the horrors of making their first picture. Witness Amy Heckerling, whose FAST TIMES AT RIDGEMONT HIGH opened the same year as Coolidge's VALLEY GIRL, and opened not only the teen market, but the door to editing in general for women. Barbara Koenig Quart, *Women Directors: The Emergence of a New Cinema* (New York: Praeger, 1988), p. 75.

   In FAST TIMES . . . what little character development there is goes to the male characters, and the girls are concerned only with how they look and which boy is cute, with Heckerling exploiting female bodies, parading them around in bikinis, moving her camera over them as they lie by pools. . . . It is shocking that during interactions between two girls, a woman director should be focusing on them as bodies, not for each other, but for the spectator. . . . [Amy Heckerling's] eye is entirely riveted on the box office: 'You know what would be great,' she says, 'if there was a female who could do what Lucas and Spielberg do: make tons of money." Tom Stempel pointed out to me that "FAST TIMES was recut by Universal at the insistence of the Ratings Board, which felt Heckerling's focusing on the women's reactions in the sex scenes made it an X-rated film.

4. Claire-France Perez, "Interview with Martha Coolidge," *L.A. Woman,* August 1985, p. 6.
5. Zina Klapper, "Movie Directors: Four Women Who Get to Call the Shots in Hollywood," *MS,* November 1985, pp. 62, 65–67.
6. Ibid., p. 65. Lee Grant would do similarly well later in 1989 with STAYING TOGETHER. Both films show a sensitive, well-developed treatment of young male coming-of-age characters. But if they do it for young men, certainly there are as many teenage girls who go to movies! There is room on the market for more than one SMOOTH TALK (1985).
7. Quart, p. 76.
8. Paul Attanasio, "The Road to Hollywood—Director Martha Coolidge's Long Trek to 'Real Genius,' " *Washington Post,* August 7, 1985.
9. Martha Coolidge, interview with Jim Brown and Ally Acker, summer 1986.
10. Dudley Clendenin, "RAMBLING ROSE Blossoms for the Screen," *New York Times,* December 2, 1990, p. C-19.
11. Sharon Bernstein, "Women and Hollywood—It's Still a Lousy Relationship. But is there Hope for the Future?" *Los Angeles Times,* Calendar Section, November 11, 1990, p. 82.
12. "Dialogue," p. 19.

Susan Seidelman

1. Vincent Canby, *New York Times,* March 29, 1985.

2. Louise Bernikow, "The Devil and Susan Seidelman," *Lears,* January 1990, p. 110.

3. "The idea of a woman's having become the man she always wanted to marry ... is a shrewd idea for a film to focus on ... but a brilliant conception is hardly enough to carry a film": Barbara Koenig Quart, *Women Directors: The Emergence of a New Cinema* (New York: Praeger, 1988), pp. 67, 68.

4. Susan Seidelman, interview with Ally Acker, summer 1988. All Seidelman quotes, unless otherwise attributed, are taken from this interview.

5. Clarke Taylor, "Seidelman's Next Film Date Is with 'Mr. Right,' " *Los Angeles Times,* Calendar Section, August 11, 1986, p. 1.

6. Bernikow, p. 111.

7. Ibid.

Donna Deitch

1. Donna Deitch, interview with Ally Acker, June 1989. All Deitch quotes, unless otherwise attributed, are taken from this interview.

Joyce Chopra

1. Joan Baez made her debut in Chopra's coffeehouse.

2. JOYCE AT 34 (1972), co-directed with **Claudia Weill,** was a personal odyssey, while her other film extreme was documenting health care in Nigeria.

Stephanie Rothman

1. Dannis Peary, "Stephanie Rothman: R-Rated Feminist" in Karen Kay and Gerald Peary, *Women and the Cinema,* (New York: Dutton, 1977), p. 179.

2. Linda Gross, "A Woman's Place is in ... Exploitation Films?" *Los Angeles Times,* Calendar Section, February 12, 1978, p. 34.

3. Peary, p. 179.

4. Ibid., p. 192.

5. Ibid.

Mary Pickford

1. Kevin Brownlow, *The Parade's Gone By . . .* (New York: Ballantine Books, 1969), p. 155.

2. Ibid., p. 154.

3. Ibid., p. 138.

4. Kevin Brownlow and John Korbal, *Hollywood/The Pioneers,* (New York: Alfred Knopf, 1979), p. 157.

5. Kevin Brownlow, interview with Ally Acker, summer 1987.

6. Brownlow, *Hollywood/The Pioneers,* pp. 156–57.

7. Benjamin Hampton, *History of the American Film Industry* (New York: Dover, 1970), p. 190. Reprint of Hampton's 1931 book, *A History of the Movies.*

8. Brownlow, *Parade's,* p. 140.

9. Ibid.

10. Adela Rogers St. Johns, "Why Mary Pickford Bobbed Her Hair," *Photoplay,* September 1929, p. 33.

Mabel Normand

1. Sam Peeples, "Madcap, the Story of Mabel Normand," *Classic Film Collector* Spring—Summer 1970, p. 27.

2. Joe Franklin, *Classics of the Silent Screen* (New York: Citadel, 1959), p. 78.

3. Ibid.

4. Ivan Butler, *Silent Magic* (New York: Ungar, 1988), p. 22.

5. Peeples, p. 24.

6. Peeples, p. 27.

7. Ibid.

8. Peeples, *Classic Film Collector* Winter, 1970, p. 26.

9. Ephraim Katz, *The Film Encyclopedia,* (New York: The Putnam Publishing Group, 1979), p. 864.

10. Peeples, p. 27.

Nell Shipman

1. Peter Morris, "The Taming of the Few: Nell Shipman in the Context of Her Times," essay placed at end of Nell Shipman's autobiography, *The Talking Screen and My Silent Heart* (Idaho: Hemingway Western Studies Series, 1987), p. 214.

2. Ibid., p. 213.

3. Tom Fulbright, "Queen of the Dog Sleds," *Classic Film Collector* Fall 1969, p. 31.

4. Morris, p. 215.

5. Ibid., p. 218.

6. Ibid., p. 215.
7. Ibid.
8. Fulbright, p. 31.
9. Morris, p. 219.
10. Ibid., p. 215.
11. In the case of these lost Shipman films, it is important to note how the decisions to archive certain films on the basis of their "critical significance" is falacious at best. Tastes from one decade to the next shift for all kinds of reasons—most of the time, as is starkly evident here, the reasons have nothing to do with the quality of the work. The reasons are based on the critical whim of the times and on the word of white male historians who have passed down a falsely skewed and biased perspective of what makes up "good" movies. The tragedy is how much artful work of women has been lost to such whim.
12. Fulbright, p. 31.
13. Ibid. Charles and Daphne Ayers were born in 1926. Shipman had married Charles Ayers, an artist, the year before.
14. Ibid., p. 30.
15. Morris, p. 220.
16. Ibid.

Lillian Gish

1. Lillian Gish, interview with Ally Acker, on the occasion of the 1984 American Film Institute's Lifetime Achievement Awards.
2. Marjorie Rosen, *Popcorn Venus* (New York: Avon Books, 1974), p. 390.
3. Rosen, p. 390.
4. Acker interview.
5. Ephraim Katz, *The Film Encyclopedia* (New York: Putnam Publishing Group, 1979), p. 485.
6. Acker interview.
7. Katz, p. 485.
8. Ibid.
9. Acker interview.

Ruth Stonehouse

1. Mae Tinee, *The Life Stories of the Movie Stars,* (Ohio: Presto Publishing Co., 1916).
2. Anthony Slide, *Early Women Directors* (New York: A.S. Barnes, 1977), p. 54 and 55.

Lucille McVey

1. Anthony Slide, *Early Women Directors* (New York: A. S. Barnes, 1977), p. 105.
2. Ibid.

Lule Warrenton

1. *Moving Picture World,* February 17, 1917.
2. Anthony Slide, *Early Women Directors* (New York: A. S. Barnes, 1977), p. 57.
3. Ibid.

Cleo Madison

1. Tom Fulbright, "Cleo Madison," *Classic Film Collector* (1968), quoting poem "I Have Known" by Cleo Madison.
2. William M. Henry, "Cleo, the Craftswoman," *Photoplay Magazine,* January 1916, p. 109.
3. Ibid.
4. Ibid., p. 111.
5. Ibid.
6. Buck Rainey, "Filmographies, Cleo Madison," *Classic Images,* no. 143, May 1987, p. 17.
7. Mlle Chic, "The Dual Personality of Cleo Madison," *Moving Picture Weekly,* June 1, 1916, p. 25.
8. Henry, p. 111.
9. Ibid.
10. "The Dual Personality," p. 25.
11. Ibid.
12. Henry, p. 109.

Margery Wilson

1. Anthony Slide, *Early Women Directors* (New York: A. S. Barnes, 1977), pp. 62 and 72.
2. Ibid., p. 66.
3. Ibid.
4. Ibid., p. 62. Anthony Slide quotes the *Moving Picture World,* (September 2, 1922) as the source of this information.
5. Ibid.
6. Ibid., p. 72.

Ida Lupino

1. Barbara Scharres, Taorimina Film Festival Catalogue, 1988.

2. Ibid.
3. Ibid.
4. Ibid.
5. Richard Koszarski, *Hollywood Directors 1914–1940* (New York: Oxford University Press, 1976).
6. Ida Lupino, "Me, Mother Directress," *Action,* May–June 1967, p. 14.
7. Carrie Rickey, "Lupino Noir," *Village Voice,* October 29–November 4, 1980, p. 43.
8. Dwight Whitney, "Follow Mother, Here We Go, Kiddies!" *TV Guide,* October 8, 1966, p. 16.
9. Rickey, "Lupino Noir," p. 43.
10. Whitney, "Follow Mother," p. 18.
11. Rickey, "Lupino Noir," p. 43.
12. Lupino, p. 14.
13. Ibid.
14. Rickey, "Lupino Noir," p. 43.
15. Ronnie Scheib, "Ida Lupino: Auteuress," *Film Comment,* January–February 1980, vol. 16, p. 1.
16. Rickey, "Lupino Noir," p. 43.
17. Paul Gardner, "Ida Lupino in Comeback after Fifteen Years," *New York Times,* October 10, 1972.
18. Mary Ann Anderson, "Ida Lupino—Director," profile from unpublished papers.
19. Sue Cameron, "Coast to Coast," *Hollywood Reporter,* November 16, 1972, p. 10.
20. Lupino, p. 14.
21. Whitney, "Follow Mother," p. 18.
22. Mary Ann Anderson in an interview with Ally Acker, June 1989.
23. Barbara Scharres, *The Film Center Gazette,* The School of the Art Institute of Chicago, vol. 16, no. 2, February 1987, p. 4.
24. One unaware reviewer remarked in 1966, "Gee, one of the crew members, who said he liked working with her, says she directs just like a man." In the same article, " 'Mother' is Ida Lupino, the first and maybe the last of the lady TV directors."

Barbara Loden

1. Margarethe von Trotta, interview with Ally Acker, summer 1988.
2. Madison's Women Media Collective, "Barbara Loden Revisited," *Women and Film,* 1: 5–6, 1974, p. 67.
3. Rex Reed, "Poignant Study of a Girl Born to Lose," *Chicago Tribune,* February 21, 1971, p. S9.
4. Madison's, p. 68.
5. Reed.
6. Ibid.
7. Ibid.
8. Ibid.
9. Ibid.
10. Ibid.
11. Elia Kazan, *A Life* (New York: Knopf, 1988), pp. 571, 572.
12. Ibid., p. 669.
13. Ibid., p. 793.
14. Madison's, p. 69.

Elaine May

1. Sharon Smith, *Women Who Make Movies* (New York: Hopkinson and Blake, 1975), p. 52.
2. Linda Malm, "Elaine May," *Dictionary of Literary Biography,* American Screenwriters, vol. 44, p. 251.
3. Ibid., pp. 251–52.
4. Ibid., p. 252.
5. Stempel, *FrameWork* (New York: Continuum, 1988), p. 222.
6. Ibid.
7. Malm, p. 251.
8. Dick Lemon, "How to Succeed in Interviewing Elaine May (Try, Really Try)," *New York Times* January 4, 1970, p. D-12.
9. Thomas Thompson, "Whatever Happened to Elaine May? *Life,* July 28, 1967, p. 59.
10. Michael Rivlin, "Elaine May Too Tough for Hollywood?" *Millimeter* 3, October 1975, pp. 16–18, 46.
11. Ibid.

Lee Grant

1. Ken Gross, "Lee Grant, *People,* October 23, 1989, p. 9.
2. Lee Grant, interview with Ally Acker, summer 1989. All Grant quotes, unless otherwise attributed, are taken from this interview.
3. Gross, p. 10.
4. Kathy Larkin, "Lee Grant Comes Home," *Daily News,* Manhattan Section, August 22, 1983.

Barbra Streisand

1. Steven Bach, *Final Cut* (New York: William Morrow & Co., 1985), p. 390.
2. Barbara Koenig Quart, *Women Directors: The Emergence of a New Cinema* (New York: Praeger, 1988), p. 81.
3. Ibid., p. 84.
4. Rebecca Vander Lende, "The Roles of Women in the American Film Musical," unpublished paper presented at the Michigan Women's Studies Association Conference, April 21, 1990 at Saginaw Valley State College.
5. Ibid., p. 3.
6. Ibid., p. 5.
7. Quart, p. 84.
8. Vander Lende, p. 11.
9. Ibid.
10. Ibid.
11. Quart, p. 85.
12. Ibid., pp. 84, 85. "Kael was right," she continues, "in feeling that a film so extraordinarily controlled by a woman would be different. They locate its difference primarily in the covert, devious, but unmistakably recognizable love (romantic love) that exists between the two women."
13. Ibid.
14. Vander Lende, p. 12.

Penny Marshall

1. Evelyn Renold, "The Marshall Plan," *Daily News Magazine,* October 5, 1986, p. 24.
2. Frank Sanello, "Marshall Directs Her Anxiety," *Boston Globe,* October 11, 1986, p. 21.
3. Ibid.
4. Renold, p. 24.
5. Sanello, p. 21.
6. Renold, p. 24.
7. Rachel Abramowitz, "Shot by Shot," *Premiere,* January 1991, p. 21.
8. Ibid.
9. Ibid.
10. Ibid.
11. Ibid
12. Ibid.
13. Sanello, p. 21.

Maya Deren

1. Anaïs Nin, *The Diary of Anaïs Nin,* vol. 4, 1944–1947, ed. Gunther Stuhlmann (New York: Harcourt Brace Jovanovich, Inc., 1971), p. 352.
2. *New York Times,* obits, October 19, 1961.
3. Nin, *Diary,* p. 76.
4. Ibid., p. 90.
5. Ibid., p. 102.
6. Ibid., p. 111.
7. One of her books includes *Divine Horseman,* an anthropologic/biographic account of her experiences with voodoo while living in Haiti. The book was requested and prefaced by Joseph Campbell.
8. Nin, p. 137.

Shirley Clarke

1. Susan Rice, "Shirley Clarke: Image and Images," *Take One,* 3:2, 1972, p. 20.
2. Ibid.
3. Ibid., p. 21.
4. Ibid.
5. Ibid., pp. 20–21.
6. Ibid.
7. Ibid.
8. Sharon Smith, *Women Who Make Movies* (New York: Hopkinson and Blake, 1975), pp. 42–48.
9. Harriet Polt, "Shirley Clarke at Venice—An Interview with Harriet Polt," *Film Comment,* vol. 2 spring 1964, p. 31.
10. Smith, p. 48.

Yvonne Rainer

1. E. Ann Kaplan, *Women and Film, Both Sides of the Camera* (New York: Methuen, 1983), p. 113.
2. Ibid.
3. Ibid.
4. American Film Institute program notes by Bill Horrigan, 1988.
5. B. Ruby Rich, "The Personal Film," *Women and Film,* 2:7, 1975, p. 23.
6. Ibid., p. 24.
7. Ibid., p. 86.
8. Carol Wikarska, "A Film About A Woman Who" *Women and Film* 2:7, 1975, p. 85.
9. Camera Obscura Editors, "Yvonne Rainer

Interview," *Camera Obscura,* no. 1, 1976, pp. 76–96.

10. Kaplan, p. 123.

Marie Menken

1. Program notes by P. Adams Sitney to the Avantgarde Film Tuesday Series, arranged and conducted by the Film-Makers' Cinematheque at the Jewish Museum in New York, 1969.
2. Ibid.
3. "Marie Menken, 61, Early Leader in Underground Movies, Dies," *New York Times,* December 31, 1970.
4. J. Pyros, "Notes on Women Directors," *Take One,* vol. 3, no. 2, 1972.

Mary Ellen Bute

1. Gregory Markopoulos, "Beyond Audio Visual Space—a Short Study of the Films of Mary Ellen Bute," *Film Comment,* summer 1962, p. 52.
2. Mary Batten, "Actuality and Abstraction," *Film Comment,* summer 1962, p. 55.
3. Ibid.
4. Ibid.
5. "Mary Ellen Bute in Conversation at The Art Institute of Chicago—May 7, 1976." Reprinted in *Field of Vision,* no. 13, spring 1985.
6. Ibid.
7. Ibid.
8. J. Pyros, "Notes on Women Directors" (quoting Parker Tyler), *Take One,* 3:2, 1972, pp. 8–9.
9. Arthur Knight, *The Liveliest Art* (New York: Mentor, 1957), pp. 260–61.
10. For an interview with Mary Ellen Bute and a discussion of FINNEGAN'S WAKE, see Gretchen Weinberg, "An interview with Mary Ellen Bute," *Film Culture,* winter 1964–65, p. 25.
11 Markopoulos, pp. 52, 53.

Reel Women of Color—Preview

1. Waters was born in 1896 and raised in utter poverty, working as a scrubwoman, laundress, and chambermaid before she went on to success in entertainment. Ironically, she rose to success in movies playing a scrubwoman, laundress, and chambermaid. She died in 1977.
2. Bell Hooks, "Black Women Filmmakers Break the Silence," *Black Film Review,* summer 1986, p. 14.
3. Michelle Parkerson, "Remembering Kathleen Collins," *Black Film Review,* winter 1988–89, p. 5.
4. Euzhan Palcy as a woman of French Martinique descent is an exception, and is included due to the film A DRY WHITE SEASON (1989) being generated and distributed through a Hollywood studio—MGM.
5. Parkerson, p. 5.
6. David Nicholson, "Conflict and Complexity: Filmmaker Kathleen Collins," *Black Film Review,* summer 1986, p. 16.

Kathleen Collins

1. David Nicholson, "A Commitment to Writing: A Conversation with Kathleen Collins Prettyman," *Black Film Review,* winter 1988–89, pp. 6–7.
2. David Nicholson, "Conflict and Complexity: Filmmaker Kathleen Collins," *Black Film Review,* summer 1986, p. 16.
3. Ibid.
4. Ibid.
5. Ibid.
6. Nicholson, "A Commitment," p. 8.
7. Ibid., p. 10.
8. Ibid.
9. Nicholson, "Conflict," p. 17.
10. Nicholson, "A Commitment," p. 9.
11. Nicholson, "Conflict," p. 17.
12. I wish to thank David Nicholson for his tributary work on Kathleen Collins. Without his efforts, she would be lost from this book.

Rita Moreno

1. Rita Moreno, interview with Ally Acker, summer 1989. All Moreno quotes, unless otherwise attributed, are taken from this interview.
2. Diana Martinez, "Lithe and Lively at 58," *Vista,* 1990, p. 8.
3. Ibid.

4. She *did* make a few "A" movies as well: SINGIN' IN THE RAIN (1952), and THE KING AND I (1956).
5. Arnold Bell, "Rita Moreno Outclasses Her Old Act," *Village Voice,* August 23, 1976.
6. Jack Hicks, "The Cutthroat Almost Got Her," *TV Guide,* January 15, 1983, p. 27.
7. Ibid., p. 28.
8. Bell.
9. Ibid.

Maya Angelou

1. Arthur Cooper, "Caged Bird," *Newsweek,* April 3, 1972, p. 85.
2. Howard Taylor, "She Wants to Change TV's Image of Blacks," *New York Times,* April 22, 1979, p. D-35.
3. Gordon R. Watkins, "Women in Film— Maya Angelou," *Millimeter,* July/August 1974, 2:7/8, p. 15.
4. Ibid.
5. John J. O'Connor, " 'Caged Bird Sings': Tales of Girlhood," *New York Times,* April 27, 1979, p. C-32.
6. Ibid.
7. Ibid.
8. Don Safran, "Finding Directing Assignments Tough," *Hollywood Reporter,* November 6, 1979, p. 3.
9. Taylor, p. D-5.
10. Ibid.

Euzhan Palcy

1. Euzhan Palcy, interview with Ally Acker. All Palcy quotes, unless otherwise attributed, are taken from this interview.
2. Mike Wilmington, "Euzhan Palcy: For All the Black Shack Alleys," *Los Angeles Weekly,* May 11–17, 1984.
3. Howard Rodman, "Between Black and White," *Elle,* October 1989, p. 132.

Ruby Oliver

1. Produced in 1990. Not yet released as of this writing.
2. Ruby Oliver, interview with Ally Acker, May 1990. All Oliver quotes, unless otherwise attributed, are taken from this interview.

Christine Choy

1. [Author and title unknown] *The Michigan Daily,* Weekend Magazine 7:10, November 11, 1988, p. 10.
2. David A. Kaplan, "Film about a Fatal Beating Examines a Community," *New York Times,* Arts and Leisure, July 16, 1989, p. 27.
3. Ibid.
4. Ibid.
5. Interview: "Women in the Director's Chair," *Profile, Video Data Bank* profile, 5:1, spring 1985. [Published four times a year by the School of the Art Institute of Chicago].
6. Interview with Peter Hanson, "Filmmaker's Battle to Make *Chin,*" *Washington Square News,* March 29, 1989, p. 10.
7. Ibid.

Julie Dash

1. Gary Tate, "Favorite Daughters, Julie Dash Films Gullah Country," *Village Voice,* April 12, 1988, p. 27.
2. Ibid.
3. Ibid.
4. Ibid.
5. Ibid.
6. Ibid.
7. Ibid.
8. Ibid.
9. Ibid.

Peaches Jones

1. Jodie David phone interview with Ally Acker, winter 1990.
2. Walter Price Burrell, "Hollywood Stunt Girl, Pert Peaches Jones Does Risky Work for the Stars," *Ebony,* December 1971.
3. Ibid.
4. Ibid.
5. Ibid.

Michelle Parkerson

1. Betsy Pisik, "In Search of a Lost Legacy," *Washington Blade,* May 1, 1987.
2. David Nicholson, "Independent, and Liking It," *American Visions,* July–August, 1986, p. 55.
3. Pisik.

4. Ibid.
5. Ibid.

Ayoka Chenzira

1. Keith Boseman, "Ayoka Chenzira: Sharing the Empowerment of Women," *Black Film Review,* summer 1986, p. 18.
2. Ibid., p. 19.
3. David Nicholson, "A Commitment to Writing: A Conversation with Kathleen Collins Prettyman," *Black Film Review,* winter 1988–89, pp. 13–14.
4. Boseman, p. 19.
5. Ibid., p. 25.

Saundra Sharp

1. David Nicholson, "From Acting to Filmmaking: Saundra Sharp's Odyssey," *Black Film Review,* summer 1986, p. 20.
2. Loretta Campbell, "Reinventing Our Image: Eleven Black Women Filmmakers," 1983. Magazine name unknown. Article brought to author's attention and obtained from Mabel Haddock, National Black Film Consortium, Columbus, Ohio.
3. Nicholson, p. 21.
4. Tom Stempel's notes to the author on the manuscript of *Reel Women,* July 1990.
5. Ibid.

Alile Sharon Larkin

1. Loretta Campbell, "Reinventing Our Image: Eleven Black Women Filmmakers," 1983. See Saundra Sharp note 3.
2. Ibid., p. 60.

Madeline Anderson

1. Michelle Parkerson, "Did You Say the Mirror Talks?" From an unpublished essay on black women filmmakers, p. 5. Many thanks to Ms. Parkerson for this and for bringing Madeline Anderson to light.

Eloice Gist

1. Michelle Parkerson, "Did You Say the Mirror Talks?" quoted with permission from her unpublished 1989 essay.

Frances Williams

1. Carroll Parrott Blue, "Sometimes a Poem Is Twenty Years of Memory," *Sage: A Scholarly Journal on Black Women,* 4:1, spring 1987.

Reel Women Producers—Preview

1. Philip K. Scheuer, "Small Girl Makes Good in Big Film Job," *Los Angeles Times,* January 21, 1945, p. 1.
2. John Taylor, "Bright as Dawn, Strong as Steel," *New York,* May 29, 1989, p. 42.
3. Ibid.
4. Sharon Bernstein, "Women and Hollywood—It's still a Lousy Relationship. But is There Hope for the Future?" *Los Angeles Times,* Calendar Section, November 11, 1990, p. 9.
5. Ibid.
6. Ibid.
7. Ibid.
8. Ibid.
9. Ibid., p. 82.
10. Ibid., p. 83
11. Ibid., p. 82.

Virginia Van Upp

1. Philip K. Scheuer, "Small Girl Makes Good in Big Film Job," *Los Angeles Times,* January 21, 1945, p. 1.
2. Ibid., p. 6.
3. Bob Thomas, *King Cohn: The Life of Harry Cohn* (New York: Bantam Books, 1967), p. 220.
4. Ibid., p. 237.

Sherry Lansing

1. Sherry Lansing, interview with Jim Brown and Ally Acker, summer 1986.
2. Meryl Gordon, "Back with a Splash," *Savvy,* October 1988, p. 46.
3. Ibid., p. 48.
4. Ibid., p. 108.
5. Ibid., p. 48.
6. Interview with Brown and Acker, 1986.
7. Ibid.
8. Gordon, p. 49.
9. Ibid.
10. Interview with Acker and Brown, 1986.
11. Ibid.
12. Gordon, p. 108.

Dawn Steel

1. John Taylor, "Bright as Dawn, Strong as Steel," *New York,* May 29, 1989, p. 42.
2. Ibid., p. 43.
3. Ibid., p. 44.
4. Ibid., p. 45.
5. Ibid.
6. Ibid., p. 46. In notes to the author, Tom Stempel wrote the following comment about FLASHDANCE: I always thought that the reason the film was a hit was not the music and the dancing, but the gumption of the leading character. She goes out and gets what she wants, her way, and she remains friends with and supportive of the women at the bar.
7. A possible exception may be **Virginia Van Upp,** who seemed almost obsessed with the *concept* of a changing woman on the screen from the looks of the screenplays she penned. Of course, the culture supported the kind of material she was writing, and the women in her pieces always ended up precisely where society wanted them, without the power and at home.
8. Nina Easton, "Tough as Steel," *Los Angeles Times,* Calendar Section, October 30, 1988.
9. Taylor.
10. Ibid., p. 43.
11. Ibid., p. 41.

Dorothy Davenport Reid

1. [No Author Cited] "Dorothy Davenport," *Universal Weekly,* September 28, 1912.
2. Gerald Peary, "Sanka, Pink Ladies, and Virginia Slims," *Women and Film* 1:5–6, 1974, pp. 82–84.
3. Kevin Brownlow, "Silent Movies Speak Eloquently of Social Issues," *New York Times,* November 25, 1990, p. 21.
4. Ruth Rankin, "Mrs. Wallace Reid Comes Back," *Shadowplay,* December, 1934.
5. Anthony Slide, *Early Women Directors* (New York: A. S. Barnes, 1977), p. 81. Quoted from the *Film Daily,* February 21, 1934.
6. Smith, Sharon, *Women Who Make Movies* (New York: Hopkinson and Blake, 1975), pp. 40–41.
7. Slide, p. 82.
8. [No Author Cited] "A Remarkable Monu-

ment to Wally Reid's Memory," *Photoplay,* September 1924, p. 74.
9. Slide, p. 74.
10. Ibid., p. 73.
11. Ibid., p. 80.
12. Rankin.

Fanchon Royer

1. Terry Ramsaye, ed., *The 1938–1939 Motion Picture Almanac* (New York: Quigley Publishing Co., 1939), p. 645.
2. Fanchon Royer entry in Jack Alicoate, ed., *Film Daily Guide* (New York: 1937), p. 247.
3. Subcaption of Parmount Pictures publicity photograph.

Hannah Weinstein

1. Dale Pollock, "Tribute Paid to Memory of Pioneer Woman Studio Chief," *Los Angeles Times,* April 14, 1984, Part V, p. 1.
2. Ibid.
3. Ibid.
4. Sharon Bernstein, "Women and Hollywood—It's Still a Lousy Relationship. But is There Hope for the Future?" *Los Angeles Times,* Calendar Section, November 11, 1990, p. 9.

Marcia Nasatir

1. Marcia Nasatir, interview with Ally Acker, 1986. All Nasatir quotes, unless otherwise attributed, are taken from this interview.

Reel Women Writers—Preview

1. Ulricka Brand, "Cinematic Pioneers: Interview with Ally Acker," *Montage* (trade publication of the IFP—Independent Feature Project), summer 1989. "The Bielby study, commissioned by the Writer's Guild in 1987, revealed that only 15.5 percent of the writing jobs at the major studios went to women. A far cry from cinema's early days when women writers outnumbered the men ten to one."
2. Gary Carey, "Written on the Screen: Anita Loos," *Film Comment,* winter 1970–71, p. 51.
3. Tom Stempel, conversation with the author, May 23, 1990.

4. Pat McGilligan, review of *FrameWork*, by Tom Stempel, *Film Quarterly*, summer 1989, p. 51.
5. Andrew Sarris, *The American Cinema: Directors 1929–1968* (New York: E. P. Dutton, 1968).
6. Tom Stempel, letter to Ally Acker, May 24, 1990.

Gene Gauntier

1. Gene Gauntier, "Blazing the Trail," *Woman's Home Companion*, (October 1928), p. 6.
2. Eldon K. Everett, "The Great Grace Cunard–Francis Ford Mystery," *Classic Film Collector*, summer 1973, p. 22. Everett says, "Kalem's Gene Gauntier seems to have created the genre in 1908–09, complete with the stunts and action so typical of later productions."
3. Ibid. (Part II, November 1928) p. 170.
4. Tom Stempel, *FrameWork* (New York: Continuum, 1988), p. 239.
5. Gene Gauntier, "Blazing the Trail," from the original, *unpublished* version of the manuscript at the Museum of Modern Art in New York, p. 21.
6. Stempel, p. 6.
7. Ibid.
8. Ibid., p. 18. Gauntier makes the claim that it was she who gave the good word about Griffith to Henry Marvin. Mrs. D. W. Griffith in *When the Movies Were Young* (New York: Dover, 1969—a reprint from E. P. Dutton, 1925), claims that it was Henry's brother, Arthur, who first mentioned Griffith. I have, however, found Mrs. Griffith's book inaccurate on many different counts.
9. Gauntier, *Woman's Home Companion*, November 1928, p. 170.
10. Stempel, p. 9.
11. Ibid. p. 10.

Grace Cunard

1. Hugh C. Weir, "She Has Written Four Hundred Scenarios!" *Moving Picture World*, September 4, 1915, p. 26.
2. Gerald Peary, "Sanka, Pink Ladies, and Virginia Slims," *Women & Film*, 1:5–6, 1974, pp. 82–84.

3. Eldon K. Everett, "The Great Grace Cunard–Francis Ford Mystery," *Classic Film Collector*, summer 1973, p. 22.
4. Ibid.
5. Ibid.
6. Obituary: "Grace Cunard, 73, Silent Film Star," [no author cited] *New York Times*, January 24, 1967.
7. Ibid.

June Mathis

1. Obituary: "June Mathis Dies While at Theater" [no author cited], *New York Times*, July 27, 1927, p. 1.
2. Thomas Slater, "June Mathis," *The Dictionary of Literary Biography*, vol. 44 (Detroit: Gale, 1984), p. 246.
3. "June Mathis Dies," p. 1.
4. Jacob Lewis, *The Rise of the American Film* (New York: Harcourt, Brace, 1939 and 1955), new ed. (New York: Teacher's College Press, 1968), p. 63.
5. Kevin Brownlow, *The Parade's Gone By . . .* (New York: Ballantine Books, 1969), p. 389.
6. Ibid.
7. Ibid.

Elinor Glyn

1. Anthony Glyn, "Now 'It' Can Be Told," *Good Housekeeping*, April 1955, p. 53.
2. Ibid.
3. Elinor Glyn, *Three Weeks*, 1907.
4. Anthony Glyn, p. 53.
5. Ibid.
6. Ibid.
7. Lenore Coffee, *Storyline* (London: Cassell, 1973), p. 26.
8. Ibid., p. 27
9. Anthony Glyn, p. 53
10. Ibid.
11. Ibid.

Frances Marion

1. Joe Franklin, *Classics of the Silent Screen* (New York: Citadel, 1959).
2. Obituary: "Francis Marion Dies on Coast; Screenwriter Won Two Oscars," [no author cited] *New York Times*, May 14, 1973, p. 34.
3. Ibid.

4. De Witt Bodeen, "Frances Marion Wrote the Scripts of Some of the Milestone Movies," *Films in Review,* vol. 20:2, February 1969, p. 76.
5. Ibid.
6. Gavin Lambert, review of "Off with Their Heads," *Academy Leader,* November, 1972.
7. Charles "Buddy" Rogers, interview with Ally Acker, summer 1989.
8. Marjorie Rosen, *Popcorn Venus* (New York: Coward, McCann & Geoghegan, 1973), p. 393.
9. Frances Marion, *Off with Their Heads!* (New York: The Macmillan Co., 1973), p. 53.
10. Bodeen, p. 76.
11. When I recounted tale to him, Kevin Brownlow said, "The problem with film history is that so much is anecdotal. So much depends on the memory of its veterans. *Everyone* likes to claim the title of 'first.' "

Anita Loos

1. Alden Whitman, "Anita Loos Dead at 93; Screenwriter, Novelist," *New York Times,* August 19, 1981, p. D-19.
2. Anita Loos, *A Girl Like I* (New York: Viking, 1966), p. 17.
3. Anita Loos, *Casts of Thousands* (New York: Grosset & Dunlap, 1977), p. 77.
4. Marjorie Rosen, *Popcorn Venus* (New York: Avon Books, 1974), pp. 391–92.
5. Sandra Schmidt, "Fun's Fun," *Newsweek* October 17, 1966, p. 113.
6. Whitman, p. D-19.
7. Anita Loos in a letter to "Women on Women In Films," *Take One,* 3:2, 1972, p. 11.
8. Loos, *A Girl Like I,* p. 167.
9. Gary Carey, "Written for the Screen: Anita Loos," *Film Comment,* winter 70–71, p. 51. *See also* Gary Carey, *Anita Loos* (New York: Knopf, 1988).
10. Ibid.
11. Ibid., p. 52.
12. John Gross, "Centenary for Author of an Indubitable Classic," *New York Times,* October 11, 1988, p. C-20.
13. Loos, *A Girl Like I,* p. 187.
14. Carey, p. 54.

15. Walter Clemons, "Loos Talk," *Newsweek,* August 12, 1974.
16. Carey, p. 54.
17. Ibid.

Mae West

1. Jon Tuska, *The Films of Mae West* (Secaucus, New Jersey: Citadel Press, 1973), pp. 69–70.
2. Ibid.
3. Ibid.
4. Ibid.
5. Ibid.
6. Ibid., p. 24.
7. Malcolm H. Oettinger, *Picture Play,* September 1933.
8. Tuska, p. 30.
9. Ibid.
10. Ibid., p. 30.
11. Ibid., p. 116.
12. C. Robert Jennings, "Interview with Mae West," *Playboy,* January 1971, p. 73.
13. Tuska, p. 189.

Dorothy Parker

1. Dorothy Parker, "Madame Glyn Lectures on 'It,' with Illustrations," *The Portable Dorothy Parker* (New York: Viking Press, 1944), p. 464.
2. Dorothy Parker, 1956 interview with Marion Capron, from *Women Writers at Work, Paris Review* Interviews, ed. George Plimpton (New York: Viking Penguin, pp. 118–19.
3. Ibid.
4. Ibid.
5. Ibid., pp. 109–10.
6. [No Author Cited] "Guinevere of the Round Table," *Time,* June 16, 1967, p. 94.
7. Ibid.
8. John Keats, *You Might as Well Live, the Life and Times of Dorothy Parker* (New York: Simon & Schuster, 1986), p. 179–80.
9. Ibid.
10. Ibid., p. 182.
11. Ibid.
12. Willa Martin, "Dorothy Parker Says Goodbye to Flippancy," *Associated Press* August 1943.
13. Ibid.

14. *Time,* p. 94.
15. Although, having seen another young husband march off to fight the Germans twenty-five years earlier, she must have felt a bit as if she was in a recurring nightmare.
16. Keats, p. 239.
17. Ibid.

Sonya Levien

1. Edith Hurwitz, *Dictionary of Literary Biography, vol. 44, American Screenwriters* (Detroit: Gale, 1984), p. 173.
2. Ibid.
3. Ibid.
4. Public Relations Flyer titled "Color Biography," published by the Fox Film Corporation, June 1932.
5. Hurwitz, p. 174.
6. Ibid., p. 176.
7. Ibid., p. 173.
8. Ibid., p. 177.
9. Ibid.

Lenore Coffee

1. Lenore Coffee, *Storyline: Reflections of a Hollywood Screenwriter* (London: Cassell, 1973), p. 101.
2. Thomas Slater, "Lenore J. Coffee," *Dictionary of Literary Biography, vol. 26, American Screenwriters* (Detroit: Gale, 1984), pp. 91–97.
3. Ibid.
4. Ibid.
5. Ibid.
6. Obituary: "Lenore Coffee, Writer of Film Romances, Dies," [no author cited] *Los Angeles Times,* July 5, 1984.
7. Ibid.

Lillian Hellman

1. Richard Hummler, obituary: "Lillian Hellman Dead at 79, Top U.S. Dramatist, Memorist," *Variety,* July 4, 1984.
2. Lillian Hellman, "Theatre Pictures," *Esquire,* August 1973, p. 65.
3. "I like fame, but I'm no good at its requirements. One must pay fame the respect it demands, or leave it alone and find someplace else to go." Lillian Hellman, from

Marsha Norman's "Lillian Hellman's Gift to a Young Playwright," *New York Times,* Arts and Leisure Section, August 26, 1984, p. 7.
4. Hellman, p. 65.
5. Ibid.
6. Ibid.
7. Hummler.
8. 1965 interview with John Phillips and Anne Hollander, *Women Writers at Work, Paris Review* Interviews, ed. George Plimpton (New York: Viking Penguin, 1989), p. 131.
9. Ibid., p. 138.
10. Norman, p. 7.
11. Stanley Young, "A Public Person's Portrait of her Private Self," *New York Times Book Review,* June 29, 1969, p. 8.

Leigh Brackett

1. Leigh Brackett, "Working with Hawks," *Women and the Cinema,* ed. Karen Kay and Gerald Peary (New York: Dutton, 1977), p. 193.
2. Leigh Brackett in *Take One* 3:6 October 1972.
3. Alain Silver and Elizabeth Ward, "Leigh Brackett," *Dictionary of Literary Biography, vol. 26, American Screenwriters* (Detroit: Gale, 1984), p. 42.
4. Ibid., p. 45.
5. Ibid.
6. Ibid., p. 43.

Harriet Frank, Jr.

1. Harriet Frank, Jr., interview with Ally Acker, summer, 1986. All quotes, unless otherwise attributed, are taken from this interview.

Jay Presson Allen

1. Nick Roddick, "Jay Presson Allen," *The Dictionary of Biography, vol. 26,* (Detroit: Gale, 1984), p. 15.
2. Ibid., p. 16.
3. Ibid., p. 16.
4. Jay Presson Allen, interview with Jim Brown and Ally Acker, summer 1986. Unless otherwise attributed, all quotes are taken from this interview.
5. Interview.

6. Paul Rosenfield, "The Prime Prose of Jay Allen," *Los Angeles Times,* October 5, 1982.
7. Donald Spoto, *The Dark Side of Genius* (New York: Little Brown & Company, 1983), p. 471.
8. Rosenfield, p. 6.

Fay Kanin

1. Fay Kanin, interview with Ally Acker, summer 1989. Unless otherwise attributed, all quotes are taken from this interview.

Julia Crawford Ivers

1. Douglas J. Whitton, "Mystery Woman Director," *Classic Images,* July 1985, p. 27.
2. Ibid.
3. [No author cited] *New York Dramatic Mirror,* February 5, 1916.
4. Anthony Slide, *Early Women Directors* (New York: A. S. Barnes, 1977), p. 111.
5. Ibid.
6. Whitton, p. 27.

Jane Murfin

1. Slide, Anthony. *Early Women Directors* (New York: A. S. Barnes, 1977), p. 113.
2. Daniel Blum, *A Pictorial History of the Silent Screen* (G. P. Putnam and Sons, 1953).

Frances Goodrich

1. Evelyn Ehrlich, "Frances Goodrich, Albert Hackett," *Dictionary of Literary Biography, vol. 26, American Screenwriters* (Detroit: Gale, 1984), p. 129.
2. Ibid.

Zoë Akins

1. Anthony Slide, "Zoë Akins," *Dictionary of Literary Biography, vol. 26, American Screenwriters* (Detroit: Gale, 1984), p. 10.
2. Edited by the great pioneering film editor, Margaret Booth. Frances Marion is also credited as a writer on this film.
3. Slide, p. 10.

Eleanor Perry

1. Judy Klemesrud, "The Woman Who Hated 'Cat Dancing,' " *New York Times,* July 29, 1973.
2. Ibid.
3. Thomas Slater, "Eleanor Perry," *Dictionary of Literary Biography, vol. 26, American Screenwriters* (Detroit: Gale, 1984), pp. 291–92.
4. Marion Weiss, "Interview with Eleanor Perry," *Women & Film,* 2:7, 1974, pp. 44–48.
5. Ibid.

Ruth Gordon

1. For trivia fans: In her 1990 Oscar-winning speech, Jessica Tandy said, "I can't tell you how encouraging a thing like this is," but she stole the line from Gordon who said it at her Oscar acceptance speech in 1968.
2. Fay Kanin, interview with Ally Acker, summer 1989.
3. Samuel G. Freedman, "Ruth Gordon, the Actress, Dies at 88," *New York Times,* August 29, 1985, p. D-22.
4. Fay Kanin, interview with Acker.
5. Mel Gussow, "Grit and Wit Made Ruth Gordon a Star," *New York Times,* Stage View, September 8, 1985, p. 10.
6. Freedman, p. D-22.

Reel Women Editors—Preview

1. Carol Littleton, interview with Ally Acker, summer 1986.
2. Geraldine Fabrikant, "Dede Allen: The Power Behind the Screen," *MS Magazine,* February 1974, p. 34.
3. Martin F. Norden, "Women in the Early Film Industry," *Wide Angle,* 6:3, 1984.
4. Ephraim Katz, *The Film Encyclopedia* (New York: Perigee Books, Putnam Publishing Group, 1979), p. 510.
5. Margaret Booth, interview with Jim Brown and Ally Acker, summer 1986.
6. Ibid.

Margaret Booth

1. Margaret Booth, interview with Ally Acker and Jim Brown, 1986. Unless otherwise at

tributed, all quotes are taken from this interview.

Verna Fields

1. Gerald Peary, "Hollywood's Mother Cutter," *Real Paper,* December 11, 1980, p. 31.
2. Ibid.
3. Ibid.
4. Direct transcript from recording of seminar given at the American Film Institute Center for Advanced Films Studies, 1975.
5. Peary, p. 31.

Dede Allen

1. *Variety,* January 6, 1971, p. 12 lists BONNIE AND CLYDE as the fourteenth highest-grossing film of the decade.
2. Dede Allen, interview with Ally Acker and Jim Brown, 1986. All subsequent quotes are taken from this interview.
3. For a fuller discussion on the work of Dede Allen see Patrick McGilligan's "Dede Allen" in *Women and the Cinema,* ed. Kay Karyn and Gerald Peary (New York: Dutton, 1977), pp. 199–207.

Thelma Schoonmaker

1. Terrence Rafferty, "His Girl Friday," *Village Voice,* November 30, 1982, p. 83.
2. Ibid.
3. Ibid.
4. Ibid., p. 84.

Carol Littleton

1. Carol Littleton, interview with Ally Acker, summer 1986. All Littleton quotes, unless otherwise attributed, are taken from this interview.
2. Linda Gross, "Littleton: What's Done in Noir, Comes to Light," *Los Angeles Times* October 16, 1981, p. C-13.
3. Ibid., p. C-1.
4. [No author cited, title unknown] *L.A. Herald Examiner,* April 8, 1983, p. E-11.
5. Interview with Acker.

Susan E. Morse

1. David Schwartz, "Helping Woody Allen Get His Art Together," *Philadephia Inquirer,* February 13, 1987, p. 1-C.
2. Ibid.
3. Ibid.

Barbara McLean

1. [No author cited], "Interesting People: She Cuts the Kisses," *American Magazine,* January 1949, p. 99.
2. John L. Scott, "Film Editors Shape Fates," *Los Angeles Times,* August 4, 1945, p. 1.
3. Tom Stempel, unpublished "Interview with Barbara McLean," for the American Film Institute. Conducted with McLean on August 4, 1970, and on August 18, 1970, pp. 51–52, 119.
4. Ibid.
5. Ibid.
6. Scott, p. 1.

Adrienne Fazan

1. Written by pioneering scriptwriter, Frances Marion.
2. Don Knox, *The Magic Factory* (New York: Praeger, 1973), p. 64.
3. From an unpublished letter from Don Weis to Anne Kail, donated as a gift to the Museum of Modern Art Film Studies Division.
4. Ibid.
5. Ibid.
6. Ibid.

Lotte Reiniger

1. Distributed by the world's first woman distributor, Margaret Winkler.
2. Lotte Reiniger, "The Adventures of Prince Achmed; or, What May Happen to Somebody Trying to Make a Full Length Feature Cartoon in 1926," *Silent Picture,* autumn 1970.
3. From the program notes of a "Lotte Reiniger Tribute," Museum of Modern Art, October 1986.
4. Ibid.
5. Cecile Starr, "Lotte Reiniger's Fabulous Film Career," *Sightlines,* summer 1980, p. 17. *See*

also Robert Russell and Cecile Star, *Experimental Animation: Origins of a New Art.*
6. Ibid.
7. Ibid.

Claire Parker

1. Claire Parker, "The Screen of Pins," *Bryn Mawr Alumnai Bulletin,* winter 1961.
2. Cecile Starr, Women's Independent Film Exchange, New York, press release, "A Profile of Claire Parker," January 1986.
3. Ibid.

Reel Stunt Women—Preview

1. Florabel Muir, "They Risk Their Necks for You," *Saturday Evening Post,* September 15, 1945, p. 26.
2. Ibid.
3. Ibid.
4. Ibid.
5. Russell J. Birdwell, "The Films' Real Heroines," *unknown newspaper,* June 13, 1925, reprinted in *Classic Images* no. 98, p. 14.
6. Muir, p. 26.

Pearl White

1. Tom Dine, "The Heroine of the Cliffs—the Story of Pearl White," *8mm Collector,* spring 1966, p. 13.
2. [No author cited], "Modern 'Perils of Pauline' Dramatizes Life Story of Pearl White, Old Time Serial Queen," *Cue Magazine,* June 7, 1947, p. 15.
3. [No author cited], "Pearl White, the Golden-haired Heroine of the Serial Silents (First Episode: The Parables of Pathe)," *The Cornell Widow,* May 1949, p. 19.
4. Ibid.
5. Pearl White, *Just Me* (New York: George H. Doran Co., 1919), np.
6. Dine, p. 13.
7. Charles W. Goddard, "Pearl White—She Did All the Tough Jobs Herself," *American Weekly,* September 4, 1938, p. 7.
8. Wallace E. Davies, "Truth About Pearl White," *Films in Review,* 10:9, November 1959, p. 537.
9. Ibid.
10. Ibid.
11. Ibid.

12. Ibid.
13. "Modern 'Perils of Pauline,' " p. 14.

Helen Holmes

1. Eldon K. Everett, "Helen Holmes—The Railroad Girl," *Classic Film Collector,* winter 1973, p. 37.
2. *Life Stories of the Movie Stars.*
3. Everett, p. 37. See Everett's article for greater detailed particulars of Holmes's life.

Helen Gibson

1. *A Bolt from the Blue.*
2. [No author cited], " 'Hazards of Helen': Those Were Days!" *Los Angeles Herald-Examiner,* September 9, 1962.

Helen Thurston

1. Florabel Muir, "They Risk Their Necks for You," *Saturday Evening Post,* September 15, 1945, p. 27.
2. Ibid.

"Behind Every Great Man . . ."—Preview

1. Sumiko Higashi, *C. B. De Mille, a Guide to References and Sources* (Boston: G. K. Hall & Co., 1985), Introduction, page 1.
2. *New York Mirror,* January 13, 1927. (From Museum of Modern Art Clipping File on Beranger).

Jeanie Macpherson

1. Caroline Lowrey, *The First One Hundred Noted Men and Women of the Screen* (New York: Moffat, Yard, 1920), p. 110.
2. Ibid.
3. Alice Martin, "From 'Wop' Parts to Bossing the Job," *Photoplay,* October 1916, p. 95.
4. Alexa Foreman, *The Dictionary of Literary Biography, vol. 26, American Screenwriters* (Detroit: Gale, 1984).
5. Ibid.

Anne Bauchens

1. Constance Sharp Sammis, "Film Editor Indefatigable," *Christian Science Monitor,* February 11, 1957, p. 4.

2. *Cecil B. De Mille, The Autobiography,* edited by Donald Hayne (Englewood Cliffs, New Jersey: Prentice-Hall, 1959), p. 119.
3. Sammis.
4. Ibid.
5. Ibid.
6. Ibid.
7. Ann del Valle, unpublished portrait of Bauchens. Gift to the Museum of Modern Art Film Studies Division, in clipping file on Bauchens.
8. Sammis.
9. Del Valle.

Claire West

1. Anne Walker, "Dressing the Movies," *Woman's Home Companion,* May 1921, p. 24.

Beulah Marie Dix

1. Evelyn F. Scott, *When the Silents Were Golden* (New York: McGraw-Hill, 1972), p. 20.
2. Ibid., p. 127.
3. Ibid., p. 21.
4. Ibid., p. 47.
5. Ibid., p. 127.
6. Kevin Brownlow, *The Parade's Gone By...* (New York: Ballantine Books, 1969), p. 276.
7. Marc Wanamaker, "Beulah Marie Dix," unpublished papers, 1986.
8. Scott, p. 121.
9. Ibid., p. 123.
10. Ibid., p. 125.
11. Ibid., p. 125.

Kay Brown

1. Carrie Rickey, "The Literary Maker of Hollywood History," *Philadelphia Inquirer,* July 1, 1986.
2. Ibid.
3. Ibid.
4. Ibid.
5. Ibid.
6. Ibid.
7. Ibid.
8. Ibid.
9. Ibid.

Joan Harrison

1. (Editorial Staff) "Joan Produces Thrillers," *Parade,* July 15, 1945.
2. (Editorial Staff) "The New Pictures," *Time,* February 28, 1944.
3. Ibid.
4. Ibid.

Helen Keller

1. Marc Wanamaker, "Helen Keller Film Corporation," from unpublished papers.
2. Ibid.
3. Grace Kingsley, [Title of article uncited] *Moving Picture World,* November 23, 1918.

Edith Head

1. Edith Head and Paddy Calistro, *Edith Head's Hollywood* (New York: E. P. Dutton, 1983).
2. Robert Windeler, "Costumes by Edith Head," *People,* March 31, 1975, p. 64.
3. Carrie Rickey, "Body by Head," *Movies,* October 1983, p. 14.
4. Ibid.
5. From a television piece done on Edith Head for KABC, Los Angeles, written and produced by Ally Acker, 1984.
6. Rickey.

Natalie Kalmus

1. Obituary: "Natalie M. Kalmus Dies at 87; A Co-Developer of Technicolor" [no author cited], *New York Times,* November 18, 1965.
2. Marc Wanamaker, "Natalie Kalmus," unpublished essay.
3. "Natalie M. Kalmus Dies."
4. Wanamaker.
5. Ibid.
6. Ibid.
7. Ibid.
8. Ibid.
9. Ibid.
10. "Natalie M. Kalmus Dies."
11. Ibid.

Brianne Murphy

1. In fact, the *Moving Picture Weekly* of June 1, 1916, said, "Men and women occupy po-

sitions of absolute equality in pictures, as they do upon the stage, so that agitation for further 'rights' [discussing the issue of women's suffrage], is foreign to their thoughts. Any position which a man has occupied in the new industry has been and is now occupied by a woman . . . including 'cameramen.' " All this may be true. In a 1989 interview, Actress/ Director Lee Grant confirmed to me, "Acting, at least, has got to be the most equitable business in the world. Both men and women performers are discriminated against equally. They either like you, or they don't."

2. Brianne Murphy, interview with Ally Acker and Jim Borwn, 1986. All Murphy quotes, unless otherwise attributed, are taken from this interview.

A Reel Female Gaze/Select Foreign Reel Women—Preview

1. Donna Deitch, interview with Ally Acker, summer 1989.
2. Barbara Koenig Quart, *Women Directors: The Emergence of a New Cinema* (New York: Praeger, 1988), pp. 97–98.
3. William M. Henry, "Cleo the Craftswoman," *Photoplay* [no month cited], 1916, pp. 109–11.
4. Ibid.
5. Mlle Chic, "The Dual Personality of Cleo Madison," *Moving Picture Weekly,* July 1, 1916, pp. 24–25.
6. Quart, p. 193.
7. Ibid., p. 146.
8. For a further examination of foreign women directors, other than the ones I have mentioned in this section, I suggest Barbara Koening Quart's *Women Directors: The Emergence of a New Cinema.*

Germaine Dulac

1. Sandy Flitterman, "Heart of the Avant-Garde: Some Biographical Notes on Germaine Dulac," *Women and Film* 1:5–6, 1974, p. 58.
2. Ibid., p. 60
3. Ibid., p. 59.
4. Surrealism, as it had been posed, had to do with male fantasy of woman, little more or less. It is not surprising to note, therefore, certain films admired by the male surreal-

ists—films that, as William Van Wert noted they tended to admire for reasons that would be offensive to women. For instance, they loved *King Kong* [1933], especially the scene in which Kong rips off Fay Wray's clothes. They loved von Sternberg's *The Blue Angel* (1930) for the many shots of Marlene Dietrich's thighs, as seen by a roving, caressing, fondling camera. . . . The portrayal of women in all of these examples is never as women actually are, but always as men fancy them to be in dream and fantasy.

How interesting that the many women artists in the surreal movement, active and involved as they were with their male contemporaries of the day—Leonora Carrington, Ramedios Varo, Leonore Fini, Dorothea Tanning, Frida Kahlo—were never solicited for their feedback or comments.

See also Whitney Chadwick's *Women Artists and the Surrealist Movement.* (Boston: Little Brown & Co., 1985).

5. William Van Wert, "Germaine Dulac: First Feminist Filmmaker," *Women and Film* 1:5–6, p. 55.
6. Marjorie Baumgarten, Museum of Modern Art Film Department Notes, for a series of films titled "Rediscovering French Films," January 1980.
7. Flitterman, p. 58.
8. Ibid., p. 59.
9. Van Wert, p.55.
10. Flitterman, p. 60.
11. Baumgarten.
12. Charles Ford, "Germaine Dulac, *Anthologie du cinema,* no. 31, January, 1968, p. 6.
13. Ford.

Musidora

1. Keith Patrick de Weese, "Musidora and the Vampires," from an unpublished paper lent to the author, 1990. I am deeply indebted to Mr. de Weese who not only brought Musidora to my attention, but also translated much of this material for me when he was on his sickbed with pneumonia!
2. *Les Vampires,* from the Jacques Doucet Library Collection, no. 7206–10. In *Musidora: La Dixieme Muse* (Paris: Editions Henri Veyrier, 1978), p. 68.
3. Ibid., p. 13.
4. Ibid., p. 17.

5. Ibid.
6. De Weese, p. 1.
7. Ibid., p. 2.
8. Ibid., pp. 3–4.
9. Patrick Casels, p. 71.
10. Ibid., p. 73.
11. De Weese.

Leni Riefenstahl

1. Kevin Brownlow, interview with Ally Acker, fall 1987.
2. Leni Reifenstahl interview with *Cahiers* (November 1964), published in *Cahiers du Cinema* (1966), p. 460.
3. Ibid., p. 456.
4. Louise Heck-Rabi, *Women Filmmakers: A Critical Reception* (Metuchen, New Jersey and London: Scarecrow Press, 1984), p. 94.
5. Richard Meran Barsam, ed., *Nonfiction Film: Theory and Criticism* (New York: Dutton, 1976), p. 85.
6. David Gunston, "Leni Reifenstahl," *Current Biography,* May 1975, p. 38.
7. Robert Gardner, "Can the Will Triumph?" *Film Comment* 3:1 winter 1965, p. 30.
8. *Cahiers,* pp. 459–60.
9. Ibid.
10. Ibid.
11. Ibid.
12. Glenn B. Infield, *Leni Reifenstahl: The Fallen Film Goddess* (New York: Thomas Y. Crowell, 1976), p. 13.
13. *Cahiers,* p. 460.
14. Infield, p. 30.
15. *Cahiers,* p. 460.
16. Ibid., p. 464.
17. Ibid., p. 465.
18. "Henry Jaworsky . . . interviewed by Gordon Hitchens, Kirk Bond, and John Hanhardt," *Film Culture* 56–57, spring 1973, p. 122.
19. Infield, p. 14.
20. Louise Heck-Rabi, p. 98.
21. Ibid., p. 111.
22. Paul D. Zimmerman, "Leni's Triumph of the Will," *Newsweek,* November 29, 1976, p. 72.
23. Ibid.
24. Richard Meran Barsam, "Leni Riefenstahl, Artifice and Truth . . . ," *Film Comment,* November 1973, p. 32.
25. Barsam, p. 255.
26. Ibid.

Marguerite Duras

1. [No author cited], "Marguerite Duras," *Current Biography,* November 1985, p. 9.
2. Ibid., p. 11.
3. Ibid., p. 10.
4. Ibid.
5. Lee Langley, "Marguerite Duras," *The Guardian,* September 7, 1968.
6. Ibid., p. 10.
7. Erica M. Eisinger, "Crime and Detection in the Novels of Marguerite Duras," *Contemporary Literature,* autumn 1974, p. 504.
8. *Current Biography,* p. 9.
9. Judith Gollub, "French Writers Turned Film Makers," *Film Heritage,* 4:2, winter 1968–69, p. 19.
10. *Current Biography,* p. 11.
11. Ibid.
12. Diane Johnson, "The Lover," *New York Times Book Review,* June 23, 1985.
13. *Current Biography,* p. 9.
14. Langley.

Agnes Varda

1. Nicholas Powell, "Agnes Varda, the Alternative Voice," *London Times,* May 31, 1986.
2. Joan Owens, "Varda at Ease in Her Own Contradictions," *Los Angeles Times,* August 6, 1978, p. 28.
3. Geris L. Carlson, "Agnes Varda: Film Master," *Village View,* July 6, 1989, p. 7.
4. Barbara Quart, *Women Directors: The Emergence of a New Cinema* (New York: Praeger, 1988), pp. 136, 137.
5. Owens.
6. Quart, p. 145.
7. Carlson.
8. "Agnes Varda," *Current Biography,* July 1970, p. 41.
9. Kevin Thomas, "Life Comes First, Films Second to Agnes Varda," *Los Angeles Times,* September 7, 1969.
10. Quart, p. 137.
11. Ibid.
12. Flora Lewis, "Varda: Is There Such a Thing as a Woman's Film?" *New York Times,* Arts and Leisure, September 18, 1977, p. 1.

13. Ibid.
14. Claire Johnston, "Women's Cinema as Counter-Cinema," *Movies and Methods: An Anthology,* ed. Bill Nichols (Berkeley: University of California Press, 1976), p. 216.
15. Quart, p. 139.
16. Jacqueline Levitin, "Mother of the New Wave: An Interview with Agnes Varda," *Women and Film,* 1:5–6, 1974, p. 64.
17. Lewis.
18. Carlson.

Margarethe von Trotta

1. Barbara Koenig Quart, *Women Directors: The Emergence of a New Cinema* (New York: Praeger, 1988), p. 97.
2. Ibid., p. 93.
3. Margarethe von Trotta, interview with Ally Acker, summer 1988. All von Trotta quotes, unless otherwise attributed, are taken from this interview.
4. Marian Christy, "Accepting Life's Dualities," *Boston Globe,* January 21, 1987, p. 61.
5. Susan Seidelman may have as many films in her oeuvre as does von Trotta, but the pressures of shared creative responsibility with the studio, including squabbles over who may have final cut, as in DESPERATELY SEEKING SUSAN (Seidelman did not get final cut), homogenizes the material as to make creative ownership nearly unidentifiable, whereas von Trotta's mark on her films is starkly evident from front to back.
6. See Quart's *Women Directors* for an in-depth discussion of these filmmakers.

Gillian Armstrong

1. Steve Ginsberg, "Gillian Armstrong's Hollywood Education," *W,* February 22–March 1, 1985.
2. Diane Jacobs, "Success against Odds," *Soho Weekly News,* February 13, 1980.
3. Chris Chase, "How Woman Director Deals with Prejudice, *New York Times,* March 4, 1983, p. C-8.
4. Stephen R. Conn, The New Australian," *Town & Country,* November 1982, p. 211.
5. Ginsberg.
6. Jacobs.
7. Ibid.
8. Jacobs.
9. Ibid.
10. Ibid.

Patricia Rozema

1. Ron Graham, "Mermaids," *New York Times,* September 6, 1987, p. 15.
2. Ibid.
3. Ibid.
4. Ibid.
5. Ibid.
6. Annette Insdorf, "Rozema Sings the Praises of Directing in Canada," *Los Angeles Times,* October 3, 1987.
7. Ibid.
8. Ibid.

Chantal Akerman

1. Linda Williams, "Feminine Mythmaking," *Chicago Reader,* Section 1, February 1, 1985, p. 12.
2. Ibid.
3. B. Ruby Rich, "Chantal Akerman's Meta-Cinema," *Village Voice,* March 29, 1983, p. 51.
4. Ibid.
5. Laura Mulvey, "Guest Appearances," *Time Out,* May 5, 1979, p. 19.
6. J. Hoberman, "Review of JEANNE DIELMAN," *Village Voice,* October 16, 1978.
7. Lynne Tillman, *Elle,* July 1989, p. 34.
8. Ibid.
9. Ibid.
10. Williams, p. 36.

Leontine Sagan

1. Patricia Erens, ed., *Sexual Stratagems,* "Leontine Sagan," (New York: Horizon Press, 1979), p. 219.
2. See Vito Russo's fascinating account in *The Celluloid Closet* (revised edition, New York: Harper & Row, 1987) of precisely how the American censors barred and subsequently (with shameful, intrusive, and censoring changes) accepted the film. For example: "Reel Four: Eliminate all views of Manuela's face as she looks at Miss von Bernbourg in the classroom," etc.

Esther Shub

1. Robert Dunbar, *The International Dictionary of Films and Filmmakers, vol. 2, Directors/Filmmakers,* ed. Christopher Lyon (Chicago: Macmillan, St. James Press, Inc., 1984), p. (uncited). Only Dziga Vertov preceded Shub in this genre.
2. Ibid.

Lina Wertmuller

1. Barbara Quart, *Women Directors: The Emergence of a New Cinema* (Praeger, 1988), p. 31.

Mai Zetterling

1. See Louise Heck-Rabi's study, *Women Filmmakers: A Critical Reception* (Scarecrow Press, 1984), for incisive looks at both Zetterling's and Box's work.
2. Joanne Stang, "In Sweden It's Easier to Play 'Night Games,'" *New York Times,* October 9, 1966.
3. Craig McGregor, "Mai is Behind the Camera Now," *New York Times Biography Edition,* April 30, 1972.
4. Judith Crist, "Filmfacts," *New York World Journal Tribune,* 1966.
5. Heck-Rabi, p. 271.

Diane Kurys

1. Barbara Quart, *Women Directors,* pp. 149–50.
2. Ibid., p. 153.

Márta Mészáros

1. Interview from the press packet, New Yorker Films.
2. Harriet Halpern Martineau, "The Films of Márta Mészáros, or the Importance of Being Banal," *Film Quarterly,* fall 1980. Note: a good introduction to Mészáros's work.
3. Quart, p. 195.
4. Ibid., p. 196.

Marion Fairfax

1. Anthony Slide, *Early Women Directors* (New York: A. S. Barnes, 1977), p. 112.

2. Ibid.
3. "Marion Fairfax Forms Production Unit," *Moving Picture World,* April 23, 1921, p. 847.

Louella Parsons

1. Charles Champlin, "Private Lives of Hollywood's Powerful Columnists," *Architectural Digest,* April 1990, p. 118.
2. Ibid., p. 64.
3. Richard Lemon, "Queens of Gossip," *People,* May 13, 1985, p. 133.
4. Ibid.
5. Ibid.
6. Louella Parsons, *The Gay Illiterate* (Garden City, New York: Doubleday Doran, 1944), p. 21.
7. Isabella Taves, "Louella Parsons," *Look,* October 10, 1950, p. 62.
8. Lemon, p. 136.
9. Ibid.
10. Ibid.
11. Ibid., p. 63. Hearst didn't mind Parsons' ability to write wonderful things in her column about Marion Davies.
12. Ibid.
13. Ibid., p. 64.
14. Ibid.

Hedda Hopper

1. Richard Lemon, "Queens of Gossip," *People,* May 13, 1985, p. 133.
2. Ibid., p. 135.
3. Ibid., p. 136.
4. Charles Champlin, "Private Lives of Hollywood's Powerful Columnists," *Architectural Digest,* April, 1990, pp. 122, 126.
5. Lemon, p. 133.

Afterword

1. There are three camerawomen that have been discovered as having worked in the era of silent films: **Margery Ordway, Dorothy Dunn,** and **Grace Davison.** As far as I know, **Brianne Murphy** was the next prominent camerawoman to gain recognition in this craft.

PHOTO CREDITS

❖ ❖ ❖

The Fronticepiece and photographs of Jane Fonda, Alice Guy Blaché, Lois Weber, Dorothy Arzner, Joan Tewksbury, Claudia Weill, Mary Pickford, Mabel Normand, Ruth Stonehouse, Lule Warrenton, Margery Wilson, Elaine May, Lee Grant, Barbra Streisand, Penny Marshall, Rita Moreno, Saundra Sharp, Virginia Van Upp (photograph by Coburn), Sherry Lansing, Fanchon Royer, Gene Gauntier, June Mathis, Frances Marion, Mae West, Sonya Levien, Lenore Coffee, Lillian Hellman, Fay Kanin, Jane Murfin, Francis Goodrich, Zoë Akins, Margaret Booth, Verna Fields, Viola Lawrence, Barbara McLean, Helen Holmes, Helen Gibson, Anne Bauchens, Claire West, Clara Berenger, Beulah Marie Dix, Edith Head, Natalie Kalmus, Brianne Murphy, Lina Wertmuller, and all art cards are made possible and with permission from *Marc Wanamaker/Bison Archives*, Hollywood, California; Photograph of Lillian Gish is made possible and with permission from Anthony Slide; Photographs of Elizabeth Pickett, Marguerite Bertsch, Dorothy Parker, Ruth Gordon, Kay Brown, Germaine Dulac, and Leontine Sagan are made possible and with permission from the *Quigley Photographic Archive, Special Collections Division, Georgetown University Library;* Photographs of Joyce Chopra, Barbara Loden, Yvonne Rainer, Leigh Brackett, Jay Presson Allen, Eleanor Perry (photography by Alix Jeffry), Joan Harrison, Marguerite Duras, and Patricia Rozema are made possible and with permission of *Photofest;* Photograph of Mary Ellen Bute is made possible and with permission from the *Yale University Film Study Center;* Kathleen Collins photograph by Ronald Gray was originally published in *Black Film Review;* Photograph of Lotte Reiniger courtesy of *Cecile Star;* Photograph of Claire Parker courtesy of the *Women's Independent Film Exchange;* Photographs of Helen Keller's film DELIVERANCE, Agnes Varda, and Gillian Armstrong courtesy of the *Museum of Modern Art/Film Stills Archive;* Photograph of Musidora courtesy of *Anthology Film Archives;* Photograph of Maya Deren from *Anthology Film Archives* postcard. Photographer unknown. Cover photo for *The Legend of Maya Deren* by VeVe Clark, Millicent Hodson, and Catrina Neiman, Volume I, Part Two, *Chambers;* Photograph of Joan Micklin Silver courtesy of Joan Micklin Silver; Photograph of Karen Arthur courtesy of Karen Arthur; Photograph of Martha Coolidge courtesy of Martha Coolidge; Photograph of Susan Seidelman, by John Clifford, courtesy of Susan Seidelman; Photograph of Donna Deitch courtesy of Donna Deitch; Photograph of Ida Lupino courtesy of Ida Lupino; Photograph of Shirley Clarke courtesy of Shirley Clarke; Photograph of Maya Angelou courtesy of Maya Angelou; Photograph of Euzhan Palcy courtesy of Euzhan Palcy; Photograph of Ruby Oliver courtesy of Ruby Oliver; Photograph of Christine Choy courtesy of Christine Choy; Photograph of Michelle Parkerson, by Leigh H. Mosley, courtesy of Michelle Parkerson; Photograph of Dawn Steel courtesy of Dawn Steel; Photograph of Marcia Nasatir courtesy of Marcia Nasatir; Photograph of Anita Loos by Christopher Alexander; Photograph of Dede Allen by Ken Regan, Camera 5; Photograph of Susan E. Morse courtesy of Susan E. Morse; Photographs of Alla Nazimova, Nell Shipman, Cleo Madison, Dorothy Davenport Reid, Grace Cunard, Elinor Glyn, Pearl White, Jeanie Macpherson, Leni Riefenstahl, Margarethe von Trotta, and Chantal Ackerman courtesy of Ally Acker.

ABOUT THE AUTHOR

$\blacklozenge$ $\blacklozenge$ $\blacklozenge$

A filmmaker and writer, Ally Acker holds an MFA in directing and screenwriting from Columbia University. She has been a segment producer for *The Today Show, Good Morning America,* and *National Geographic's Explorer.*

Acker was the first recipient of the Los Angeles Women in Film/Annenberg Scholarship for excellence in screenwriting in 1986, and was a finalist for a Nichols fellowship for her screenplay "Crystal Crystal Burning Bright" in 1988. Her first 16mm film, "Silver Apples on the Moon," which she directed, wrote, produced, and edited, won a Student Academy Award in the late seventies.

Acker has written on film for *MS* and other magazines and lectures on women in film at colleges and film festivals across the country.

Acker is completing a *film series* based on *Reel Women.* In it, top industry people behind the scenes speak about their craft. Replete with clips from their films, and footage of them at their work, the films include interviews with many of the directors, screenwriters, producers, editors, and other craftspeople included in *Reel Women.* The films are suitable for college, library, and homes. For more information write to Reel Women Videos, c/o Stanlite Corporation, 16 E. 38 Street, New York, NY 10016 or call (914) 424-3083.

INDEX

◆ ◆ ◆